Global Conflict Resolution Through Positioning Analysis

Peace Psychology Book Series
Series Editor: **Daniel J. Christie,** *The Ohio State University, Marion, Ohio*

GLOBAL CONFLICT RESOLUTION THROUGH POSITIONING
ANALYSIS
Edited by Fathali M. Moghaddam, Rom Harré and Naomi Lee

A continuation Order Plan is available for this series. A continuation order will bring delivery of each new volume immediately upon publication. Volumes are billed only upon actual shipment. For further information please contact the publisher.

Global Conflict Resolution Through Positioning Analysis

Edited by

Fathali M. Moghaddam
Georgetown University, Washington, DC, USA

Rom Harré
Oxford University, Oxford, UK

and

Naomi Lee
Georgetown University, Washington, DC, USA

 Springer

Editors
Fathali M. Moghaddam
Department of Psychology
Georgetown University,
Washington, DC,
USA
3700 O Street NW
Washington 20057
301 B White-Gravenor Hall

Naomi Lee
Department of Psychology
Georgetown University,
Washington, DC,
USA
3700 O Street NW
Washington 20057
306 White-Gravenor Hall

Rom Harré
Oxford University
Linacre College
St. Cross Road
Oxford, UK OX13JA

ISBN: 978-0-387-72111-8   e-ISBN: 978-0-387-72112-5

Library of Congress Control Number: 2007930195

Printed on acid-free paper.

9 8 7 6 5 4 3 2 1

springer.com

To Jerome S. Bruner

Series Foreword

Although the UNESCO charter claims that "war begins in the minds of men" the discipline of psychology, which places human cognition center-stage, is often not explicitly acknowledged in academic programs on conflict and peace, nor among practitioners in international relations. The Peace Psychology Book Series recognizes that the successful pursuit of human security and well being in the 21st century requires transdisciplinary approaches that include psychologically-based theories and practices. During the past 20 years, peace psychology has emerged as a specialty in psychology with its own knowledge base, perspectives, concepts, advocates, and preferred methodologies. Peace psychologists seek to understand and promote cognitions, emotions, and actions that prevent and reduce violent episodes and mitigate the insidious form of violence called structural violence, which kills people slowly through the deprivation of human need satisfaction.

It is fitting that the first book in the Peace Psychology Book Series focuses on conflict. Unlike violence, which is manifest in behavior, conflict is primarily a cognitive phenomenon. The distinction between cognition and behavior can be traced back to Decartes's dualism, which conceptualized mind and body as two separate and interacting processes, a perspective very similar to the one proposed in the fourth century B.C. by Plato. Today, psychologists continue to draw a sharp distinction between thought and action; so it is not surprising that conflict, often defined as the perception of incompatible goals, is distinguished from violence, which implies some kind of destructive action. This sharp distinction raises the possibility of managing conflicts effectively before violent episodes occur.

The specific focus of the current volume edited by Moghaddam, Harré, and Lee is the use of Positioning Theory to understand global conflict. Positioning Theory examines the talking and writing that surround a conflict. A positioning analysis yields narratives that people use to position one another, and themselves, as a conflict unfolds. These narratives can be thought of as the story-lines of community talk. For example, the Editors point out that one story-line that is ubiquitous in conflicts around the world is the positioning of one group as the "good guys" and the other as "bad guys." Other story-lines include the "axis of evil" versus "Great Satan," a complementary and interlocking set of story-lines that capture the shared beliefs of political actors who are attempting to position one another in a global conflict. The chapters in the current volume span micro and macro levels of analysis and illustrate how Positioning Theory can make explicit the ebb and flow of narratives that support and sustain conflicts. By looking at conflict through Positioning Theory the scholars in the current volume are contributing to a new conceptual framework for understanding and resolving conflicts.

At the dawn of the 21st century, we face the complex problems of terrorism, weapons of mass destruction, nuclear proliferation, failed states, ideological struggles, growing resource scarcities, disparities in wealth and health, globalizing trends, violations of human rights, the continued use of force to advance state interests, and more. The Peace Psychology Book Series is positioning itself within the domain of peace and conflict studies and demonstrating the explanatory power of linking macro-level problems with micro-level analyses where the dynamics of human psychology come into play. Such a transdisciplinary analysis can deepen our understanding of macro-level threats to human security while informing actions that are needed to address some of the most urgent and profound issues that bear on human well being and survival in the 21st century.

Daniel J. Christie
Series Editor

Preface

The medical and engineering advances of the last century have been spectacular and might even inspire us to envisage humans as "...noble in reason...infinite in faculties, in form and moving...express and admirable, in action...like an angel, in apprehension...like a god: the beauty of the world, the paragon of animals!?" Hamlet (II, 2, 303-308). Landing on the moon, creating artificial intelligence, discovering cures for major diseases - humans seem sublime and 'like an angel' in these performances. But this admirable picture is ruined when we consider that we continue and even increase the pattern of aggression, genocide, and war that has blackened our history. In this respect, we are the loathsome "quintessence of dust" Hamlet sees. Our challenge is to discover new ways to overcome violent conflict, to reach closer to being 'like an angel'.

This volume explores a radical new path toward understanding and resolving conflict. The new path is part of the cultural-narrative turn and emerges primarily from research in psychology, linguistics, micro-sociology, and philosophy. The core of the new path is positioning theory, with its ability to reveal the exquisitely subtle undercurrents of meaning and moral framing in conflict situations. Our contention, justified by research presented here, is that by paying close attention to these undercurrents we can better understand and resolve conflicts.

The intended audience for the volume are students and researchers in psychology, political science, linguistics, sociology, and philosophy, interested in conflict at intra-personal, intra-group, and inter-group levels. The chapters have been written in accessible and fairly uniform style, even though the authors come from very different research backgrounds. Thus, this volume builds on an important strength of positioning theory, its multidisciplinary tradition.

Fathali M. Moghaddam, Rom Harré and Naomi Lee
Georgetown and Oxford

Contents

Part 4   Conclusion and Glossary

Contributors

Tom Bartlett
University of Northern Virginia and Institute of Conflict Analysis and Resolution
USA

Julie Caouette
McGill University, Canada

Daniel J. Christie
Ohio State University, USA

Rom Harré
Oxford University, UK

Karen Grattan
George Mason University, USA

Thomas Duus Henriksen
Danish University of Education, Denmark

Kathryn A. Kavulich
Georgetown University, USA

Michael King
McGill University, Montréal, Québec, Canada

Naomi Lee
Georgetown University, USA

Erica Lessem
Georgetown University, USA

Winnifred R. Louis
School of Psychology, University of Queensland, Australia

Fathali M. Moghaddam
Georgetown University, USA

Cristina Jayme Montiel
Ateneo de Manila University, Spain

Christine Redman
The University of Melbourne, Australia

Daniel Rothbart
George Mason University, USA

Steven R. Sabat
Department of Psychology, Georgetown University, USA

Robert Schmidle
American University, USA

Nikki R. Slocum-Bradley
UNU-CRIS Belgium

Donald M. Taylor
McGill University, Canada

Esther Usborne
McGill University, Canada

Part 1
The Concept of Positioning

1
Positioning and Conflict: An Introduction

FATHALI. M. MOGHADDAM, ROM HARRÉ AND NAOMI LEE

Mr. Bush said he regretted challenging insurgents in Iraq to 'bring it on' in 2003, and said the same about his statement that he wanted Osama bin Laden 'dead or alive' (Sanger & Rutenberg, 2006, p. A1)

When in May 2006 the United States President George W. Bush made a rare admission of mistakes made following the 2003 invasion of Iraq by U.S. led forces, he also helped to highlight the fundamentally important role of narrative in conflict. Of course, the continuing war in Iraq involves real tanks, aircraft, bullets, suicide bombings, and hundreds of thousands of deaths and serious casualties, but like all conflicts the fighting takes place in a narrative framework, and is ascribed meaning through discourse of various types. By admitting he was wrong to challenge the insurgents to 'bring it on', Mr. Bush acknowledged that through those words he had stamped a particular, unfortunate meaning to the conflict, daring and goading the opposition to fight as hard as they possibly could. Moreover, Mr. Bush's 'dead or alive' phrase framed the conflict as a 'fight to the death', one in which there would be no compromise.

The particular focus of this volume is the narratives people use to position themselves and others, in the course of conflicts. By bringing together in one volume the latest ideas of leading scholars on conflict looked at through positioning theory, our goal is to add a much needed new perspective on how to better understand and perhaps resolve conflicts. This new perspective moves us to re-think story-lines about conflict, which in the traditional literature become taken-for-granted scenarios. For example, a conflict is frequently represented according to the 'good guys' against the 'bad guys' scenario, a story-line found in all cultures. The 'axis of evil' with its complement the 'Great Satan' is just such a story-line.

However, conflicts do not just occur out of nowhere. In this book we emphasize the unfolding of conflicts. Many years may go by as hostilities become more and more dangerous and more and more violent emotions appear.

Nor do resolutions occur over night. Conflicts may evolve over hundreds of years, reproduced from generation to generation, such as conflict between

Protestants and Catholics in Northern Island. The resolution of conflict may evolve through complex, long-term interactions between cultural, economic, political, technological and psychological factors – as in the case of Northern Ireland.

In all cultures ways are provided for formal resolution of disputes, evolving into legal systems with authorities whose decisions apropos of conflicts have binding force. The neighbors object to the noisy parties thrown by the people next door, and a court order is issued forbidding them after a certain hour. If the rowdy family do not obey the magistrate's edict, the police will try to make sure they do. Notice that compliance usually leaves a smouldering resentment ready to burst into hostile action if the opportunity arises. Is the court order a resolution of the conflict? Maybe not!

Moreover, there are a great many conflicts which are not easily dealt with by the routine invocation of standard procedures. Numerous examples of this are readily available, from conflicts within families that continue for generations, to conflicts between large groups, as is the case in the Middle East, that seem endless.

The positioning theory approach involves a shift of focus, from a study of conflicts themselves, towards the flow of talking and writing within which the hostile actions of the conflict is usually set. We believe that there are patterns of belief, customs and habits that nourish conflict. In the talk of a community, people's explicit beliefs become visible, and much that is implicit can be brought to light. In the talk around a conflict we can find the norms realized in actions.

At the heart of such talk, and the literature that condenses and crystallizes it, are narratives, the story-lines of community talk. In so far as these narratives are implicit their authenticity and viability cannot be brought into question. Positioning theory is not the only approach to the understanding of conflicts and to taking steps to revolve them, but the emphasis on narrative opens up another dimension from the idea of negotiating issues, such as real or imagined grievances. From the early days of this approach to social psychology (Harré & Secord, 1972) the coincidence of the actors' story-lines and the psychologists' hypotheses about the narratives that underlie the unfolding of social episodes has been a major methodological principle. It has been enshrined in the slogan 'Why not ask them?' in researching the dynamics of social processes. We will be working with the hypothesis that the narratives proposed by the psychologist interpreting a conflict and the story-lines animating the actors should ultimately coincide.

This Volume in the Context of Traditional Literature

There is a large and growing literature on conflict resolution and psychological theories related to conflict. For example, in the area of conflict resolution there are general texts (Ramsbotham, Wood, & Miall, 2005; Wallensteen, 2002) and handbooks (Deutsch, Coleman, & Marcus, 2006). There are also texts that emphasize case studies of conflict resolution (e.g., Fisher's, 2005, analysis of multiple cases in different contexts, and Paden's, 2005, case study of conflict in Nigeria). Perhaps inevitably, some researchers have tried to harness the power of computer modeling to facilitate conflict resolution (e.g., Trappl, 2006).

Since the 1970s, there has been considerable growth in the literature on conflict resolution and theories of intergroup relations (Brewer & Miller, 1996; Hogg, 2001; Moghaddam, in press; Taylor & Moghaddam, 1994; Worchel & Austin, 1986). This literature has been strongly influenced by the earlier writings of Karl Marx (1818–1883), Sigmund Freud (1856–1939), and Vilfredo Pareto (1884–1923) (although the influence of Pareto is seldom explicitly acknowledged). It is useful to consider the major theories of conflict around four main themes: irrationality, competition for material resources, identity, and perceived justice (Moghaddam, in press).

Irrationality

Are humans aware of what they do and why? In answering this question, Freud argued that humans are very good at providing rationalizations of why they fight (for example, 'We go to war to spread democracy' or 'We must fight in order to secure peace'), but seldom able to fathom out the deeper root of why they are fighting. The theme of irrationality as influenced by Freud (see Taylor & Moghaddam, 1994, ch. 2) is present, explicitly or implicitly, in a number of major theories. Freud's influence is explicit in research on frustration and aggression, from the classic studies of Dollard, Bood, Miller, Mowrer, and Sears, 1939, to the contemporary research of Miller and his associates (Miller, Pederson, Earlywine, & Pollock, 2003). This research informs us that frustration does not always lead to aggression, but is an important mechanism through which displacement can take place. Displacement of aggression, behavior intended to harm other(s), is often associated with group cohesion and stronger support for aggressive leadership, although the concept of aggression/frustration can be criticized as vague.

Another example of a contemporary theory strongly influenced by Freud is Terror Management Theory (Pyszczynski, Solomon, & Greenberg, 2003). This theory begins with two simple claims: first, that all living creatures are motivated to preserve their lives; second, humans recognize that they will die. The theory proposes that the combination of the self preservation motive and the awareness of impending death creates the potential for overwhelming terror. Humans cope with this potential terror by constructing cultural world views (including religions and nationalist ideologies) that serve a protective role. Conflict tends to arise when we are confronted by outgroup members who threaten our worldview, and potentially raise feelings of terror within us. If I believe the world was made in seven days out of cow milk and you believe the world was created instantaneously at the command of a divine monkey, we can't both be correct. The recognition that we could be wrong leads to feelings of terror, which is seen as 'irrational' because we are not aware of why we experience terror.

The theme of irrationality is also present in an implicit way in a number of other theories. For example, system justification theory (Jost & Banaji, 1994), influenced by Marx, argues that minority group members are not aware that they often adopt and act on worldviews that reflect the interests of dominant groups rather than themselves.

Conflict and Material Resources

A second theme in traditional research is conflict and material resources. The two main topics addressed, how material conditions shape consciousness and how competition for material resources is at the heart of all conflicts, are both influenced by Marx's writings.

The most rationalist materialist theory in psychology is realistic conflict theory (Sherif, 1966). Support for this perspective was provided by the famous field studies involving 11 and 12 year old white boys attending a summer camp. The basic sequence of events can be summed up as follows: In stage one, the boys arrived at camp and friendships developed between them. In stage two, the researchers (acting in the guise of camp councelors) divided the boys up into two groups, making sure that best friends were separated and placed in different groups. During stage three, the two groups engaged in competition for resources (actual material prizes as well as status). Competition for resources led to intense negative attitudes toward the outgroup, and even physical conflict. In stage four, superordinate goals were introduced (goals that all groups want to achieve, but no group can achieve without the cooperation of outgroups [starting the truck that was going to get lunch for the whole lot]), with the result that conflict ended. Of course, Freud would reject such as rationalist account, and claim that material factors are often used as an excuse to fight. For example, the United States could have bought a great deal of oil on the open market with the money it spent invading and occupying Iraq in 2003. The material gains in such a conflict do not support a rational explanation.

Another very influential rationalist approach to conflict is the so-called contact hypothesis, the most important version of which was presented by Allport (1954). For about half a century after Allport (1954) landmark publication *The Nature of Prejudice*, it was assumed that under certain conditions contact between people would lead to less conflict. The four conditions identified by Allport were: the groups should have equal status; the groups should have common goals; the contact should be cooperative and not competitive; and contact should be sanctioned by the community. But subsequent meta-analytic research suggests that these preconditions are not necessary, and that mere contact can be enough to improve relations and reduce conflict (Pettigrew & Tropp, 2006). This approach is rational because it assumes that the root of conflict is ignorance: once we have contact and knowledge of the outgroup, conflict ends.

Three more recent theories have added to the materialist perspective. Resource mobilization theory (McCarthy & Zald, 1977) argues that those who control resources (e.g., television stations) can shape psychological feelings, such as discontent, and create or diminish collective antagonism and conflict. Similarly system justification theory (Jost & Banaji, 1994) proposes that those who control material and cultural resources shape an ideology that justifies the system, and those with less power tend to 'buy into' the dominant ideology, and thus accept rather than revolt against the system. Social dominance theory (Sidanius & Pratto, 1999) points out that stratification and group-based inequalities are universal, and postulates an evolutionary basis for inequality. Of course, the basic propositions of these theories are not new; what is new is the psychological measures used to try to empirically support the propositions.

Identity

The most exciting new theme in conflict research is identity, meaning what sort of person an individual believes she or he is. In answering the question, 'what sort of person am I?', individuals typically refer to groups ('I am an African American woman', 'I am a Latino', 'I am an English rugby fan', and so on). Social identity theorists (Tajfel & Turner, 1979) have argued that individuals are motivated to achieve an identity that is positive and distinct. Because personal identity is to a large extent dependent on social identity, 'that part of an individual's self-concept which derives from his knowledge of his membership in a social group (or groups) together with the value and emotional significance attached to that membership' (Tajfel, 1978, p. 63), individuals strive to belong to groups that have a positive and distinct identity.

What happens when disadvantaged group members are unable to exit from their group, and are at the same time unhappy with their social identity? If they perceive the social system as illegitimate and unstable, disadvantaged group members will attempt to mobilize and directly challenge the advantaged group. This leads to various kinds of 'conflict', from the 'soft' confrontations, as in the case of the women's liberation and Black Power movement in the 1960s, to the 'hard' confrontations that resulted in revolution and regime change in Iran in 1978. The identity tradition suggests that at the heart of such conflicts are attempts to reconstruct identity.

Social identity theory, but not the traditional research it has stimulated, fits in with a normative, discursive account of thought and action (Moghaddam, 2006). First, the need assumed in the theory for a positive and distinct identity is presumably socially derived. People can be socialized to have other needs. Second, because conflict is seen to arise from perceived inadequate social identity, conflict can presumably be avoided by reinterpreting social identity as positive and distinct. Of course, it might be claimed that such 'reinterpretation' is part of system justification and 'false consciousness'.

Perceived Justice

At the heart of conflict is often perceived injustice: people who are engaged in fighting tend to justify their actions with explanations such as, 'We want our legitimate rights, that's all!' or 'They have treated us unfairly!' or simply 'We are fighting for justice!' Of course, both sides in conflicts have their own perceptions of justice, and they both claim to be fighting for a just cause. How do we explain this situation?

Similarly puzzling are situations where on objective criteria there seems to be great injustice, but the disadvantaged group apparently accepts their low status. Consider, for example, the worsening situation of the poorest 30% of the population in the United States in the 21st century. The growing gap between the rich and the poor is well documented even in the U.S. media, including in mass circulation papers such as the New York Times where it was reported that,

'Between 1972 and 2001 the wage and salary income of Americans at the 90th percentile of income distribution rose...about 1 percent per year...But income at the 99th percentile rose 87 percent; income at the 99.9th percentile role 181 percent; and income at the 99.99th percentile role 497 percent' (Krugman, 2006).

Given that the growing gap between the richest and the poorest is no secret, why do the poor not react against this trend, at least by voting in elections? Since the Second World War, participation in elections has declined in the United States (Teixeira, 1992), just as income disparities have increased. Do people not see this situation as unjust?

An enormous psychological literature addresses perceived justice, most of it around the conceptual themes of the justice motive (Hafer & Bègue, 2005; Lerner, 1980), equity theory (Tyler & Huo, 2002; Walster, Walster, & Berscheid, 1978) and relative deprivation theory (Runciman, 1966; Stouffer, Suchman, De Vinney, Star, & Williams, 1949; Walker & Smith, 2002). Three central ideas underlie this vast literature (Moghaddam, in press). First, that people are motivated to see the world as just and fair. To maintain this view, people will psychologically distort their views of the world and their treatment in it. Second, that perceived justice can depend not so much on the outcome of procedures, 'what we get out of it', but the perceived nature of procedures themselves, 'how fairly we see the decision making process to be'. A third important theme in the justice literature is the idea that perceptions of justice arise through social comparison processes and how fairly we feel we are treated can be manipulated by changing social comparison targets. The poor in the United States feel less deprived when they compare themselves to the poor in Africa.

Traditional Theories and Positioning

The traditional theories of conflict have explored rationality, material factors, identity, and perceived justice mainly through laboratory experimental procedures. Such procedures have typically involved various kinds of 'gaming paradigms' (this long tradition is discussed in Taylor & Moghaddam, 1994, Ch. 3). The traditional approach has led to interesting insights, but because most traditional studies have examined the interactions of strangers (undergraduate students) in brief encounters (an hour or so) in laboratory contexts, we still have very little insight into the longer term, dynamic processes of conflict. A small subset of conflict resolution theory and practice looks in more detail at the interactive, discursive, and dialogic dimension of conflicts (see Ramsbotham et al. 2005, Ch. 14). Jabri (1996), for instance, develops a discursive approach to conflict analysis by combining Giddens structuration theory with discursive psychological theory and social identity theory.

Positioning Theory extends these discursively-oriented approaches by proving a framework by which to analytically organize complex and dynamic social interactions. The nature, formation, influence and ways of change of local systems of rights and duties that influence small scale interactions all become more comprehensible. Positions, as clusters of rights and duties, exist more in the practices of social actors than in structural demands.

Introducing Positioning Theory

Positioning Theory is to be seen as complementary to the older framework of Role Theory, rather than an alternative approach. Roles are relatively long lasting norms determining what a person in role is able to do. Role conformity determines action by training, by reminders of what is to be expected of someone as 'student', 'professor,' 'mother', 'friend', 'President' and so on. Roles are often formally defined, delineating possible and forbidden kinds of actions. Roles are sometimes realised in people's shared beliefs about what they can do, but often the location of role-content is in the living structure of the social world. The role of 'police officer' in Western societies, at least, allows an occupant of that role to arrest alleged wrong doers but does not permit torturing them. Most police officers believe this is how they should act – but if doubts arise then statues and other structural items can be invoked. Even such phenomena as *role distance*, displaying one's personal independence, and *role strain*, the stress consequent on trying to fulfill the demands of two incompatible role prescriptions at once, presuppose the stability of the roles to which they are related. Positioning Theory concerns conventions of speech and action that are labile, contestable and ephemeral.

However, that said, it is important to emphasize that the distinction between Positions and Roles lies along a spectrum. Assignments of rights and duties arising through an act of positioning can become crystallized into the long requirements of a role. One can say that in certain cases positioning acts are the birth place of roles.

Positioning acts are themselves episodes. In this respect they are closely related to Goffman's procedures by which someone establishes a 'footing' in a conversation or some other social process (Goffman, 1975, 1981b). This idea can be expressed in the image of a conversation going on, with someone on the periphery of the group wanting to have a say. How does this person get a footing in the group and gain the right to intervene? Goffman identified some of the ways that an outsider gets a footing in among the existing occupants of the microsocial world in which the conversation is going on. No doubt Goffman's 'footing' picks up an aspect of positioning acts. However, establishing a footing is the work of the outsider, while positioning is often the work of someone else, who positions the aspirant with or without consent. Here we encounter the way social power is salient in many encounters, both at the interpersonal and intergroup levels. Furthermore Goffman differentiated between 'footings' and 'frames', corresponding to our 'story-lines' as independent features of social episodes, whereas for us positioning acts and evolving story-lines are indissolubly integrated.

Positioning Theory is also independent of considerations of motivation, except in so far as declarations of motives are social acts, aimed at making one's actions intelligible to others and sometimes to oneself. Positioning Theory is particularly opposed to explanatory theories of human action that posit motives as causes. For the most part Positioning Theory sees people as trapped within discourse conventions, ways of making sense of whatever is going on. Actions are identified by their then and there meanings for the people engaged in an episode.

Of course the meanings one group of actors assigns to what is going on may be very different from the meanings assigned by other people involved in the very same episode. This is important, since it leaves open the possibility that the same conversational actions may have more than one set of meanings as acts. This, in itself, is a prime source of conflict. It is also the key to the resolution of at least some of the impasses that arise from multiple meanings of this sort. 'Oh! That's what you meant!' can be the beginning of a deep resolution, since it gets to the heart of the conflict. Sometimes antithetical meanings are so deeply embedded in a form of life that the very idea of an alternative to the assigned significance of an act may be felt to be deeply immoral. The conflicts in the European Union over the right of Muslim women to wear the veil arise from the irreconcilable antithetical meanings ascribed to this practice by Muslim fundamentalists and by the secular authorities. One Muslim cleric put forward the idea that 'One should cover the meat so that the flies do not come'.

Conditions of Meaningfulness

There are three relevant background conditions for the intelligibility of a flow of meaningful interactions. The media of such interactions include not only linguistic utterances, performances, but also religious icons, road signs, gestures and so on.

a. There is a local repertoire of admissible social acts, in each kind of everyday episode. Positioning Theory borrows the term 'illocutionary force' from philosophy to describe the social significance of a speech, gesture or social action (Austin, 1959). The same verbal formula, gesture, flag or whatever it might be, may have a variety of different social forces, may be the performance of a variety of different social acts, depending on who is using it, where and for what. Saying 'I'm sorry' may, in certain circumstances, be an apology. It may also, in the UK, be a way of asking someone to repeat what has just been said. It may be a way of expressing incredulity. There are no doubt other uses for the phrase.

b. Second, there is the implicit pattern of the distribution of rights and duties taken for granted in a small group, a family, a work force and so on, to make use of items from the local repertoires of the illocutionary forces of various signs and utterances. Each such distribution is a position. A father has the right to encourage his male child to take part in whatever dangerous sports in whatever way law and custom allow. As a default position fathers have this right and many think it also a duty. However, this right is not role related, though it may at first seem so. Tender hearted mothers may challenge this paternal positioning, and so the rights and duties to act in certain ways and to say certain things that go along with it. Conflicts flare up.[1] By way of contrast the fact that Catholics have a duty to confess their sins individually, while Protestants do not, is not a matter of adopting positions, but of roles. Positions have this in common with roles, that they pre-exist the people who occupy them, as part of the common knowledge of what is right and proper in a community, family, sports team and so on. However, positions are not supported by regulations, edicts or laws.

c. The flow of actions and interactions in an evolving social episode is structured by one or more story lines. The study of origins and plots of the implicit repertoire of story lines current in a culture is the work of narratology. Story lines surface in many ways.

For example, autobiographical episodes take their shape in accordance with locally valid narrative conventions. A train journey may be told as a 'heroic quest'. The lateness of the arrival could be a 'complainable' according to one story line. In the 'quest' it becomes an obstacle to be resourcefully and bravely overcome in another. A solicitous remark can be construed as nurturant (having the social force of sympathizing) according to the story line adopted by one actor, but as condescending (having the social force of denigration) according to the narrative conventions adopted by another actor in the same episode (Davies & Harré, 1990b). The philosophical question as to whether, in these circumstances, it is the same episode, is not just a theoretical puzzle. Positioning Theory emphasizes the variety of story lines that may be realised in an encounter bounded in space and time. Any encounter may realize more than one story line, and be the enactment of more than one episode. If the above example is one episode then a common meaning might be negotiable. If it is two different episodes the situation appears to be hopeless.

Among the sources of story lines are folk tales and fairy stories, histories as beliefs about the past, even soap operas and the like, persistent media presentations of traditional plots. Traditions and customs are a rich source of Positions.

They are rarely explicitly formulated. Complex patterns of rights and duties emerge even in such mundane activities as introducing a stranger to the members of one's family. Usually traditions and customs are passed on one to another informally, for example to whom, when and how much should one give as a tip. The roles of diner and server are fairly formally delineated, so that the fine detail of interactions in restaurants become matters of Positioning. Informal episodes analyzable on Positioning Theory lines contrast with formal or semi-formal constraints on actions, such as ceremonies, managed by an existing script, rule book or manual.

The Positioning 'Triangle'

The three aspects of the cognitive conditions for the unfolding of meaningful episodes mutually determine one another. Presumptions about rights and duties are involved in fixing the moment by moment meanings that are to be given to what people are doing and saying. Both are influenced by and influence the story line drawn implicitly from a local repertoire. We can represent this mutuality schematically as follows (see figure 1.1):

Each such triangle is accompanied by shadowy alternatives, into any one of which it can modulate as an episode unfolds. Sometimes, and this is particularly relevant to the use of Positioning analyses in the study of persisting conflicts, alternative patterns can exist as competing and simultaneous readings of events.

There is a possible fourth vertex, the physical positions and stances of the actors, for example, the doctor is standing while the patient is lying down on the examination couch. In Chaplin's Great Dictator, 'Hitler' and 'Mussolini' try to establish social dominance one over the other, by competitively elevating their chairs.

Challenges to the way an episode is unfolding can be directed to any one of the three aspects. 'You do not have the right to do that! [rummage around in my bag]'; 'That's not what I meant'[my remark was a joke]; 'I am not your doctor!'[so don't ask me for medical advice].

Throughout this exposition we have been invoking the idea of a 'moral order'. By this we mean the cluster of norms that are tacitly subscribed by the actors in some cultural setting. Such a cluster includes not only norms of action, what it is proper to do and even to feel in this or that situation, but also norms of person presentation, what sort of person it is proper to display oneself as.

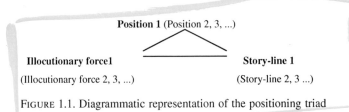

FIGURE 1.1. Diagrammatic representation of the positioning triad

In Positioning Theory only one aspect of a moral order is invoked explicitly, namely the rights and duties that surround a person's possibility of acting. In any moment and among some particular group of people in a certain social setting there is what people can do, their skills and capacities, what people actually do, and the constraints of the moral order, what people in these circumstances may do. Positioning Theory is the tool for exploring the relation between what is possible and what is permitted.

The expanding literature on positioning theory has inevitably resulted in an expanded terminology, as researchers explore different avenues and adopt and adapt terms to new uses. In orer to facilitate communication, in this book we have provided a glossary of positioning terms (pp. 291–292). Our goal is to help clarify the meaning of basic positioning terms and encourage greater consistency in the use of terms.

The Studies in this Book

The rapid development of Positioning Theory in recent years has involved not only the enrichment of the original insights into the dynamics of social episodes, but has also led to more careful distinctions between the leading concepts of 'position' and 'role'. In Part I the place of positioning theory in social psychology is developed against the background of existing approaches to the understanding of the sources of conflict. None of these theories can be applied without reservations both as to the psychological presumptions they make and the generality with which they can be applied. A critical survey enables us to locate their strengths and weaknesses, making clear how positioning theory is an essential addition to the methodology of conflict studies.

In the course of the present chapter positioning theory is distinguished from two other leading theoretical approaches, namely role theory and Goffman's concepts of 'footing' and 'frame'. While Goffman's concepts find their place within positioning theory, as aspects of the positioning approach, role theory has a distinct domain of application. Nevertheless as Louis (Chapter 2) and Henriksen (Chapter 3) show, there is some overlap between the two concepts. Positions can crystallize into roles, and roles can dissolve into positions. The upshot of these considerations is an eclectic methodology, in which 'role' and 'position' are drawn upon as the basis of complementary analytical tools.

Parts II and III encompasses a variety of studies of the development of conflicts as episodes, sometime of considerable duration, as they unfold and positions are established, contested, taken up and abandoned. In each of the case studies the possibility of the ultimate aim of resolving the conflict is examined. A variety of resolutions emerges. There is no sure-fire formula which can shape a guaranteed permanent resolution to a conflict, so these studies seem to show.

The chapters present researches which gradually enlarge in scale. We begin with intrapersonal conflicts in which a person is somehow at odds with his or herself. Resolution of intrapersonal conflicts may involve several different denouements, in which psychiatry can play a major part. In many cases the resolution comes about through the adoption of an alternative story-line with which to conceive of one's life.

In examining the fate of people diagnosed with Alzheimer's Disease (AD) Steven Sabat makes us of Positioning Theory to investigate the problems posed by 'procedural justice. In the treatment of such people. At the root of the failure of the system to accord a proper standing to such people lies the malignant positioning of someone by which that person's diagnosis becomes a kind of license to depersonalization. In particular the generalization without warrant from word finding difficulties to across the board 'memory loss' is one of the main ways that malignant positioning can adversely affect the standing and so the fate of the sufferer. The perception of the Self 2, the psychological being of a human individual, can be so distorted by the influence of a diagnosis of AD that even the most devoted care giver can feel that 'this is not the person I once knew'. Of course he or she is now the person he or she is! That person may feel, if confronted consistently with 'the person he or she once was', a hopeless purposelessness invading their lives. Here the reactivation of purposefulness is tantamount to recovering personhood.

Redman's study (Chapter 6) follows the genesis and resolution of a tiny conflict in the course of a single conversation among four people well known to each other. Positioning moves are countered by repositionings legitimated in turn by implicit recourse to reminders of role. Though the scale is small the pattern of positioning moves and the resistances they encounter is exemplary of the unfolding of episodes of much greater import.

In dialogue with social identity theory, Lee, Lessem, and Moghaddam (Chapter 7) consider how reconceptualizing 'social identity' as 'positions in moral orders' and 'intergroup strategies' as 'mutual positioning' highlights the relationally negotiated and open-ended character of what are fundamentally 'identity projects' (Harré, 1983). In two studies, the authors focus on how lower status persons (less qualified job candidates and 'lower class' Venezuelan women) manage personal distinctiveness in threatening social comparison situations. The studies reveal how through mutual positioning acts distinctiveness is assigned positive, negative, and at times ambiguous moral valence. The ambiguity of some positioning acts is characteristic of social episodes. It is argued that such ambiguity provides great latitude for attaching storylines that can deepen or avert social conflicts.

Enlarging the scale again Grattans' analysis (Chapter 8) of the well known case of Teri Schiavo shows how a conflict gradually grows in both scope and intensity, as the participants engage in mutual and hostile positioning. The study emphasises the importance of character assassination in the way the positioning of each of the parties to the conflict depends upon mutual denigration. The case is also important for the way that as the conflict escalated over more than a decade, more and more people were drawn in to it. Some of them were 'moral entrepreneurs' seeking a public platform for their views on the issue of the proper grounds for termination of the use life support systems to sustain a vegetative existence. Finally the scale of the conflict enlarged to include even the President of the United States himself. The resolution, if it can be so-called, came about by the decision of the courts to support the position claimed by Michael Schiavo, the husband of the injured woman, of his absolute right and indeed his duty to terminate the vegetative existence of the being who had once been his wife. Once bodily death had supervened on the death of personhood, long gone from the scene, the conflict ended. This is one kind of resolution, in stark contrast to the mannerly negotiations of Redman's three school teachers.

In Chapter 9 Taylor, Caoutte, Usborne, and King use positioning theory to understand the apparent paradox when people from seemingly disadvantaged groups actively support the existing system. This is the very system within which they have come to be disadvantaged. Other studies have shown Moghaddam (2007) that being seen as disadvantaged by those in the seeming dominant position can be exploited as a covert advantage. Taylor et al demonstrate the same phenomenon. Equity considerations are a 'two edged sword'. By achieving equity with the previously advantaged group, the disadvantaged now lose their bargaining power in society. Individuals, successfully positioning themselves as having the rights and even the duties of members of the advantaged soon disavow their previous group membership. While people's motives may seem paradoxical according to social identity theory they become entirely intelligible if analyzed in terms of the establishing and contesting of positions.

Bartlett (Chapter 10) opens up another dimension of positioning theory in his analysis of the interplay between a government edict, a political speech and a discussion of sustainable management. Not just one positioning triangle of rights (duties), story-line and social meaning is required to carry through the analysis, but eleven different positioning structures come and go, interweaving as the focal episode unfolds within the long term context of positions generated by the beliefs people had in the force of the original law. In the course of the analysis we are presented with an almost pure case of positioning by character assassination as a speaker insists on the incompetence and arrogance of one of those who works with the official edict. The incipient conflict between the official line and the rights of people to manage their environment is resolved in the sense that through a shifting pattern of positionings and repositionings the 'chips are never down'.

Enlarging the scale of events still further Schmidle (Chapter 11) takes us into the councils of war of two great military commanders, Napoleon and Lawrence of Arabia. Why did Napoleon lose his grip on the Battle of Borodino, while Lawrence succeeded triumphantly in bringing the Arab irregulars victory over the army of the Turks? The key lies in the maintenance of a clear vision of the relevant positions that commanders can take. Napoleon, being both Emperor and General-in-command, positioned himself as the former conflicting with the positioning as the latter was essential to successfully managing the battle. The conflict was never resolved. Lawrence made no such mistake. His subtle and flexible positioning of himself in relation to the Arab leaders, and his subsequent choice of style of warfare that these positioning made possible, explained his extraordinary success as a commander. Here we have a study of second order positioning which had a profound significance for the first order conflict. Napoleon's confused positioning of himself led to the ultimate defeat at the hands of the Russians, while Lawrence's very clear conception of his relations to the Arab leaders brought victory. In each case the first order conflict was resolved – by defeat in the one case and by victory in the other.

Genocide, as Slocum-Bradley shows (Chapter 12), is made possible by positioning of the two parties to systematic mass murder so that the aggressors not only have the right to slaughter their opponents but the duty to do so. She shows how a story-line was deployed to legitimate the massacres, that is establish them as right and proper and their commission a duty. The analysis focuses on the broadcasts by Rwandan radio, which depended on a prior 'ethnicization' of the Hutu-Tutsi distinction. From being a weakly defined social distinction the antithesis became an a priori ethnic differentiation. 'Tutsi' does not even describe an empirically determined ethnic category. However, once in currency the preliminary moves, particularly character assassination, on which subsequent positioning acts were grounded, became possible rhetorically. The story-line of the previous behaviour of the Tutsi is a sustained background available for each and every local positioning act. Slocum-Bradley's analysis leaves the Rwandan world in the aftermath of the genocide. In a way this is a macabre resolution of the conflict engendered by clever use of positioning tactics.

Rothbart and Bartlett (Chapter 13) look at the very same conflict from the point of view of the Hutu story-line and the consequent positioning of the Tutsi. Looking in more detail at the ethnicization of the Hutu-Tutsi distinction they open out a wider context of Bantu-Hamitic antagonism. This move allows for a systematic stigmatization of the Tutsi in class terms – the arrogant lords. The scale of analysis opens out beyond Slocum-Bradley's historical story-line of Tutsi and Hutu relations into a vast space of an axiology of mythic events. As the scale increases so does the virulence of the character assassination that underpins the call to genocide. The mythic dimension crystallizes into one term, 'cockroach'. The key to the enlargement is the conflation of historic myth with stories illustrating the current situation. The resolution, it seems, is evident and immediate – eliminate the Tutsi before they can regain their power as oppressors. Once again as social researchers we must eschew the naïve idea that conflict resolution comes about by negotiation and the development of mutual respect among the parties.

In the next chapter the positioning agents are political leaders but the entities being positioned are nation states, particularly Iran and the United States. The conflict is wholly one of positions, that is the rights and duties of the contending parties to carry on certain activities, with disputes focused particularly on supererogatory duties. The meaning of these activities, the enrichment of uranium, interacts with the positioning moves, the story-line evolving in this case as the dependent component of the positioning triangle. In the Hutu- Tutsi conflict story-line was the most important factor, positioning and act interpretations following in its wake. However, as the conflict continues a potent story-line begins to appear – the community or 'family' of nations. By refusing to accept the rules that this community has put together for the welfare of all people, and positioning itself as having the right to do what it likes with its own industrial plants, Iran forfeits its place in the family. The US administration ascribing faults and vices to Iran positions the Iranian administration as having a duty to obey the 'family values' and so not to have the right to pursue its uranium program as it wishes. The Prime Minister of Iran, Mahmoud Ahmadinejad refuses that position, particularly the claim by the US and the rest of the 'family of nations' to be so positioned as to have the right to question to the intentions of the Iranians. So far no resolution is in sight.

In the last analysis Montiel and Christie (Chapter 15) apply positioning theory to the conflicts inherent in the idea that authoritarian regimes should be 'toppled' to be replaced by some of a 'democratic' cast. As an analytical device the authors suggest a four level format for the analysis of democratization: society, state, informal organizations, families. All four levels are in interaction, and so are engaged in mutual positioning acts across these scale boundaries. On these boundaries an individual may take up a variety of positions with respect to the nature of the structures. For example, a pro-democracy activist might take up a position comprised of natural rights in conflict with a repertoire of rights conceded by a state. A family might position itself as having the right to discipline its own members in conformity with the rights ascribed to the members by virtue of their religious affiliation. During the process of democratization an individual may take up as many as six different positions.

Conclusion

The advent of Positioning Theory can be seen as a development of one the dimensions of Vygotsky's (1986) conception of the person growing up to live in an ocean of language, in intimate interaction with others in the construction of a flow of public and social cognition. Looking at social episodes in such a dynamic way opens up all sorts of insights and research opportunities. Moving beyond the overly restrictive frame of Role Theory it offers a conceptual system within which to follow the unfolding of episodes of everyday life in new and illuminating ways. By changing the scale of the investigation of conflicts from communities, ethnicities or nations to that of the everyday encounters to which people bring their implicit beliefs about what it is right and proper to say and do, one can begin to redress the balance between rights and duties. At the same time one is making visible the moral orders of those close encounters which make up the greater part of our lives.

Positioning Theory shows how there are psychological matters under-lying many conflicts, particularly beliefs about rights and duties. Negotiating techniques may be targeted only on superficial aspects of a dispute, for example trying to establish a common norm of equity. In so doing they may not addressing the underlying psychological issues at all. These often take the form of antithetical moral orders in which rights and duties are defined in conflictive ways. In the United States justice as equity is a dominant factor in the implicit establishment of Positions. Not so in Spain, where matters of justice as the defence of honor generally outweighs equity considerations (Finkel, Rodriguez, & Harré, 2003). Positioning theory offers a way to reach into the background of persistent conflicts to at least make clear the psychological frameworks of beliefs that underlie them. It is our contention that exploring this dimension of depth in the analysis of conflicts is one of the most fruitful ways of looking for ways in which resolutions could be sought.

There are three sources of persistent and damaging misunderstandings that the use of Positioning analysis could, and in some of the cases presented in this book, actually does remedy, resolving the conflicts that arise from it. Different meanings may be given to the same action by some of the people involved in an episode. Resolution comes from simply pointing this out. But it is not always so simple. The antithetical meanings come from discordant story-lines, sometimes on the scale of cosmic narratives. Explaining to each side the cosmic myths of the others may lead to enthusiastic attempts by each side at proselytizing, making things a great deal worse. 'The people who believe this rubbish must be less than human! It is our duty to save them from their folly, by force if necessary!' Making and publicizing a positioning analysis is no guarantee that a resolution will eventually follow. At least it is a way of reaching into the underlying background on which the superficial conflict rests.

Though the material in this book is largely directed to the resolution of conflicts, it must also be acknowledged that sometime we need to amplify or create a conflict. Just as Socrates remarked that doctors make the best murderers so Positioning Theorists who understand the source of many conflicts in positioning incompatibilities have the skills to help bring conflicts to the boil. They should be the best agents provocateurs. It may be necessary to bring allies onto one's side in a conflict. It may necessary to incite the team one is coaching to position the opponents as people we have a duty to defeat, and so on. Exacerbating one conflict may be just as morally meritorious as resolving another. The study of electioneering maneuvers in the formalized conflicts at the polls in representative democracies reveals positioning acts in a very overt way.

Note

1. This happened in the family of one of the authors, who went to play lots of rugby and to be a member of the university boxing team.

References

Allport, G. W. (1954). *On the nature of prejudice*. Cambridge, MA: Addison-Wesley.
Austin, J. (1959). How to do things with words. Oxford: Oxford University Press.
Brewer, M. B., & Miller, N. (1996). Intergroup relations. Pacific Grove, CA.: Brooks/Cole.

Davies, B., & Harré, R. (1990a). Positioning theory. *Journal for the Theory of Social Behaviour, 20,* 1–18.

Davies, B., & Harré, R. (1990b). Positioning: The discursive production of selves. *Journal for the Theory of Social Behavior, 20,* 43–63.

Deutsch, M., Coleman, P. T., & Marcus, E. C. (Eds.) (2006). *Handbook of conflict resolution.* 2nd. Ed. Jossey-Bass.

Dollard, J., Bood, L., Miller, N., Mowrer, O., & Sears, R. (1939). *Frustration and aggression.* New Haven: Yale University Press.

Finkel, N.J., Harré, R., & Rodriguez, J. (2003). Commonsense morality across cultures: notions of fairness, justice, honor and equity. *Discourse Studies, 3,* 5–27.

Fisher, R. J. (Ed.). (2005). *Paving the way: Contributions of interactive conflict resolution to peacemaking.* Lanham, MD: Lexington Books.

Goffman, E. (1975). *Frame analysis.* London: Penguin Books.

Goffman, E. (1981a). Replies and responses. In E. Goffman, *Forms of talk* (pp. 5–77). Philadelphia, PA: University of Pennsylvania.

Goffman, E. (1981b). *Forms of talk.* Philadelphia: University of Philadelphia Press.

Hafer, C., & Bègue, L. (2005). Experimental research on just-world theory: Problems, developments, and future challenges. *Psychological Bulletin, 131,* 128–167.

Harré, R. (1983). Personal being. Oxford: Blackwell.

Harré, R., & Secord, P. F. (1972). *The explanation of social behaviour.* Oxford: Blackwell.

Hogg, M. A. (2001). A social identity theory of leadership. *Personality and Social Psychology Review, 5,* 184–200.

Jabri, V. (1996). *Discourses on violence: Conflict analysis reconsidered.* Manchester, UK and New York, NY: Manchester University Press.

Jost, J. T., & Banaji, M. R. (1994). The role of stereotyping in system-justification and the production of false consciousness. *British Journal of Social Psychology, 33,* 1–27.

Krugman, P. (2006). Graduates versus oligarchs. The New York Times, February 27, p. 23.

Lerner, M. J. (1980). *The belief in a just world: A fundamental delusion.* New York: Plenum.

McCarthy, T. D., & Zald, M. N. (1977). Resource mobilization and social movements: A partial theory. *American Journal of Sociology, 82,* 1212 1241.

Miller, N., Pederson, W. C., Earlywine, M., & Pollock, V. E. (2003). A theoretical model of triggered displaced aggression. *Personality and Social Psychology Review, 7,* 75–97.

Moghaddam, F. M. (2006). Interobjectivity: The collective roots of individual consciousness and social identity. In T. Postmes & J. Jetten (Eds.), *Individuality and the group: Advances in social identity* (pp.155–174). London, UK: Sage.

Moghaddam, F. M. (2007). Multiculturalism and intergroup relations: Implications for democracy in global context. Washington, D.C.: American Psychology Association Press.

Paden, J. N. (2005). *Muslim civic cultures and conflict resolution: The challenge of democratic federalism in Nigeria.* Washington, D.C.: Brookings Institution Press.

Pettigrew, T. F., & Tropp, L. R. (2006). A meta-analytic test of intergroup contact theory. *Journal of Personality and Social Psychology, 90,* 751–783.

Pyszczynski, T., Solomon, S., & Greenberg, J. (2003). *In the wake of 9/11: The psychology of terror.* Washington, DC: American Psychological Association press.

Ramsbotham, O., Wood, T., & Miall, H. (2005). *Contemporary conflict resolution: The prevention, management and transformation of deadly conflicts.* Cambridge, UK: Polity.

Runciman, W. G. (1966). *Relative deprivation and social justice.* Harmondsworth, UK: Penguin.

Sanger, D. E., & Rutenberg, J. (2006). Bush and Blair concede errors, but defend war. The New York Times, May 26, 2006, pp. A1&A12.

Sherif, M. (1966). *Group conflict and cooperation: Their social psychology.* London: Routledge & Kegan Paul.

Sidanius, J., & Pratto, F. (1999). *Social dominance: An intergroup theory of social dominance and oppression.* Cambridge, UK: Cambridge University Press.

Stouffer, S. A., Suchman, E. A., De Vinney, L. C., Star, S. A., & Williams, R. M. (1949). *The American soldier: adjustments during army life (vol.1).* Princeton: Princeton University Press.

Tajfel, H. (1978). Social categorization, social identity, and social comparison. In H. Tajfel (Ed.), *Differentiation between social groups* (pp. 61–76). London and New York: Academic Press.

Tajfel, H., & Turner, J. C. (1979). An integrative theory of intergroup conflict. In W. G. Austin & S. Worchel (Eds.), *The social psychology of intergroup relations* (pp. 33–47). Monterey, CA: Brooks/Cole.

Taylor, D. M., & Moghaddam, F. M. (1994). *Theories of intergroup relations: International social psychological perspectives.* Westport, CT: Praeger.

Teixeira, R. A. (1992). *The disappearing American voter.* Washington, DC: Brookings Institute.

Trappl, R. (Ed.). (2006). *Programming for peace: Computer-aided methods for international conflict resolution and prevention.* Dordrecht: Springer.

Tyler, T. R., & Huo, Y. J. (2002). *Trust in the law.* New York: Russell Sage Foundation.

Vygotsky, L./S. (1986). *Thought and language.* Trans. A. Kozulin. Cambridge MA: MIT Press.

Walker, I. & Smith, H. (Eds.). (2002). *Relative deprivation: Specification, development, and integration.* Cambridge, UK: Cambridge University Press.

Wallensteen, P. (2002). Understanding conflict resolution: War, peace and the global system. Sage. Thousand Oaks, CA

Walster, E., Walster, G. E., & Berscheid, E., (1978). *Equity: Theory and research.* Boston: Allyn & Bacon.

Worchel, S. & Austin, W. G. (1986) (Eds.), *Psychology of intergroup relations.* Chicago: Nelson-Hall.

2
Intergroup Positioning and Power

WINNIFRED R. LOUIS

This chapter aims to review positioning theory and discuss its utility for the analysis of intergroup conflict; to discuss the implications of considering intergroup behaviour and conflict in the analysis of positioning theory; and finally to combine the insights of positioning theory and intergroup research to understand group power and the operation of social influence in conflict contexts. A primary goal is to explore theoretical consistencies and contradictions and identify directions for future research in the analysis of conflict dynamics.

Positioning Theory in Intergroup Conflict: Insights and Challenges

Positioning theory, as noted by Harré and Moghaddam (2003) aims to analyse social interaction over time, as "unfolding sequential structures of meanings, ordered in accordance with local rules, conventions, and customs of correct conduct" (p. 3). This science produces a "catalogue of situation-specific meanings and sets of context-sensitive rules that explained the pattern of the evolving social episode, as an actual sequence of meaningful social actions" (p. 3). Positioning theory is an essential complement to the ahistorical snapshot of the experiment and the cause and effect reasoning of mainstream psychology. Group conflict and cooperation is profitably modelled with universalist models (e.g. Moghaddam, 2005) but there is also "unexplained variance": group conflict is particularist and probabilistic (see e.g., Reicher, 2004). To paraphrase Tolstoy, all harmony is alike, but each conflict unfolds in its own unique history. And many or most large scale social conflicts could have developed along multiple paths, far from being the inevitable result of determinist processes (see e.g., Churchill, 1950). In short, conflicts by definition involve more than one individual;[1] they imply a temporal relationship and a constructed, contested social reality. In this sense the core insights of positioning theory define the essentials of conflict.

Positioning theory also proposes three specific concepts to be used to understand social interactions and conflict (Harré & Moghaddam, 2003;

Harré & van Langenhove, 1999): positions, acts, and story lines. Each of these may be discussed in relation to research in intergroup conflict, along with the operationalisation of conflict and the role of power.

Positions

Positions define what is socially possible without incurring reprobation or punishment (Harré & Moghaddam, 2003; Harré & van Langenhove, 1999). They are emergent and ephemeral clusters of rights of access to particular repertoires of action, and/or duties of access to others. In my position as a chapter author, I have the right to pontificate at length about my views; in another position as a conversational partner I have the duty to curtail my self-centered eloquence, invite comments, and respond to others.

Actors beyond the individual. Essential to the study of positioning and conflict is the study of groups. But while positioning theory understands itself as a science of social interactions and meaning, it is common to see an underlying individualism in the writing, for example when positions are defined as clusters of rights and duties attached to persons (Harré & Moghaddam, 2003; Harré & van Langenhove, 1999). An analysis of disputes which does not extend from I to consider the implicit collective actors, we, you and they, is inherently incomplete and partial. Most positioning theorists would doubtless agree! The social cognition of the individual and collective self and of the perceptual relationship between one we-group and another they-group has been elaborated by researchers in social identity and self-categorisation (see Tajfel & Turner, 1979; Turner, Hogg, & Oakes, Reicher, Wetherell, 1987). These and others have argued that all rights and duties – and thus all self-positioning – are shaped by groups, intergroup relations and collective identities (Louis & Taylor, 2005; see also Taylor, Bougie, & Caouette, 2003; Worchel, 2005). The conflicts of individuals take place in the context of their mutual relationship to group authorities (e.g., Tyler & Smith, 1999). In this sense, the positioning of individuals with respect to each other can never be understood without addressing their relational concerns to be, and to be seen to be, valued and respected group members.

Many conflicts – and many of the most pervasive and intractable conflicts – also go beyond individual enmities. If one American soldier kills an insurgent Iraqi, or vice versa, the killer acts as a group member for group goals, and typically as individuals the killer and victim are strangers to each other. But more broadly group conflicts may include collective actors (such as armies, bureaucracies, political parties, parliaments, nations, or multi-national coalitions of the willing and unwilling) and their actions (wars, missions, marches, riots, conferences, treaties, and so on). The social identity approach helps us to understand that group conflict implicates group-level factors, without an understanding of which the "position" of the individual actor cannot be derived.

The closest concept to positions in intergroup theory is the salient self-categorisation or identity (Tajfel & Turner, 1979; Turner et al., 1987). Turner and colleagues have theorised in many papers how individuals define themselves along continua from personal identity (I) to social identities (we, e.g., we women, we academics). Each identity has associated norms defining rights and duties, each is innately relational, and the salience of different self-categorisations is thought to be highly consequential for interactions. My self-categorisation as an academic may lead me to perceive you as an ingroup member, which will lead to increased perception of similarities on dimensions that define the group, positive self-stereotyping, and normatively prescribed action (talking shop, etc.!). By contrast if I self-categorise as an Australian I may perceive you as an outgroup foreigner, with salient group boundaries leading to increased perception of differences on dimensions that define the relationship (e.g., nationalist stereotyping). The group context is evaluated in terms of secure or threatening relationship perceptions, giving rise to normatively prescribed cooperative or competitive behaviour. Like positions, salient social identities are dynamic and responsive to context.

Beyond coherence. Positions have been defined as "patterns of beliefs [about rights and duties] in the members of a relatively coherent speech community" (Harré & Moghaddam, 2003: p. 3). In the consideration of intergroup positioning and conflict, however, one must move away from the frame of the coherent speech community. Harré and Moghaddam specify that people can access positions deliberately, or deliberately eschew them; they may be pushed into them, or be displaced from them; in this sense, the concept of position need imply neither coherence nor consensus across individuals.

Moreover, the transient and relationally defined position aims to capture the swift changes in social influence and dominance of conflict contexts, in a way that its ancestor, the stable, static concept of role, does not (Harré & Slocum, 2003). In positioning theory people are proposed to occupy more than one position simultaneously. This discordance occurs both when perceptions are not mutual (I think of myself as the teacher and you as the student; you think of me as the tyrant and you as the rebel). It also occurs when people are simultaneously working on multiple social projects (I am the facilitator of a research forum with the right and duty to choose speakers; I am also a sexist man preferentially choosing men; I am also a friend choosing a friend; and so on). These positions can interact with each other. For example, my personal identity as absent-minded compared to my friends may reinforce a social identity as an academic, or a position as a teacher with the right to pontificate may conflict with my position as younger, with the duty to listen to elders (Taylor et al., 2003). This explicit consideration of multiple simultaneously active identities, possibly internally inconsistent and externally contested, is an important difference from most intergroup research.

A second theoretically interesting difference between positioning theory and most intergroup research is that the salient psychological positions need not imply a mental first person, nor define the self exclusively. As noted above, many positions may be salient at the same time for the same individual: some of these may be social wes, others personal Is, and others subjectively recognised as complex clusters that make up a single phenomenological I. For example,

I might be positioned as an academic female aspiring to leadership in my subdiscipline who is a loyal friend to a peripheral department member disliked by the male dean of the faculty. In this sense, positioning theory contravenes the principle of functional antagonism as proposed in the original formulation of self-categorisation theory: that identities can be ordered on a continuum from personal to social and that the salience of one category inhibits the salience of others (Turner et al., 1987). McGarty (1999) and others have also thoughtfully reconsidered functional antagonism from within the self-categorisation framework. But certainly, positioning theory encourages researchers to consider multiplicity and salience across personal and social levels, as well as resistance to and rejection of a situationally-relevant or imposed position.

Self-categorisation theory also poses important empirical questions to positioning researchers: for example, out of the multiple positions identified, how many can really be subjectively experienced at one time? While the inevitability of functional antagonism between identities has been challenged by McGarty (1999) and others, it is surely aversive and unusual to feel like several different people; it is part of our understanding of psychosis! Although positioning theorists point to the multiplicity of positions that may be experienced within an interaction, little research has demonstrated that these multiple positions are subjectively real, or common, or behaviourally important. Out of the multiple positions identified, how many can really influence behaviour? Granted that I may feel conflicting imperatives for writing papers or playing with children, don't my choices demonstrate one tendency in one context? I do not oscillate at random between being an academic and mother: I feel and act like an academic at work (albeit angsting about children neglected) and a mother at home (albeit angsting about papers unwritten).

Elaborating this point: rather than choosing strategically to express particular positions, is not the "choice" often environmentally-driven? I might work 9–5 as an academic, or stay late to meet a deadline, or suddenly feel parental when I receive a phone call that my child is ill. Thus rather than strategically choosing to position myself and others, I might show adaptation to the environment, consistency regulated by the activation of particular identities and norms. In short, although positioning theory positions itself as phenomenological, it remains to be established through empirical research whether and how often people subjectively feel as though they choose positions (or story-lines, or acts – see below). By contrast the unconscious activation of identities in response to environmental cues and the subsequent expression of group normative action is well supported in the literature (e.g., Terry & Hogg, 2000).

A related question open to empirical research is: To what extent does the activation of multiple positions resolve itself (particularly over time) in the construction of a new, internally coherent subgroup identity: working mother, feminist academic, and so on? The experienced position – the subjective position – has internal consistency pressure within contexts (Festinger, 1954), though it may change across contexts as the social identity approach has shown.

Positioning theory has yet to grapple with these issues empirically, although a theoretical position against determinism is clear.

And one final question: how can post-hoc reifications be avoided in "positioning" if inconsistencies in people's actions are ascribed to the operation of infinite salient positions? Is all behaviour strategic, and if so, what is happening when people respond to malignant positioning (below)? Little research has been conducted on these issues, and thus, it yet remains to demonstrate the limits of either position (sic!).

Actions and Acts

As a second tool to understand social conflict, positioning theory introduces a distinction between actions (behaviours that are intended performances, such as writing to the newspaper) and acts which are what the behaviour means socially (a plea to achieve a goal, a protest about another's behaviour, etc.). Thus "speech and other acts" (Harré & Moghaddam, 2003: p. 6) are the second concept proposed as necessary to understand social interactions. The study of conflict almost by definition implies the consideration of acts, as socially understood behaviours; the "act" vs "action" distinction is particularly useful here. However, conflict studies lead to a greater focus on non-speech behaviour.

Beyond utterances. Harré and Slocum describe the application of positioning theory to a dispute as a cataloguing of the positions, story lines, and "speech acts" available to persons or institutions (2003: p. 132). Humans talk a lot, especially academic humans, and perhaps that's reason enough for positioning theory to privilege words. The theory also offers conflict researchers a useful elaboration of the concept of lexical adequacy, for example as analysed in Harré and colleagues' work on "greenspeak" in the environmental movement (Harré, Brockmeier, & Mühlhäuser, 1999). This research proposes that every social movement must achieve success in language creation/co-option: referential adequacy, or available words [lexical resources] to discuss a topic in sufficient detail; systematic adequacy, or words which can be structured to promote efficiency, and social adequacy, or words acceptable to speakers in a target community, promoting unity and intercommunication, and catering to needs. An analysis of rhetorical resources available is likely to deepen the understanding of group's conflict choices and social power. And a group approach can increase the sophistication of the analysis by fleshing out the concepts of acceptability (injunctive vs descriptive referent group norms, etc.), target community, and so on (see e.g. Gallois, Ogay, & Giles, 2005; Terry & Hogg, 1996).

However, as noted by Slocum and van Langenhove, in their analysis of positioning in the political science of regional integration, "The act is what is accomplished socially through a particular action, which can be constituted by linguistic and/or **non-linguistic** discourse" (2003: p. 225; bold added). They discuss "the action of allowing an Arab to hold a seat in the Knesset, which was interpreted by some people as an act of compromise to promote democracy and peace, and by others as an act of treason" (p. 225). In short, conflict commonly calls for an expanded scope of study, beyond the utterance. It may include non verbal conversations of body language and spatial distance, as well as written words and physical actions. It calls for an understanding of behaviours which may not have a single target or "conversational" partner, but rather be like plays be designed to be witnessed by audience(s). One actor, such as a leader, may perform to collections of individuals, or to a collectivity, or to multiple groups; groups may perform to each other, to individuals, and to third parties. In these conversations, monologues and plays the positions may be expressed non-verbally through physical action (holding hands, punches), symbolism (wearing colours, waving placards), and collective actions (marches, rallies, voting), as well as speech. In this sense the study of conflict pushes theorists to take the useful distinction between act and action far beyond the "speech act".

Story Lines

As the third element proposed as necessary to understand the unfolding of conflict, positioning theory deploys the concept of story lines, which are narrative conventions according to which social episodes unfold. These may indirectly determine positions, actions and acts. For example, as a facilitator of a public forum, I position myself as the person who calls on audience or panel members to speak. I might directly position you as a speaker by inviting you to speak, or indirectly position you as a speaker by attributions of expertise ("Dr. Y has done research on this"). Alternatively, I may adopt a story line that positions you according to my goals, such as "we are going around the circle so that everyone speaks in turn" (you will get a chance) or alternatively "we are hearing from eminent experts" (I can exclude you based on non-eminence).

A story line is like a script, directing behaviour according to positions which may be implicit or explicit (Abelson, 1976). But whereas scripts are often researched as consensual and evoked by a situation, story lines are proposed to be actively constructed and contested. Story lines give meaning to actions and define them as acts; they order goals and strategies as well as tactics and means. In applying positioning theory to an analysis of conflict, Slocum and van Langenhove (2003) identify story lines around European regional integration that link integration to either prosperity, peace, power, defense against American hegemony, etc., or to lost identity, lost sovereignty, harm to the environment, the poor, etc..

The construction of these story lines is a project of actors positioning themselves and others. Once constructed, the story lines are spread through speech and other acts targeting media and political outlets as well as individual conversation partners. Actors' unequal access to media and political outlets; their unequal abilities to reach and sway audiences with coercion, bribes, or credibility: All these reflect unequal power to promote storylines which in turn frame interpretations of a conflict and direct behavioural responses (this point is elaborated below). Cultural fit too is unequally distributed, and essential for the creation and survival of a story line. Ability to recognise and express the culturally meaningful patterns of a storyline, the values that are embraced by a culture versus rejected, and the historical experiences that make new analogies believable and relevant versus far-fetched: This not only motivates the actors intrinsically as they create their story lines but also extrinsically, as actors strategically shape the stories to be accepted and disseminated by other audiences.

Beyond the present. The concept of the story line, with behaviours unfolding over time in a sequence ordered and legitimised by narrative, may be a valuable import to the study of conflict. In the social identity/self-categorisation approach, the choice of particular tactics is understood as determined proximally by group norms, which in turn arise from perceptions of three dimensions of intergroup relations: permeability, legitimacy, and stability. If people perceive (in the present) that group boundaries are permeable, so that group members can freely exit disadvantaged groups and join advantaged ones; that they are legitimate or fair, and that they are stable or unchanging; then they do not perceive alternatives to the status quo. In this case their behaviour is secure (low salience of group threat) and may be oriented to intergroup cooperation or to intra-group, individualistic concerns. As perceptions of illegitimacy, impermeability, and instability arise, the salience of the group identity increases, a sense of threat is experienced, and norms arise favouring explicitly competitive intergroup actions (e.g., discrimination by advantaged groups, or demonstrations and rallies by disadvantaged groups).

A comparison of the models raises the question of whether concepts such as socio-structural beliefs about stability, legitimacy, permeability, and norms could benefit from being unpacked and temporally ordered. For example, the idea that one past behaviour legitimises a second future behaviour is a theoretically interesting and socially important aspect of conflict (e.g., "first try voting then protest then terrorism then revolution") yet it is rarely studied in cross-sectional intergroup research (cf. Drury & Reicher, 2000). So too observed interactions between permeability, stability and legitimacy (e.g., Johnson, Terry, & Louis, 2005) may be implicitly regulated by temporal sequencing, so that changes in legitimacy induce changes in perceived stability, and so on. Behind the socio-cognitive processes of perception and emergent norms there is also an active construction and negotiation, between and within groups, which must be addressed – as indeed Reicher and others have argued from within the social identity tradition (see below).

Beyond the particular? Consideration of the social identity approach also highlights a complementary need for positioning researchers to delineate the dimensions according to which story lines are psychologically experienced. Granted that I may know a wealth of details about the historical relationship between our groups, as well as imagine our future(s): All of this complexity may not be salient or influential to me. What is it about "history" that impacts on how I think, feel, and act? Positioning researchers often take mainstream psychology to task for failing to grapple with the construction of personal and collective meaning. However, by identifying at least three core aspects of story lines that change intergroup psychology and action, the social identity/intergroup approach has arguably taken an important step towards understanding the phenomenology of group conflict. By analysing intergroup positions, acts, and story lines as complex particularist narratives, psychological similarities and commonalities across particular conflict contexts may be overlooked and minimised.

Similarly, the emphasis on the active construction of story lines rather than "determinist" responding to the social environment raises the question of how often there are alternative positions and story lines available psychologically to individuals? As noted above, it has not been demonstrated whether and how often people feel as though they choose a position whereas social identity and social influence studies show that people often do respond to determinist cued identities and norms. Even given the theoretical possibility of more than one storyline, factors such as cultural norms, environmental cues, and personal values – what the social identity approach might identify as the perceptual and normative fit of an identity – may constrain strategic positioning for most people most of the time (Oakes, Turner, & Haslam, 1991).

Finally, social identity work on pro-group action provokes the comment that one sees little work by positioning theorists about benevolent or pro-social or self-sacrificing positions and story-lines. An underlying individualism which neglects groups and cooperation at the expense of stories of individual quests for advantage can only produce a partial understanding of any social behaviour, including group conflict itself (cf. Tan & Moghaddam, 1999a).

The Operationalisation of Conflict

Finally, positioning theory helps us to reflect on the operationalisation of conflict itself. In positioning theory, conflict protagonists are thought to work actively to choose story lines in order to position themselves to access useful repertoires of action, and position opponents to cut them off (Harré & Slocum, 2003). In order to privilege the desired story line, disputants may define the conflict differently, implicating different actors and goals. This focus on agency for action rather than "wired" cognitive responses is a key component of positioning research in conflict. Thus, positions are relational, but vary in the extent to which they are consensual as well as in the extent to which they are intentionally chosen.

Some actors may passively accept another's positioning in conflict, as when a child or a newcomer accepts the authority of a parent or oldtimer in framing an interaction; in other cases positioning may be not only non-intentional but unsuc-cessfully resisted. What has been called malevolent or malignant positioning can be used to deprive people of access to particular repertoires of social behaviour; for example when minor incapacities are used to position people with Alzheimer's disease as demented (Sabat, 2003). Benson (2003) notes that a position of deprivation sometimes results in the target's self-censoring (the action becomes unthinkable) and sometimes in emotional self-regulation (considering the action triggers revulsion); in the latter case particularly, the target's position is internalized as an identity as non-performers of the action. Other times a position of deprivation can mean that the deprived target's act cannot be socially or psychologically seen or heard by the target's partners, as when a judge rules to strike a comment from the record (Harré & Moghaddam, 2003, p. 8), or when a heterosexist cannot "hear" that a lesbian has identified a same-sex partner.

These concepts – asymmetric identity positions for conflict participants, strategically chosen or deployed in narratives to limit action/power, or passively accepted, or unsuccessfully resisted, or internalized to produce self-regulation and self-censorship – are interesting when applied to conflict studies' social identities and self-categorisations (see e.g., Reicher, 1996). These are often studied as independent variables in theory made salient by an intergroup context and in practice operationalised as symmetric, consensual and non-embedded (as when participants self-identify according to experimenter-given category labels, and then rate the salience or strength of identification along experimenter-given dimensions). Moreover, experimental social psychology offers a wealth of fascinating research on processes that might be involved. For example, Baumeister and colleagues' work on the impact of exclusion could draw attention to undermined executive function as a possible precursor to unsuccessfully resisted malignant positioning (Baumeister, Dewall, Ciarocco, & Twenge, 2005), or my own work could point to changing deliberative cost-benefit analyses as a potential mediator of the link between new positions and new behavioural choices (e.g., Louis, Taylor, & Neil, 2004, 2005). In this sense, intergroup research might readily apply the insights of positioning theory using the tools and micro-theories of experimental social psychology.

Understanding the interaction. The methodological procedure of research in positioning theory is to delineate hypotheses regarding the three components of the positioning triangle: to identify possible positions, story lines, and actions/acts. Though positioning theory may discover these components in the accounts of research participants, like discourse theory, positioning theory emphasizes that multiple story lines can be experienced at the same time as only one is verbalized to a particular audience (Harré & Moghaddam, 2003; Harré & Slocum, 2003). Thus the positioning researcher attempts to analyse an episode from various points of view and to catalogue "shared and unshared beliefs about the story lines unfolding and the rights and duties of participants" (Harré & Moghaddam, 2003: p. 9). In this sense, positioning theorists attempt to identify psychological motives – beliefs and emotions – within narratives (story lines).

The role of the positioning researcher is to identify what conflict participants believe the actors and the goals are: how they define the groups, and position themselves and the other, with a story line in which people's actions are being identified and taken to signify particular acts. In positioning theory, however, social actors' "beliefs" are not taken as face value but are treated as discursive constructions, and this understanding of beliefs is quite different from the usual treatment of the term in psychology. Likewise, it can be suggested that positioning theory is only interested in "motives" insofar as they are used by speakers to position people in particular ways according to particular story-lines. The argument that beliefs and motivations are strategic constructions begs the question of which strategies are being pursued, however, and answering this question requires reference to internal beliefs and motives. A positioning theory that conceptualises beliefs and motives as inextricably linked to particular relationships and identities, and that sees the expression of these as structured by narrative and oriented to achieving contested political goals, which in turn shape salient beliefs and motives, is compatible with existing intergroup conflict work by Reicher and his colleagues (see Reicher, 1996, 2004).

In this sense, both interactionist approaches remind conflict researchers to go beyond two-group conflict models to include third parties (see also Simon & Klandermans, 2001), to study the internal dynamics of positions of groups with respect to leaders and vice versa (e.g., Moghaddam, Hanley, & Harré, 2003; see also Reicher, Haslam, & Hopkins, 2005), to include the active contestation of asymmetric frames rather than assuming that the categories in a conflict are consensually understood and static (e.g., Harré & Slocum, 2003; Reicher & Hopkins, 1996; Sani & Reicher, 1998, 1999), and to include the temporal unfolding of conflict according to narratives including a past and a future (e.g., Drury & Reicher, 2000; Hopkins & Reicher, 1997). These are essential insights for conflict studies.

Power

The final goal of applying positioning theory in disputes, according to Harré and Slocum (2003), is to identify who does and does not possess positioning power, the basis on which the power is allocated, and the role of differences in positioning power in the conflict (e.g. in making certain story lines more dominant). Dispute resolution is proposed to occur with new story lines that remake the local moral order and create a discursive space for a new norm to allow both parties to satisfy their long term goals. Perhaps a key insight of positioning theory is that a new position will be viable to the extent it is embedded in a mutually acceptable story line.

In this sense, positioning theories again complement and expand the work of interactionist intergroup theories. Turner (2005) applies a social identity/self-categorisation approach to the study of power which proposes that group formation and ideology underpin the capacity for social influence, which in turn allows for resource control. This paper is theoretically important because it proposes a reversal of the traditional causal path, in which resource control yields social influence. If we substitute positions and story line for group formation and ideology the arguments of the two approaches are strikingly similar. Again, the social identity approach may help positioning researchers to identify the probable characteristics of "mutually acceptable story lines" – narratives of permeability, stability, and legitimacy.

What the self-categorisation model also adds to positioning research is a fleshed out model to understand the socio-cognitive processes involved in the construction of power. This research and theory shows that individuals position themselves relative to groups through self-categorisation and identification, and groups relative to other groups through socio-structural perceptions (permeability, etc.) and norms. These socio-cognitive processes are the underpinnings of individual and group power. The processes define clusters to look for in the universe of infinite possible positions, acts, and stories. What positioning theorists add to the study of conflict and power is a methodological directive to include the study of discourse, and a conceptual integration beyond the present to the past and the infinite possible futures. As noted above, this methodological and conceptual expansion is also well underway within the social identity approach, through the work of Turner, Reicher, Giles and others.

Where Next?

Agentic Norms and Normative Influence

While positioning researchers speak of positions, story lines, and actions, and while identity researchers speak of group identity, norms, and power, most applied decision-making research, even in conflict, has been more proximally oriented and focused on individual-level cost-benefit analyses (e.g., Ajzen, 1991; see, Feather, 1982). These "rational choice" theories propose that individuals choose among actions by weighing the costs against the benefits in terms of the total subjective expected utility (von Neumann & Morgenstern, 1944). The evaluation is a function of two interacting variables: the subjective probability (expectancy) that a cost or benefit will occur if behavior is performed, and the subjective utility, or extent to which an individual values each of the costs and benefits. The rank order of preferences among the behaviours (i.e., from best to worst outcomes) may be determined quantitatively.

Expectancy-value models have been criticized because both cognitive and social deviations from linear expectancy-value processes have been observed in collective and conflict behavior (see e.g., Halpern & Stern, 1998; Ostrom, 1998). The narrow economic model, which understands rational choices as maximizing individuals' immediate material self-interest, has been found to underpredict cooperation substantially and overpredict conflict and competition (e.g., Bazerman, Gibbons, Thompson, & Valley, 1998). In social contexts, studies show individuals are motivated by intangibles such as personal moral imperatives and internalized societal norms for fairness and reciprocity (e.g., Manstead, 2000; McLean Parks et al., 1996). They can use social abilities such as trusting to achieve outcomes in excess of the economic model's predictions (e.g., Insko et al., 2001). Moreover, individuals are influenced by others' outcomes in social contexts (e.g., McLean Parks & Smith, 1998). As noted above, an individual's self-concept can expand to include interpersonal and group others ("we" as well as "I"), changing considerations of rational self-interest (see also, Aron et al., 2005; Tajfel & Turner, 1979).

Some consideration of social factors in rational decision-making is clearly warranted, as few intergroup or positioning researchers would disagree. But how does it work? One class of individualistic models implies that social processes shape decision-making when they impact on individual-level outcomes (e.g., Ajzen, 1991). This approach, in which group-level incentives are thought to be irrelevant unless they touch on the actor directly, suggests that a mechanism for dispute resolution will be effective to the extent that individual-level material or social rewards for cooperation can be generated for group members (see Olson, 1968). In this case, there is no role for group positions except indirectly, and individual positions should change choices only via their impact on perceived costs and benefits for the individual actor.

A second approach focuses on processes which operate in parallel to cost-benefit analysis, such as social influence via self-stereotyping (e.g., Simon & Klandermans, 2001) or motivation by group-based emotions, such as anger on behalf of a group (van Zomeren, Spears, Fischer, & Leach, 2004). Importantly, this large and empirically-supported body of work suggests that because only one's own groups can trigger processes of self-stereotyping and define one's emotions, other groups' views are ignored unless a superordinate group identity can be activated to frame the conflict as within-group. That is, in the absence of coercive power afforded by surveillance and control over rewards and punishment, dispute resolution resting on outsiders' interventions may be irrelevant to group members' decisions (see also Hornsey, Oppes, & Svensson, 2002).

Adopting the logic of this research, positioning processes could be proposed to operate in parallel so that the expression and active construction of positions within story lines could function independently of rational cost-benefit analyses, with the positioning processes being an alternative path to impact on action. In this sense, unconscious and automatic self-stereotypes would operate alongside conscious, deliberative cost-benefit analyses for salient identities as well as conscious, deliberative discursive construction. Or alternatively the three may fall into a causal sequence, whereby an objective intergroup relationship makes salient a social identity which determines the dimensions and values attached to cost-benefit analyses which motivate an actor to deploy a particular rhetorical position to achieve a group-normative goal. Such an argument could be compatible with social identity approaches, but it would be more theoretically controversial to argue that strategically adopting a particular social identity in order to position oneself could trigger self-stereotyping and group-normative action, or cost-benefit analyses in line with consensual group goals. The relative frequency and influence of conscious invocations of identity through positioning, versus unconsciously determined self-categorisation based on the salience of environmental cues remains to be empirically addressed, as noted above.

In the day to day process of living, when one's self-categorisation and behaviour changes from parent-making-breakfast to commuter to worker and back again, how often and how importantly does positioning occur? In conflict, however, which breaks routinisation by introducing change, negative affect, and salient cognitive alternatives to the status quo, conscious deliberation may be more frequent (Louis, Taylor, & Douglas, 2005). On a theoretical level, moreover, positioning theorists would resist any argument in which primacy is given to psychological processes that are elicited by the social environment, rather than to the agents who perform the acts of positioning, stereotyping, and cost-benefit analyses themselves.

A more optimistic prospect for social influence is delineated in my own research, in which I developed a hierarchical model of group-level rationality to study the evolution of conflict and the possible bases for successful cross-group interventions (Louis & Taylor, 2002; see also Louis & Taylor, 2005; Taylor & Louis, 2004). In this model, when individuals psychologically identify with social groups, the actor's evaluations of the consequences to themselves of a behaviour (e.g., grumbling vs. voting) are derived from perceptions of the consequences for their group (see also, Turner et al., 1987). Perceptions of group-level consequences thus indirectly motivate behavior by shaping perceptions of individual-level consequences when people identify. But following the social identity approach, it is proposed that when people identify with a group, group level consequences are also directly motivating. Moreover, the model argues that people strategically conform to or violate outgroup (they-group) norms as well as ingroup (we-group) norms, because these norms signal how individuals in intergroup conflict can act to benefit themselves and their group. This process of social influence via changed perceptions of costs and benefits to the group has been called agentic normative influence – normative influence for action.

Previous research has demonstrated these processes in field contexts (Louis et al., 2004, 2005). In a series of studies, Anglophone Quebecers were asked to evaluate ways in which they could react to conflict with Francophones, e.g. by accommodating linguistically or by demanding service in English, and federalist Quebecers were asked to evaluate political actions they could use in their political dispute with sovereigntist/separatist Quebecers, e.g. by voting versus speaking to individual outgroup members personally. Those who identified strongly with their ethnolinguistic or political group were observed to associate group- and individual-level consequences (Louis et al., 2004, Study 1). For people committed to their identity, actions that benefited the group were seen to benefit the self, whereas "selfish" actions that harmed the group were seen as harming the self. The link between identification and higher intentions to act was mediated by these group-level consequences (Louis et al., Study 2). More specifically, benefits for the group were found to drive action both directly (cf., Olson, 1968) and by shaping individual-level cost-benefit analyses and thus attitudes to the behavior.

These perceptions of group- and individual-level consequences were found to arise from group norms, as is expected on the basis of social identity research (Louis et al., 2005; see, Tajfel & Turner, 1979; Terry & Hogg, 1996; Turner et al., 1987). Importantly, however, both ingroup and outgroup norms impact on perceptions of consequences for the group, and both are found to be significantly mediated in their impact on action by perceived costs and benefits

(Louis et al., 2005). That is, outgroups can influence people not just by coercively controlling individuals' reward contingencies (Reicher & Levine, 1994) and ingroups can influence not just by "irrational" processes of internalized in group norms and self-stereotyping (Terry & Hogg, 1996) or emotionality (van Zomeren et al., 2004). Rather, rational cost-benefit analysis can concern the path forward for groups as well as individuals, and be triggered and shaped by identity factors – factors such as the norms of one's own group, but also the norms of other groups in interaction.

This model thus proposes that when group identities are salient in conflict, both high and low power groups use the norms of other groups to evaluate the costs and benefits of inaction, conformity, and outgroup norm violation for the ingroup. A high power group (e.g., a government) attempting to change rather than coerce the behaviour of a low power group (e.g., disgruntled farmers) must evaluate the status quo and alternative actions, and then strategically anticipate the low power group's reactions. Will a concession appease the low power group, or will it fuel further demands? The anticipated reaction of the low power outgroup shapes the perceived benefit or cost to the high power group of making a concession.

So far so good! The extent to which decisions are influenced by the relative views of interaction partners in the present model, and by anticipated future interactions, is complementary with positioning theory, and indeed with the approach of many researchers in the social identity approach. From the text above, however, it can be seen that positioning researchers would direct attention to the positioning of individuals within the group, to multiple simultaneous possible positionings, and to the role of history and narrative. An additional fundamental question, moreover, and a problem for all three theoretical models, is to identify when outgroups will be able to influence cooperation vs escalation positively. A high power group, by definition, may be more capable of inflicting costs on or offering benefits to low power groups, so that low power groups are more motivated to attend to outgroups' norms (see Moscovici, 1985; e.g., Reicher & Levine, 1994). Empirically, however, high power groups do not rely exclusively on coercion. Rather than ignoring other groups' norms, it is common to have explicit discussions of what lower power groups expect, and to debate the response that the outgroup position should elicit. The conditions under which urban people will attend to rural norms, or White Australians to indigenous Australians' norms, etc., are not well understood.

Since high power groups benefit from the status quo, by definition, high relative power may increase a group's focus on the benefits versus the costs of inaction. In this sense, high power groups may be biased to inertia. They may strategically promote duties to uphold the status quo, while disadvantaged groups assert rights to change (Louis & Taylor, 2005; Moghaddam & Riley, 2005). However, field studies suggest that if low power groups anticipate that outgroups will ignore their normative actions, escalating violence is a common result (see also, Moghaddam, 2005; e.g., Rouhana & Bar-Tal, 1998). If high power groups can predict this dynamic, they in turn will strategically pay attention to frustrated low power outgroups. Thus, for both high and low power groups, agentic normative influence processes may occur as a common, natural part of conflict interactions.

In short, the present theoretical model hypothesizes that people do pay attention to other groups' views, regardless of power, and that they will make strategic concessions or strategically offend other groups in order to achieve group goals. This process makes sense when people consider the interests of their group in ongoing conflict relationships, even though it seems irrationally risky and counter-productive when analysed at an individual level.

By demonstrating that groups attend to outgroups' norms and strategically respond even at high power, an agentic model will contribute significantly to interactionist theories of conflict evolution, as well as improving the theoretical understanding of how cost-benefit analyses for conflict behaviours are shaped by social influence. For positioning theory, again, the model offers the opportunity to structure the wealth of social data on acts and actions along two theoretically interesting dimensions: the degree to which actors, in their construction of acts, attend to the norms of others versus ignoring them; and the degree to which actors in attending to the norms of others strategically violate versus conform to them. At the same time, positioning theory can enrich research on the operation of agentic norms by suggesting an analysis of sequences of behaviours, temporally ordered and supported by narratives in which the perceived permeability, stability, and legitimacy of the present intergroup relationship are wedded to selectively represented actions and acts.

Summary and Conclusions

This chapter aimed to consider the utility of positioning theory for the analysis of intergroup conflict, the implications of intergroup conflict for positioning theory, and how positioning theory and intergroup research can be jointly applied to further the understanding of group power and the operation of norms in conflict contexts. The chapter has identified important theoretical complementarities, but also theoretically interesting inconsistencies. Positioning theory offers intergroup research a coherent set of concepts – positions, acts vs actions, and story lines – with which to address two critical issues in conflict: temporal sequencing and meaning construction. Intergroup research offers positioning theory an understanding of the socio-cognitive processes involved in positioning, of the phenomenologically experienced regularities in perceptions of self and group, of intergroup relationships, of the creation of power through identity dynamics, and of intergroup choices through strategic norm violation and conformity. Despite the story line that positions positioning theory and experimental intergroup research as parallel psychologies, the blending of these theoretical traditions in future research may well contribute to the understanding, analysis and resolution of intergroup conflicts.

Note

1. Or at least more than one individual identity! Internal conflict within the individual will not be dealt with in this chapter, except as the outcome of multiple collective actors or interpersonal relationships represented within the self (e.g., conflicts between the interests of self-Australian and self-peacenik, or conflicts between self-mother and self-wife). See also the existing work developing the concept of reflexive positioning (e.g., Tan & Moghaddam, 1999b).

References

Abelson, R. P. (1976). Script processing in attitude formation and decision making. In J. S. Carroll & J. W. Payne (Eds.), *Cognition and social behavior* (pp. 33–45). Hillsdale, NJ: Lawrence Erlbaum Associates.

Ajzen, I. (1991). The theory of planned behavior. *Organizational Behaviour and Human Decision Processes,* 50, 179–211.

Aron, A., McLaughlin-Volpe, T., Mashek, D., Lewandowski, G., Wright, S. C., & Aron, E. (2005). Including others in the self. In W. Stoebe & M. Hewstone (Eds.), *European Review of Social Psychology* (Volume 14) (pp. 101–132). Hove, UK: Psychology Press.

Baumeister, R. F., Dewall, C. N., Ciarocco, N. J., & Twenge, J. M. (2005). Social exclusion impairs self-regulation. *Journal of Personality and Social Psychology,* 88, 589–604.

Bazerman, M. H., Gibbons, R., Thompson, L., & Valley, K. L. (1998). Can negotiators outperform game theory? In J. Halpern & R. N. Stern (Eds.), *Debating rationality* (pp. 79–99). Ithaca: Cornell University Press.

Benson, C. (2003). The unthinkable boundaries of self. In R. Harré & F. Moghaddam (Eds.), *The self and others* (pp. 61–84). Westport, CT: Praeger.

Churchill, W. (1950). *The second world war,* volume 4: The hinge of fate. London: Houghton Miflin Company.

Drury, J., & Reicher, S. (2000). Collective action and psychological change: The emergence of new social identities. *British Journal of Social Psychology,* 39, 579–604.

Feather, N. T. (Ed.). (1982). Expectations and actions: *Expectancy-value models in psychology.* Hillsdale, NJ: Lawrence Erlbaum Associates.

Festinger, L. (1954). A theory of social comparison processes. *Human Relations,* 7, 117–140.

Gallois, C., Ogay, T., & Giles, H. (2005). Communication accommodation theory: A look back and a look ahead. In W. Gudykunst (Ed.), *Theorizing about intercultural communication* (pp. 121–148). Thousand Oaks, CA: Sage.

Halpern, J. J., & Stern, R. N. (Eds.). (1998). Debating rationality: Nonrational aspects of organizational decision making. Ithaca: *Cornell University Press.*

Harré, R., Brockmeier, J., & Mühlhäuser, P. (1999). Greenspeak: *A study of environmental discourse.* London: Sage publications.

Harré, R., & Moghaddam, F. (Eds.). (2003). The Self and Others: *Positioning individuals and groups in personal, political and cultural contexts.* Westport, CT and London: Praeger.

Harré, R., & Slocum, N. (2003). Disputes as complex social events: On the uses of positioning theory. In R. Harré & F. Moghaddam (Eds.), *The self and others* (pp. 123–136). Westport, CT: Praeger.

Harré, R., & van Langenhove, L. (1999). The Dynamics of Social Episodes. In R. Harré & L. van Langenhove (Eds.), *Positioning theory* (pp. 1–13). Oxford: Blackwell.

Hopkins, N., & Reicher, S. (1997). The construction of social categories and processes of social change: Arguing about national identities. In G. Breakwell & E. Lyons (Eds.), *Changing european identities* (pp. 69–93). London: Butterworth.

Hornsey, M. J., Oppes, T., & Svensson, A. (2002). "It's OK if we say it, but you can't": Responses to intergroup and intragroup criticism. *European Journal of Social Psychology, 32*, 293–307.

Insko, C. A., Schopler, J., Gartner, L., Wildschut, T., Kozar, R., Pinter, B. et al. (2001). Interindividual-intergroup discontinuity reduction through the anticipation of future interaction. *Journal of Personality and Social Psychology, 80*, 95–111.

Johnson, D., Terry, D. J., & Louis, W. R. (2005). Perceptions of the intergroup structure and Anti-Asian prejudice among White Australians. *Group Processes and Intergroup Relations, 8*, 53–71.

Louis, W. R., & Taylor, D. M. (2002). Understanding the September 11th terrorist attack on America: The role of intergroup theories of normative influence. *Analyses of Social Issues and Public Policy, 2*, 87–100.

Louis, W. R., & Taylor, D. M. (2005). Rights and duties as group norms. In N. J. Finkel & F. M. Moghaddam (Eds.), *The Psychology of Rights and Duties: Empirical Contributions and Normative Commentaries* (pp. 105–134). Washington, DC: APA Press.

Louis, W. R., Taylor, D. M., & Douglas, R. L. (2005). Normative influence and rational conflict decisions: Group norms and cost-benefit analyses for intergroup behaviour. *Group Processes and Intergroup Relations, 8*(4), 355–374.

Louis, W. R., Taylor, D. M., & Neil, T. (2004). Cost-benefit analyses for your group and your self: The rationality of decision-making in conflict. *International Journal of Conflict Management, 15*(2), 110–143.

Manstead, A. S. R. (2000). The role of moral norm in the attitude-behavior relation. In D. J. Terry & M. A. Hogg (Eds.), *Attitudes, behavior, and social context: The role of norms and group membership* (pp. 11–30). London: Lawrence Erlbaum Associates.

McGarty, C. (1999). *Categorization in social psychology.* London: Sage publications.

McLean Parks, J., Boles, T. L., Conlon, D. E., Desouza, E., Gatewood, W., Gibson, K. et al. (1996). Distributing adventitious outcomes: Social norms, egocentric martyrs, and the effects on future relationships. *Organizational Behavior and Human Decision Processes, 67*, 181–200.

McLean Parks, J., & Smith, F. L. (1998). Organizational contracting: A "rational" exchange? In J. Halpern & R. N. Stern (Eds.), *Debating rationality* (pp. 125–154). Ithaca: Cornell University Press.

Moghaddam, F. M. (2005). The staircase to terrorism: A psychological exploration. *American Psychologist, 60*, 161–169.

Moghaddam, F. M., Hanley, E., & Harré, R. (2003). Sustaining intergroup harmony: An analysis of the Kissinger papers through positioning theory. In R. Harré & F. M. Moghaddam (Eds.), The self and others: *Positioning individuals and groups in personal, political, and cultural contexts* (pp. 137–155). Westport, CT: Praeger.

Moghaddam, F. M., & Riley, C. J. (2005). Toward a cultural theory of rights and duties in human development. In N. J. Finkel & F. M. Moghaddam (Eds.), *The psychology of rights and duties* (pp. 75–104). Washington, DC: APA Press.

Moscovici, S. (1985). Social influence and conformity. In G. Lindzey & E Aronson (Eds.), *The handbook of social psychology* (3rd ed., pp. 347–412). Hillsdale, NJ: Erlbaum.

Oakes, P. J., Turner, J. C., & Haslam, S. A. (1991). Perceiving people as group members. *British Journal of Social Psychology,* 30, 125–144.

Olson, M. (1968). *The logic of collective action.* New York: Schocken Books.

Ostrom, E. (1998). A behavioural approach to the rational choice theory of collective action; Presidential address, American Political Science Association 1997. *American Political Science Review,* 92, 1–22.

Reicher, S. (2004). The context of social identity: Domination, resistance, and change. *Political Psychology,* 25, 921–945.

Reicher, S. D. (1996). 'The Battle of Westminster': Developing the social identity model of crowd behaviour in order to explain the initiation and development of collective conflict. *European Journal of Social Psychology,* 26, 115–134.

Reicher, S. D. & Hopkins, N. (1996). Seeking influence through characterizing self-categories: An analysis of anti-abortionist rhetoric. *British Journal of Social Psychology,* 35, 297–311.

Reicher, S. D., Haslam, S. A. & Hopkins, N. (2005). Social identity and the dynamics of leadership: Categorization, entrepreneurship and power in the transformation of social reality. *Leadership Quarterly,* 16, 547–568.

Reicher, S., & Levine, M. (1994). Deindividuation, power relations between groups and the expression of social identity: The effects of visibility to the outgroup. *British Journal of Social Psychology,* 33, 145–163.

Rouhana, N. N., & Bar-Tal, D. (1998). Psychological dynamics of intractable ethnonational conflicts: The Israeli-Palestinian case. *American Psychologist,* 53, 761–770.

Sabat, S. R. (2003). Malignant positioning and the predicament of people with Alzheimer's disease. In R. Harré & F. Moghaddam (Eds.), *The self and others* (pp. 85–98). Westport, CT: Praeger.

Sani, F., & Reicher, S. (1998). When consensus fails: An analysis of the schism within the Italian Communist Party. *European Journal of Social Psychology,* 28, 623–645.

Sani, F., & Reicher, S. (1999). Identity, argument and schism: Two longitudinal studies of the split in the Church of England over the ordination of women. *Group Processes and Intergroup Relations,* 2, 279–300.

Simon, B., & Klandermans, B. (2001). Politicized collective identity. A social psychological analysis. *American Psychologist,* 56, 319–331.

Slocum, N., & Langenhove, L. V. (2003). Integration speak: Introducing positioning theory in regional integration studies. In R. Harre & F. Moghaddam (Eds.), *The self and others: Positioning individuals and groups in personal, political, and cultural contexts* (pp. 219–134), Westport, CT: Praeger.

Tajfel, H., & Turner, J. C. (1979). An integrative theory of intergroup conflict. In W. G. Austin & S. Worchel (Eds.), The social psychology of intergroup relations (pp. 33–47). Monterey, CA: Brooks/Cole.

Tan, S. L., & Moghaddam, F. M. (1999a). Positioning in intergroup relations. In R. Harré & L. van Langenhove (Eds.), *Positioning theory: Moral contexts of international actions* (pp. 178–194). Boston: Blackwell.

Tan, S. L., & Moghaddam, F. M. (1999b). Reflexive positioning: culture and private discourse. In R. Harré & L. van Langenhove (Eds.), *Positioning theory* (pp. 74–86). Oxford, England: Blackwell.

Taylor, D., Bougie, E., & Caouette, J. (2003). Applying positioning principles to a theory of collective identity. In R. Harre & F. Moghaddam (Eds.), *The self and others: Positioning individuals and groups in personal, political, and cultural contexts* (pp. 197–215). Westport, CT: Praeger.

Taylor, D. M., & Louis, W. R. (2004). Terrorism and the quest for identity. In F. Moghaddam & A. J. Marsella (Eds.), *Understanding terrorism: Psychosocial roots, consequences, and interventions* (pp. 169–185). Washington, DC: APA Press.

Terry, D. J., & Hogg, M. A. (1996). Group norms and the attitude-behavior relationship: A role for group identification. *Personality and Social Psychology Bulletin, 22,* 776–793.

Terry, D. J. & Hogg, M. A. (Eds.). (2000). *Attitudes, behavior, and social context: The role of norms and group membership.* London: Lawrence Erlbaum Associates.

Turner, J. C. (2005). Explaining the nature of power: A three-process theory. *European Journal of Social Psychology, 35,* 1–22.

Turner, J. C., Hogg, M., Oakes, P., Reicher, S., & Wetherell, M. (1987). *Rediscovering the social group: A self-categorization theory.* New York: Basil Blackwell.

Tyler, T. R., & Smith, H. J. (1999). Justice, social identity, and group processes. In T. R. Tyler, R. M. Kramer, & O. P. John (Eds.) *The psychology of the social self,* pp. 223–264. London: Lawrence Erlbaum Associates.

van Zomeren, M., Spears, R., Fischer, A. H., & Leach, C. W. (2004). Put your money where your mouth is! Explaining collective action tendencies through group-based anger and group efficacy. *Journal of Personality and Social Psychology, 87,* 649–664.

von Neumann, J., & Morgenstern, O. (1944). *Theory of games and economic behavior.* New York: Wiley & Sons.

Worchel, S. (2005). The rightful place of human rights: Incorporating individual, group, and cultural perspectives. In N. J. Finkel & F. M. Moghaddam (Eds.), *The Psychology of Rights and Duties* (pp. 197–220). Washington, DC: APA Press.

3
Liquidating Roles and Crystallising Positions: Investigating the Road Between Role and Positioning Theory

Thomas Duus Henriksen

In this chapter, the relationship between rigidity and dynamics in conflicts is addressed as a relationship between role and positioning based approaches to understanding social interaction. Positioning theory has, with its emphasis on interactivity, movement and fluidity, been ground-breaking in the post-modern critique of classical social-psychology, and especially with role-theory as a static tool for understanding social interaction. In this change, the emphasis of rigidity rather than change has been replaced by an emphasis on dynamics and change, but rather than allowing one perspective to replace the other, there seems today to be a need for an approach that allows us to think in terms of both firmness and sluggishness, as well as in terms of dynamics and change. Such need is, for instance seen when working with the staged conflicts of learning games, which allow their participants to experience the meeting between the firm and the fluid in social interaction. Seeing social interaction as a meeting between such, calls for an understanding of how rules and structures blend with the dynamics of social interaction, as well as how such firm perspectives are adopted by concrete persons and enacted as their own.

There is little doubt that social interaction is too finely grained to be grasped by role theory, but instead of throwing away roles in favour of positions, it is interesting to see both as individual contributions to a shared understanding on how firmness and change meet and interact in the social. In respect to conflict, the structural and rigidity emphasis of role-theory seems to hold a potential for grasping the rigidity of conflicts, as well as the emphasis on dynamics employed by positioning theory allows the dynamic elements to be addressed. The concepts of crystallisation and liquidation are introduced to address the transition between role- and positioning-based participation in conflicts, with special attention on how power is deployed in the situation. This transitional perspective, as well as the attempt to bridge the concepts of role and positioning, is illustrated through the experiences from a learning game. The analysis of the conflict taking place between the participants during the game is used to provide a view on how the different approaches can inform our conception of conflicts. In order to follow such an ambition, I find it important to investigate the individual contributions to understanding social interaction provided by the diverse theories, as such an approach allows a nuanced integration into an understanding that allows us to address both the dynamics and firmness of social interaction, and with it a third road into social psychology.

Positioning as an Approach to Social Interaction and as a Critique on Role Theory

Positioning theory represents a contemporary line of thinking that emphasises the active component of social interaction. It originated as a critique against certain trends in social psychology, arguing that they built upon a static approach to understanding social interaction and human behaviour (see e.g. Harré & van Langenhove 1999b; Harré & Moghaddam 2003b), and that it attempted to analyse interaction by freezing the moment (Harré 2000). This critique has addressed the shortcomings of emphasising the static elements when trying to grasp social interaction, rather than diving into the social dynamics on their own premises. Positioning theory thereby attempts to take on an immanentist perspective while addressing the operational elements of social interaction. Within social psychology, the emergence of positioning theory represents a turn towards a more dynamic paradigm, as it attempts to distinguish itself from the more structurally based approaches that followed the anthropologist Ralph Linton (1936) and his conception of roles. A key issue in this distinction is the emphasis on the element of negotiation in social interaction; rather than seeing it as a mere extrapolation of structural representations, the key for understanding its cause is seen as the social interaction itself. By doing so, positioning theory distinguishes itself from a role-based approach, which is accused for being static (van Langenhove & Harré, 1999), prescriptive (Tan & Moghaddam, 1999) and ritualistic (Davies & Harré, 1999), constituting itself as a replacing (ibid) alternative to role theory. Several influential lines of thinking have presented a similar critique in order to propose a more active approach to social psychology, e.g. the constructionist approach, as well as to the whole movement of discursive psychology (see e.g. Potter & Wetherell, 1987a,b).

Within positioning theory, roles are considered a structural approach to understanding social interaction, one that emphasises the person and situation-external factors as determinate. Instead, positioning theory seeks to address the interaction itself, which from a poststructuralistic perspective can be seen as a co-constructed game of power, taking place between the participants. One key concept in positioning theory is the continuous definition of categorical distinctions, through which the participants define positions of self and others, as well as the relationship between them (Harré & van Langenhove 1999b). Rather than seeing them as descriptive or performative according to Austin's (1962) distinction, both should be seen from the Deleuzian idea that we are unable to describe anything discourse-externally, because any description would either seek to manifest or challenge a discourse. According to this point of view, all acts must be considered, as Butler (1990) calls it, performative, and thereby as acts of positioning. Such an approach would, according to Deleuze (1994), allow us to unsettle current approaches and explanations of social interaction, and in contrast to the role-based approach, establish access to radical new understandings of a given problem or context.

Through the acts of positioning, subjects position themselves and others into more or less desirable or troublesome positions, forming the basis for further acts of positioning. According to van Langenhove & Harré (1999), positions can be understood as a cluster of rights and duties, which affect the subject; some actions are rendered socially acceptable or unavailable, whereas others become mandatory to the subject. Within positioning theory, the acts of positioning and the positions are contextualised within a storyline, consisting of already established patterns and conventions, which the acts follow (Harré & Moghaddam, 2003b) in a mutually constituting relationship. Although more dynamic, the storyline is, in many respects, comparable to social structures of role theory, which are addressed further below. One key difference between the two is, however, that storylines allow positions to emerge, rather than seeing them as given prior to the situation.

Understanding Conflict from the Positioning Perspective

Positioning theory is of particular interest for conflict analysis, as it provides a view on how conflicts and solutions are negotiated among its partners. In contrast to this negotiation, a role-based approach would emphasise the structurally provided solutions. Within positioning theory, attention is paid to the social dynamics of conflicts, rather than seeing it as something itself. From this perspective, the utterances and acts occurring within a given storyline are addressed, and instead of seeing conflicts as a choice between two more or less opposing perspectives, positioning theory allows the negotiation of nuanced solutions to be addressed, and to consider solutions as something created in the interaction, rather than something constituted prior to the negotiation. Such an approach is distinct from that of role-theory, which sees conflicts and solutions as constituted by social structure and enacted through roles. An example could be an employee, having a conflict with a manager about working hours. While discussing the issue, the employee may have arguments for starting late, whereas the manager may want to place the working hours early due to company politics. Whereas a positioning approach might provide a view on how to find a solution that fits both company politics and the employee, whereas the role-based approach might provide a view on the perspectives the two bring into the negotiation.

Roles as an Approach to Social Interaction

Positioning theory delivers extensive criticism of role-theory as a tool for understanding social interaction. Rather than considering positions as a replacing alternative to roles, as proposed by van Langenhove & Harré (1999) and Davies & Harré (1999), the concepts can be combined into an integrated approach to understanding social interaction. Although active in the same sphere of social life, roles and positions address two entirely different phenomenons in social interaction: Positions address an immanent aspect of social interaction. Roles bring about an enactment of the social structures under which the interaction takes place. Although roles have been criticised for promoting a structural approach to understanding social interaction (see Harré & van Langenhove, 1999a), the concept should be recognized for highlighting both the ritualistic, static and formal aspects, which role-theory according to Davies and Harré (1999) addresses, and for the deterministic and organising aspect of the social interaction that it, according to Harré & van Langenhove (1999b) addresses. Slocum & Harré (2003) criticise roles for being a too coarse-grained tool for analysing social interaction, but do so from an interpretation of roles as persistent and pervasive to someone's life, making roles, in all respects, too cumbersome for addressing the dynamics of the micro social. The key elements of role-theory are presented below in order to address the contribution that roles may present to the analysis of social interaction.

The Concept of Roles

According to Krysia Yardley-Matwiejczuk (1997), the concept of 'role' was originally introduced in the social sciences by G.H. Mead (1934) and Ralph Linton (1936). The use of the concept is, however, much older. Erving Goffman (1959) draws his inspiration from the classical Greek theatre as the foundation for his work on the concept. According to Michael Banton (1965), the semantic origin of 'roles' is the scroll or roll that actors were to recite. Despite the fact that the concept has been in use in different settings, no coherent definition seems to have been accepted generally. Several theorists have proposed a clear definition on the concept; according to Yardley-Matwiejczuk (1997) without much luck. One reason for this has been that the proposals have built upon an assumed, shared understanding or consensus of the concept with the reader. Although the attempts have not established a uniform definition of the concept, each definition provides a perspective on the key characteristics of the concept 'role'.

Linton's Structural Approach to Roles

Linton (1936) provides one influential approach to the understanding of roles. Linton uses a structuralist approach to propose that roles are an operationalisation of social structure and social status. 'Structure' is here understood as lines of socially embedded thinking, rights, duties, perspectives and values, which have a deterministic effect on the interaction. In Linton's line of thinking, roles become representations of these structural issues, thereby providing a top-down deterministic approach to understanding social interaction.

Linton provides an interesting perspective on how to understand the relationship between structure and social interaction as mediated by roles. By considering roles representations of macro-social structures (issues), which can be enacted in the social interaction through these roles, he provides a perspective on how to understand the relationship as deterministic. Roles can therefore be considered to be representations of macro-social structures and issues to be enacted in the social interaction, an understanding that, according to Yardley-Matwiejczuk (1997), has meet a general support throughout the literature.

Linton's structural-deterministic approach has had a major impact on the functionalist tradition of sociology, which has been taken up by theorists like Parsons and Merton. The approach has also been criticised widely within both social psychology and sociology. One major critique of the structural-deterministic concept of role is provided by Turner (1968), who argues that the approach leaves little room for individual action, a critique that later has been elaborated within positioning theory, which criticises the structural-deterministic approach to roles for not seeing the finer grains of social interaction (see e.g. Harré & van Langenhove, 1999a; Harré & Moghaddam, 2003a). From their critique, structural determinism frames social interaction with a sluggish repetition of predetermined issues, which Turner argues makes it unsuitable for addressing the interaction that takes place beyond structural determination. A more individualised approach to understanding roles and social interaction is provided by Mead (1934), as presented below.

Mead and the Interactionsist Approach to Roles

George Herbert Mead's (1934) approach to roles was closely linked to the matter of developing an identity within society, considering roles as means for analysing social structures and the means of social participation embedded in those. Mead considered the concept of role and role-taking as a way to address the socially embedded means of participation within society, thereby allowing the participant to address the social through an enactment of certain roles. This provided the individual with the means to reduce the complexity of the social, as well as the means to acquire an understanding of the social. According to Mead, the participant explored what he termed 'the generalised other', a stereotypical understanding of other roles and role enactments that can be utilised for exploring presumptions about social processes, values, etc. By providing the individual with a generalised concept of ways to enact structurally given concepts, means of participation could be provided, and thereby explored for further development.

Mead made an effort to distinguish his theory from the deterministic line of thinking of his time, proposing a more interactive approach to the relationship between structure and individual. Rather than considering role to be a tool of structural determination, Mead considered roles to be subject to personal interpretation and construction. Mead designed his approach to roles to be dynamic (Yardley-Matwiejczuk, 1997) in comparison to the more static structuralist approach. However, the whole concept of roles has been framed as static or ritualistic by positioning theory since (see e.g. Harré & van Langenhove, 1999a; Harré & Moghaddam, 2003a). The criticism was aimed on the analytical granularity of the analysis; whereas Mead and Linton were concerned with the relationship between individual and structure, positioning theory seeks to look upon social interaction itself and in relation to communicative connotations. Rather than presupposing a pre-given understanding, positioning theory is concerned with how such understanding is negotiated socially.

An interesting critique of Mead's symbolic interactionist approach to roles has addressed the theory's limited attention to the social span of social interaction (see Stryker & Statham, 1985). Whereas Mead operates within a social context, more contemporary approaches have appointed the need for including a cross-contextual element. From the positioning theory point of view, symbolic interactionism can not be criticised for looking at social interaction as taking place within a storyline. Howeger,symbolic interactionism overlooks the fact that each participant in the interaction participates in one or more individual storyline, and that the given context is a situated conjunction of those individualised storylines.

Between Structural Determination and Individual Opportunity

Erving Goffman (1959) provides another interactionist approach to the concept of role, following Mead's lead on an interactive approach to roles. Throughout many publications Goffman drew on theatre as his main source of inspiration, embedding concepts of theatrical enactment into his understanding of social interaction. Even though Goffman challenged contemporary sociology by focussing on the operationalised content of face-to-face interaction, he basically accepted a structuralist element, seeing roles as a deterministic representation of structure, or, as Yardley-Matwiejczuk (1997) puts it, considering roles as '... constitutive and prior to the individual' (p. 62). Goffman's contribution to understanding roles can be considered to be a step towards bridging the two extremes; he accepts the element of structural determination, but only in a semi-scripting manner, which allows some opportunity for personal interpretation and construction.

Turner's (1968) critique addressed the element of agency within a social structure as a feature of social action. From the point of roles, there is very little room or opportunity for individual interpretation and action. An even more immanistic approach to roles is provided by George Kelly (1955), who suggested the use of 'part' as alternative to role. Kelly sought to undermine the element of social determinism; as the part is independent of societal issues. Playing a part allows the social interaction to free itself from structural issues. Such a decoupling approach is interesting for designing therapy, theatre and role-play, but represents a very radical perspective when we try to address social interaction in general. Another view is provided organisational theory by Boonstra (2004), who claims that existing structures often act as stumbling blocks in organisational change, which is interesting for addressing the perspective rigidity of conflicts. Boonstra's claim supports viewing role-based enactments of structure as an obstacle to conflict resolution. Whereas a role-based approach to participating in a social context might be a overly rigid, a role-based approach to understanding elements of social interaction may provide a valuable view on how rigidity is introduced and how it is accepted in social interaction.

Defining Roles

The presented perspectives each provide, in their differences and similarities, contributions to an understanding of roles. The main contribution seems to be from Linton who presented roles as a representations of structural issues, thereby providing the social interaction with values, norms, etc. This points to roles as given by structure, and as something that makes certain lines of action available to the participant through the definition of a collection of certain rights and duties associated with each role. The second contribution is provided by Mead, who sees taking a role as involving the assumption of the generalised other. By the notion of assuming a role, Mead paves the way for including an individual interpretation of the role to be enacted. Although both reside firmly within the symbolic interactionism, this perspective is countered by Goffman's way of considering a role to be something constitutive and preceding the individual, thereby accepting a larger degree of social determination than Mead. Linton and Goffman would disagree with Kelly when he attempts to remove or minimize the element of structural determination though an immanist approach, as he, at the same time distances himself from the concept of role. On the basis of Mead, Linton, Goffman and Kelly, I will propose the following clarification on the concept of roles:

A role consists of a structurally determined and legitimated collection of privileging rights, duties, norms and values (perspectives) which applies to a social situation within the determining structure according to the interpretation of the enactor.

In the clarification, I would like to emphasise that role is subject to interpretation by the enactor (see e.g. Henriksen, 2004). A role has to be enacted, by a subject, in a social interaction that is taking place within the structure that determines the role in order to be able to act legitimately in the situation. The legitimacy of action is bound to a certain structure. Under these circumstances, the role allows some and prevents other lines of action. The concept of role-assumption is considered less relevant to the definition itself, as the theorists largely agree upon the role as something given, whereas the element of personal interpretation seems less prominent. This element is, however, relevant when considering how different roles are enacted within different storylines, and is therefore a key issue when it comes to building a bridge to positioning theory.

Between Roles and Positions

Based on the definition deployed above, roles and positions would be similar in many respects, but would also differ with respect to how they are created and occupied. One key difference is the two approaches' understanding of structure. Just as in the Saussurean structuralist line of thinking, the role-based approach employs a one-way relationship between structure and role-enactments; roles are constituted by structure, but structure is unaffected by the enactments of these roles. In comparison, the post-structuralist line of thinking employed by positioning theory considers the relationship between the positioning and the structuring storyline as mutually constituting. Whereas roles are given by structure, positions are created, occupied, held and abandoned through social interaction. Similarly, norms, values, rights and duties are structurally provided within role-theory, whereas they are negotiable within positioning theory. Another important difference is the power associated with the social positions. Negotiated positions rely on the power achieved through negotiation and the position already achieved. Roles are, on the other hand, based on structural issues, and can therefore draw upon the power of these issues. While both approaches address the perspectives employed by participants in a social interaction, their differences contribute to the analysis of social interaction by providing a view on different aspects of the interaction.

Role-Enactment as the Active Component

One often-heard argument from positioning theory is the notion that roles are either ritualistic and formal (Davies & Harré, 1999), or static (van Langenhove & Harré, 1999), framing role-theory as a passive concept for understanding social interaction. This argument is frequently heard within social psychology due to the widespread scepticism towards theories that consider 'frozen moments' rather than the processes and dynamics (see Harré 2000). But is it possible, perhaps even fruitful to challenge this critique? By looking into the active element of role-theory, a view emerges on how they can be used to bring structural issues into the interaction. Heading (1972) suggested seeing roles as the active dimension of a social position (or structure), allowing him to emphasise the enactment of social issues through roles. By enacting a role, its socially legitimated rights, duties, values, norms and perspectives are brought into play.

If roles are to be considered to be dynamic representations of structural perspectives, they must demonstrate these perspectives by enacting them in the social interaction. If we listen to the post-structuralist argumentation, only the perspectives that are performed in the social interaction are affecting it. If roles (and through them the structural issues) are not enacted, they lose their effect. Roles must therefore provide operational lines of action that can be enacted in order to have an effect. This enactment must be conducted in the social interaction by the participating subjects (or institutions), or constituted through physical cues.

The concept of such active component, and especially of its significance to social interaction, has been widely debated among sociologists and social psychologists. One example of this is provided by Coutu (1951), who, on the basis of a rather orthodox reading of Mead, attempts to set the concepts of role-playing and role – taking straight. While doing so, he defines 'role-playing' as the performance of an ascribed role, as opposed to role-taking, to which he ascribes an element of pretending, effectively turning the concepts upside down in comparison to latter practice. Although both the concepts of role-playing and role-enactment can be considered active components of roles, allowing the otherwise passive concept to have an active dimension, only the concept of role-enactment is examined in this chapter.

From the perspective of role-enactment, a position is just as static as a role, even though it may derive from a more dynamic process. There is little sense in comparing one of two men, who are standing still, to one of two cars that are moving, and claiming that the difference between the two is whether they move or not. Rather than just calling roles static and positions dynamic, the active component is addressed, allowing positions to be compared to roles and positioning to be compared role-enactment or role – playing.

Enacting Roles

The concept of role-enactment was introduced by Sarbin & Allen (1954), who used the concept to address the active component of structural issues in social interaction. With this concept, emphasis was moved from roles as static representations of structural matters to the active performance of these matters in the social interaction. According to Sarbin & Allen (1954), role-enactment refers to the application of an otherwise passive role in a social context. Performance of a role implies the enactment of the role's perspectives onto the issues of the context.

Although not embraced by functionalistic social science of the time, role-enactment has been picked up by later studies. Forward et al. (1976) picked up the term without much elaboration, probably in attempt to avoid the contemporary discussions on role-play. A more contemporary study conducted by Fitzergerald et al. (2006) used the term to add an active component to the otherwise passive roles in their study of discrepancies between role definition and execution in organisational change. Such a distinction is interesting, as Fitzgerald et al. see roles as '... defined via social interaction, and cannot be addressed in isolation from relationships ...' (ibid. p. 14). Whereas the distinction between role definition and execution can be recognized as a distinction between roles as static representations of structural forms and roles as something enacted. Such definition of roles undermines the existence of a static definition of a role that is independent to the enactment, and utilises Banton's (1965) understanding of roles, as opposed to the structuralist approach. Rather than understanding roles as a product of structure, Banton takes a bottom-up approach by stating that roles are defined through, what in terms of positioning, would be an occupation of a position in the social context. In many respects, Banton foreshadows elements of positioning theory, but instead of attempting to replace the concept of roles, Banton studies the construction of roles. Fitzgerald et al.'s use of Banton's approach to roles is interesting when we try to bridge the two concepts, as it provides a view on the interaction or transition that from a post-structuralist approach would be taking place between them. The role-enacting approach does however provide a view on the differences and similarities between role enactment and positioning, which is addressed below.

Between Role-Enactment and Positioning

As with the concepts of position and roles, the active components of both approaches have their differences and overlaps. As role-enactment is tied to the role-based approach, it is closely linked with structural issues. Positioning is, on the other hand, concerned with achieving a position from which to act. Whereas role-enactment draws upon power that is structurally legitimate in a specific context, the positioning acts on behalf on what is negotiated and achieved, and can only draw on the power of positions that are already taken in the situation. Another difference between the two means of participation is the level of intentionality. Role-enactment concerns the enactment of certain structural issues or perspectives, whereas positioning concerns achieving legitimate means for participating.

Role-enactment is in many respects comparable to the concept of moral positioning, which, according to van Langenhove & Harré (1999), is comparable to roles with respect to drawing on values, understandings or situational drivers defined by the storyline. In doing so, power is sought in a manner comparable to role-enactment, which relies on the role's structural legitimation. The main difference between role-enactment and moral positioning does however lie in the purpose of the enactment. Moral positioning is interesting here, as it exemplifies the difference between positioning and role-enactment. Role-enactment seeks to perform the perspectives of a role in a given context with the purpose of enacting the role; moral positioning may draw upon the same arguments in order to mobilise the power to define certain issues, but it is the use of such power, and not the enactment of the role itself that is the purpose here. Such distinction may be beneficial in determining whether a participant is 'enacting' or 'positioning' in a given situation.

Between Structural Issues and Storylines

One important element in understanding the differences and similarities between role enactments and acts of positioning is how acts and enactments become meaningful. According to the linguist Saussure (1916), meaning arises as a consequence of the contextualisation of an utterance. This is also the case within both role and positioning theory, although the two have different approaches; positioning theory employs the concept of storylines, whereas role theory contextualises in respect to social structure.

The concept of storyline can be seen as a critique against Mead's (1934) symbolic interactionism, which, according to (Stryker & Statham, 1985), does not take situation external issues into account. According to Harré & Moghaddam (2003b), social episodes do not unfold in a random manner, but follow already established patterns, referred to as 'storylines'. Such storylines are tied to the subject, who acts out one or more storylines in a given situation, effectively making a social situation a conjunction of overlapping storylines. One important point within positioning theory is that storylines and social interaction are mutually constituting. The storyline has a determining effect on the social interaction, distinguishing the socially legitimate from the logically possible actions, but is at the same time constituted through the interaction.

The concept of structure employed within role-theory is somewhat more rigid, and is easily compared to Saussure's game of chess (see e.g. Broch, 2000). A chess game is constructed by a number of invariant, structure-constituting elements (board, colours, figures), which can be moved according to a constituted set of rules, allowing some actions to take place, while inhibiting others. Within its set of structuring rules, an astronomic number of socially legitimate acts can be conducted. One key consequence of such a structuralist approach to social interaction, is that the structure, while having a determining effect on the social interaction taking place, it is unaffected by the individual acts taking place within it. Such an approach deploys a much more static and deterministic approach to understanding social interaction, thereby addressing the occurrence and enactment of external, but still determining issues within the social interaction.

Although both concepts seek to provide an act or enactment with meaning through contextualisation, the two operate differently. Storylines are linked to the enacting subject, who carries the storyline across contexts, whereas the structurally enforced discourses are linked to a specific context, like the chess game. As a road going through several countries, one behaviour, or set of rights and duties, may be applicable to one section of the road, but not to another. It may not be meaningful to attempt to enact rights and duties that were structurally legitimate in one context in a different part of the storyline. Whereas the role-based approach emphasises those perspectives that are determined by structure, the positioning approach allows us to grasp those which are not. Such a combination provides an analytical model for grasping both the lived lives of subjects, as well as the process of subjectivation.

Understanding Conflicts from the Role Perspective

With respect to roles, conflicts can be considered a matter of role unclarity in a given situation, barring from the situation a fixed set of norms, rights, duties and values that the participants can use to navigate the situation. Such unclarity can unfold in many ways; either as something being challenged, attempted to be introduced or something disestablished, or simply inappropriate to the situation. In terms of positioning, roles can be understood as privileged positions, provided by structure and given to specified subjects. These privileged positions, allowing the occupant to enact certain rights and duties in the situation, are not available to the participants on equal terms. As an example, a structurally appointed manager has privileged rights that are unavailable to an employee. In such case, the role may either dampen conflict as a result of role clarity, or it may create conflict as the employee challenges either the enactment or the legitimating structure. Of particular interest are the situations where certain roles are not recognized, either as a consequence of being enacted outside the enforcing structure, or because something is being challenged. In this type of situation, previously defined roles cannot be used to determine the outcome of the conflict, but can still provide a valuable contribution for the understanding of the perspectives enacted in the conflict.

Understanding Conflicts from a Combined Approach

When trying to understand conflicts solely from the perspective of roles, conflicts quickly turn into a struggle between opposing perspectives, which can be handled with respect to the determining structure. Such an approach has repeatedly been criticised for not grasping the dynamics of social interaction. As an alternative, positioning theory addresses the dynamics that take place beyond the scope of structural determination, but doing so with less attention paid to the structural issues. By combining the two perspectives, the dynamics of non-recognized social structures can be addressed as a meeting between determination and dynamics, and in particular as the transitions between the two, which I would like to explain further.

Understanding the Transition Between Roles and Positions: Crystallisation as the Movement from Positions to Roles

One distinct feature that separates roles from positions is that roles are given by a structure that reaches beyond the particular interaction, whereas positions are continuously negotiated in the particular here and now social interaction. Whereas positions have to be re-negotiated over and over again, roles provide a ready made set of privileged positions, which can be occupied by the bearer of the role without further ado. A role consists, in other words, of a number of positions, which are ascribed to the role by structure. Roles can therefore be considered a catalyst to social interaction as it allows the participants to skip certain steps of negotiation, especially re-negotiation, allowing them to save time and effort. One example of such a time-saving role would be that of a manager, who is given the rights (positions) to lead and distribute tasks, providing a very powerful means for determining the outcome of the interaction, and eventually occupying further positions. In such situation, power and the distribution of power is already embedded in the role and legitimated by structure, allowing its enactor to perform certain rights and duties.

The acquisition of such roles is therefore interesting to the participants in the social interaction, as it provides the means for occupying and governing specific positions or clusters of positions without continuous re-negotiation. A defined, formal role provides the binding that protects certain positions from being challenged. I will describe the constitution of such protective binding as the process of crystallisation. This kind of processes can be illustrated from the following case example:

John works in a large, private Danish company. He is rather committed to his work, and thinks that he could do things better if he was in charge. With a strong opinion on how the place should be run, he sets out to get a promotion to become some kind of manager in the organisation, and in order to become a manager, he starts out by thinking like one. He analyses the objective; 'to become a manager'; and assuming that he reads the organisation correctly, he fairly quickly figures out that it is not in his hands to become one, it is a role that is given by the organisation. In order to achieve his objective, he analyses what could lead to getting such position, and decides to a) make a show of himself by achieving some outstanding results, contribute in meetings and be on the ball; b) to leave the right impression in the right places by making sure to talk to the right people at the right time, attend social events, and be a good storyteller on social occasions. Having made this plan, John sets out to get his promotion.

When framed within the concepts of building a business plan, John's plan can be broken down to the following components:

Vision:	To become a boss of some sort in the organisation.
Strategy:	To think like a boss
	Make a show of himself
	To leave the right impression with the right people
Tactical:	Achieving some outstanding results, contribute in meetings and be on the ball.
	Talk to the right people at the right time, attend social events, and be a storyteller on social occasions.
Operational:	All the positioning legwork

In the example, John decides to occupy the position of a manager in the company and takes a very goal-orientated approach to the task. By occupying the specified positions in respect to his colleagues and managers, John takes on the tasks of a manager, but without becoming one. This positioning only provides the content of the role, but not the formal recognition. The last step can only be conducted through a formal promotion, only then will the occupied positions be given the 'protective wrapping' of a role, making the achieved positions unchallengeable. Without the structural acceptance that lies in the formal promotion, John would continuously have to re-negotiate the positions in order to maintain them. The protective wrapping would in this case probably consist of a formal promotion, a title, and a job description that relates John's new role to the other roles in the organisation.

Crystallisation can take place in any social institution or system that has the power to define roles. One very interesting aspect of crystallisation is that it provides social interaction with fixed enactments, which forces the turn of events into specified trajectories across the social interaction. As the crystallisation of positions into roles becomes determinate and thereby resistant to further change, time is saved by having to negotiate the duties and rights that emerge in the course of the interaction over and over again. This process is useful for conducting what Schein (1962) refers to as refreezing, a process that allows the learner to stop evolving a perspective while indicating that a sufficient level has been reached, as well as for constituting means for preserving the new perspective. By manifesting power through the crystallisation, the negotiation of perspectives ceases, allowing the current understanding or relation to be formalised and gain structural legitimation. The process of crystallisation can therefore be considered a process that finishes processes of change or negotiation for the time being, for instance in respect to an agreement on how to handle a conflict. By formalising the agreement through crystallisation, the structural integration provides the partners involved with power to enact the agreed solution by reference to the agreement.

The crystallisation of one's own positions is a powerful means for positioning others in the social interaction due to the defined, protected character of crystallised positions. No crystallisation is, however, more solid than the legitimating structure that it is part of and, for instance, the norms that it represents. Despite the protective wrapping, roles can incite attempts of counter-positioning, either through self-positioning as being independent of the role ('you have no authority here/over me!') or by questioning the integrity of the role and bearer of the role. Such unbinding attempts of counter-positioning are considered acts of liquidation, which are addressed below.

Liquidation as the Movement from Roles to Positions

The concept of liquidation is a contrast to crystallisation. Rather than trying to construct roles through social interaction, the process of liquidation seeks to remove the protective wrapping and deconstruct the role into positions, which then can be challenged through negotiation. The key issue of liquidation is to challenge either the structure that is represented or the structural representation that is enacted by the role-carrier or subject that occupies a protected set of positions. The aim of the liquidation is to nullify the rights and privileges (or duties), which structure has provided the content of the role, e.g. the power to distribute tasks or define what is right from wrong in a given situation.

Liquidation seeks to unsettle the current discourses by questioning the commonly accepted meanings of what goes on. A reason for doing so could be to either change the current practice, or to position oneself within that practice. Foucault argues that the movement of definitorial power allows a movement of understandings, allowing fixed understandings to be challenged. By liquidating a fixed perspective, the enactors are allowed to look for new approaches to a given problem or situation, rather than having to stick to the fixed approach.

The liquidated roles can both be desired or undesired. In line with the cognitive stress associated with a perturbation (see von Glasersfeld, 1995) or the process of unfreezing a conceptual understanding (see Schein, 1962), the process of having one's role liquidated cannot be expected to be a pleasant experience; although it may be the role of an underdog, the role still represents a means for participating in a certain practice. A liquidation of the role allows the duties of the role to be challenged (as they are embedded in the positions), but also the rights and privileges that role would provide. Liquidation of such roles is, however, considered an exception, as liquidation generally would be attempts to attack the fortified positions of desirable roles, allowing these positions to be occupied by the attacker. Being able to liquidate a role in a social interaction is a desirable tool for undermining the means of others for positioning, allowing the protected positions to be challenged. It also provides the opportunity to free and occupy desired positions, although this is a more complex move, consisting of several positioning acts.

Moral Positioning and Roles

The process of liquidation is closely associated with the concept of moral positioning, describing the situations where the positioning takes place on the basis of positions provided by the storyline, rather than emerging in the situation (van Langenhove & Harré 1999). Liquidation can be seen as a process of decoupling the acts and enactments from the deterministic elements of storylines and structural frames.

The issue of moral positioning is addressed by van Langenhove & Harré (1999) as a matter of expectational deviance from the roles in a given situation. Positioning can take place as a consequence of the moral order provided by a situation or storyline, which is similar to the roles made available by structure. As an example, van Langenhove & Harré (1999) uses a situation between a nurse and a patient; the latter is complaining to the nurse for not having made the patient's bed, after which the nurse excuses herself by giving personal reasons; 'I am sorry I forgot to make your bed, but I am a bit confused today as I just received this letter in which ...' (Ibid, pp. 21–2). In this situation, the nurse is unable to explain her own behaviour from the basis of the moral order of the nurse-role. She is required to find particular reasons for the misconduct, e.g. personal means of explanation and through that achieving a re-positioning against the patient's critique. The nurse just cannot say that 'I haven't made your bed because I'm a nurse' as this would challenge the integrity of the nurse-role as bed-making is a part of the job description.

As mentioned earlier, moral positioning is in many respects comparable to role-enactment, which referred to the process of representing structural issues in the social interaction, as both moral positioning and role-enactment draws upon issues that are defined prior to the situation. According to Harré & van Langenhove (1999c), acts of positioning always include an element of both personal and moral positioning, which can be seen as a framework for integrating role and positioning theory.

Maintaining Roles and Moral Positions

The nurse's positioning is necessary in order to maintain the legitimate role of being a nurse; if this personal positioning did not take place, or was unsuccessful, the nurse's role would be challenged, which could position the nurse as a bad nurse. Rather than allowing the patient to challenge the nurse-role, the nurse decides to make a personal positioning that is independent of the nurse-role, which then remains intact and unchallenged. This allows us to draw a distinction between roles and positions; whereas the moral positioning is associated with the role, acts of moral positioning can therefore be said to take place in correspondence to this role, compared to personal positioning, which concerns the positioning act that takes place beyond the scope of the role.

Engaging the Acts of Liquidation

What would have happened if the nurse had answered
'As a nurse, I have given other duties priority over making your bed'
- thereby denying the patient his moral right for having the bed made by the nurse? Obviously, by denying such a request, the reactive second order positioning challenges the moral order (or role-conception) of the patient, which according to van Langenhove & Harré (1999), breaks the current social ritual.

Rather than playing out a sound social ritual of two roles meeting and engaging in a social interaction, the moral enactment of the roles results in a conflict of the two as the nurse challenges the conceived rights and duties of the patient. Through this moral positioning, the nurse uses her role as means for positioning both herself, and at the same time challenges the integrity of the patient's role. Such a positioning is likely to result in a mutual role-enactment, in which the perspectives, values and norms of both roles are challenged, or in a personal positioning from 'either side of the bed', attributing the conflict to something independent to the roles involved. If one side agrees to yield to the other part's

role-battering, the result would be a liquidation of that side's role. If the patient decided to yield to the challenge saying
'Oh, you are probably right, you have more important things to do'
- his enacted role would be a liquidation of the otherwise crystallised role of the patient, allowing the nurse to invade the rights associated with this role.

If we assume that a role merely consists of a series of positions, held together by a protective wrapping of structural recognition, the liquidation would take away the structural approval. The main consequence of this would be that previously bundled positions now could be challenged individually, rather than being able to hide behind the structural approval of the role. It would now be possible for the nurse to challenge each of the positions this particular patient would call for with a claim to being a patient. The enacted role can therefore both be seen as a means for positioning, as well as an objective for positioning.

If the relationship between the roles involved or the perspectives that applies are to be changed, they have to be addressed and readdressed through application. According to Butler (1990) change is made possible through repetitive re-addressment. If the position is hiding behind the protective wrapping of a role, it is not addressed in its application, but if the position and their mutual relationships are addressed as individual positions, change is made possible.

Integrating Liquidation and Crystallisation

If we look at the perspectives put forward in a conflict, the enactment of roles can be illustrated as clenched fists, whereas positions can be viewed as the individual fingers. By clenching the fist, the fingers provide a protective wrapping around each other, making them an effective tool for winning a conflict. When clenched, only the role as a whole can be addressed, making it difficult to challenge the enacted perspectives. Through the liquidating removal of the protective wrapping, the hand is opened, allowing the individual perspectives to be challenged individually. Instead of being a take-it-or-leave-it-package, the enacted perspectives can be addressed, positioned and negotiated individually, and eventually provide an agreement to resolve the conflict.

A new approach can then be found and decided on. Rather than leaving the enactor with a cluster of liquidated perspectives, the new perspective can be re-crystallised by reestablishing the protective wrapping. This process is both important to ensure that the new perspective is enacted, but also in order to get the process started to begin with; being allowed to step back into the privilliged position can be an important incentive for letting the role be liquidated in the first place. If the liquidation would challenge the right to occupy a certain role, not in respect to how it is enacted, but in respect to being alowed to enact it, the participant would not be expected to play along. Another reason would be the need for obtaining strucutal legitimation (or constitution) for the new approach. According to Schein (1962), social integration is a powerful means to ensure that a perspective is enacted. An example would be a case of five managers (see below), who after having solved a conflict among themselves, explicitly agree and thereby ensure each other will enact an agreed upon solution. Through such agreement, the consensus is integrated socially between the involved parts, and through that provides the enactment with structural legitimation. The recrystallisation does in other words help the participants in returning to a sitiation where they can enact their roles legitimately.

Roles and Positions in Practice

A situation among group of managers during the EIS learning game can be used to illustrate the dynamics of role, positioning and the transition between them. In the EIS, the group of participants was to decide on what initiatives to take in order to implement an organisational change in a fictional company . The main instruction for staging the game was that the participants, as group, were to achieve the highest possible score, which is intimately linked to the quality of the change management performed. Initially, the participants must decide on a strategy to implement a defined, organisational change. After each initiative, the game provides the participants with feedback in terms of reactions and progress. During the game, the participants decide what initiatives to deploy in order to implement their initial strategy. While doing so, the participants discuss viable approaches and what initiatives that would have the desired effect. The effect can be seen immediately after making a choice. The EIS was deployed as part of an international course for young managers, with the purpose of providing the participants an unsettling practical experience on change management.

   While playing the game, a group of participants, who had a very conflict-filled game and scored very low, employed two different types of argumentation for characterising the game ; one can be seen as situational, the other as personal. The situational argumentation was put forward as an argument, based on the logic of the situation. One example of this would be to hold one initiative back until the group had had a chance to talk to a specific character in the game about it, and then go through with it. This argument was based on the situation, both with respect to the group and value consensus, and allowed the other members to take part in the decision. The personal argumentation was on the other hand, not based on the current situation, but attempted to draw on personal features. One example would be the utterance 'We should go informal' or 'Do the covert lobbying', which in the situation could be seen as presentations of decisive and final decisions, rather than as suggestions to the group. Presenting the utterances in isolation reflects the way they were uttered. They were not prepared or followed by supporting argumentation by the utterer, but were presented as something to be authoritative in itself in attempt to shape the decisions of the group. From a positioning perspective, the participant attempted to take a position, either to shape the decision, or to achieve a more powerful position to act from within the group. From the role-perspective, knowing that the utterer was a manager, the enactment can be seen as an attempt to draw upon the mundane role of being a manager, as well as attempting to employ the personal access to structural power that the role would provide.

Both lines of argumentation would have the purpose of framing a specific initiative as vital, but employed different sources of legitimating power. The situational, position based-approach clearly draws upon distinctions and arguments that were validated in the group. The scope of the storyline was limited to the learning game itself, and did not attempt to draw on arguments from situations or relations outside the game. In contrast, the personalised, role-based approach drew upon storylines that transcended the situation; as the participants were managers, and the EIS was played as a part of a management course, the game-based situation can be seen as a conjunction between the participant's personal manager-storylines, allowing the utterances to be seen in a management perspective. The utterances can be seen as acts of management, employed in an attempt to define the situation. In doing so, the utterer would attempt to draw upon a situation-external legitimation to distinguish and define within the situation, rather than drawing on the situational consensus. These attempts were not accepted by the group, but were often ignored, resulting in more group tension.

The two decisional approaches resembles that of a positioning approach, using the situational features, logics and values in order to make decisions in the game, and also resembles that of the role approach, drawing upon external legitimation in order to define decisions in the game. Both approaches can provide the situation with viable solutions to the game-based problem, but there is a key difference in how. With the role-based approach, it can be seen as an attempt to bring clarity into the decisional process (by appointing a manager or decision maker), or it can be seen as an attempt to perform management in the situation. When attempting to draw upon such situational-external legitimation as a source for definitorial power, the situation became a conflict as the attempt was not recognised by the other participants. If the attempt had been successful, it might have provided the situation with some clarity on the decisional process, but as it failed, it only brought fuel to the fire. With the positioning approach, clarity is provided in the situation by the negotiation of rights, duties, and especially rules for the interaction, that is a schematic script or storyline. Such an approach may provide an unforeseen opportunity for unsettling other issues than the conflict addressed by allowing power to be re-negotiated, slowing down the process. Slowing down the conflict negotiation may provide an incentive for employing strong-arm tactics through the mobilisation of powerful roles and structures to determine the solution, but slowing down may also provide an opportunity for finding solutions that exceed the immediate conflict. The mobilisation of the role should however not be seen as illegitimate; as learning games and the participant's mundane reality are expected to be mutually permeable, allowing non-game issues to be explored through the game and the game to affect non-game situations, the enactment of mundane issues can be seen as a contribution to the issues addressed during the game. The enactment can however be seen as unproductive with respect to the pedagogical objective as the specific game-session fuelled a conflict beyond the scope of the game.

The interaction taking place between the role-enactment and positioning acts raises the question of intentionality of the performance. Did the manager try to provide clarity, or was it a tactical move in a crystallisation plan that reached beyond the learning game? As a poststructuralist approach, positioning theory would, according to Wetherell (2003) be a problematic framework for investigating intentionality. Such shortcomings may be met through the role-perspective, as it provides an opportunity to look for structurally embedded intentionality. One hypothesis would be that the role-enactor had a self-experience of having a more informed, and thereby more effective perspective on how to solve the challenge; another would be that the actor saw the game-based learning environment as an opportunity to achieve a situation-external objective, and navigating politically as result. A third possibility could be that the enactor performed the role in order to build a particular sense of self as being a manager. This line of thinking would, according to Wetherell (2003) be closer to psychoanalysis than to post-structuralism. The situation can both be understood as a case of role-enactment and as a case of positioning, which provides a view on the dynamics of the conflict between the participants, as well as an opportunity for grasping the conflict taking place. At the same time, none of the acts in the situation can be seen as either role or position-based, emphasising the need for a framework that is able to grasp both the perspectives as well as the transition between them.

Liquidation and Crystallisation in Practice

During the learning game, some of the participants allowed their managers roles to be liquidated, thereby basing their participation on the situation rather than on their external role. As the purpose of the game was to attempt to disturb and unsettle the participants' current understanding of change management, it is most likely that holding on to current understandings has had a negative impact on the pedagogical yield. The retainment of the role is also likely to have had a significant impact on the conflict that occurred between the participants, who spent much of the game-time trying to establish the decisional process of the group, rather than interacting with the game and trying to solve the challenge on change management. The attempt to draw upon power that was not legitimate in the situation clearly had a negative detrimental effect on solving the task.

The occurring conflict can be understood on several levels; as the situationally provided conflict, which was to be solved corporately; another as the introduced conflicts, which are related to situation-external issues, but are deployed through the roles. In such a situation, the conflict can be understood through the concepts of roles and positions, whereas crystallisation and liquidation provides a view on the transition or change ability, thereby providing means for interacting with the conflict, and eventually making the conflict manageable. One interventional move would be to promote a member to lead the group, thereby crystallising a position; another would be to state a number of rules for the group, thereby creating an explicit, shared conception of values in the group, and through that use liquidation to prevent the members from drawing upon group-external means. By performing one of the two, the conflict may have become manageable, thereby allowing the participants to work with the game-provided conflict instead

The Process of Liquidating Roles in Conflicts

Role analysis provides a powerful tool for addressing the enactment of structural issues in the social interaction, allowing us to identify and distinguish between different levels of conflicts that take place at the same time. In the case of the five managers, resolving the counter destructive part of the conflict regarding the personal, managerial level would most probably have paved the way for the group to work with the game-provided conflict in a more expedient manner. By using role theory to address the structurally defined roles, these roles and their perspectives can be addressed in a conflict and used for drawing distinctions on the legitimacy of objectives and power in the situation. By addressing and explicating power and objectives in a group, the positioning of different objectives and the legitimacy of power can indicate that liquidation is on its way, which may be helped along by clarifying what consequences it might bring the partners in the conflict.

The Process of Crystallising Positions

After liquidating the enacted roles, the process of negotiating the conflict can be seen as a positioning game on arguments, allowing the partners to establish a mutual way of understanding and handling the conflict. At the end of the negotiation, the agreed decisions must somehow be institutionalised in order to be enacted effectively outside the negotiation. From the role-perspective, the decisions would be integrated into the roles of the partners before re-crystallising their roles. As Schein (1962) pointed out, perspective changes must be integrated either personally or interpersonally in order to retain their effect. From this point of view, the role integration would provide the partners with the structurally legitimated rights and duties to enact the negotiated decision. By re-crystallising the role with the agreed changes, the agreement would become a part of the structurally legitimated power that the role drew upon.

In the case of the five managers, the participants would have had to liquidate their roles as managers in order to avoid the destructive conflict, but that would only be possible under the condition that they all could re-crystallise their roles afterwards. The managers would not lose their jobs by stepping down from them during training neither would they be forced to abandon their personal objectives for good as a consequence of the liquidation. These objectives could freely be pursued afterwards, but only in respect to the agreed solution.

Conclusion

Although unable to deal with the dynamics of conflict negotiation, role-theory provides insights into how structural issues and situation-external objectives are enacted in a conflict. It provides insights into how the enactment of roles may either work as means of clarity, as stumbling blocks when trying to change perspectives, or even as means for escalating conflicts. Positioning theory provides a powerful tool for addressing the dynamics of conflicts and conflict negotiation, while the role-based approach provides insights into its more persistent elements.

Although the presence of roles in a social context may make the situation inflexible due to role-deployed agendas and structural issues, the problematic presence of roles should not be seen as an incentive to abandoning the perspective. Rather, it should be considered in connection with the more situationally orientated perspective of positioning theory, thereby creating a framework that is able to encompass the factors that create and maintain conflicts, as well as the factors and means that may help in managing and solving them. Through the combination of the structuralist approach of roles and the post-structuralist approach of positioning, the transitional perspective appears as a third road between them, allowing us to address how sluggishness and dynamics interact in the social. Examining roles and positioning separately allows us to address opportunities and obstacles in a given conflict, whereas the transitional, integrative perspective of liquidation and crystallisation provides us with means for not only understanding, but also for intervening in conflicts.

References

Austin, J. (1962). *How to do things with words.* Oxford, UK: Oxford University Press.
Banton, M. (1965). *Roles. An introduction to the study of social relations* New York, US: Basic Books Inc.
Boonstra, J. J. (Ed.). (2004). *Dynamics of organizational change and learning.* West Sussex, UK: Wiley.
Broch, T. (2000). Strukturalisme. In H. Andersen & L. B. Kaspersen (Ed.), *Klassisk og Moderne samfundsteori.* Copenhagen, Denmark: Hans Reitzels Forlag.
Butler, J. (1990). *Gender trouble. Feminism and the subversion of identity.* London, UK: Routledge.
Coutu, W. (1951). Role playing vs. role taking: An appeal for clarification. *American Sociological Review, 16,* 180–187.
Davies, B., & Harré, R. (1999). Positioning and personhood. In R. Harré & L. van Langenhove (Eds.) (1999), *Positioning theory: Moral contexts of intentional action* (pp. 32–52). Oxford, UK: Blackwell Publishers. [Original version published 1990, Journal for the Theory of Social Behavior, *20,* 43–63].

Deleuze, G. (1994). *Difference and repetition*, London, UK: Athlone Press.

Fitzergerald, L., Lilley, C., Ferlie, E., Addicott, R., McGivern, G., & Buchanan, D. (2006). Managing Change and Role Enactment in the Professionalized Organisation [www.sdo.lshtm.ac.uk/pdf/Change%20Management/ finalreport_fitzgerald_21.pdf] (18 of July 2006)

Forward, J., Canter, R., & Kirsch, N. (1976). Role Enactment and deception methodologies, *American Psychologist*, *31*, 594–604.

Goffman, E. (1959). *"The presentation of self in every day life"*, Doubleday Garden City, NY, US.

Harré, R. (2000). Acts of Living (book review). *Science*, *289*, August.

Harré, R., & Moghaddam, F. (2003a). Introduction: The self and others in traditional psychology and in positioning theory. In R. Harré & F. Moghaddam (Eds.), *The self and others* (pp. 1–11). Westport, CT: Praeger.

Harré, R., & Moghaddam, F. (Eds.). (2003b). *The Self and Others: Positioning individuals and groups in personal, political and cultural contexts*. Westport, CT and London: Praeger.

Harré, R., & Van Langenhove, L. (1999a). The Dynamics of Social Episodes. In R. Harré & L. Van Langenhove (Eds.), *Positioning theory* (pp. 1 – 13). Oxford: Blackwell.

Harré, R., & van Langenhove, L. (1999b). *Positioning theory: Moral contexts of intentional action*. Oxford, UK: Blackwell.

Harré, R., & van Langenhove, L. (1999c). Epilogue: Further Opportunities, In R. Harré & L. van Langenhove (Ed.), *Positioning Theory*. Oxford, UK: Blackwell Publishers.

Heading, B. (1972). The man and the mask. In J. A. Jackson, *Role*, Cambridge, Cambridge University Press

Henriksen, T. D. (2004). On the Transmutation of Educational Role-Play. A Critical Reframing of the Role-Play in Order to Meet the Educational Demands, In M. Montola & J. Stenros (Ed.), *Beyond role and play. Tools, toys and theory for harnessing the imagination*. Preceding papers for Knudepunkt, Helsinki, FI.

Kelly, G. (1955). *The psychology of personal constructs*. New York: Norton.

Linton, R. (1936). *The Study of Man*. New York: Appleton

Mead, G. H. (1934). *Mind, self and society*. Chicago, US: Chicago University Press.

Potter, J., & Wetherell, M. (1987a). *Discourse and social psychology: Beyond attitudes and behaviour*. London: Sage.

Potter, J., & Wetherell, M. (1987b). *Discourse and social psychology*. London, UK: Sage.

Sarbin, T. R., & Allen, V. L. (1954). Role theory, In G. Lindzey & E. Arnson (Ed.), *The handbook of social psychology*, 2. ed. Vol. 1, Texas, US: Addison-Wesley Publishing Company.

Saussure, F. de (1916). *Course in general linguistics*. London, UK: Duckworth.

Schein, E. (1962). Management Development, Human Relations Training and the Process of Influence, In I. R. Weschler & E. H. Schein (Ed.), *Selected readings series five, issues in training*. Washington, US: National Training Laboratories, National Training Education Association.

Slocum, N., & Harré, R. (2003). Integration Speak: Introducing Positioning Theory in Regional Integration Studies, In R. Harré & F. Moghaddam (Ed.), *The self and others. Positioning individuals and groups in personal, political, and cultural contexts*. Westport, CT: Praeger Publishers.

Stryker, S., & Statham, A. (1985). Symbolic interactionism and role theory, In G. Lindzey & E. Aronson (Ed.), *The handbook of social psychology* (Vol. 1, pp. 311–79). Random House, New York, US.

Tan, S. L., & Moghaddam, F. M. (1999). Positioning in intergroup relations. In R. Harré & L. Van Langenhove (Eds.), *Positioning theory: Moral contexts of international actions* (pp. 178–194). Oxford, England: Blackwell.

Turner, R. H. (1968). The self-conception in social interaction. In C. Gordon & K. Gergen (Ed.), *The self and identity in social interaction*, vol. 1. Wiley, New York, US.

Van Langenhove, L., & Harré, R. (1999). Introducing Positioning Theory. In R. Harré & L. Van Langenhove (Eds.), *Positioning theory* (pp. 14 – 31). Oxford: Blackwell.

von Glasersfeld, E. (1995). *Radical constructivism. A way of knowing and learning.* London, UK: The Falmer Press.

Wetherell M. (2003). Paranoia, ambivalence, and discursive practices: Concepts of position and positioning in psychoanalysis and discursive psychology, In R. Harré & F. Moghaddam (Ed.), *The self and others. Positioning individuals and groups in personal, political, and cultural contexts.* Westport, CT: Praeger Publishers.

Yardley-Matwiejczuk, K. (1997). *Role-play. Theory & practice.* London, UK: Sage.

4
Intrapersonal Conflict

ROM HARRÉ AND FATHALI M. MOGHADDAM

> 'Was it the old hag I killed? No, I killed myself, and not the old hag. I did away with myself at one blow and for good. It was the devil that killed the old hag, not I.'
> (Dostoyevsky, 1866/1966, P. 433)

A major theme in literature is the 'internal struggle' experienced by central characters, who often develop, 'grow', to become better persons because of that struggle. One of the most exhaustive studies of such characters is found in Dostoyevsky's novel Crime and Punishment, in which Raskolnikov kills an old woman for her money, and then struggles to the realization that he must confess his crime in order to live and die at peace with himself, and reconnect to the rest of humanity.

Intrapersonal Conflict and the Transformed Self

A common theme in discussions involving intrapersonal conflict, such as cases where a religious person is guided by a priest to 'sruggle against sin' or a patient reporting mental illness is guided by a therapist to 'fight against depressing thoughts', is a transformation in the self. Through intervention and an 'internal struggle', involving a battle fought using religious, clinical, or other value systems and languages, an individual can change and become 'renewed', or 'born again'.

Colloquially we often speak of a person as being 'at war with him or herself' or as suffering from some kind of 'internal conflict'. No doubt in many cases this is some kind of metaphor for vacillation of intentions or shifting from one project to another before completing what one has started out to do. However, there are some kinds of psychopathology where such expressions are not far short of literal descriptions of a kind of intrapersonal 'civil war'. Manic-depressive cycles seem to be something like this. How can I be cheerful and upbeat at one time and miserable and suicidal at another? These seem to be clusters of characterological and personality characteristics that characterise one person but which are in contradictory opposition to one another. Even less metaphorical are the rare kinds of oppositions that have been reported in studies of the few genuine cases of multiple personality syndrome. In Morton Prince's classic study Sally and Christine, the alternative versions of Miss Beauchamp, expressed considerable hostility to one another. Does it make any sense at all to approach the analysis of interpersonal conflict and proposals and strategies and means of resolution or exacerbation with positioning theory as one of the main analytical tools? We believe that the conceptual structure on which positioning analyses of interpersonal conflicts are based can usefully be applied to some cases of intrapersonal discord. In post traumatic stress disorder (PTSD), individuals who have experienced life in highly stressful situations, such as war, 'fight with themselves' to avert flashbacks and a 'reliving' of stress-provoking past events.

Looked at more analytically there seem to be a variety of situations for which the expression 'intrapersonal conflict' would seem appropriate.

a. There are cases where one and the same person performs actions that seem to embody contradictory intentions. He might pull someone towards him and then give that apparently valued person a sharp pinch.
b. There are cases in which a person expresses an attitude or belief and then performs an action that is at odds with it. A person might scorn the rituals of superstition but yet be seen to cross his fingers if a black cat crosses his path. A person may be well known for his reactionary beliefs but at the polling booth, almost without thought, he puts his cross by the name of the radical candidate.
c. There are cases in which a person seems to hold quite sincerely beliefs that seem to be at odds with one another. He declares that democracy will perish unless everyone votes, and yet omits to vote himself because he asserts that his vote will not make any difference.

Positioning Theory

The first step in pursuing this development of the technique will be to ask whether and how far positioning theory can be modified to serve the purpose of intrapersonal analysis. As an analytical scheme it involves three components:

1. The local cluster of rights and duties about which people have beliefs and prejudices, cite edicts and rules, and so on, with which they frame their thoughts and actions. It does not seem to make any sense to talk 'rights over oneself' but notions like 'duties to oneself' are widely cited in explanations and exhortations.
2. The story-lines that are taken to be unfolding within the framework of such beliefs and customs which shape patterns of action in episodes of conflict according to local conventions of meaning. Familiar conflictual story lines include such remarks as 'I couldn't make up my mind', 'I had a great struggle with myself to keep to the diet' and so on.

3. The thoughts the actors have and the actions they carry out given meaning as acts according to the story-lines and the moral principles associated with them. Thus doing the proper or correct thing is told as 'overcoming temptation' or 'my better self came to be the fore' and so on. The meanings given to moments in recounting commonplace episodes seem to draw on local moral orders in which such achievements as giving up smoking are lauded as praiseworthy and story lines feature the tale teller as 'hero'.

Can any of this be applied to an individual suffering some kind of personal trouble, from indecisiveness right through to the various ways that personality, character and even the very self can disintegrate into antagonistic fragments?

To provide a framework for answering this question we need to lay out the structure of the concept of 'self'. It is the unity and diversity of 'selves' that the possibility intrapersonal conflict must lie.

Summarizing a vast literature there seem to be several root ideas in the notion of selfhood (Harré, 1998, 5–10; Chapter. 4). Using the grammar of the first person as a starting point the pronoun 'I' indexes the content of what is being said with the place of the speaker's body in space and time. This aspect of selfhood is the stable core of identity. However, it also indexes what the speaker has said with his or her taking responsibility for what is said, be it apropos of its truth or be it some commitment to action. This aspect of 'the self' is highly mutable and context sensitive. However, psychologists have coined the term 'self-concept' for the beliefs a person has about him or herself, including beliefs about that person's life course, their autobiography. There is plenty of evidence that 'telling one's life' is often shaped by immediate strategic considerations rather than the 'whole truth'. This aspect of self-hood is closely tied to Goffman's (1959) conception of the display or presentation of self. This is a performance in the course of which other people form opinions about the nature, character and personality of the speaker/actor. This can sometimes be Machiavellian, but it is certainly always highly context dependent.

When people talk about the 'social construction of self' they are usually referring to such matters as one's moral standing, beliefs about oneself, the self as presented in social action and so on, since these aspects come to be and are shaped by social conditions and relations. However, that there should such contingency requires that there be something conserved and self-identical. That is the embodied core of the person, the point from a human being perceives the world and acts upon it.

Forms of Personal Conflicts

The next question to be addressed is how the troubles of individuals could be construed as conflicts? It seems to be part of the grammar of the word 'conflict' that there is more than one party involved. If the conflict is not between two human beings, families, tribes or nations, between what is there a conflict?

Heroism

An obvious case that comes to mind is when an individual is not confronted by another human being or association of human beings, but by some external entity, process or condition which may be believed to be threatening. Story lines featuring heroes in various postures come to the fore.

Rarely is the right to attack conceded to the non-human entity, be it avalanche, tsunami or grizzly bear. But it was not always so. The wrath of God as embodied in such menaces was a rightful wrath. The Black Death was a punishment for Sin, humanity in conflict with God. But this takes us back to interpersonal positioning again. This kind of talk surely presupposes a personal God.

Nevertheless, heroic individuals do describe their adventures as struggles with the forces of nature, obstacles to be overcome, conditions to be circumvented. In these stories the hero has the right to take measures against that which opposes him and more recently her as well.

Not so long ago individual people were thought to behave strangely because they had been entered by a demon, an incubus or a succubus. Sometimes the original person and the demon fought it out. Sometimes more than one demon struggled to obtain mastery over the soul of the person in whose body they had taken up residence. Exorcism proved an effective end to the conflict by expelling one or more of the warring parties. Here again the analysis draws on the very same conceptual structure as the original interpersonal cases.

We will not pursue this kind of one-person conflict any further since analytically it seems to depend for its force on the personification of the non-personal oppositions. Or perhaps it may be that the demons are persons too.

Self-deception

More to the point, because more radical in the way an individual becomes the scene of conflict, there are a number of psychological processes that look conflictual. These are the various forms that Self deception can take. At least the grammar of self-deception accusation seems to underpin a discourse in which a person's conscious thoughts and feelings are pitted against some unacknowledged aspect of him or herself. Some Freudian crises rooted in the story-line of a conflict between the Id and the Superego, often presented as independent aspects of the self, the self that is overt and the self that is suppressed.

The structure of self-deception as a continuing cognitive process raises questions about reflexive personal knowing and its relation to consciousness.

Freud's theoretical account of the human psyche makes conflict and resolution the abiding feature at all levels and stages (Freud, 1905). The cosmic duel between Good and Evil reappears in the energy of the Id as the manifestation of biological forces in the individual in conflict with the shaping influence of the Superego as the manifestation of social forces in the individual. The Oedipal stage involves the resolution of the conflict between the male child and his father.

The child's love for the mother, with its sensual tinge, pits him against the father as the actual lover of the mother. Despite all these family relationships between real people this is an intrapersonal conflict. The emotional attitudes are all those of the child. The fear of castration is fantasy, if it exists at all. Similarly the girl child's fantasy love for her father, envy of the male genitalia and eventual absorption into her mother's world of child bearing is an intrapersonal saga. Freud was forced to give up the idea that real sexual relations existed in the family circle. The fantasy theory that succeeded it seems to have been the result of an intrapersonal conflict in the psyche of Dr Freud himself (Gay, 1988).

In Freudian psychology, conflict internal to the individual is directly connected with conflict internal to, and between, groups. All libidinal ties binding individuals to one another in intimate relationships are assumed to involve both positive and negative sentiments. For example, two lovers, a married couple, parents and children, and all others who feel strong sentiments toward one another experience a mixture of love and hate. In order for love and positive sentiments to dominate the relationship, hatred and negative sentiments residing inside each individual in a 'loving' relationship must be re-directed onto targets external to the relationship. Thus, in his discussion of 'Why war?', Freud (1930/1953) argued that the 'conflict within' is revolved by displacing negative sentiments onto dissimilar others. This insight led to a tradition of research on displacement of aggression (Miller, Pederson, Earlywine, & Pollock, 2003).

The irrationalist model of Freud in two key respects prepared the ground for the 'balance' models that emerged by the mid twentieth century as part of the first cognitive revolution. Freud's irrationalist model assumed that individuals, first, struggle to in some ways 'deceive themselves' and, second, maintain a balance in their psychological states (by keeping a lid on suppressed motives, wishes, and so on).

There are two main modes of self-deception. Freud's is based on the idea of 'denial'. The fact that someone vigorously denies that some event took place or that some fantasy was entertained is the best reason for believing that it did or had.

Not quite so well known generally, but important and influential nevertheless, was Jean-Paul Sartre's concept of 'mauvaise foi', bad faith (Sartre, 1966).

Both Sartre and Freud can be thought of as claiming that it is possible to juxtapose a conscious cluster of beliefs with an unconscious cluster which would contradict those held consciously. For some reason this person is not willing to entertain the second cluster of beliefs, so that they remain unattended to. This distinguishes the liar from the self-deceiver. There is no doubt that, in some sense, there is a conflict in such a situation. However, it is only a potential conflict. As long as the unattended beliefs are not attended to and made conscious there is no psychological conflict for a person to resolve. The potential conflict is resolved by the shunting off of one set of beliefs to the limbo of the unconscious or the unattended.

The evident paradox in this story has been much discussed. Surely this 'shunting off', this repression, is motivated. But how can one be motivated to deal with something of which one is not conscious?

Sartre emphasises the paradox in the following passage: 'I must as deceiver know the truth that is masked for me as the one deceived. Better yet, I must know that truth very precisely, in order to hide it from myself the more carefully – and this not at two moments of temporality, which would permit us to reestablish a semblance of duality, but in the unitary structure of one and the same project (Sartre, 1966: 87).[1]

Wood (1988:220) offers an exegesis of Sartre's way of resolving the paradox. Sartre seems to be claiming that belief is always an imperfect epistemic state. A belief held in good faith is open to critical revision, while a belief held in bad faith is not. This gap between final and rigorous confirmation leaves room for someone to consciously hold two contradictory beliefs. There is no need to create such an elaborate and implausible psychology as Freud's complicated processes of rendering the distasteful psychologically invisible by consigning it to the unconscious and blocking its return except in the form of a symbolic transformation into something seemingly morally different. In short Freudian psychology is irrelevant to the paradoxes of self-deception.

However, if Freudian accounts of cases of neurotic behaviour are right then, so argues Erwin (1988: 228–245), they are not irrelevant. He considers how like and how unlike Freudian self-deception is to deceiving another person. It is unlike deceiving another because there need not be inconsistent beliefs. It is the defence mechanisms that reshape unconscious beliefs into acceptable forms. Of course, Freudian 'hang ups' are like deceiving another person because the apparatus of repression and defence is an attempt to hide the truth.

Cognitive Dissonance

Current applications of Positioning Theory have been based on only one aspect of local moral orders, the prevailing system of rights and duties, and the beliefs people have about their own involvement with them. However, there are other norms than these active in the affairs of everyday living. In the nineteen sixties and seventies a great many studies were made of the role of norms of consistency in how people adjusted discrepant actions and beliefs. The alleged phenomenon of 'cognitive dissonance' was analysed as a conflict between a person's beliefs and what a situation seemed to require someone to do (Festinger, 1957). Shifts of attitude were identified, and were explained as the result of a person's trying to adhere to a norm of consistency. Festinger tried to get people to change their beliefs or at least their expressed beliefs by 'forced compliance', that is inducing someone to say or do something inconsistent with a previously expressed belief or previously displayed attitude.

The theory itself is something of a mess. Dissonance is supposed to arise between 'cognitions', but this concept is so wide as include attitudes, beliefs and behaviour. Quite how an action is also a cognition, that is a thought, is never explained. Probably it is the thought about what one has done or expressed in action that is dissonant with another thought or belief. Be that as it may, the theory inspired interesting studies of 'buyer's remorse', wishing that one had not bought the item one did but had decided to buy something else or not buy anything at all. Here indeed both contradictory poles are thoughts. Trading in an old car for a new model is an oft-cited example. Thinking about the situation after taking delivery of the new car can lead to the feeling that the added monthly payments are more of a burden than originally one thought they would be. Dissonance has emerged. Perhaps one should not have traded in the old car after all. One strategy to restore consonance in one's pattern of thoughts is to emphasise to oneself all the good points of the new vehicle (Brehm, 1965).

In this and many other cases there is a kind of intrapersonal conflict between beliefs or between a belief and an action and so on. Positioning Theory identifies the familiar story-lines well enough. Such actions as moving to a new house are interpreted in accordance with whatever story-line is salient at that point in someone's life. However, to make sense of these episodes other aspects of local moral orders than the distribution of rights and duties must be taken into account. There does seem to be a consistency norm to which people strive to adhere in how they present their actions. Indeed further studies of such phenomena as 'buyer's remorse', which might include all sorts of other situations where regrets come to the fore, might show how close the norm of consistency come to a moral principle. People do seem to blame each other for inconsistencies. Kant based his entire moral theory on the use of contradiction to identify immoral actions. For example, he argued that lying is wrong because if one wills to make one's own maxim of telling untruths to escape censure to be a universal moral rule, then lying will cease to be an effective strategy since no one will be ready to take what the liar says as truth. The distinction between lying and truth-telling collapses (Kant, 1787/1996).

Vacillation

Another feature of local moral orders is revealed in the way that vacillating between two or more alternative beliefs, attitudes, actions and so on is frowned upon. Vacillation is treated by most people to be a kind of vice. Moreover, it is clearly an example of intrapersonal conflict, as now this, now that alternative seems to be the right one.

Aristotle might be our guide here. Weakness of will or akrasia is manifested in those only too common cases in which after hesitating between doing the right thing and doing what one wants, one chooses the lesser good. Confronted by a dessert trolley on which there is Tin Roof Fudge Pie and a 'healthy alternative' I hesitate and hear myself saying 'I'll try some of your TRFP'. The conflict is resolved. Leibniz discusses the more difficult theoretical question of how choice is possible between two alternatives identical in all respects, the ultimate situation for vacillation. He declares that there is an original power of action which is not simply a response to the better of alternatives. There never is a situation which there is no reason for choosing between alternatives. As he says '... let us not pretend to that harmful ... liberty, of being in uncertainty and perpetual embarrassment, like that Ass of Buridan ... who, being placed at an equal distance between two sacks of wheat, and having nothing that determined him to go to one rather than the other, allowed himself to die of hunger' (Quoted in Russell, 1949: 194) There are any number of popular story-lines to make sense of weakness of will. Duty appears naturally in these contexts. One does have a duty to oneself to choose the best. Here is one of those situations in which a manifest duty does not seem to be linked to a complementary right.

Temptation to Sin

In Christian tradition human life is shot through with personal conflicts between the two components of the person – body and soul. The body is the source of those impulses that drag us downward while the soul strains upward towards God.

This form of personal conflict depends on two unquestioned theses.

a. A human being is an embodied soul. The soul is eternal and indivisible. It survives the death of the temporal and divisible body.
b. The cosmic conflict between the fallen angels, led by Satan, and God and his angels is played out in individual people.

These theses offer both an ontology of pairs of beings between whom conflicts can and almost certainly will arise and a story-line according to which individual lives unfold. This story-line comes in two versions, one with a good ending in some kind of union with God, and the other with disaster, as the errant soul is hurled into the pit of fire to be tormented for all eternity. This story-line is found in both Islam and Christianity. Here is a description of the conflict from the writings of the Sufi poet.

Analysed in the framework of Positioning Theory two of the three features of that theory are evident. There is a story-line which reflects the unfolding of a life reveals a deep seated and enduring conflict. The resolution of the conflict also follows Positioning Theory principles since it depends on the outcome of contested distributions of rights and duties between the personified aspects of the person. This becomes clearer still when we turn to another Medieval example, the psychodramas played out in the Miracle Plays.

The underlying psychological progression goes something like this: impulse, intention or plan for execution. We can see how framing this progression in Positioning Theory shows us how the Medieval dramatists created interpersonal conversational models of intrapersonal conflictive cognition. In this model conflicting impulses and intentions appear as the positions taken up in a debate between pseudo-characters. Here is an example from Skelton's Magnyfycence of c 1516. The hero, Magnyfycence, has been led astray by vices disguised as virtues. He comes to believe that 'liberty' means doing anything he likes. But the personified virtue Measure assures the personified attribute Liberty that 'Yea, Liberty with Measure need never dread'. Liberty retorts 'What, Liberty to Measure would then be bound?'. Measure replies '... if Liberty should leap and run where he list, it were no virtue, it were a thing unblest'. The story-lines are simple tales of someone being tempted in various ways by the attractions offered by the vices, yet by listening to the advice of the virtues sin is avoided. None of this would make sense unless itself embedded in a moral order in which the virtues have the right to be heard and the hero the duty to take heed. Interestingly in such a play as Magnyfycence, the illocutionary force, the real meaning of the honeyed talk of the disguised vices, must be reinterpreted by the hero in the light of the story-line revealed to him by the virtues.

In some versions of this story-line, particularly associated with Sufism and other movements of mysticism, a good ending is achieved when the self is emptied of all 'bad' characteristics. Thus, the Persian mystical poet Feyz Kashani declares:

'I emptied myself of me so that I could be filled with his love' (our translation)
and Khajeh Abdollah Ansari writes:
'Bravo to people who have said goodbye to slavery
Given up being worldly and freed themselves of all' (our translation)
Emptying oneself of all worldly desires leave space for 'his love' to enter.

Multiple Personality Syndrome

In some case histories the stories told by the patients reveal situations in which there is quite evidently conflict between person-like beings though they are not fully realised as persons. In what may be the only two genuine cases reported in the literature, 'Sally and Christine', Miss Beauchamp's alter egos, and 'Eve White and Eve Black', some of the conditions for ascribing personhood to the 'beings' conjured up in the talk are met. Some are not. For example, in neither case were there multiple bodies. So a key necessary condition for distinctive persons was not met. In the fiction of Robert Louis Stevenson, Dr. Jekyll and Mr. Hyde have very different bodily forms. Lycanthropic transformations in the movies show the hands turning to claws and hair sprouting on the skin while the mouth and nose elongate to become a muzzle. More recently 'The Incredible Hulk' bursts out of the modest physique of the doctor and turns green. These may be metaphors for aspects of a person, but they trade on the singularity of embodiment to present a story-line of conflict.

In looking closely at the case histories the power of proper names and personal pronouns to sustain independence of persons becomes evident. Miss Beauchamp used the two proper names, 'Sally' and 'Christine' in her conversations with Morton Prince. In the write up of the 'Eve' case by Thigpen and Cleckley the woman who presented such startlingly different appearances is described as refusing to accept her married name at one point in the story as rightfully hers. In both cases, the conflict between the distinctive 'personas' was expressed in conversational moves with pronouns, usually 'I' and 'she'.

It is worth noting that persons are distinguished in phone conversations, chat rooms and so on without benefit of visible concrete embodiment of the beings in question. Telemarketeers try to gain our confidence by offering 'I'm Michael' or some such as the opening move. Ringing up an institution, after making one's way through the jungle of 'Press One for So and So' instructions until we reach the comforting terminus of 'Stay on the line if you wish to speak to an agent' after a long wait being entertained by music, we usually get 'How can I help you?', one person to another person. Tones of voice are physical evidence of distinctive persons, but as Peter Strawson showed, in a brilliant analysis of individuality in a sonic world, without the possibility of reidentification that material embodiment makes possible 'I' would fade away.

Miss Beauchamp, at first only under hypnosis, would talk about things she had herself done, as if they had been done by someone else. This was expressed by the use of the ordinary system of personal pronouns. 'I' indexed an action, thought or speech as the speaker's, Chris's, while 'she' referred to someone other than the speaker, a person Sally, whose thoughts and actions could be commented on. Later Miss Beauchamp talked this way without being hypnotised. The key moment for Morton Prince was when the speaker began to use the first person to recount events that had been previously recounted as those of the 'she' of the original conversation. The clinching stage for the diagnosis of 'dissociation of personality', the idea of two persons in the one body, came when the recollection of events began to be distributed between the speakers Chris and Sally without any overlap between them.

That this phenomenon had its origins in and expressed some form of intrapersonal conflict was evident in the content of the talk of the two primary speakers. Sally claimed to have a man friend and to be able to speak French, while Chris presented herself as solitary and poorly educated. The ingredients of a situation appropriate for a Positioning Theory analysis seem to be here. There is a familiar story-line. One young woman jealous and resentful of another. Sally has things Chris would like. Indeed some of Chris's remarks suggest that it is she rather than Sally who has a right to them. Duty does not appear in these conversations, at least as reported by Morton Prince.

Sally, one of Miss Beauchamp's alter egos, writing a letter to herself as Chris, says (ironically) 'I have such good news for you, my dearest Chris ...I'm going to get them [some small snakes] to amuse you at night ...' (Prince, 1978: 166). Chris describes the situation to Morton Prince as follows: 'They [the letters] were really dreadful ... ['I'] would almost swear she was bitterly jealous ...' (Prince, 1978: 167). The content of the letters that Sally addresses to herself as Chris two story lines unfold in accordance with this assessment. In one, Sally shows herself to be jealous of Chris wishing to hurt and humiliate her. In accordance with the logical grammar of 'jealousy', Sally is working with the moral belief that Chris is not entitled to whatever good things she has. Sally sees this as humiliating her. The familiar strategy is to get revenge by turning the humiliation in the opposite direction. The other story-line, developed by Chris and by Morton Prince, is to see Sally's actions and her manner of talk as immature, driven by an irresponsibility for what she says and does.

In The Three Faces of Eve, Thigpen and Cleckley give a detailed history of their relations with the young mother who appears first as Eve White, married to Reginald White with a daughter Bonnie. She consults the doctor about headaches. She is quiet, modest and conscientious in her life. Sometime later she is back, but with a very different manner and appearance. Now she is Eve Black (her maiden name). She reveals a very different kind of person, flirtatious and mildly dishonest. She claims to know what Eve White is thinking. However, Eve White denies any knowledge of Eve Black, either her thoughts or her actions. When she finds out what Eve Black has done she is chocked and surprised. Later a third style of thinking and behaving manifests itself in a sufficiently coherent way to be identified as a third 'person', Judy. Gradually Eve comes to be Judy-cum-Eve Black, a human being with a stable personality and character. This Eve divorces her dull but worthy husband.

Person identification is indexical, based on the grammar of the personal pronouns. Eve Black tells Thigpen and Cleckley 'I got nothing against her [Eve White]... I don't wish her any bad luck. But I got myself to think about too'. Here is a rather different story-line from the Miss Beauchamp case. She goes to remark 'I can't keep my mind on her and her doings and sayings [about her husband as Eve White and her daughter] all the time'. (Thigpen & Cleckley, 1957: 68).

The conflict opens up between two contrary story-lines. Eve White's life is lived as a conscientious and hardworking wife and mother. Eve Black is a carefree, flirtatious good time girl. Reflecting on the obvious possibility that it was all a fake, Thigpen and Cleckley lay a good deal of weight on the asymmetry of partial amnesia. Summing up their skepticism they remark that 'she can live it up as Eve Black and then return to her status as the innocent wife and mother without troubling her conscience. Who would not find such an arrangement remarkably convenient?' (Thigpen & Cleckley, 1957: 163). It might have been just a more elaborate version of the claim of the injured innocent – 'It wasn't me!'.

Past and Present Selves

There can surely be clashes between one's remembered self and what one now takes oneself to be, from mild shame or regret right through to manic-depression or cyclic disorder as it is now called. Emil Kraepelin describes a patient in these terms for his audience of young doctors: 'The patient's illness began in her fourteenth year with an attack of depression, which was followed two years after by a state of excitement. Two years later another attack of depression came on with self-accusations ... In her states of depression she felt deep repentance for her behaviour during the excitement ...' (Kraepelin, 1923: 65). Kraepelin gives some vivid descriptions of the reckless, grandiose and loquacious goings on of people in the manic phase. These are well remembered and often regretted in the depressed phase of the cycle.

In a similar vein the story-lines that are presented by the 'born again' in reflecting on their transformation turn on contradictions between the actions and beliefs of the old self and those of the new self just born. It is notable though that this contradiction does not lead to intrapersonal conflict. The old and the new do not co-exist in conflict with one another for the soul of the afflicted. St Paul, the great exemplar of the art of being 'born again', says ... Paul replaces Saul, and so Paul has nothing to regret. Of course, he now has a preacherly opportunity to comment on the moral weaknesses of his previous self. St Augustine makes this retrospective commentary the centre piece of his famous salvation story.

The enormously popular 'self help' industry is clear evidence of the eagerness of many people to try to change themselves. There are numerous self help books, films, and programs intended to guide clients become more assertive, more sociable, a better decision maker, more creative, more popular, less shy, a better leader, and so on. But in some situations the change we seek in ourselves is more strategic and temporary: it is a change needed to get us out of a passing difficulty. For example, at an interview for a government job that he desperately needs, Joe positions himself as supportive of large government programs, even though he always votes for political parties that try to cut such programs.

A classic example of this kind of 'temporary' change is found in Hamlet. After the ghost appears and tells Hamlet of his father's murder by his uncle, Hamlet's struggle within himself intensifies: what should he do? Hamlet expresses iron resolve to avenge his father, but his actions fail to follow up on his words. When he discovers his uncle alone, kneeling in prayer, Hamlet does not kill, on the flimsy excuse that he should not kill the king 'in the purging of his soul' but, rather, kill him,

'When he is drunk asleep, or in his rage,
Or in th'incestuous pleasure of his bed' (III.3.90–91)

In his efforts to keep his uncle and mother from discovering his suspicions too early, Hamlet feigns madness. But his uncle plots a scheme to kill of him, and Polonius remarks on his behavior, 'Though this be madness,yet there is method in't' (II.2.205–206). In an impulsive moment, Hamlet lunges at a figure behind a screen in his mother's chambers, imagining he is striking at his uncle, only to kill Polonius by mistake. At the end of the play, when Hamlet has been manoevered to fight a dual with Laertes, who seeks to avenge the murder of his father Polonius, Hamlet explains away his actions by claiming that it was his madness, not him, that did the deed,

'Was't Hamlet wronged Laertes? Never Hamlet.
If Hamlet from himself be ta'en away,
And when he's not himself does wrong Laertes,
Then Hamlet does it not. Hamlet denies it.
Who does it then? His madness. If't be so,
Hamlet is the faction that is wronged.
His madness is poor Hamlet's enemy.' (V.2.227–233)

Thus, at the end of the play, and his life, Hamlet has changed again and climbed out of madness – if he ever did fall temporarily mad. His transformation is complete when he persuades Horatio to not join him in death, but to live 'To tell my story' (V.2.343), which Horatio proceeds to do.

Conclusion

In each of the cases discussed the dominant feature seems to be the story-line. According to Positioning Theory this is not just a reflection of the structure of what happens to be the structure of a life episode. It the very schema that shapes the way the relevant slice of personal history unfolds. It is in terms of the story-line that the various events in that history are given meaning. The third component of Positioning Theory, the local distribution of rights and duties in line with the prevailing moral order, is not so immediately visible. Yet in the way that the story-lines tell of the triumph of good over evil, which must surely be the desired outcome of the intrapersonal conflicts, tacit distributions of rights and duties from the person to the pseudo-persons in conflict is clearly to be seen. That this intuition is right becomes clear when one turns to the plots of the Mystery Plays, the psychodramas that present the stories of personal struggles with a caste of human propensities.

Though the content of the local moral order is evident in many of the cases discussed above, the emphasis on rights and duties that is at the heart of inter-personal Positioning Theory is displaced by other features such as the seeming moral status of consistency. Duty sometimes appears as a personal imperative, but without the correlative right.

These discussions of different ways in which a person may be the site of conflicts lead to the recognition of a variety of ways in which intrapersonal conflicts can come about and several ways in which such conflicts can be resolved Even if not resolved conflicts can be held at bay so as not to disrupt a person's life. The Freudian story-line makes available ways of interpreting thoughts and actions that would be contrary to professed beliefs and actions so that they do not intrude on the smooth workings of life.

Note

1. This passage is quoted in an excellent article by A. W. Wood (1988: 207).

References

Brehm, D. J. (1965). An experimental analysis of self-persuasion. *Journal of Experimental Social Psychology*, *1*, 199–218.

Dostoyevsky, F. (1866/1966). *Crime and punishment*. (Trans. D. Magarshack). Blatimote, MD: Penguin.

Erwin, E. (1988). Psychoanalysis and self-deception. In B. P. McLaughlin & A. O. Rorty, *Perspectives on Self-deception*. Berkeley, CA: University of California Press.

Festinger, L. (1957). *A theory of cognitive dissonance*. Stanford, CA: Stanford University Press.

Freud, S. (1900–1901/1953). *The interpretation of dreams (part two) and on dreams*. (J. Stachey, ed. and trans.). London: Hogarth.

Freud, S. (1905). *The Ego and the Id. In The complete Works of Sigmund Freud* (Vol. 19) London: Hogarth.

Freud, S. (1930/1953). Civilization and its discontents. In J. Stachey (ed. and trans.), *The standard edition of the complete psychological works of Sigmund Freud*. Vol. 21. London: Hogarth Press.

Gay, P. (1988). *Freud: A Life for our Time*. New York and London: W. W. Norton.

Goffman, E. (1959). *The Presentation of self in everyday life*. Garden City, NY: Doubleday.

Harré, R. *The singular self: An introduction to the psychology of selfhood*. London: Sage.

Kant, I. (1787/1996). *Critique of pure reason*. (Trans. W. S. Pluhar). Indianopolis, IN.: Hacket.

Kraepelin, E. (1923). *Manic-depressive insanity and paranoia* (trans. R. M. Barclay). Edinburgh: E. & S. Livingstone.

Miller, N., Pederson, W. C., Earlywine, M., & Pollock, V. E. (2003). A theoretical model of triggered displaced aggression. *Personality and Social Psychology Review, 7*, 75–97.

Prince, M. (1905) [1978]. *The dissociation of a personality*. Oxford: Oxford University Press.

Russell, B. A. W. (1949). *The Philosophy of Leibniz*. London: Allen and Unwin.

Sartre, J. -P. (1966). *Being and nothingness*. New York: Bantam Books, 75–97.

Thigpen, C. H., & Cleckley, H. M. (1957). *The three faces of eve*. London: Secker and Warburg.

Wood, A. W. (1988). Self deception and bad faith. In B. P. McLaughlin & A. O. Rorty, *Perspectives on self-deception* (pp. 207 – 227). Berkeley, CA: University of California Press.

Part 2
Interpersonal Positioning

5
Positioning and Conflict Involving a Person with Dementia: A Case Study

Steven R. Sabat

Interpersonal interactions with and among older people can be affected by the ways in which older people position themselves (reflexive positioning), and how older people are positioned (a) by younger people (interactive positioning), (b) by other older people (interactive positioning) and (c) the degree to which interactive positioning is accepted or rejected by the person being positioned. Negative positioning, which can, in some cases, become malignant positioning (Sabat, 2001; 2004) often results from the presence of cognitive deficits that occur as a result of brain damage as seen in cases of dementia in general and Alzheimer's disease (AD) in particular. When a person's behavior is prematurely explained as being dysfunctional, the person is being positioned in a negative way. If the negative positioning leads to treatment that is depersonalizing, then we can say that the positioning is "malignant", or dangerous to the personhood and self-worth of the person in question. It is extremely important to explore the effects of positioning of people with diagnoses of AD in particular and dementia in general, because (1) the incidence of people thus diagnosed is expected to triple by mid-century, which will mean that (2) the number of people affected directly and indirectly (as professional and informal caregivers) will reach into the tens of millions in the developed world alone, and this will mean that (3) the financial costs required to care for and sustain those diagnosed will reach into the hundreds of billions of dollars (Alzheimer's Association, 2000).

Although advances in biomedical treatment have not reached the point at which AD can be cured, prevented, or reversed, some gains have been made regarding the slowing of the progress of the disease. Still, the behavior of people thus diagnosed is affected by more than brain damage alone; people with AD and other forms of dementia react to the losses they sustain in aspects of memory and language function and to the ways in which they are treated by others (Sabat, 2001). To the extent that such people are treated in dysfunctional ways, their quality of life will suffer and the extent to which they will be able to use cognitive abilities that remain intact will be diminished.

One of the ways in which the social environment can affect people with AD and, more generally, dementia, is how they are positioned (Harré and van Langenhove, 1992) by healthy others. In many instances, malignant positioning can occur wherein the person with dementia is seen as being defective in one or another way, is then treated as such in a variety of situations, and reacts negatively to such treatment. The negative reaction itself can then be interpreted as yet another symptom of AD, thereby validating the original story line behind the initial positioning. As a result of the malignant positioning and the reaction of the person thus positioned, conflict can ensue between persons and also within an individual person, be it the person with the diagnosis or the caregiver. The purpose of this chapter is to explore the nature of such conflict, the role that positioning can play in the entire process, and to offer some suggestions as to how to reduce such conflict via alterations in positioning.

Conflict and Positioning Following Diagnosis

Snyder (1999) interviewed people who had been recently diagnosed with AD and she revealed a great deal about how her subjects reacted to the symptoms, the diagnosis, and the ways in which others treated them. In some cases, her subjects reacted quite strongly and negatively to the way the medical personnel who were involved in arriving at and communicating the diagnosis treated them. For example, Bea commented about the neurologist who interviewed her: "He was very indifferent and said it was just going to get worse…If he had just shown a little compassion. He was there to diagnose my problem, but he wasn't there to understand my feelings. He had no feelings for me whatsoever. I've hated him ever since. Health care professionals need to be compassionate" (p. 18). Another of Snyder's subjects, Betty, a retired social worker and former faculty member at San Diego State University, said about health care professionals whom she encountered during the process of being diagnosed, "They're busy wanting to climb up to the next rung on the ladder. That's very human. I don't blame them. But they don't really accept the significance of illness for people. They know the diagnosis, but they don't take time to find out what it truly means for that person. This casualness with which professionals deal with Alzheimer's is so painful to see…You have to really be willing to be present with the person who has Alzheimer's. But there are some people who don't want to learn, and it's the looking down on and being demeaning of people with Alzheimer's that is hard to watch" (pp. 123–4).

In both of the above cases, the women were essentially being depersonalized by the health care professionals who informed them of their diagnosis, but who seemed to lack any interest in exploring with them what the diagnosis meant to them, how they felt, or in extending to them any human compassion or caring. It would be incorrect to assume that the professionals in question were callous, uncaring people. So why did they behave as they did? Among the possible reasons is the way in which the professionals positioned Bea and Betty as well as how they positioned themselves. That is to say, the professionals in question saw their roles as being limited to communicating the facts of the diagnosis and nothing more. They did not think that they had any reason to discuss anything further with their patients, perhaps because there was nothing they could do to stop the disease from progressing toward its eventual conclusion. Tacitly, however, they were incorrectly positioning Bea and Betty negatively as people who, because of their illness, would either (a) have no particular reaction to the news, given that they have a form of dementia, or (b) lack the ability to engage in any kind of discussion about what the news meant to them. Thus, the process and presence of conflict can be seen to begin as early as the moment of the revelation of the diagnosis: the person being diagnosed is essentially objectified and reacts negatively to that treatment. Part of the negative reaction can be understood in terms of the diagnosed persons' ability to understand and evaluate the lack of "procedural justice" being accorded to them.

The Role of Procedural Justice and Reactions to Treatment Accorded to "Patients"

Social psychologists have explored the phenomenon that, in a striking percentage of situations in which people report having been treated unjustly, it was not the outcome or decision that the person faced that led to their sense of injustice, but rather the manner in which they were treated (Messick, Bloom, Boldizar, & Samuelson, 1985; Mikula, Petri, & Tanzer, 1990). Furthermore, people seemed to accept third-party decisions made if they believed that the decisions in question were arrived at through what they saw as fair processes (Tyler and Huo, 2002). And, finally, with regard to the situations faced by Bea and Betty described above, underlying a person's judgments about procedural justice is the quality of the treatment that the person has received. Bea was quite clear in her reaction to what she perceived as the lack of compassion and indifference on the part of the physician who communicated the diagnosis to her. Betty spoke of the lack of the professionals' acceptance of the significance of the illness for, and their demeaning of, those diagnosed, and so both women can be heard as decrying the unfairness of the treatment they were given. So it was not the outcome, the diagnosis, that drove the women's negative reactions to the medical professionals, but rather how they were treated by those who conveyed the diagnosis: as if their feelings thoughts and goals were irrelevant.

This is not to say that such interactions occur in each and every situation between health care professionals and their patients, but it surely was true in these cases, as well as in the case of Dr. B (Sabat, 2001), whose internist commented that "treating a person with Alzheimer's is like doing veterinary medicine." In such cases, the person with AD begins to feel ignored, unworthy of being treated as a human being, and someone who is defined to a great extent, if not completely, by his or her diagnosis. Betty commented that, "A person with Alzheimer's disease is many more things than just their diagnosis. Each person is a whole human being" (pp. 123–4). Once persons are positioned socially as nothing more than instantiations of a diagnostic category, their essential humanity, including their intellectual and emotional characteristics, needs, and their social personae beyond that of "demented, burdensome patient" become more and more obscured and can ultimately become erased. Under these circumstances, the extent to which such people can enjoy any semblance of a good quality of life is correspondingly reduced and this, in turn, will require increasing expenditures of resources in order to "manage the patients" instead of interacting with them as persons in ways that would not lead to conflict and the need for "management".

As Snyder (1999) reported, following the diagnosis, Bea commented that she often felt "nearly invisible" in social situations, although she did perceive others' apparent discomfort about her being thus diagnosed and having problems with aspects of her memory, as well as having some problems organizing and directing bodily movements such as shaking hands. As a result, others in her social milieu positioned her negatively as someone who was far more disabled than she actually was, and treated her as if the negative positioning were actually valid, thus leading to a dramatic constriction of her social world to the point of her being isolated and thereby becoming increasingly dependent upon her husband. She was well aware of this fact and of the fact that her dependence on her spouse essentially resulted in his becoming more and more isolated from the larger social community, and characterized the situation by saying, "I'm isolating him as well as myself and I'm not being fair to him" (p. 24). Feelings such as these, that spring forth in the wake of being negatively positioned by others and then treated in socially malignant ways such as being ostracized and banished (Kitwood, 1998) create internal conflict within the person with AD and work to diminish the person's sense of self-worth.

It may seem odd, at the very least, to the reader at this point, that the two women whose reactions were quoted verbatim above could be treated as they were. Specifically, here we have two women who have expressed themselves clearly, cogently, and even with some grace. There is nothing in their words or syntax that could conduce to the idea that they were cognitively compromised, and yet they were still treated in ways that could be described as "dysfunctional" and "malignant" by healthy others. It is precisely this confluence of facts that underscores how powerful an influence a diagnosis of probable AD can be, for in the minds of everyday persons, the diagnosis seems immediately to lead to the negative positioning of the people thus diagnosed and to what those diagnosed perceive as being a lack of procedural justice. What is the foundation of this sort of positioning? One possibility is that there is a stereotypic view, promoted by professionals, the public press, entertainment media, and the like, that focuses on the defects that AD can ultimately cause, and simultaneously ignores the persons' remaining intact abilities. Likewise, there is the tendency to assume that all reported "defects" in people thus diagnosed are due to the disease alone and not to the ways in which the people thus diagnosed are then treated by others. So to summarize, stereotyping of people diagnosed with

AD is based on a medical view that every instance of seemingly "abnormal" behavior seen in the person diagnosed is due to brain damage, and that such people are immune to being treated in dysfunctional ways by others. So, for example, if a person with a diagnosis of probable AD is treated in a way that is humiliating and embarrassing, and if that person reacts with anger or grief or by pulling away from others or avoiding them completely, the anger, grief, social isolation are viewed as symptoms of AD instead of symptoms of dysfunctional social treatment, such as to validate the original malignant positioning of the person.

In the cases above, we see that, from the earliest stages following the initial diagnosis, because of the malignant ways in which the person diagnosed is positioned by healthy others (medical personnel as well as informal caregivers and friends), there are clear conflicts created (1) between the person diagnosed and healthy others, and (2) within the person thus diagnosed. Some of the building blocks of the original malignant positioning can be found in misunderstandings harbored by medical professionals as well as informal caregivers and friends. One of the most basic of these misunderstandings involves what are, to many people diagnosed with AD, the first signs that something is amiss: memory problems. In the following section, I shall explore this misunderstanding.

The Problem with the Notion of "Memory Loss"

All too often, formal as well as informal caregivers believe that people with AD or other forms of dementia have "memory loss", that they cannot remember anything that has happened recently. This incorrect belief is exemplified in the following comment from a caregiver whose husband had been diagnosed with early stage, or mild, dementia:

He does have a logical mind, but without a memory it can't help him.

The caregiver in this instance had come to believe that her husband had no memory because he had, on a number of occasions, failed to recall events that occurred a short time ago, sometimes asking her the same questions repeatedly and receiving the same answers. In this case, the caregiver mistakenly assumed that recalling information was the same thing as remembering information. Thus, if her husband did not recall things, he had no memory of those things and, as a result, his logical mind could not be of any use to him.

It is the case, however, that contributions of cognitive psychologists (Grosse, Wilson, & Fox, 1990; Howard, 1991; Morris & Kopelman, 1986; Randolph, Tierney, & Chase, 1995; Russo & Spinnler, 1994; Schacter, 1987; Squire, 1994) have enhanced our understanding of memory such that we know that there is explicit memory, which includes retrieval of information from memory by recall as well as by recognition, and that there is also implicit memory, which is often revealed by a change in a person's behavior as a result of an experience that the person is not consciously aware of having had. It is clear that people with AD have intact implicit memory and that they can be affected significantly by the ways in which they are treated (Sabat, 2006). It is possible, for example, for a person with AD or another type of dementia to fail to recall a recent event, but (1) still have an implicit memory of that event, or (2) be able to recognize correctly that the event in question occurred. Likewise, it is possible for the same person to be able to recall some events that carry important meaning to him or her. This latter phenomenon was revealed in the same caregiver's comment about her husband:

I again asked "Do you remember Steve Sabat" and he said "Yes, he came to dinner." That is pretty remarkable. You made quite an impression.

In this case, the husband had recalled, a month after the fact, my having joined them for dinner, even though he did not recall other events that occurred at approximately the same time or even more recently. What the caregiver revealed in saying that "This is pretty remarkable", was based upon her previous belief that her husband's ability to recall recent events was defective regardless of how meaningful the events might be to him. It may be instructive in the present context to examine at least one of the reasons that, according to the wife, I "made quite an impression." It was at the end of the main course of the dinner in question that the wife and one of the adult children began to clear the dinner table. During this time, the husband commented to me, "I don't even remember what I ate." My reaction was to say, "Well, let's see about that. Did you have chicken?" He replied, "No, I think it was fish." I replied, "That's exactly correct. We had salmon." He then addressed his wife and said with a clearly pleased look on his face, "When is this guy going to come back again?" Although he couldn't immediately recall what he had for dinner, when I explored the issue by beginning to use a "multiple choice" format that avoids recall but depends upon recognition instead, he correctly retrieved the information he had initially thought he'd forgotten.

It is under these conditions that conflicts can arise between the person with dementia and his or her caregiver because the caregiver may be assuming, incorrectly, that the person with dementia "has no memory" and may therefore say things in the presence of the person with dementia that are embarrassing to that person or may do things that the person does not like, assuming that there will be no long lasting effect. If then, the person with dementia becomes angry or hurt and remains that way, the caregiver will assume that the anger is caused by the presence of "dementia" and not by the fact that the person with dementia remembers being treated badly or spoken about in a negative way. And, it is not uncommon under these conditions for the caregiver to report to physicians that the person with dementia has behaved angrily "for no reason" and for the behavior to be labelled "irrational hostility" (instead of "righteous indignation"), requiring pharmaceutical intervention.

Clearly, the entire conflict can be avoided if professionals educate caregivers about the different aspects of memory so that such incorrect assumptions about recall and remembering are avoided entirely and incorrect malignant positioning is likewise avoided.

Problematic Social Interactions

Beginning with the diagnosis, it is often the case that there is a fundamental change in the social world of people with dementia. As Snyder's (1999) subjects noted and as Kitwood (1997, 1998) discussed at length, the reactions of healthy others to the fact of the diagnosis can serve to undermine the social life of the person with dementia in that others remove themselves and thereby constrict the person's social world tremendously. There is still other "fallout" that follows in the wake of the diagnosis and the problems with recalling some recent events demonstrated by the person with dementia. Another result that is often observed is that the person's social self, or persona, is compromised. In order to appreciate this dynamic, let us first examine the different aspects of selfhood as viewed through the lens of a Social Constructionist approach.

From a social constructionist point of view (Harré, 1991b; Sabat, 2001), there are three aspects of selfhood, called Self 1, Self 2 and Self 3. Self 1, the self of personal identity is experienced as a singular point of view from one time to another time. We express that singularity through the use of pronouns such as "I", "me", "myself", "my", "our" (yours and mine). Through the use of these pronouns, we index experiences, obligations, and responsibilities, as being our own. A person might have a retrograde amnesia such that he or she cannot recall all sorts of autobiographical information, but might still reveal an intact Self 1 merely by saying, "I can't recall anything about who I am." Indeed, a person might not be able to speak at all and still express an intact Self 1 through the use of gestures.

Another aspect of a person's selfhood, according to social constructionist theory, is what is referred to as Self 2 (Sabat, 2001), and is comprised of a person's physical and mental attributes, past and present, along with the person's beliefs (political, ethical, religious, etc.) and beliefs about his or her attributes. For example, one may be proud of some attributes, but ashamed of others. The diagnosis of "probable AD" becomes one of a person's many attributes, as might problematic recall of recent events, and the inability to recall the words one wants to use from time to time. It is not uncommon for people with AD to be embarrassed by dysfunctional Self 2 attributes.

A person's social persona, or Self 3, is multiple in nature. Each of us has many different social personae, revealed in unique patterns of behavior. For example, the behavior patterns related to being a loving spouse, are quite different from those associated with being a demanding professional at work, from those associated with being a devoted and loving parent and those associated with being a deferential child. In addition, each social persona, cannot exist without the cooperation of at least one other person. For example, the social persona of "devoted spouse" cannot be constructed if one's husband or wife, as the case may be, does not recognize the person as being his or her spouse. One cannot be a "loyal friend" if one's friends disappear from one's life, and one cannot be "the authoritative professor" if one's students do not attend class or if they are all engaged in activities that result in ignoring the existence of the person standing behind the lectern.

When the Self 2 of the individual becomes dominated in the eyes of others by the attributes relating to the diagnosis of AD or another form of dementia and problems with aspects of memory and the like, and when the Self 3 of the person is reduced to being a "burdensome patient", interpersonal misunderstandings can arise easily and lead to conflict.

For example, let us listen to the words of the wife and caregiver of the man who was diagnosed with "mild dementia" to whom I referred to earlier. Keep in mind that the couple was married for more than fifty years.

What I find so difficult is realizing that he is no longer the man I knew and in fact, I think I have almost forgotten the man he was.

Clearly, if "he is no longer the man" that his wife knew, then she might treat him in ways that are very different from the ways in which she treated the man "she knew". And if, in fact, he still is in many ways the man she knew, problems might arise quite easily.

Therefore, my initial reply to her was the following:

I don't think that you've forgotten the man he was, because if you had forgotten that man, you wouldn't be nearly as saddened by what you see in his present condition. It may be the difference between him now and him "then" that is so hurtful to you and you have to have a sense of him "then" in order to feel that way.

This led to the following exchange, illuminating the beginnings of conflict between the husband and wife, beginning with the wife's comment:

At times he resents my taking over his life completely and I resent having to do it. He also has physical problems and I am constantly worrying about his falling so I won't let him do anything (even taking out the garbage).

In this case, the wife/caregiver is not necessarily seeing her husband's resentment in terms of the man he always had been throughout their marriage. She is aware of his resentment, but not of some of the important reasons behind that resentment. Thus, it was useful for me to try to call her attention to the nature of her husband's present subjective experience in the context of the attributes that he always had during their marriage and continued to have despite the diagnosis and some of the problems he was having with retrieving some information via recall:

I can understand your husband's resenting your doing so much for him; it's not so much that he resents you, however. I think that he's probably feeling guilty that he is in a situation in which you have to do so much for him that he used to be able to do for himself. He probably resents the fact that you are carrying so much on your shoulders and he could very well feel as though he is a burden to you. He is a man whose life as an adult was all about being in command and now he's not. That is a huge, bitter pill to swallow. He has to have injured pride and he likely needs to have something to do to help out–even taking out the garbage if nothing else. If you worry so much that he'll fall, but prevent him from doing anything that allows him to feel as though he's a man who's taking care of something to help around the house, you may be "protecting" him into a state of anguish. My point is that he has to have something that gives him a sense of purpose.

It is often the very lack of a sense of purpose that plagues people who are experiencing the problems that stem from the brain damage associated with dementia and the social treatment that they then receive. As one man with probable AD said to me when I was about to administer a battery of neuropsychological tests to him, "Doc, you've gotta find a way to give us purpose again" (Sabat, 2001). Despite the variety of cognitive problems that are part and parcel of the brain damage that results in a diagnosis of dementia, a person can still retain the cognitive ability to evaluate situations and interpret their meaning. That is, a person can still be a "semiotic subject" (Sabat & Harré, 1994). So it was for the man with whose wife I was engaged in the conversation reported herein. Indeed, upon my conveying to her the above notions, she replied by saying,

You certainly make some excellent points. Right on the button. I don't know why I should be surprised, that's your field… He does feel very guilty that I have to do so much for him and constantly tells me that he knows he is a burden.

So we see from the wife's report that her husband has verbalized to her that he feels that he is a burden to her and, from all accounts, he has every reason to feel that way, given that he still remained a semiotic subject (a person whose behavior is driven principally by the meaning the person derives from the situations he or she confronts) despite his problems with some aspects of retrieving information from memory and the diagnosis of mild dementia.

As I discussed above, a person's Self 2, the self of physical and mental attributes, including beliefs about one's attributes past and present, can endure long into the course of AD and other forms of dementia. This aspect of selfhood was revealed yet again in the following exchange between his wife and me:

One thing that puzzles me about my husband is that he has never become angry over his memory loss. He just mentions that he can't remember lots of things, but then he goes on to something else. Wouldn't a person be frustrated and angry when they can't remember and they know it's permanent?

Although we still see in her question the misunderstanding regarding the relationship between memory per se and the ability to retrieve information via recall, indicating how powerful this misconception truly is, the main focus of this part of the conversation was her puzzlement regarding why her husband did not become angry about what were, in fact, his problems with recalling particular pieces of information. My response to her was based upon the idea that long established Self 2 attributes from the past can persist despite the problems in her husband's everyday life with which she was familiar:

That (your husband) hasn't become angry about memory problems–how has he handled adversity in the past? Whether that was adversity in (his profession) or wherever, how did he typically react? Also, how important has it been to him, during all the years you know him, to move through things gracefully–being "cool" under fire, keeping his poise? The issue is not whether "some generic person" (un-named) might become angry/annoyed/frustrated when not being able to recall something simple. It's not what

9 out of 10 people "out there" might feel or do. It's about (your husband) and what he does and how, if at all, his way of reacting in this situation is anything like his way of being during previous decades of his life when adversity struck. Remember whom you're talking about. You cannot compare him to others or think of him in terms of how you or anyone else might react. You have to think about this only in terms of (your husband).

Upon my encouraging her to think in terms of her husband's way of dealing with adversity in the past, focusing her upon his Self 2 dispositions and personality characteristics, she replied:

You amaze me. Of course, you are right. That is exactly how he has handled adversity. He has had disappointments, but he never let his feelings show.

Thus, his Self 2 attribute of how he handled adversity in the past was still functioning in the present, despite his diagnosis. The act of calling his wife's attention to this aspect of his selfhood, and allowing her to see that it was still very much intact, also accomplished something else that was extremely important to the way she viewed him. Specifically, it allowed her to think about (and position) her husband in a way that was not limited to his rather new Self 2 attributes of having recall problems and not being able to do, with ease, some of the things he did quite automatically in the past. And, in so doing, she was able to see that aspects of him that she always admired were still alive in him:

I also feel I have much more respect for the man that he is... I have more respect for (him) now because of how well he is handling adversity. When I was younger I never thought about that aspect of (my husband's) personality. Now that I am older I have come to appreciate that wonderful quality.

Although her reaction above was certainly helpful to her in terms of her respect for and appreciation of her husband's way of dealing with adversity, it also indicated something important about an entire process of re-thinking (and re-positioning) that she did about her husband. Recall that, at the outset of this conversation, she said the following:

What I find so difficult is realizing that he is no longer the man I knew and in fact, I think I have almost forgotten the man he was.

She had positioned her husband in a negative way, based primarily on one of his relatively new Self 2 attributes that was caused by brain injury, saying in a sad way that he was, in her view, no longer than man she knew. By focusing upon his dysfunctional attributes almost exclusively, she effectively blinded herself to the admirable qualities that her husband still possessed and that she had admired as she grew older. As our conversation progressed, however, she came to realize that she had "much more respect for the man that he is" because she realized that one of his abiding Self 2 attributes, how he handled adversity, was still alive and well. It is instructive to examine a significant part of this process, namely that because she had focused so keenly on his dysfunctional recall ability, she then came to interpret his lack of anger and frustration about that particular dysfunctional ability as yet another "defect" in him. So, the negative or, dysfunctional story line that she wove, or was beginning to weave about him, was itself based upon the fact of his diagnosis and problems with recalling particular recent events, even though his reaction, as we came to see, was perfectly in accordance with his life-long way of dealing with adversity. Here we see that the seeds of conflict between the husband and wife were sown by how the wife began to interpret one of her husband's virtues as a defect because she had already positioned him in a negative way.

Another important aspect of this process is that we are herein discussing a type of interactive positioning, wherein one person positions another in a negative way. It is often the case that when an otherwise healthy person is positioned in an unfavorable way by another person, the person being thusly positioned can refuse to be positioned as such and can work to redress the social dynamic that he or she finds objectionable. It is also the case, however, that when people with dementia are positioned in negative ways, they may not be able to reject that positioning because (1) their language skills may be compromised, or (2) they are essentially unaware that they are being positioned in a negative way. In the present case, it was the latter condition that was in effect and thus, in order for the wife to reposition her husband in a positive way, what was required was a careful examination of the objective facts (his reaction to his recall problems) in terms of the way he always dealt with adversity in the past. Clearly, a third party can be extremely helpful here in facilitating such an examination.

Conclusion

Although I make no pretense about generalizing from the present case study to all people with diagnoses of dementia, what is reported herein is a phenomenon that has been reported previously (Sabat, 2001, 2004, 2006) and that could very well be occurring in a host of interpersonal situations. Further research will establish the extent to which these dynamics are common in the relationships between formal and informal caregivers on the one hand and people with dementia on the other. What is clear from the foregoing is that

(1) conflicts that arise within people with AD and other kinds of dementia, as well as between such people and their caregivers can be seen to have their roots in the ways in which healthy others negatively position and then treat those people;
(2) at least some of the negative positioning results from misunderstandings about the exact nature of the dysfunctional attributes of the person with dementia ("memory loss");
(3) some of the negative positioning occurs because caregivers focus more and more upon the dysfunctional Self 2 attributes of the person with dementia, while simultaneously ignoring other healthy and virtuous Self 2 attributes that remain intact and, as a result,

(4) fail to see that the negative reactions elicited in the person with dementia as a result of the ways in which he or she is treated, are not themselves "symptomatic" of dementia, but of the dysfunctional ways in which the person is treated; and

(5) the resolution of such conflicts requires that caregivers (a) begin to recognize and pay more attention to the existence of worthy remaining Self 2 attributes in their loved ones who are diagnosed with dementia, (b) understand that many of the negative reactions they observe in their loved ones are evidence of semiotic behavior which, itself, reflects a high level of cognitive functioning, (c) think about the extent to which the reactions they observe in their loved ones are consistent with long established Self 2 attributes, and if such reactions are thus consistent, realize that the person for whom they are providing support is still, in many ways, very much the same person they've known for years;

(6) the resolution of such conflicts may also require the assistance of a third party who can help the caregiver in his or her efforts to become aware of all of the above and thereby re-position the person with dementia; and

(7) people diagnosed as being in the mild stage of dementia react as do otherwise "normal" people to the lack of procedural justice accorded to them. Thus, the "meaning-making" ability regarding issues of fairness is not compromised in people in the mild stages of dementia and their reactions to and feelings about situations, therefore, should not be ignored. Rather, such people should be treated with the same concern, sensitivity, and politeness as one would any human being regardless of his or her medical status.

Positioning Theory would seem to be a very useful heuristic in helping to illuminate the nature and resolution of interpersonal conflicts in the interactions between caregivers and people with dementia. As such, it lends further support to the idea that what people with dementia say and do is not merely a reflection of biological pathology, but also of the incorrect assumptions that are made about them based upon dysfunctional Self 2 attributes, the misunderstanding of the exact nature of those attributes, and the subsequent dysfunctional treatment that they are then subjected to by healthy others. Thus, in principle, applications of Positioning Theory can be extremely useful in improving the quality of life of people with dementia as well as that of their formal and informal caregivers.

References

Alzheimer's and Related Disorders Association. (2000). *A race against time*.Chicago, IL: ADRDA.

Grosse, D. A., Wilson, R. S., & Fox, J. H. (1990). Preserved word stem completion priming of semantically encoded information in Alzheimer's disease. *Psychology and Aging, 5*, 304–306.

Harré, R. (1991a). *Physical being: A theory for a corporeal psychology*. Oxford: Blackwell.

Harré, R. (1991b). The discursive production of selves. *Theory and Psychology, 1*, 51–63.

Harré, R., & van Langenhove, L. (1992). Varieties of positioning. *Journal for the Theory of Social Behavior, 20*, 393–407.

Howard, D. V. (1991). Implicit memory: An expanding picture of cognitive aging. In: K. W. Schaie (Ed.), *Annual Review of Gerontology and Geriatrics* (Vol. 11), New York: Springer-Verlag Publishing Co., pp. 1–22.

Kitwood, T. (1997). *Dementia reconsidered: The person comes first.* Philadelphia, PA: Open University Press.

Kitwood, T. (1998). Toward a theory of dementia care: Ethics and interaction. *The Journal of Clinical Ethics, 9*, 23–34.

Messick, D. M., Bloom, S., Boldizar, J. P., & Samuelson, C. D. (1985). Why we are fairer than others. *Journal of Personality and Social Psychology, 21*, 480–500.

Mikula, G., Petri, B., & Tanzer, N. (1990). What people regard as unjust: Types and structures of everyday experiences of injustice. *European Journal of Social Psychology, 22*, 133–149.

Morris, R. G., & Kopelman, M. D. (1986). The memory deficits in Alzheimer's type dementia: A review. *The Quarterly Journal of Experimental Psychology, 38A*, 575–602.

Randolph, C., Tierney, M. C., & Chase, T. N. (1995). Implicit memory in Alzheimer's disease. *Journal of Clinical and Experimental Neuropsychology, 17*, 343–351.

Russo, R., Spinnler, H. (1994). Implicit verbal memory in Alzheimer's disease. *Cortex, 30*, 359–375.

Sabat, S. R. (2001). *The experience of Alzheimer's disease: Life through a tangled veil.* Blackwell: Oxford.

Sabat, S. R. (2006). Implicit memory and people with Alzheimer's disease: Implications for caregiving. *American Journal of Alzheimer's Disease and Other Dementias, 21*, 11–14.

Sabat, S. R., & Harré, R. (1994). The Alzheimer's disease sufferer as a semiotic subject. *Philosophy, Psychiatry, and Psychology, 1*, 145–160.

Sabat, S. R., Napolitano, L., & Fath, H. (2004). Barriers to the construction of a valued social identity: A case study of Alzheimer's disease. *American Journal of Alzheimer's Disease and Other Dementias, 19* (3), 177–185.

Schacter D. L. (1987). Implicit memory: History and current status. *Journal of Experimental Psychology: Learning, Memory, and Cognition, 13*, 501–518.

Snyder, L. (1999). *Speaking our minds: Personal reflections from individuals with Alzheimer's.* New York: Freeman.

Squire, L. R. (1994). Declarative and nondeclarative memory: Multiple brain systems supporting learning and memory. In D. L. Schacter & E. Tulving (Eds.), *Memory systems* (pp. 203–232). Cambridge, MA: The MIT Press.

Tyler, T. R., & Huo, Y. J. (2002). *Trust in the law: Encouraging public cooperation with the police and courts.* Russell Sage Foundation: New York.

6
The Research Planning Meeting

CHRISTINE REDMAN

Introduction

In the episode to be analyzed in this chapter we see a short term challenge to the established rights and duties of people enacting roles. A tiny conflict flares up and is resolved as positions are challenged, occupied and abandoned. It all takes place within the course of a research planning meeting in a large Australian school. Four people were involved, all well acquainted with one another. Three were teachers in the school and one, the author, was a researcher from the university.

The school had been providing specialized computer classes in a computer lab for four years that all grades regularly attended. Each classroom had installed a number of internet connected computers.

The research project concerned the ways teachers could utilise a website found at www.fourmilab.ch in their classes. I, the researcher, had previously introduced the website to them. The website shows photo-like pictures of the surface of the Earth in space in real time. Mountains, deserts and the undulating seafloor can be discerned. Night and day are easily located. I also intended to investigate the meanings afforded primary aged students by the website as they interpreted the site. In the course of the meeting subtle rearrangements of rights to make plans and control the way the research material was incorporated in the teaching programme came and went.

Introducing the Three Teachers

Dot is the most senior of the three teachers and her duties include overseeing the teaching in the level three area of the school. This teaching unit encompasses two grade levels; grades three and grade four. Dot teaches in one of the grade four classrooms. There are six teachers working in this level three unit. The school structure of the school is provided in Figure 6.1.

Wyn is a member of the same teaching unit as Dot. Wyn teaches a grade three and leads the team of grade three teachers. She works with and reports to Dot and so is accountable to Dot, who in turn is responsible to the Principal class members of staff.

Joi is the third teacher in this meeting and she is a grade five teacher. Joi is in the level four teaching unit and leads a team of three people like Wyn, and is accountable to her unit leader.

This institutional framework endows each teacher with a role and the rights and duties that it defines.

As the occupant of a role a person has certain prescribed relatively long term rights and duties, known to and generally accepted as legitimate by other members of the social order in which the role has an established place. In contrast, by establishing a position in the course of a then-and-there conversational manoeuvre, a person takes on or has thrust upon him or her a repertoire of rights and duties that are usually ephemeral. They rarely hold good (that is are taken up by the others involved) for more than the course of the episode in which they are created. In the episode to be analyzed a positioning challenge to a standing role structure opens up a small conflict. By undermining the positioning move, the senior role holder reoccupies the moral high ground momentarily conceded to the challenger.

This study also brings to light the importance of acquiring allies and supporters in even so tiny a conflict as the one to be described. For the most part, the antagonists, Wyn and Dot, amplify their resources by recruiting Joi, first for one side and then the other. In this microworld we see some of the fateful processes of the larger world played out in miniature.

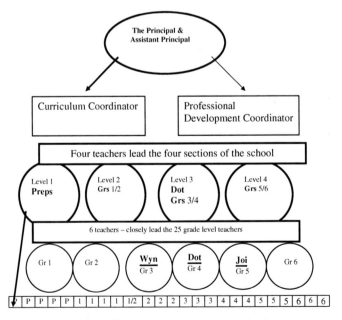

FIGURE 6.1. Relative positions of the three teachers in the school structure.

Each of the people engaged in the episode to be analyzed had a well-defined and mutually understood role, determined by each one's place in the school hierarchy. The interest of the episode lies in the way momentary positionings interacted with the more permanent and stable role structure. The positioning 'flux' depended on the introduction of a story-line ('busy busy') which had no place in the role defining story-line of schooling Australian-style.

The Episode

Dot, Wyn, Joi and I now gathered in the computer lab to plan ways that they could organise their participation in this research project. It had been explained to the teachers in the initial letters inviting them to partake in the research that the focus of the study was to see how a particular website could be utilised.

Wyn had called the meeting in order to get the research project moving along. This meeting was taking place after a six months delay with repeated phone calls from me that had failed to produce a starting date. Wyn had now asked me for practical support to help them begin to implement the project. I was now positioned as having a duty with respect to the purpose of the meeting.

The meeting took place in the schools' computer lab that had 32 computers around the edges of the room and we four sat in the middle at tables. I began by asking the teachers to identify the themes of their integrated units. The school policy is that an integrated topic is taught each term and it has a specific or shared discipline focus. So the topic could be Transport and teachers could choose to take a Technology or Science or Historical emphasis and quite often an integrated topic could take several discipline areas and merge them together.

As the conversation unfolds we see Wyn repeatedly using positioning moves to challenge Dot's presumptive leadership, based on her role position.

The Conversation Unfolds

Joi has just told the meeting that her area will focus on the 'function of plants' and Wyn has stated that her topic would be Australian History but qualifies this,

Wyn   we're actually doing, um... Australian History more...and cultural...

In using the pronoun 'we' Wyn seems to be indexing the group of six teachers in her teaching unit who would all be doing the same integrated topic. In this way Wyn positions herself as having the right to speak for all six teachers in her unit and not just the three she officially was responsible to lead. She had immediately and actively positioned herself as leader. This could be seen as a possibly a challenge to Dot's more senior position. As the official leader of the unit, Dot added 'geographical ...basically Australia'. Wyn agreed and then Dot added, 'and the things around...oceans'.

The First Challenge to Dot's Role Status

Then Wyn immediately qualified Dot's comment stating again, 'it's more of a cultural focus…' Dot agreed with her, confirming Wyn's moral advantage. As the school science coordinator she had perhaps seen this as an opportunity for a more scientific focus, using the research project as a step towards a stronger science emphasis. Dot had allowed the possibility of such a focus when she described it as 'geographical … and oceans'. Wyn continued to use 'we'.

> Wyn.   Where as next term, we'll be doing more the physical side of things. So, but, the water one, we have …got next week the water The Water Watch Week, whether we can just do some stand alone lessons, and just… do something interesting…look at the earth, as you…perhaps looking at the drought areas as you mentioned on the phone, or something.

Developing the initial positioning move Wyn began a critical commentary on the status quo, thus casting doubts on Dot's competence as leader. She suggested not only that they 'do something interesting' but that they consider doing 'some stand alone lessons'. This does not normally happen in the well-planned curriculum, as there are no empty spaces in which to place lessons.

Wyn changed her pronoun to 'you' and this effectively served to draw me into the conversation, recruiting support for her challenge to Dot. Wyn referred to one of our phone conversations. I had suggested that the website could contribute to their topic of Australia if it included a focus on the weather/drought. Wyn said that she thought this focus would fit in with their integrated unit. I had arrived at the meeting with support materials related to teaching about Australia's climate. As the school's Science Coordinator Wyn would be looking for ways to add a science focus to their curriculum. Wyn's reference to this prior communication had acted to affirm her position as a proactive leader in this research project.

However, Wyn had repeatedly qualified and diminished her vision by her use of the words 'just' twice and the word 'perhaps' leaving an ill defined description, shown by the use of 'something' twice and drought only once. Qualifying words like 'perhaps', 'possibly', 'maybe' and 'just' weaken the illocutionary force of a person's commitment, belief or confidence. Words like 'actually', 'really' and 'basically' can can strength it. Attending to the qualifying words can help in tracking subtle changes in relationships, weakening and strengthening challenges such as Wyn's positioning moves vis à vis Dot's role-defined hegemonic status. Wyn had used these qualifying words to distance herself both in a professional and personal sense from her critique and proposal. Wyn had been able to suggest that she sought a change and that it could make the teaching more interesting. This would be assumed to be a positive focus for a leader to take but suggesting 'stand-alone' lessons was risky as it goes against the schools existing practices as evident in the social rhetoric.

Joi Establishes a 'Footing' in the Conversation

Goffman's (1981a) concept of 'footing' is useful in emphasizing the way in which a person has to establish rights to intervene in the unfolding of an episode. By picking up the 'science' theme, Joi not only supports Wyn's positioning move but provides herself with a position as a speaker to be attended to, that is she has a footing.

> Joi   That's what you were talking about the other day was it? We were talking, I couldn't remember who it was. Yeah, see we're doing eco...like eventually, down the track, we'll be looking at ecosystems, and probably endangered environments, and maybe the Antarctica, a little bit, so whether we could... you know, look at the, the melting, ice caps and... how, how does that come up, very... the Antarctica, does it come up?

Joi chose to begin with a rhetorical question, serving momentarily to control the conversation and hold the listener's attention. She then seemed to devalue the importance of the past conversation she had with Wyn by dismissively saying she couldn't remember 'who it was'. Joi then established herself as a leader of two teachers in grade five by her use of the collegiate encompassing form of 'we' and her capacity to manage the project.

Joi, like Wyn, had drawn upon words and phrases that acted as qualifiers to her statements. This had created a sense that she perhaps lacked confidence in the vision she was building. Joi had used 'probably', 'maybe', 'a little bit' and 'whether' in quick succession. Joi was aware that perhaps she was exposing herself in an uncertain and unfamiliar teaching area.

Joi had used 'you know' to imply everyone knew what she meant and had simultaneously included everyone she knew to agree with her. By this strategy the listeners were being positioned to agree with her. But listeners could have chosen to accept or reject this position, though they did not.

Strengthening and Weakening a Challenge

The expression 'you know' can be used to enlist someone to your point of view or to show that you assume the listener(s) understands what you mean. Sometimes this phrase strengthens a person's position in a conversation because it shows that the person is familiar with everyone's experience and understanding of the topic under discussion. But it can also weaken a position if it implies everyone has the same understanding and they don't. It can also be used to avoid having to explain anymore about the topic and so weakens a person's position because it creates doubt that the person does understand and can explain. It can strengthen or weaken a position in a conversation because it can appear to manipulate others to your position or move a conversation on without providing any further details. 'You know' must be considered both in its context and for its subsequent affect on the listener(s).

> CR   Are you looking at, did someone say explorers?
> Wyn   Well, we were…!

In this institutional place and setting Wyn's three words had assumed and implied a shared significance. It seemed Wyn understood the topic Explorers was no longer a component of the integrated unit. It had been changed. Wyn expected at least two people understood the intent and significance of her words. One person was me who Wyn had already been informed that the topic would include Australian Explorers. The other unknown person(s), probably Dot, was the person responsible for changing the topic. Wyn had expressed apparent exasperation and she had used 'we' as though, again, she was speaking as a leader.

These three words were not uttered in isolation but were connected to a series of past social episodes and practices. At this point a story-line is beginning to emerge. 'This is what we did and so this is what we will do'. These practices reveal the local moral order in action and show how it permits the distribution of rights, duties and obligations to persons in an institution.

Wyn had previously discussed with me the option of introducing a new and an additional focus. It seemed Wyn had sought to change the focus in the integrated unit and perhaps to have 'Drought' included in the topic since our phone conversation. But someone had either overridden or ignored Wyn suggestion. Wyn had drawn on threads of other conversations, practices and events and laid them out now as a critical challenge at the centre of this group. Wyn had been establishing her authority or warrant but now it could be seen as limited and her position weakened. She had made clear that this latest change in the focus of teaching had irritated her and she distanced herself from it. Was Wyn irritated at the change in the teaching focus or the processes involved that produced the change? This still remained uncertain.

Strategic Re-positioning

Wyn has now actively sought to position Dot as the senior leader who would acknowledge and take responsibility for this latest change. Dot responds as so positioned and then proceeds to inform Wyn that there may have also been another change. Wyn implied that the focus on Explorers had changed but now Dot qualifies this stating,

> Dot   Yeah, that will be one part of the topic.

It appears either Wyn did not know this or had not understood the intended change. This is a serious loss of face.

Dot and Wyn are both leaders. In the previous run of speech acts the two speakers had different levels of moral force by their standing in this institution, that is reference to role. Wyn had less institutional and moral power than Dot but had used her moral standing here in relation to her public commitment to my project in calling the meeting and has now actively expressed her frustration. Wyn positioned Dot to assume the responsibility that her moral standing and rights gave her. The moment Dot said, 'yeah', she had assumed responsibility for the change. Dot had also taken responsibility for the frustration implied in Wyn's previous utterance. Dot indicated that she understood the intent and meaning of Wyn's three words 'Well we were!' The words had not been explicit in their intended meaning but rather implicit as Wyn seemed to criticise a change. Dot then denied the change and this may have embarrassed Wyn by undermining her personal authority and demonstrated commitment to the research project.

The Re-positioning Rejected

The micro-conflict now expands. Wyn responded; even more disgruntled now,

> W   But with … we've got so much in one term, we've got, we've got Aborigines, we've got this, we've got that, its ridiculous!

Strengthening her position by calling on her allies Wyn spoke as a representative of others, using the collegiate 'we' five times. She could have said 'I' but she had chosen to remind Dot that she held a position as a team leader and expressed her criticisms succinctly, and on behalf of others. But Dot held the more senior and more powerful position as leader of the unit. Wyn now faced the meeting with the faces of several other teachers crystallised behind her. This intimated that it was not Wyn alone who thought 'it's ridiculous', but implied instead a team of teachers. Wyn must have considered there would be strength and or safety in these numbers. A new story-line, that becomes more and more salient as the episode unfolds, now appears. In the discursive history of this setting Wyn had chosen to represent herself and her absent colleagues as very busy, too busy! Let us call this the 'busy-busy' story-line. In accord with this story-line Wyn positions herself as a teacher who was 'too busy' rather as one whose rights in the local moral order had been ignored. Wyn chose the well-known and accessible story lines of the 'busy teacher' who was already trying to fit too much into the 'crowded curriculum'.

Goffman describes this as the least 'self-threatening' (Goffman, 1981b, pp. 325–6). Wyn sought to maintain her place in the local moral order and had chosen to position herself as both frustrated and angry. Dot had again been positioned as responsible for the unpopular changes. Dot could choose to ignore Wyn's latest positioning efforts to force her to take responsibility for this unexpected change that could mean an increase in the amount of material to be taught.

Wyn had actively repositioned herself. Wyn's self-repositioning had placed the emphasis on the collective agency evident in her repeated use of 'we'. This 'we' did not exclude Dot, but rather signaled to all present Wyn's acceptance of Dot's authority and responsibility for this change. Positioning had not only been used to define a person's place in the action but it had been used with skill. Wyn had assumed the moral authority in her initial negotiations with me to use the website in the work on Drought but now it had been made apparent she did not have the institutional authority to deliver this.

By re-positioning herself Wyn tacitly accepted Dot's authority and actively pointed out both the responsibility and accountability that came with the authority. Wyn had spoken and acted as a leader, but not as Dot's equal. She positioned herself as a victim, one whose rights had been violated. Things done 'to her' that were not desirable rather than things being done 'for her' that were beneficial.

Harré explains that in the discursive construction of these story lines as a person narrates their autobiography we can see how they conceive of themselves at that moment in the conversation (Davies and Harré, 1990b). Wyn had portrayed herself as a leader with limited authority, and with a right to be frustrated, angry and too busy. Wyn's attempt to reposition Dot could be confirmed or denied by the next response. Wyn's storyline was about to be accepted or rejected by the listeners (Harré, 1991, p 56).

'Getting Off the Hook'

Dot   But that's what it's meant to be though, it's really just meant to be that overview, that taste, what happens, cause they do have aborigines in 5/6

Dot accepted responsibility and Wyn's positioning of her and acted as though she was obliged to explain. But instead of justifying the addition of Aborigines to the Explorers topic Dot had objectified the curriculum and pedagogy as externally mandated 'it's' ...'just meant to be that overview, that taste.' Did Dot accept Wyn's positioning her back in role? It seems not. Dot needs to reposition herself as lacking the relevant responsibility and accountability. 'They' could have meant the students/teachers and 'have' implied a degree of ownership outside her influence or control.

Dot began to say 'what happens' as though she was about to explain a series of events that she seemed to view as not in her control, but mandated by others. Dot then repeated, 'So, it's just a taste of...'impling a summary of conclusions and finality. Dot was aware Wyn was dissatisfied with the impending busyness of the curriculum. From the lack of surprise this was probably not the first protest about busyness. Wyn had positioned Dot to defend and justify the busy curriculum as if she had a duty so to do. The use of the qualifying word 'just' appeared to weaken Dot's leadership position. Dot had implied there were other forces influencing the decisions about what and how much would be taught.

Wyn Regains Her Position and Loses It

Wyn restated that the topic was cultural, recruiting the outside researcher as a supporter. Thus positioned I had the duty to explain ways the website could support that focus. Wyn then declared

Wyn   That's actually really, really spot on for next years topic.
Dot   It is, yeah.
Wyn   Yeah.
Dot   Perfect, we should actually use it next year as well.
Wyn   Yeah, mmm.
CR   As for explorers you can see how much had to be explored, how much is desert.
Wyn   Yeah, that's true.
Dot   Oh, yeah that's true.

The disagreement and challenges had evaporated from their conversation. Both Wyn and Dot appeared to be in agreement. Dot agreed with Wyn statements. Dot affirmed 'we' could do this and 'we' was a team working together and building a shared vision. Dot and Wyn were a team again. But Dot had repositioned herself as someone who had control over the content of the curriculum. Wyn suggested the topic but it is Dot who approves Wyn's suggestion as 'Perfect' and states that they should use it.

The Junior Member Rejoins the Conversation

Joi enters the conversation and discusses her options and ways that she might use the website for her focus on plants adapting to rainfall and climates. The Fourmilab website provides a global perspective of where plants grow and so could be used as an introduction to Joi's topic. I begin to distribute the material on climate that I brought for Wyn and Dot's unit because now it seemed it could be useful for Joi's topic too. On seeing the weather resource materials Wyn affirmed,

Wyn   Yeah, I think that's what I would prefer...now...

Wyn now positions herself as 'in charge' with the rights and duties that go with that position. In that position she could say 'I would prefer.' Wyn then punctuated her sentence with the addition of the word 'now.' 'Now' had referenced the annoying changes that had not been explored in this meeting but still cast a long shadow over it. This one word had linked Wyn back to the critical comments she had uttered previously. This was a timely reminder of her frustration. She had drawn her previous frustration into this conversational moment. Her double use of 'I' indicated her strong personal commitment and or stance. She had laid down a challenge. She said 'now', but this had been her focus prior to this meeting and she had stated this in her phone conversation with me.

Wyn's suggestion of the weather as a focus meant an additional topic to teach that supported her position as 'science director'. Wyn was trying to reposition Dot as obliged to agree with her. She used the oblique threat of her earlier frustration and anger and importantly, and most effectively, her personal commitment. Although this would add more teaching it would give the term's work a more science-orientated focus and therefore perhaps more power and influence to Wyn. Story-line 2, 'science in the school' overcame story-line 1, 'busy-busy'.

Dot responded immediately and agreed. She did not add any suggestions, directions or decisions. Wyn had suggested what she wanted to do and doubly indexed herself to the position and Dot had capitulated. Dot may have been positioned by Wyn's indirect reference to herself as annoyed. Wyn may have been repositioned by Dot's recent affirming comments. Dot had just used the collegiate 'we' and reformed their team stance. In this pattern of dynamic relations Wyn had negotiated herself into a position of influence. Her place in the local moral order allowed her to access rights (Jones, 1999 p. 51). The positions, and repositioning, were changing moment by moment. Wyn had just secured Dot's agreement to add another focus to the unit and so to do more teaching. It seemed that Wyn's use of 'I' had more impact on Dot than Wyn's collegiate 'we'.

Story-lines in Conflict

Wyn begins to respond to Dot's statement,

> Wyn   I, cause it's just a one off sort of thing, yeah, but, it's still…

Wyn began with 'I' and stopped. Her strength dissipated and dissolved into a verbalised sequence of qualifying words such as, 'just', 'one off', 'sort of', 'thing' and 'but.' Perhaps she now sensed that she had to understate the demand of the research project in order to acknowledge her storyline of busyness. These qualifying words contrasted with the sense of conviction she had expressed seconds earlier. Wyn seemed unsure about what to say. She stopped herself; seemingly uncertain of how to resolve the problem of the willingness she had created.

> Dot   Well, plus the droughts in the paper, we've been talking about it, water restrictions and all that…sort of…you know, it would fit, you know, tie in with something, at least, so…

Dot completed Wyn's unfinished sentence. 'Well' implied the justification would follow. Dot understood Wyn's 'but it's still…' Wyn had suggested a stand-alone science focus on the weather topic. But stand-alone lessons were not a normal practice. Wyn needed the more senior Dot to approve and justify this change in their practices. Dot reintroduced again the familiar grammar of the integrated unit and affirmed that this would 'tie in' and 'fit in'.

The 'it' is the new focus of drought. This focus has been approved and can now be added and seen to be part of their accountability to their integrated unit. Only Dot could affirm this change in emphasis in the teaching. Wyn had waited because she needed Dot to endorse and validate the change in their practices. Wyn had finally secured a change that added another focus to the unit, more teaching and an emphasis on science. These 'busy-busy' teachers needed this approach to be defensible or they couldn't honour their commitment to the research project.

Dot spoke to Wyn as someone who understood and shared the same perception of this need for justification. Dot needed to ensure Joi and I understood. Dot had no need to reposition Wyn; this was Wyn's idea. Dot needed to justify her stance to Joi who was from another area of the school. Dot had justified the change by using the school's institutional practices that valued the integrated unit approach for teaching. These changes could only be accepted against the acceptable social rhetoric of 'we are busy' because Dot could point to how it 'fitted in' and 'tied in' to the existing integrated unit that they were held accountable to have taught. 'Busy-busy' is overcome both by 'this school values science' and 'this school has integrated courses'. The conflict has been resolved by adjusting the relevant salience of the available story-lines.

Confirming the Resolution

Once again Wyn and Dot occupied the same side of the argument. Wyn seemed to relax and she made the following comment,

> Wyn   We watched some clouds this morning.

Wyn used 'we' and meant the members of her grade. Wyn presented herself as a proactive science teacher and the comment was directed to me.

> Dot   Oh did you…!

Dot had spoken with surprise at Wyn's personal revelation.

> W   mmm, going across, the other ones were actually going east and the lower level ones south, we we're watching the clouds (laughs)

Wyn had briefly responded to Dot's question with a paraverbal 'mmm.' But then re-immersed herself in the story and her memory of it and spoke directly to me.

But her laughter had seemed uneasy. It was though she had registered she had surprised Dot and perhaps had been challenged.

> Joi   That's good!

Joi now rejoined the conversation. These two words were spoken slowly. Wyn offered justification.

> Wyn   It was one of my reading groups, actually.

Wyn had responded defensively. She had not seemed to me to behave like a renegade! But no longer was Wyn sharing her reverie of the uniqueness of the cloud behaviour. Instead she had begun to justify her actions by linking it to the higher moral authority that literacy practices offered her. Joi becomes an ally, since she had been coordinator of literacy activities. Wyn had worked with Joi in the literacy area in previous years and together they had set up successful reading group activities. Wyn knew from her lived experiences and habits past (Dewey, 1929/1958) that Joi valued literacy, as did the school's practices. Wyn anticipated her apparently surprising behavior would be validated by reference to literacy practices. The word 'actually' qualified, emphasised and connected Wyn actions to literacy.

> Joi   Oh, Ok, yes

Implicit in Joi's response of 'Oh' was that this had explained the surprising and unusual action. Joi's use of 'Ok' implied she understood and approved. 'Yes' affirmed that this behaviour was acceptable. But Wyn seemed to sense more reasons could still be needed.

> Wyn   My 'acrobats', they had a book on um, weather and climate, and there was a double page on cloud formation.

Wyn was responding to her sense of obligation to the mandated two-hour time block used for literacy teaching. Literacy now dominated Wyn's narrative. Wyn had revealed to Joi and Dot that literacy time had been used elsewhere, in the area of science and in children 'looking at clouds.'

> Joi   Oh, OK

Joi continued to respond and perhaps she sensed it was her duty as a literacy coordinator to cast judgment over Wyn's actions, perhaps having been inadvertently repositioned by Wyn. This had been apparently unusual and unexpected behavior and was in conflict with anticipated cultural practices. Joi still seemed to express surprise and continued to offer Wyn acceptance of the actions.

But Wyn continued to explain and offered even more elucidating comments to redeem her position in the local moral order of duties.

Wyn   So we went out and named them and looked at them, so that was just one group, just one group.

The qualifying word 'just' was used twice to de-emphasise her unusual actions. Wyn pointed to naming of clouds as a learning activity that perhaps could be judged as acceptable. This registered with me as an extraordinary moment. A teacher continued to express her strongly felt need to justify children observing, identifying and naming real moving clouds. Wyn had taken the opportunity to connect children with real clouds and this seemed to be an appropriate and laudable teaching action. But Wyn had to justify, clarify, specify and minimise her actions to her colleagues. Wyn actively linked her actions to the efficacy of the acceptable practices of literacy and the intimacy of small group teaching. I inserted a comment

CR   You can make clouds in the classroom
Wyn   Oh, I have done that.

Wyn seemed to be familiar with the activity, and used the pronoun 'I' as an indicator of her personal experience and familiarity with the activity. 'Oh' had implied surprise but it was followed by a recall of the activity and the experience

Dot   Yeah, I've done that ... really good.
Wyn   I vaguely remember doing that.

Dot had returned to the conversation, taking up the 'looking at clouds' story-line and positioning herself as having a right to comment on it. But after Dot had also recalled and affirmed her knowledge of the 'cloud activity' Wyn murmured that she now had reduced recall of the experience.

A New Positioning Challenge

Wyn's position in the local moral order had been challenged and weakened, by the way the 'looking at clouds' story-line had given Dot's position a boost. But moments later Wyn reasserts herself as one positioned with the duty to check out the viability of incorporating 'fourmilab' in Joi's course plan.

Wyn   Does this suit you Joi or did you want to do something different?

This was a positioning move as Wyn was aware Joi had not yet specified what she would be teaching. Joi was now positioned as one with the duty to respond then and there. Wyn had isolated Joi from the team of Wyn and Dot. Wyn may have thought Joi and Dot had acted together when challenging her about 'clouds' and so had an unexpected alliance. This question to Joi demonstrated that Dot and Wyn shared the same focus. They were an official team in this structure in this institution. Joi worked in a different teaching unit and a part of the school and this question had served to disconnect Joi from Dot and Wyn. Joi responded,

> Joi   Well… yeah I'm fine to fit in, I think we'll… I mean Christine what…
> with this what do you want us to present to you, like obviously you
> need some…data, research to present, how, how…?

Joi spoke in first person 'I' only for the second time in this meeting. But now she did so three times and included her own important reference to 'fitting it in.' Joi deflected the focus from Wyn's question 'will this website suit you?' to my needs as the researcher whom Wyn and Dot had shown they were able to assist. In this social episode, in a moment, Wyn positioned Joi as separate to the team of 'Wyn and Dot'. Wyn challenged both Joi's professional and personal positions. 'Positions can be challenged, negotiated and denied or subverted' (Harré, 1997, p. 181). Joi subverted the challenge to her position and instead sought clarification from me. This shifted the focus to an area equally concerning to all three of them. Joi repositioned herself as a leader and as a member of the team again experiencing the same impending demands.

The issue of alliances remained open. For several minutes the discussion focuses on the details of when and where the research material would be taught. Wyn made a comment that she did not mind missing out on her extra time in the computer lab. Dot and Joi, allies again, ignored Wyn's comment.

> Dot   We might not even know where we're going, mightn't we? (laughs)
> Joi   We might discover where we're going!
> Dot   That's exactly right, and that's what usually happens (laughs)
> Wyn   (seriously) So, as I… trial run, only from my point of, as well, pop in
> for grade four, I, probably, it would be good practice to have a look
> around for next year. It would, yeah, but also we are also looking at
> the water challenge too.

Dot and Joi spoken light heartedly, but Wyn did not laugh. She remained serious and distanced herself from the comments about the 'we' of Joi and Dot. Using 'I' twice she spoke for herself and emphasised it stating 'only from my point of view.' Then she inserted and referenced another 'we', all teachers in the school, and repositioned herself as a leader within the whole school. She concluded using 'we' speaking as a leader of a school wide team, not the 'we' of Dot and herself. Joi and Dot have formed a partnership.

The 'Busy-busy' Story-line Again

The final turn in this episode involved positioning of 'the researcher', the author of this chapter. I asked if any of them are planning to teach using the website on computers in their classrooms, Dot explained

D   Um, Oh I was hoping to, but it is just too difficult to try and fit it in and yeah... I was going to try and fit it in as part of a reading thing...like just make it a whole guided reading session that each group would have their own... something based at their own level, which is something, you, you'd, it would really be a great thing to do, you know, you could use big books at the same time, and um, and you could use a whole heap of things, but, just the time, I, you'd have to plan something like that, very well, so that you could have your groups working on things that they were capable of doing, and the other, and then the kids at the other end, the extension kids, could really go ahead and, I mean research things, you know, using this site, so yeah, that would be a great way to use it, I reckon.

Despite Fourmilab's appeal to Dot she said it will be found to be too difficult to manage and to 'fit in.' Dot detailed the pressure of time and juxtaposed this against her personal desires and ideas. The continual choice of the pronoun 'you' has acted to distance Dot from any real sense of personal responsibility. But it identified and located her sense of duty and obligation and seemed to demonstrate that she had considered, comprehensively, the possibilities. The shift from I to the use of the pronoun 'you' located the moment Dot changed from expressing her personal commitment of 'I was hoping/going' and instead now indicated how these were only possible events that were part of a potential vision. Literacy events were the only place Dot had imagined 'it' fitted into. Dot had seen 'it' as 'a reading thing' and even then as only 'part of a reading thing.'

Dot was unclear about the details of a learning focus that could be obtainable from the website. Three times she had used 'something' as an imprecise reference that implied only vague possibilities. Dot used 'things' five times to reference formless activities. Dot planned for what children could do rather than what they could learn. She created the sense that she had pictured ways to effectively use the website when she stated, 'that would be a great way to use it', but what that was and what could be learnt still remained unclear. The lessons she envisaged referenced the use of familiar teaching strategies from the literacy program approach. The 'this school does science' story-line is tacitly abandoned.

After her initial uses of 'I' the rest of the text was about the world of institutional artifacts and routines. There was no longer a sense of her as a person just management and organisation of materials and what they afforded, along with the accompanying, acceptable, rhetoric of 'no time'. In this way she could present the adverse positioning of 'the researcher' as emanating not from her as a person, but from the institution and other abstractions.

The organisational problems that surrounded the practical use of the website were identified and dealt with, but no attempts were made to resolve the larger surrounding issues. In this meeting if something 'sort of' (Dot) fits in, then that justifies the change. Only Dot had the institutional power to authorise this but first Wyn had to position Dot to give approval, and then wait for the endorsement needed to continue. But the bigger and long lasting issue of the 'over crowded curriculum' remained. It remains as a useful tool to bargain for a personally desired position. The dominant discourses of busyness and the crowded curriculum have become reified reasons that can be used in the subsequent struggles for influence or autonomy. These story-lines are the basis of acceptable reasons allowing us to interpret the speech acts of the interlocutors as a repertoire of excuses that mutually define an institution and which often fail to be challenged.

'Cover stories' emerged and disappeared, as I came to better 'understand the teachers' personal professional knowledge, in the context of teachers professional knowledge landscapes' (Clandinin & Connelly, 1996, p 29). It is significant that the question of what the students might learn from their use of the website were not specifically considered in this meeting by the teachers.

Conclusion

The episode illustrates how the means for the management of practical tasks interact with settling expressive matters, such as relative standing of the two leading characters. Even in such a small scale episode as the one analyzed here it is possible see the influence of background beliefs about who has which rights and duties in the situation as defined by institution, however small it might be. In working towards an agreed way of dealing with the 'left field' request of the researcher for some of the most valued commodity of all, time, one sees the shifting influence of moment by moment negotiations of authority. In this case we witness the subtle ways in which the leading actors recruited their colleague and, of course, the outsider. Role gave way to Position and in turn Position gave way to Role. Dot's recovery of her 'role privileges' required her to engage in positioning moves, rather than just go along with being positioned as lacking the rights that Wyn had claimed. Dot did not say 'Just a minute – I am in charge of these matters!'. Rather she engaged in positioning moves, especially recruiting Joi's support, that left her back where she began.

The website itself appeared in a variety of guises – modulating from 'resource' to 'nuisance'. How its presence was brought into the illocutionary force of various utterances depended on the dominant story-line at that point. Was it 'busy busy' or was it 'this school's commitment to science education'?

In this social exchange many mental phenomena, attitudes or emotions familiar to these primary teachers emanated from the discursive activities themselves (Harré and van Langenhøve, 1991, pp. 394–5). In these discursive utterances about the planning for participation in this research project the conversation was 'overlain with qualifications, open to dispute, charged with value, already enveloped in an obscuring mist or, on the contrary, by the 'light' of alien words that have already been spoken about it' (Bakhtin, 1981, p. 275).

Acknowledgement

Thank you to Dr Rod Fawns, The University of Melbourne, for his considered suggestions for analyzing this social episode.

References

Bakhtin, M. M. (1981). *The dialogic imagination: Four essays* (C. Emerson & M. Holquist, Trans.). Austin: University of Texas Press.

Clandinin, D. J., & Connelly, F. M. (1996). Teachers' professional knowledge landscapes. *Educational Researcher, 25*(3), 24–30.

Davies, B., & Harré, R. (1990a). Positioning theory. *Journal for the Theory of Social Behaviour, 20,* 1–18.

Davies, B., & Harré, R. (1990b). Positioning: The discursive production of selves. *Journal for the Theory of Social Behavior, 20,* 43–63.

Dewey, J. (1929/1958.). *Experience and nature.* New York: Dover.

Goffman, E. (1981a). Replies and responses. In E. Goffman, *Forms of talk* (pp. 5–77). Philadelphia, PA: University of Pennsylvania.

Goffman, E. (1981b). *Forms of talk.* Philadelphia: University of Philadelphia Press.

Harré, R. (1991). *Physical being: A theory for a corporeal psychology.* Oxford: Blackwell.

Harré, R. (1997). Forward to Aristotle; the case for a hybrid ontology. *Journal for the Theory of Social Behavior, 27*(2/3), 173–191.

Harré, R., van Langenhove, L. (1991). Variates of positioning. *Journal for the Theory of Social Behaviour, 21,* 393–409.

Jones, R. (1999). Direct Perception and Symbol Forming in Positioning. *Journal for the Theory of Social Behaviour 29* (1), 37–58.

7
Standing Out and Blending in: Differentiation and Conflict

NAOMI LEE, ERICA LESSEM AND FATHALI M. MOGHADDAM

A major development in psychology since the 1960s has been an increase in theorizing on the self and identity. Social identity theory (Tajfel & Turner, 1979) has fueled the most sustained theoretical and empirical efforts in this area. A central assumption of social identity theory is that individuals universally strive to achieve and maintain a positive and distinct social identity. While the centrality of 'positive' identity seems intuitively obvious and generally agreed upon (after all, positive evaluation seems so universally desired), that distinctiveness is desirable is a more complex and intriguing proposition. Distinctiveness can be rewritten as too different, alien, and bizarre. How do we handle the delicate balancing act between standing out and blending in to achieve a comfortable state, the 'optimal distinction' that Brewer (1991) postulated? In this chapter, we take up this relatively neglected topic and show how positioning theory offers a new understanding of social differentiation, one that can inform the study of intergroup conflicts. We will illustrate our perspective by presenting two empirical studies on the role of differentiation in social conflicts.

Previous Research

Lemaine's (1974) studies remain seminal in the social differentiation literature. He created 'open situations' where research participants could introduce their own criteria of social comparison. For instance, children at a summer camp were organized into two groups and competed to build the best hut. One group was 'disadvantaged.' It had less suitable building material, an unclear division of labor, unstable leadership, and comparatively poor organization. This group planted a garden and argued with the judges and other team for recognition of this 'new criteria' of comparison. Lemaine interpreted these actions as the disadvantaged team's attempt to gain equivalence to a superior opponent, to be different but of equal value. Because one team had a garden and the other did not, an 'apples-to-apples' comparison was contestable, a situation the disadvantaged team tried to exploit.

In a second study by Lemaine (1974), psychology students wrote two job applications, one before and one after they were given information about their competitor. The competitor was either very similar to subjects, had unique work experience, or studied at a highly regarded university (Grande Ecole) in France. Participants who competed against the latter two types of opponents used a compensatory differentiation strategy; they added the criterion of 'clinical' knowledge to their original job application letters and also emphasized their positive personality traits. Both new criteria are difficult to measure and thus prevent easy comparisons between candidates.

In 'open' comparison situations, Lemaine (1974) remarked, those with disadvantaged positions may try to gain equal recognition for new dimensions of comparison by 'bringing into play the appropriate verbal strategies' (Lemaine, 1974, p. 36). Though Lemaine did not analyze these 'verbal strategies' in detail the way discursively-oriented psychologists might today, he did explain the team's behavior by relying on the team's account of its intentions. We can elaborate on Lemaine's remark and note that planting a garden is not in and of itself a compensatory social differentiation strategy. The disadvantaged team's 'verbal strategies' provide the indispensable evidence for this interpretation. Had this team built a garden but then proceeded to deride it as a useless addition, it would have been inappropriate for Lemaine to have labeled their actions as a compensatory differentiation strategy.

Our more general point is that one observable activity can take on many different meanings, and to understand which is in play, we need to consult with the social actors themselves. As Lemaine noted, the garden-planting team members 'engaged in a vigorous discussion with the children in the other group and the judges – the adults – to get them to admit that what they wanted to do was legitimate (ibid., p. 35).' The children displayed what value and function they wanted assigned to their garden. While Lemaine's brief comment above can be criticized – for tending to use discourse as a transparent 'window' into motives and for ignoring the role judges and the opposing team played in upholding or undermining the disadvantaged team's claims – his attention to how participants assign meaning to their activities afforded him insights that escape the purview of the dominant research paradigm.

With few exceptions (see e.g. Branwaithe, Doyle, & Lightbrown, 1979), nearly all experimental studies of differentiation to follow Lemaine's (1974) have precluded research participants from explaining their behavior in their own terms. Instead, they are asked to rate pre-formulated statements or distribute points in ways that are pre-categorized by the researcher as denoting such and such intergroup strategy. Pre-formulated statements are treated as participants' own utterances, though only rarely is inquiry made into participants' interpretation of such statements or their reasons for circling 'mostly agree' versus 'completely agree.' Just as one activity (building a garden) can take on a variety of meanings depending on the context and perspective of the social agent, so too can a pre-formulated statement.

Assigning a single, universal interpretation to an act (or statement) abstracts situated activities from the specific circumstances and normative concerns of the agent. 'Responses' are treated in purely representational terms, e.g. as merely denoting a pre-existing and rigid social identity. In this way, social identity and intergroup strategies are reified into things as concrete and unchanging as the 0 to 5 scales with which participants are required to communicate. Intergroup strategies become divorced from the evaluative process by which actors select one course of action over another. Since research participants usually complete these questionnaires in solitude, there is also a tendency to presume that relations of self to others (or even self to self) are built uni-directionally rather than relationally.

Despite their tendency to reify and atomize social identity as an entity existing in individual minds, the predominant experimental methods do not conduct individual level analysis. Instead, the ratings participants give to various statements are aggregated, though even earlier work questioned the meaningfulness of group means. Branthwaithe et al. (1979) for instance, pointed out that group means obscured the bimodal distribution of intergroup behavior in the minimal group paradigm – discrimination on the one hand and fairness on the other. Such convenient and conventionalized statistical manipulations erroneously transform mean scores into mean strategies for managing intergroup relations. Lost in these calculations are the strategies of actual persons.

The prevailing research paradigm also mislabels phenomena occurring in very specific laboratory conditions as generalizable. This situation results from allowing methods to drive theory. Revealing just such a mistep, Mummendey and Schreiber (1983) demonstrated that ingroup favoritism, theorized as a basic means of positively distinguishing one's group, is an artifact of the experimental procedures used to study this phenomenon and not a universal human tendency. Specifically, they showed that when people are allowed to evaluate ingroup and outgroup on different criteria, they do not exhibit ingroup favoritism. Hence, outgroup derogation might conceivably only arise when ingroup members are forced to compare themselves directly to an outgroup on identical criteria. If given the option – as is frequently the case in life outside the laboratory – people might tend to evaluate in- and outgroup members on different dimensions, allowing members to position their groups as different but equivalent. Mummendey and Schreiber (1983) suggested that a norm of fairness may guide such differentiation: 'As soon as a good result is possible for both groups at the same time ... it appears that the judgements are influenced in the sense of fairness (ibid., p. 395).' At the same time, the authors cautioned that positively judging an out-group's performance on a less valued dimension can be a subtle form of discrimination. This point underscores crucial to any analysis of differentiation is the meaning that participants themselves ascribe to comparison dimensions.

(Mummendey, Simon, Dietze, Grünert, Haeger, Kessler, Lattgen, & Schaferhoff, 1992) identified a second means by which ingroup favoritism vanishes, namely when people are told to distribute punishments rather than rewards. They referred to this phenomenon as the positive-negative asymmetry in social discrimination (Mummendey, Brown, & Smith, 1992). In an attempt to explain this pattern, Blanz, Mummendey, and Otten (1997) studied how onlookers judged the normative appropriateness of various positive and negative outcome allocations. Participants rated equal distribution as the most appropriate allocation of both rewards and punishments. Ingroup favoritism, i.e.disproportionately allocating negative outcomes to an outgroup, was deemed the least appropriate response within the minimal group situation. Blanz, Mummendey, and Otten (1997) suggested that people may apply a norm of fairness when distributing punishments. Their research again demonstrates how tried-and-true research methods may so narrowly limit participants' options that they foreclose meaningful, realistic alternatives and tempt psychologists to overgeneralize. Part of this situation results from adopting an unwaveringly causal account of human actions in the laboratory.

Mummendey and Schreiber (1983) are exceptional in that they explain social differentiation in the laboratory setting in normative terms. Most such research treats the person as a conduit of forces (independent variables) rather than a social actor oriented to cultural norms. This causal framework is built into the way that social differentiation is operationalized as a dependent variable, whose characteristics are fully determined by causally powerful independent variables. Indeed, the empirical research on differentiation has been so prolific that meta-analyses have already been conducted that measure the influence on intergroup differentiation of such proposed causal forces as level of intergroup distinctiveness (see Jetten, Spears, & Postmes, 2004), size and nature of groups (Mullen, Brown, & Smith, 1992; Mullen, Migdal, & Hewstone, 2001), self-esteem (Aberson, Healy, & Romero, 2000), and the legitimacy, stability and permeability of status relations (Bettancourt, Dorr, Charlton, & Hume, 2001).

Intergroup Strategies As Self and Other Positioning in Normative Space

Positioning theory begins from the proposition that in social situations people are active (agentic) and oriented to norms that are socially upheld and historically situated. Hence, we can view intergroup strategies as acts of mutual positioning, i.e. evaluating the characteristics and actions of self and other in moral terms and with respect to relationally negotiated norms. The potentially reified notion of 'social identity' can be re-theorized as the positions people occupy (whether forced or willfully) in the 'local moral orders' (Harré & Moghaddam, 2003) brought about through mutual positioning. Achieving a positive social identity thus involves claiming positions – in a field of alternatives and in concert with relevant others – that are normatively upheld as morally good. This rendering is a direct descendant of Harré's (1984) identity projects.

This perspective challenges those approaches that treat the person as a passive medium through which independent variables exert causal force. The positioning theory approach to intergroup relations treats intergroup activities as intentional activities: people select from among a range of alternative actions that are granted moral valence and have moral implications. To understand how one intergroup strategy is chosen over another, we inquire into social actors' account for their actions with respect to alternative actions and to the people they deem relevant. The current convention of matching manipulated variables to outcome variables involves just the opposite, as this practice grants interpretive hegemony to the researcher's presuppositions about the social actor's apprehension of what was at stake during the episode under study.

The normative approach espoused by positioning theorists also recognizes that the meaning of people's activities are socially and historically contingent. This theoretical perspective is not inimical to laboratory experimentation as a method of inquiry. Even in a laboratory setting, actors position themselves in relation to relevant others (the researcher, other participants) and attend to perceived norms. Again, 'relevant context' is defined by the participant, rather like the 'psychological field' recognized by Gestalt psychologists. Although the respondent may complete his questionnaire in solitude or perform activities in a barren observation room, he does not cease to be a socially-embedded and normatively-oriented actor. In nearly all of the social differentiation literature, though, responses are analyzed strictly with respect to the manipulated independent variables picked out by the researcher. This practice enables precise statistical manipulations, but it either underplays or outright ignores the possibility that participants' activities are contingent on concerns not operationalized as independent variables or not obviously present in the experimental setting, either temporally or spatially. From here, it is a short step to interpreting laboratory-based responses as resulting mechanistically from factors endogenous to the brief episode under study.

In contrast, we see participants as actively negotiating intergroup positions for selves and others in a normative context. 'Intergroup strategies' are 'achieved through social interactions, collective discourse, and collaborative negotiation' (Moghaddam, 2006, p. 166). This process is inherently relational, a quality under-scored by reframing 'social identities' and 'intergroup strategies' in positioning theory terms. Viewing social identities as positions in local moral orders helps illuminate how concerns about social identity are bound up with concerns about intergroup relations. Approaching intergroup strategies as mutual positioning in local moral orders emphasizes how strategies for securing 'positively distinct social identities' are also intergroup strategies.

Because we view people as invariably oriented to norms, we also see mutual positioning as an ongoing activity, a perpetual identity project (Harré, 1984). One's social identity concerns are ever present in social situations, even though empirical studies often create the opposite impression by reporting on 'results' and 'outcomes.' Our view is that there is no stepping outside of the continuous process of social identity construction, to view social identity or intergroup relations as 'completed,' because each attempt at capturing 'social identity' or 'intergroup strategies' is a new act of construction carried out in a new context. Participants' reports (including questionnaire ratings) are enactments rather than mere representations of intergroup strategies; they are still photos of an ongoing and interactive process. While patterns may be discerned, specific instances are not 'instantiations' of transcendental causal laws. Instead, following Davies and Harré's (1990/1999) 'immanentist' perspective, orderliness in human activities is evidence of the normative orders that people actively negotiate.

In reframing intergroup strategies as interactive positioning and social identities as positions, we substitute a parlance that has tended to reify and mechanize activities like social differentiation with one that unequivocally treats humans as agentic, evaluative beings who continually position self and other in relation to relevant others and according to communally negotiated under-standings of right and wrong, good and bad. While patterns may be extracted from people's actual interactive positioning practices, these patterns are always abstractions whose meaning and effects can only be discerned in locally situated activities as experienced from the participant's vantage point.

Differentiation and Social Conflicts

The concept of differentiation has been discussed in relation to economic production, following Adam Smith, the search for vacant spaces, following Charles Darwin, and the division of labor, following Emile Durkheim. In dialogue with these early thinkers, Mulkay and Turner (1971) developed a concept of social differentiation in their analyses of North African Islamic religious leaders, 19th Century French paining, and the scientific community. More recently, Moghaddam (1997) developed a critique of specialization in academia, the economy, and civic culture. Below, we report on two empirical studies that address a relatively neglected topic: differentiation as a means of managing conflict.

Study 1 – Job Applicants

In this study we used traditional experimental methods minimally supple-mented with a free response task that allowed participants to communicate their understanding of the experimental manipulation. Following Lemaine (1974), we looked at how men (n = 34) and women (n = 52), Georgetown students, competed with fictitious 'higher' and 'lower' status opponents for a prestigious summer internship. Recruits were placed in one of four conditions. They either competed individually or were paired with either a local community college student or a Columbia University student. Profiles of the Columbia University or community college students' GPA and work experience were provided to participants. Students were asked to rate on a scale of 1 to 9 (1 = little / no importance, 9 = highest importance) how much consideration the prospective employer should give to each of three dimensions: academic institution, work experience, and grade point average. Students also rated the degree to which they were better than and different from their competitor (or partner) along these three dimensions on a scale of 1 to 9 (1 = not at all, 9 = completely). For each dimension, participants were asked to explain (in essay form) their ratings.

We will limit our discussion here to how Georgetown students rated themselves in comparison to a Columbia University student competitor or partner on the dimension of 'institution attended,' as this situation was thought to best exemplify the canonical one in social differentiation research, whereby a participant orients to a presumably higher status target. The Columbia student was described as having a GPA of 3.9 (of 4.0) and two previous internships at high profile organizations similar to the one for which they were applying. We were curious to see how Georgetown students would mutually position themselves in relation to this high status reference person. Based on similar work by Lemaine (1974) and Branwaithe et al. (1979), we predicted that Georgetown students would emphasize unique aspects of themselves and position these as assets. Previous literature provided less guidance on how Georgetown students would behave when paired with a high status partner to win a competition. Two possibilities seemed likely: 1) Georgetown students would distinguish themselves from their high status partner in order to complement the partner, or 2) Georgetown students would rate themselves as highly similar to the partner, so as to 'blend in' with the high status partner.

On average, Georgetown students gave their institutions similarly high importance ratings in both competitive and cooperative conditions (see Table 7.1). As predicted, Georgetown students who were told to compete with a Columbia student rated their own institution as more 'different from' than 'better than' Columbia University ($t[19] = -1.85$, p<.10). Only four of the twenty participants (20%) in this condition gave their institution a higher 'better' than 'different from' rating. Georgetown students' accentuation of difference rather than superiority was even stronger when they partnered with the high status Columbia student ($t[21] = -2.86$, p<.01), although average difference ratings were higher in the competitive versus the cooperative condition ($t [40] = 1.75$, p<.10). In the

TABLE 7.1. Mean scores (and standard deviations) of ratings given to academic institution as a job application criteria when partnered or competing with Columbia University student.

	The level of importance I want a prospective employer to give this dimension is	I am **better** than my partner / opponent on this dimension	I am **different** from my partner / opponent on this dimension	t
Competing (n=20)	6.7(.80)	4.95(2.06)	6.15(2.37)	-1.85*(df = 19)
Partnering(n=22)	6.73(1.03)	3.45(2.06)	4.91(2.22)	2.86**(df = 21)

*p<0.10, **p<.05

cooperative condition, only four of 22 (18%) participants assigned Georgetown a 'better' rating that exceeded its 'difference' rating. Georgetown students who formed cooperative pairs with the Columbia student also rated themselves on average as more equal to this high status reference person than did Georgetown students who competed with the Columbia student (t[42] = 2.34, p<.05). In future research, it would be interesting to investigate the reasoning of those participants who deviated from the mean pattern. For now, we will focus on those who conformed to the central tendencies of each condition.

Many studies on intergroup relations report statistical tables with mean scores as we have in Table 7.1 The conventional next step is to discuss how comparison with a competitor results in greater social differentiation (as measured by the difference ratings) than does comparison with a partner. Notice in this assertion the presumed cause-effect relationship between the manipulated independent variable and the participants' ratings: the social agent disappears from view. Furthermore, the 'finding' is discursively constructed as decontextualized and generalizable. To better understand how recruits actively managed the social comparison situations into which they were placed, we now turn to the participants' own explanations for their ratings.

Case 1: Distinguishing Oneself from a High Status Competitor

The Georgetown student below assigned high importance (7 of 9) to this aspect of her profile, although she did not rate Georgetown as far superior to Columbia (5 of 9). She did, though, rate her institution as more different from (6 of 9) than superior to her competitor's. Her ratings are in line with the aggregated results reported in Table 7.1. Given the pattern of her ratings, one might guess that she constructed 'difference' as a positive attribute. She did assign high importance to her institution even though she did not rate herself as far superior to the competitor in this regard. Her written justification displays her account of the experimental situation:

Student A – I would like this trait to be given somewhat of a high importance because I think that people should be rewarded for hard-work & accomplishments. I do not think, however, that too much emphasis should be based on the prestige of the university attended b/c personal characteristics should also be taken into account.

This student briefly relates her avowed principles for how hiring decision should be made. First, she deems 'university prestige' as indicating 'hard-work & accomplishments.' This reading is evidenced by her contrastive use of 'however' in her second sentence. On the one hand, 'people should be rewarded for hard-work & accomplishments,' but on the other hand, 'prestige of university attended' (i.e. a symbol of hard-work & accomplishments) should not overshadow 'personality characteristics.' Her use of depersonalizing language – 'people' should be rewarded rather than 'I should be rewarded,' and disembodied 'personal characteristics' rather than 'my personal characteristics' – helps her caste her point of view as a general principle or rule rather than her own personal opinion.

We can observe how she uses these principles to her competitive advantage. While she rates herself as not much better than her competitor along the dimension of university prestige, she can be heard mutually positioning herself as having positive personal characteristics that can overrule any disadvantage along the 'university prestige' dimension. It is notable that Student A spontaneously draws attention to a dimension of evaluation that is difficult to measure, just as did Lemaine's (1974) job applicants.

Students B also rated her institution as more 'different' (8 of 9) than 'better' (6 of 9) than her competitor's, and she assigned very high importance (8 of 9) to this criterion. Her justification was as follows:

Student B – Although admission to Columbia is lower than to Georgetown, both are highly respected universities. Depending on the career field of the internship, Georgetown might have prepared me better than Columbia prepared the other candidate.

She can be heard refining the definition of a 'better' academic institution. While she submits that Columbia is more competitive, she subsumes both universities under a flattering, superordinate category of 'highly respected' schools. She bolsters the value of Georgetown too by suggesting that the fit of educational preparation to career field matters more than the pedigree of the educational institution. Thus, student B can thus be heard introducing a new, complex criterion of comparison that affords her potential advantages over her high status competitor. Hence, she mutually positions herself as positively distinct from her competitor.

Georgetown students who competed with Columbia students frequently positioned themselves as positively distinct from their opponent. While Table 7.1 shows that students reported being more 'different from' as compared to 'better than' their competitor, these ratings do not constitute unequivocal proof that Georgetown students positively distinguished themselves from competitors. Instead, participants own written justifications provide some a modicum of evidence for this interpretation.

Similar to Lemaine's (1974) job applicants, Georgetown students introduced and argued for the value of new comparison criteria that are difficult to measure. Georgetown students were also explicitly invited to supplement the three dimensions chosen by us (institution, GPA, and job experience) with up to three evaluative criteria of their own choosing, and to which they also assigned 'importance' ratings. Personality (n = 12, Mean = 8.0, STD = .4), extracurricular participation (n = 10, Mean = 6.5, STD = 1.1), and career goals (n = 6, Mean = 8.3, STD = .80) were the most popularly cited additional criteria. The high importance ratings assigned to these self-selected criteria suggest that students used these new dimensions to enhance their competitiveness, although we do not pretend to have access to the students' reasoning at the time.

The most convincing evidence for interpreting participants' judgment of their own 'difference' from their competitor as positive distinction is contained in their essay-form justifications. There, students argued for the relative importance of alternative as compared to original criteria. As in the case of Lemaine's

(1974) summer campers who employed 'verbal strategies' to gain recognition for their hut garden, our participants too deployed arguments that mutually positioned themselves as positively distinct from their high pedigree competitor. This strategy allowed them to avoid head-to-head competition along identical criteria.

Next, we will examine the pattern of responses from those Georgetown students who were partnered with a Columbia student to compete as a cooperative pair. We will then consider a field study and discuss the relevance of both studies to the general issue of social conflicts.

Case 2: Blending in with a High Status Partner

In this condition, Georgetown students were partnered with the Columbia student who had a GPA of 3.9 and two previous, relevant internships at high profile organizations. As in Case 1, after rating their academic institution along the three dimensions (importance, better, different), students were asked to justify the importance they gave to this aspect of their background. Students overwhelmingly emphasized how similar Georgetown and Columbia are. Comments included:

Student C (importance = 8, better = 5, different = 3) – University attended is important because there is a big difference between the education received at a very prestigious 4-year university versus, for example, a state school or junior college.

Student D (importance = 8, better = 2, different = 1) – I would [like an employer to give high importance to institution attended] because Georgetown and Columbia are both prestigious universities.

Student E (importance = 8, better = 5, different = 5) – We would have an advantage since Columbia's a good school and Georgetown is a good school.

These students position their academic institution as equivalent to their partner's. They can be heard attempting to 'blend in' with their high status partner by creating a superordinate category ('prestigious university', 'good schools') that includes them both and puts them on equal footing. Ten of the eighteen students who wrote essay responses in this condition spontaneously positioned the two universities as belonging to one high status category; the other eight did not draw comparisons. Three of the ten who displayed the pattern could also be heard attending to the charge that Georgetown is not as prestigious as Columbia, a situation that threatened to make the Georgetown student a detriment to the pair's competitiveness.

Student J – Columbia U. is a very high prestige school, but Georgetown is as well. I would like to see it [academic institution attended] considered, but not of total importance. (importance = 5 better = 3 different = 5)

Student K – I am surely different in that I have attended a different university, but in many cases if the student is serious about their education it doesn't make much of a difference. However, Georgetown may have provided me with some expanded opportunities. (importance = 6, better = 7, different = 5)

Student L – We both attend prestigious universities and therefore deserve almost equal credit. (importance = 7, better = 1, different = 1)

Student J argues that Columbia University is not unique in having 'high prestige.' Her contrastive but (Schiffrin, 1987), 'but Georgetown is as well,' functions to rebut any assertion that Columbia is more prestigious than Georgetown. This student rates Georgetown as more distinct from (5 of 9) than superior to (3 of 9) Columbia, but her written justification downplays the universities' differences and allots them equal status. This case illustrates our earlier point about how mutual positioning is ongoing: providing ratings constitutes one positioning act and essay responses a subsequent one. For this reason, the ratings and written justifications must be seen as sequential acts of positioning. The essay is not a simple 'representation' of the ratings.

Student K positions herself as 'different,' however she immediately diminishes the significance of this difference in her contrastive 'but' clause. This discourse marker signals to us that the unit to follow ('...but in many cases if the student is serious about their education it doesn't make much of a difference') undermines any attempt to equate difference with inferiority. Student K argues that earnest study may mitigate her being from a 'different' (i.e. lower status) university. She constructs this contentious claim in depersonalized language ('if the student is serious...') but then applies this 'rule' to her specific case in arguing that Georgetown may have afforded her 'expanded opportunities.' Student L places Georgetown and Columbia into one category ('prestigious universities'), and she assigns them equal status (1 of 9) and complete similarity (1 of 9). However, she only demands 'almost equal credit,' displaying her reluctance to mutually position her university as equal in quality and kind to Columbia.

In sum, Georgetown students who partnered with Columbia students overwhelmingly emphasized their institutions' equivalence by assigning them to a superordinate category. As partners, some Georgetown students also countered the unspoken charge that their school was less esteemed than Columbia. In contrast, Georgetown students who competed with Columbia students emphasized their differences. They constructed this difference as either 1) compensating for disadvantaged positions along other dimensions (e.g. university's admissions rate or prestige) or 2) as new evaluative criteria that made direct comparisons more difficult and claims of equivalency more convincing.

'Difference' thus carried dual semantic potential, as either positive or negative distinctiveness. Students' could explain their ratings in an essay, which constituted a second act of positioning. Without these essays, the dual semantic potential of difference would have been unsubstantiated and likely overlooked. Indeed, the paucity of such qualitative data in the social differentiation literature may help explain why, in theorizing positive distinctiveness as a primary motivational force, to our knowledge no traditional empirical studies have examined how people use similarity claims to ward off negative distinctiveness. While our results show a pattern of positive differentiation in competitive situations and similarity claims in cooperative situations, calling out these patterns inevitably abstracts social activities from their local meaning and functions. By performing a ground-up analysis using participants' own reports of their reasoning, we could identify patterns in function as well as form.

Study 2 – 'Poor' Women Doing Beauty

The first study we reported involved university undergraduates in a constrained experimental setting, where they provided limited explanations for their differentiation strategies. We now turn to a very different cultural context, Caracas,Venezuela, and an open-ended interview method designed to elicit less constrained narratives reflecting differentiation. A total of 64 women were interviewed in Spanish by the first author. Our analysis here is based on ten interviews selected because the participants identified themselves as 'low class,' 'poor,' from a 'humble family,' or a 'slum' resident. Most interviews took place at a community clinic, where interviewees were patients and employees referred to us by a female gynecologist. One participant was approached at an open market. Interviews were transcribed by the first two authors, resulting in a 13,300-word document in Spanish. Analyses were conducted on the original Spanish transcripts, though our English translations are provided here.

The interview situation permitted participants to mutually position themselves and others in an on-going conversation with the first author. The general topic of conversation was a quotidian practice, female beauty. Venezuela has won more international beauty contests than any other country in the past 50 years, and its beauty industry flourishes. Venezuelans spend one-fifth of their income on beauty products (Sosa, 2001), and two-thirds of Venezuelan women report thinking about their looks 'all the time,' compared to under one-third of U.S. women (Society, 2001). However, as in other industrialized societies, female beauty in Venezuela is tightly linked to financial resources. The extracts below are from interviews with women who could not afford the costly beauty rituals of wealthier women. While it is tempting to presume from market research that our interviewees value beauty, participants' own talk provides the only evidence for what beauty signifies to them. In the following extracts we show how they positioned themselves using social categories in ongoing conversation about female beauty.

Case 1: Gaining Positive Distinction – Standing Out

After talking casually about Rosalinda's beauty rituals and her opinions about cosmetic surgery, the interviewer asks her how she justifies her expenses on beauty products.

Excerpt 1 [42.8:50]

1 Rosalinda: Well, I think he who has money, and he who can spend it however
2   he wants, can spend it however he wants. In that respect, (I) don::'t,

3	(continuing) to use money to be more attractive which is, or to be
4	um, beautiful. If it has to be done, hey. If there is (money), that, that is
5	each person's decision. If you have it, you spend it the way you want.
6	Because those who don't have (it) restrain themselves in many ways,
7	right?

8 Naomi: Yes.
9 Rosalinda: The same in my, in, in my particular case I don:::'t, don:'t, uh…
10   don::'t . Since I don't have money to spend on that I don't, I just
11   don't spend it. I spend it on things that are useful for me and for my
12   children.

Rosalinda evades the interviewer's question. Instead of justifying her consumption of beauty products, she constructs a depersonalized narrative with two central characters: the 'haves' ('he who has money' in line 1) and the 'have-nots' ('those who don't' in line 6). Whereas the 'haves' are free to consume as they wish, the 'have-nots' 'restrain themselves.' In line 9 Rosalinda locates herself within this narrative as a 'have-not': she does not 'have money to spend on that,' where 'that' indexes beauty products. Instead of conforming or attempting to conform to wealthy women's beauty rituals, Rosalinda distinguishes herself as spending her money on 'things that are useful' for her and her children. She insinuates that beauty products are useless, and she contrasts these with her own rational and responsible purchases.

Thus, Rosalinda mutually positions herself before the interviewer and in relation to the characters she voices as a virtuous and devoted mother. While she may deviate from the beauty standards established by the 'haves,' she deflects this negative distinction by introducing a new criterion of social comparison – 'useful' consumption – that affords her positive distinctiveness vis-à-vis the 'haves.' Rosalinda's positioning move resembles that observed in Georgetown students who competed with higher status Columbia students and argued for the importance of personal characteristics, extracurricular activities, etc. Both introduce new criteria of comparison by which they may gain positive distinctiveness and compensate for shortcomings along other dimensions.

Rosalinda's strategy involves making a virtue of a necessity. Instead of, for example, complaining about the wealth inequalities that prevent her from conforming to the wealthy women's beauty practices, Rosalinda constructs her fiscal restraint as responsible mothering. She unwittingly neutralizes the injustice of economic inequalities.

Case 2: Averting Negative Distinction – Blending in

Excerpt 2 [43.5:45]

1 Naomi: And how often more or less do you go to the salon?
2 Marta: No ((I)) always. No, no, I hardly ever go to salons.

3   But I do try to have my hair a little like that.
4   I color it, I (blow-dry) it, I ( ).
5 Naomi: You do that?
6 Marta: Yes, I make myself a ( ) and I end up like this.
7 Naomi: Wow, fantastic.
8 Marta: So, I got to the salon on special occasions.
9   But the rest of the time I try to fix myself up a little.

Marta reports 'hardly ever' going to salons, an admission that introduces a threat to her positive face (Brown & Levinson, 1987): Marta fails to value female beauty and willfully neglects her personal appearances. She counters this threat with a 'contrastive but' clause (Schiffrin, 1987): 'But I do try to have my hair a little like that (line 3),' where 'like that' indexes the 'look' acquired at salons. Her utterance functions as a defense to convince the interviewer that Marta at least tries to conform to culturally normative expectations of beauty. By blow-drying and coloring her own hair, Marta can look 'like this,' where 'this' is discrepant from 'that' salon look. In line 8 Marta again admits her infrequent use of salon services. Once again she follows a face threatening admission with a contrastive but clause (Schiffrin, 1987): 'But the rest of the time I try to fix myself up a little (line 9).'

Thus, we can identify parallel structures in this excerpt. Marta's admission of counter-normative beauty practices (not attending salons) raises negative moral implications. She deflects these by positioning herself as striving to conform to beauty norms through at-home care. Her positioning strategy resembles that of Georgetown students who were paired with Columbia students and emphasized their similarity to their high status partner. Both Marta and the Georgetown students used similarity claims to combat negative distinctiveness.

Case 3: Standing Out and Blending in

The remaining excerpts from a conversation with Elena show how interactive positioning unfolds over a complex series of conversational turns. Elena was interviewed at a hot, congested street corner in the informal market, where she sells women's lingerie. The first interview question follows.

Excerpt 3 – Elena [38.0:40] Standing out

1 Naomi: Why do the Venezuelans win so many international beauty prizes,
2   for what reason do you believe?
3 Elena: But, well, apart from that beauty, to only be beautiful is not, is
4   not important. It's important to be a person who is lucky, and simple,
5   uh –intelligent, uh, and that one is interested in one's country's affairs.
6   Beauty isn't everything because, you see, what's it worth you to be
7   beautiful on the outside and on the inside you're a monster? And then
8   you don't think about anything and nothing is important to you.

Elena evades the interview question and, like Rosalinda in Excerpt 1, asserts the value of characteristics unrelated to beauty (i.e. 'luck,' 'simplicity,' 'intelligence,' and interest in one's country). External beauty and inner virtue are dichotomized, such that beauty is worth little if 'on the inside' one is thoughtless and indifferent, in short a 'monster.' Elena suggests a moral order in which women who lack beauty can positively distinguish themselves by possessing 'inner' virtues that compensate for or outweigh the value of beauty 'on the outside.' Such virtues provide an alternative basis for social comparison and moral evaluation, much as did 'responsible mothering' in Rosalinda's case or 'personality characteristics' for Georgetown students competing with Columbia students. In Excerpt 4, Elena is asked to personally confront normative beauty expectations.

Excerpt 4 – Elena [38.3:00] Blending in

1 Naomi: As a Venezuelan woman, do you feel pressured to look good?
2 Elena: Yes, I like looking good, uh. I have to say, I'm turning thirty-eight
3   and sometimes I look at my face in the mirror and see that
4   yes I have many little wrinkles,
5   but one goes out on the street to work and what happens (to
6   one) is that one gets full of the soot of car exhaust.
7   But one always has one day on which to
8   put:: on one's make-up, go about pretty, well-groomed.

Elena assents that as a Venezuelan woman, she likes to look good. Instead of claiming to embody her ideal, though, she complains about her 'many little wrinkles.' She indirectly explains her predicament by talking about the proto-typical female street vendor (referred to obliquely as 'one') who 'gets full of the soot of car exhaust.' Elena attends to the implication that street workers are always full of soot in her second 'but' clause (lines 7–9); 'but one always has one day' (per week) to look beautiful. This clause can be heard to shield Elena from the insulting inference that she never looks any better than at present. Furthermore, by using the inclusive pronoun 'one', she positions all street vendors as complying with Venezuelan norms of beauty at least one day per week. Elena could have chosen a compensatory strategy and, for instance, argued that soot is the price responsible mothers must pay to support their children. Instead, Elena positions street vendors as 'blending in' with normative beauty culture when they can. Her strategy resembles Marta's, who admitted her infrequent salon visits but mutually positioned herself vis-à-vis wealthier women as also wanting to achieve a 'salon look.'

Notably, Elena's narrative is not a call to protest poor working conditions or social pressures to look attractive. Her use of the simple present tense ('one goes out on the street,' 'one gets full of the soot, 'one always has one day,' etc.) indicates repeated or usual activities and lends her narrative a timeless and naturalized quality (Thompson, 1990), as if the routines of working in grimy conditions and spending one's only day off 'going about pretty' have always been and will always be part of the natural order of things. While this narrative does not challenge economic inequalities, it does help female street vendors preserve a positive moral position: far from being social deviants, street vendors use the scant time and resources they have to look 'well-groomed,' i.e. to display that as Venezuelan women, they too 'like looking good.' Excerpt 5 continues from Excerpt 4 and exemplifies a more ambiguous series of positioning moves.

Excerpt 5 – Elena [38.3:30]

```
 9 Naomi: Do you go to the salon, too?
10 Elena: Yes, I go to the salon once in a while.
11 Naomi: Frequently? Like, how many times a month, more or less?
12 Elena: Well, I go at least weekly to (blow)-dry my hair.
13 Naomi: Weekly? Wow.
14 Elena: Yes. I fix my hair, I (blow)-dry my hair.
15         But to color it, not, not, very often. I already have roots ( ).
16         At the very least
17         the Venezuelan woman likes to go about very well-groomed.
18         With any little detail but always well-groomed.
```

Elena positions herself ambiguously in relation to the prototypical street vendor she voiced in prior talk (in Excerpt 4). Initially, she responds that she goes to the salon 'once in a while.' After the interviewer's request for specification (Garvey, 1979), though, Elena aggrandizes this claim to 'at least weekly,' a frequency surpassing that of the prototypical street vendor voiced in Excerpt 4.

However, Elena signals that her beauty rituals are inadequate when she complains of her conspicuous 'roots' (line 15). As in Excerpt 4, she follows her personal complaint with a depersonalized narrative. The central character ('the Venezuelan woman') indexes the prototype of all Venezuelan women, not only street vendors. 'At the very least,' the Venezuelan woman 'likes to go about very well-groomed (line 16–17).' Elena can be heard constructing 'being well-groomed' as a normative preference – and not necessarily the achievement of Venezuelan women. This interpretation grants Elena moral cover: her roots may show, but she can still claim to like being well-groomed. However, this utterance is not univocal. Being well-groomed may also be heard as a Venezuelan woman's duty and a minimum social expectation, one that Elena fails to meet.

Elena's final utterance in Excerpt 5 is also rich in implications. 'With any little detail but always well-groomed' (line 17) may index the minimum virtue all Venezuelan women naturally possess (at the very least they are always well-groomed) or the minimum standard by which all are judged as deviant or compliant (they might have other accessories, but they should always be well-groomed). Elena's previously expressed complaints ('many little wrinkles' and exposed 'roots') threaten to locate her as a deviant woman before the interviewer, herself, and the ideal Venezuelan woman whom she voices. She can be heard mitigating this threat by characterizing the Venezuelan woman as requiring very little to qualify as 'very well-groomed': she needs just 'any little detail,' indexing perhaps Elena's own nominal salon expense (blow-drying). Elena is not fully redeemed in this interpretation, though, because the prototypical Venezuelan woman is 'always well-groomed.' This achievement lies beyond the reach of the street vendor voiced in Excerpt 4, who has only one day to be 'well-groomed.' Whether Elena would argue for a position among the perennially well-groomed is conveniently left ambiguous.

General Discussion

Elena's interview illustrates our central reasons for suggesting a positioning theory approach to social differentiation, whereby social differentiation is understood as a form of interactive positioning, and achieving a positively distinct social identity is reframed as achieving a positive position in locally (i.e. in the conversation) negotiated moral orders. First, the extract demonstrates how people achieve their moral positions through mutual positioning, even in a research interview. Both Elena and the interviewer index characters from the social world, and together contribute to constructing normative beauty practices. Rosalinda too voiced characters and staged a dialogue among the 'haves,' 'have-nots,' interviewer and herself.

Second, Elena's interview demonstrates how positions often can not be univocally characterized as 'positive' or 'negative', 'distinct' or 'similar.' Elena could be heard both deviating from and conforming to normative beauty practices. Furthermore, normative expectations are left ambiguous. 'Any little detail but always well-groomed' can be taken either to indicate that Elena's beauty practices meet or fall short of social expectations. This ambiguity and Elena's indirectness (in using the third-person narratives) serve meaningful relational functions: she can make claims and assume positions without having to explicitly defend them and risk engaging in a mutually face-threatening debate with her interviewer (or with the narrative characters she creates). This socially useful ambiguity is obliterated in traditional social differentiation research, where participants are forced to take a fixed and univocal position, for instance by rating themselves as enduringly 'better' or 'different' from members of another group. Study 1 shows how even in a brief free response task participants mutually position themselves in more nuanced ways than traditional questionnaires lead one to believe.

A pattern present in both studies is that people displayed their concern to be positively distinct and positively similar, where 'positive' is normatively constructed in the local context. Stated another way, 'distinctiveness' carries dual semantic valence and is contextually contingent. Study 1 shows how, when placed in direct competition with a high status opponent, people construct themselves as positively distinct, whereas when paired with a high status partner, people position themselves as similarly 'high status.' In Study 2, Elena's excerpts serve as an exemplar of the complex maneuvers all interviewees employed in negotiating positive moral positions in conversations, where conformity and deviance are locally and mutually defined and redefined, often ambiguously. Interviewees confronted with face-threatening talk about beauty at times introduce alternative dimensions on which to measure human worth, such as responsible mothering, intelligence, patriotism, humility, and generosity. Such criteria serve as compensation for shortcomings along other dimensions, just as in Lemaine (1974) and in the Georgetown competitors of Study 1.

What stands out most in applying positioning theory to actual conversations is that distinctiveness never completely ossifies as 'positive' or 'negative.' As long as the possibility exists for another turn in the conversation, for another act of mutual positioning, there is an open-endedness to intergroup relations and identity projects. It is this open-endedness that permits both mutual repositioning over time and entrenchment into set storylines. This potential can be harnessed by actors, including practitioners of conflict resolution, to avert conflicts or deepen them. As analysts of social conflicts, we can examine the moves of various actors and come to some reasonable interpretations of events. We can attach narratives that appear to fit. However, we should take care not to over-determine what may be intrinsically ambiguous acts, for we may be surprised by what the next positioning move brings.

Appendix: Transcription Notations

always	Underlining indicates stress or emphasis in the speech
don::'t	Colons indicate drawn-out speech
( )	Inaudible
(blow-dry)	Partially audible
((I))	Double parentheses indicate words not present in Spanish transcription
It's mostly from the –?	Hyphen indicates cut off word or phrase
But I do try	Bold indicates element(s) discussed in the analysis

References

Aberson, C. L., Healy, M., & Romero, V. (2000). Ingroup bias and self-esteem: A meta-analysis. *Personality and Social Psychology Review*, *4*, 157–173.

Bettancourt, B. A., Dorr, N., Charlton, K., & Hume, D. L. (2001). Status differences and in-group bias: A meta-analytic examination of the effects of status stability, status legitimacy, and group permeability. *Psychological Bulletin*, *127*, 520–542.

Blanz, M., Mummendey, A., & Otten, S. (1997). Normative evaluations and frequency expectations regarding positive versus negative outcome allocations between groups. *European Journal of Social Psychology*, *27*, 165–176.

Branwaithe, A., Doyle, S., & Lightbrown, N. (1979). The balance between fairness and discrimination. *European Journal of Social Psychology*, *9*, 149–163.

Brewer, M. B. (1991). The social self: On being the same and different at the same time. *Personality and Social Psychology Bulletin*, *17*, 475–482.

Brown, P., & Levinson, S. C. (1987). *Politeness: Some universals in language usage*. Cambridge, UK: Cambridge University Press.

Davies, B., & Harré, R. (1990). Positioning: The discursive production of selves. *Journal for the Theory of Social Behavior, 20,* 43–63.

Davies, B., & Harré, R. (1999). Positioning and personhood. In R. Harré & L. van Langenhove (Eds.) (1999), *Positioning theory: Moral contexts of intentional action* (pp. 32–52). Oxford, UK: Blackwell Publishers. [Original version published 1990, Journal for the Theory of Social Behavior, *20,* 43–63].

Garvey, C. (1979). Contingent queries and their relations in discourse. In E. Ochs & B. Schieffelin, *Developmental pragmatics* (pp. 363–372). New York, NY: Academic Press.

Greimas, Algirdas Julien. (1987). On meaning: selected writings in semiotic theory. translation by Paul J. Perron and Frank H. Collins. London, UK: Pinter.

Harre, R. (1984). Personal being: A theory for individual psychology. Cambridge, MA: Harvard University Press.

Harré, R., & Moghaddam, F. (2003). Introduction: The self and others in traditional psychology and in positioning theory. In R. Harré & F. Moghaddam (Eds.), *The self and others* (pp. 1–11). Westport, CT: Praeger.

Jetten, J., Postmes, T., & Spears, R. (2004). Intergroup distinctiveness and differentiation: A meta-analytic integration. *Journal of Personality and Social Psychology, 86,* 862–879.

Lemaine, G. (1974). Social differentiation and social originality. *European Journal of Social Psychology, 4,* 17–52.

Moghaddam, F. M. (1997). *The specialized society: The plight of the individual in an age of individualism.* Westport, CT: Praeger Publications.

Moghaddam, F. M. (2006). Interobjectivity: The collective roots of individual consciousness and social identity. In T. Postmes & J. Jetten (Eds.), *Individuality and the group: Advances in social identity* (pp.155–174). London, UK: Sage.

Mulkay, M. J., & Turner, B. S. (1971). Overproduction of personnel and innovation in three social settings. *Sociology, 5,* 47–61.

Mullen, B., Brown, R., & Smith, C., (1992). Ingroup bias as a function of slience, relevance, and status: An integration. *European Journal of Social Psychology, 22,* 103–122.

Mullen, B., Migdal, M. J., & Hewstone, M. (2001). Crossed categorization versus simple categorization and intergroup evaluations. A meta-analysis. *European Journal of Social Psychology, 31,* 721–736.

Mummendey, A., & Schreiber, H. J. (1983). Better or just different? Positive social identity by discrimination against, or by differentiation from outgroups. *European Journal of Social Psychology, 13,* 389–397.

Mummendey, A., Simon, B., Dietze, C., Grünert, M., Haeger, G., Kessler, S., Lattgen, S., & Schäferhoff, S. (1992). Categorization is not enough: Intergroup discrimination in negative outcome allocation. *Journal of Experimental Social Psychology, 28,* 125–584.

Mummendey, B., Brown, R., & Smith, C. (1992). Ingroup bias as a function of salience, relevance, and status: An integration. *European Journal of Social Psychology, 22,* 103–122.

Schiffrin, D. (1987). *Discourse markers.* Cambridge, UK: Cambridge University Press.

Society (2001). "Vanity in Venezuela." January/February, *38* 2–4.

Sosa, R. (2001). "Under the sun, under the knife" The UNESCO Courier, July/August 2001.

Tajfel, H., & Turner, J. C. (1979). An integrative theory of intergroup conflict. In W. G. Austin & S. Worchel (Eds.), *The social psychology of intergroup relations* (pp. 33–47). Monterey, CA: Brooks/Cole.

Thompson, J. B. (1990). *Ideology and modern culture.* Cambridge, UK: Polity.

8
The Dispute Over the Fate of Terri Schiavo: A Study of Positions and Social Episodes in the Formation of Identity

Karen Grattan

For several weeks in early 2006 Americans were transfixed at the emotional family feuding, legal acrobatics and public spectacle that surrounded the fate of Terri Schiavo. News of Terri Schiavo and her would-be rescuers from both sides filled our lives in every medium; print, radio and television. As we listened and watched, we saw clearly the two distinct and seemingly polar opposite stances that existed around the right thing to do for one individual: Two readings of the same circumstance. Should Terri's feeding tube be removed in respect of her rights of privacy and her right to die? Or, should the feeding tube remain, acknowledging Terri's personhood and her intrinsic right to life? It is not that the issues of the action under dispute were unique in their rarity or special circumstances; such complex moral decisions regarding life and death are made by families every day. Rather, it was the bitterness and rancor between the family members and their willingness to go to great lengths for their cause that thrust this story in to the center of the public debate over rights to life, rights to privacy and how end-of-life decisions are made.

So exactly how was it that Terri Schiavo and the fight over her life became a news event to rival a Hollywood suspense blockbuster? This chapter will explore Terri Schiavo's story by analyzing "strips of life", using positioning theory— identifying speech acts employed by the actors, clusters of rights and duties both claimed and assigned, and the underlying narrative structures taken up by the characters. Three periods along the 15-year saga are explored in detail via various, publicly available, texts. In the first, a written communication, we see how a trigger event establishes the context for first order positioning between the two parties who had, by all accounts prior to this event, been working in concert on Terri's behalf. The second strip, brought to life through interviews conducted on U.S. national television, demonstrates a move to the use of presumptive positioning (ascription of character traits used to mediate the positioning) and shows how each of the disputants see their relationship with Terri as a resource for the positions they take and ascribe to others.

Finally, nearing the end of the battle, we see the deepening effects of special interest groups as the discourse takes on a meaning and implication far beyond the central characters. Here, acts undertaken by an enlarging cast are demonstrative of positions being contested at a more metaphysical level where the very existence of the positions, both assumed and ascribed, is called into question. The perlocutionary force of the acts employed; the drama, desperation and unparalleled intervention, has set off a debate that continues today.

Background

Teresa Marie Schiavo (Terri) suffered a collapse and cardiac arrest in her home in Florida on February 25, 1990. She was 26 years old. Terri and Michael Schiavo had been married for over five years when the tragic accident occurred, leaving her brain deprived of oxygen for an extended period. She spent almost three months in an acute care hospital after which she was discharged to a skilled care and rehabilitation facility. In June of 1990 the courts appointed Michael Schiavo as Terri's guardian without objection from her parents, Robert and Mary Schindler. For the next six months Terri's husband and parents sought aggressive rehabilitation, including two months of experimental treatment in California, in hopes of improving Terri's functional abilities. As a result of the severe anoxic brain injury, and despite all efforts, clinical assessments revealed no changes in motor or cognitive function and the formal diagnosis was that Terri was in a chronic vegetative state (CVS).

Michael returned to Florida with Terri in January of 1991 where she continued to receive 24 hour skilled care as well as physical, occupational, speech and recreation therapies at various facilities for the next three years. Meanwhile, he initiated a medical malpractice suit against physicians treating Terri for infertility prior to her injury. It was Schiavo's contention that the potassium imbalance thought to have caused the cardiac event should have been detected. The case was concluded in 1993 with the courts ruling in favor of the plaintiffs, Michael and Terri Schiavo, for an amount totaling slightly more than one million dollars. It was shortly after the money was awarded that hostilities between Michael Schiavo and Terri's parents, Robert and Mary Schindler, erupted and became public.

In early 1994 Michael Shiavo elected not to have Terri treated for an active urinary tract infection and simultaneously enacted a "do not resuscitate" order. Though he reversed his course in that particular instance, it was the first documented indication that Michael's perspective on Terri's condition had changed. Michael's directive occurred whilst the Schindler's were actively pursuing the first, among multiple, attempts to have him removed as Terri's guardian. In 1997 Michael initiated action aimed at eliminating all artificial life supports for Terri. According to Florida statute CVS is listed amongst other terminal conditions for which "life prolonging procedures" can be refused. Further, Florida law is specific to delineate "artificially provided sustenance and hydration" as among the techniques and treatments of artificial life support and, as such, eligible for discontinuation. Because Terri Schiavo had neither advance directives nor a living will to assert her wishes should she become incapacitated, the law required that her proxy, Michael, provide clear and convincing evidence to support his contention that his efforts to withdraw life support were what his wife would have wanted. This contest over which of the parties really knew Terri and what she would have wanted was the primary platform on which the positions where established and contested.

Until the late stages of the legal wrangling between Terri's husband and guardian Michael and her parents, Robert and Mary Schindler, they shared the opinion and medical consensus that Terri was in a chronic vegetative state (CVS). When the Schindlers posit that Terri is not in a CVS rather, in that she is in a 'minimally conscious state', the debate is expanded from multiple directions.

Modeling the Dispute Dynamics

While applying the positioning framework will best illuminate the changing social relationships between the Schindlers and Michael Schiavo, the dynamics of the dispute might initially be represented by Figure 8.1.

The circles within each bounded area represent the positions of primary disputing parties; Michael Schiavo on the one side and Robert and Mary Schindler on the other. The first box of the diagram can be used to imagine how the two parties might have functioned before their dispute became public. After Terri Schiavo's catastrophic anoxic brain injury in 1990, her husband Michael and parents, Mary and Robert Schindler, by all accounts, worked tirelessly side-by-side to see Terri regain some of her pre-injury functioning. Together they shared in Terri's constant care, sought aggressive rehabilitation and even traveled great distances to receive experimental treatments. Michael went back to school and studied nursing with the self-expressed goal of becoming better able to care for Terri. The parties, 'on the same page' and working toward the same goals, operate within the same, conceptually closed, set of meanings and positions from the time of Terri's injury up until the dispute began. The arrows represent speech acts occurring in this relatively private world that serve to constitute and strengthen the local moral order (i.e. positions or clusters of rights and duties). Within this contained moral space and if given the opportunity to witness the actual conversations, it is possible we might uncover signs of divergent meanings in the daily discourse, but the narrative project that both Schiavo and the Schindlers are pursuing (e.g. Terri can improve with appropriate treatment) is strong such that the boundaries of shared meaning and purpose are never breached. The overlap area dominates the discourse.

On February 14, 1993 a fight occurred between Michael Schiavo and Robert Schindler in the halls outside Terri's hospital room. Modeled in Figure 8.1 as

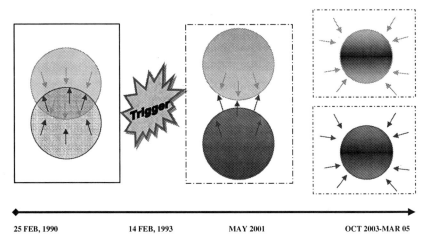

FIGURE 8.1. Representation of the dynamics between Michael Schaivo and the Schindlers.

the "Trigger" both parties identify this event as the beginning of overt hostilities. Prior to this point, there are no transcripts available because this was simply another story of a family coping with a terrible tragedy. Not long after this date, legal action is initiated by both Schiavo and the Schindlers and interview transcripts emerge from interviews with the various parties or their representatives. Indeed, it is not clear that Michael Schiavo and the Schindlers ever communicated in person again after this fateful day. Perhaps one of the last direct communications that is not mediated through a legal representative is a letter written on July 16th of 1993 by Terri's parents to Michael Schiavo. Certainly neither party knew at the time how far they would end up taking their fight and the extent to which their projects would be taken up by the media, interest groups, the high courts, legislatures and even the executive branches of the state and federal government.

The second bounded area of Figure 8.1 shows circles completely separated with arrows, representing speech acts, constituting the boundaries of each party's own position while also suggesting the boundaries of the others'. After the triggering event, the preponderance of discourse suggests positions asserted and contested through speech acts that assign character. Schindler ascribes character traits to Schiavo that simultaneously suggest his own position and legitimize his actions, while contesting the rights of Schiavo. Conversely, Schiavo positions Schindler through attributions of character that further reinforce his duty to continue at all cost toward his project. The box bounding the circles is broken, demonstrating the increased permeability of the moral space as Terri's plight becomes a public issue and the possibility for the actors to become part of a broader discourse is opened.

In the final episode of the model, we see the positions of the primary parties become more rigid as a multitude of outside actors seek to shape their positions relative to special interests. Neither Schiavo nor the Schindlers are immune to the effect of these larger social forces as they each use the growing cast to bolster their increasingly entrenched positions in this now intractable conflict.

Moral Positioning Meets Legal Positioning

As stated previously, Michael Schiavo, as Terri's husband, was awarded legal guardianship of Terri shortly after her injury, which included making medical decisions on her behalf. Because Michael also believed that the potassium imbalance purported to have caused Terri's collapse should have been picked up by their fertility specialist, he sought damages for Terri and himself. In January of 1993, Terri was awarded $750,000 and Michael, $300,000 as part of the settlement. Not much more than a month after the award was made, a fight occurred between Robert Schindler and Michael Schiavo. The date was February 14, 1993 and both sides clearly recall this as the point that their collaborative efforts on Terri's behalf ceased and their relationship became heated and adversarial.

In the 1993 letter, the Schindlers clearly engage in first order positioning of Michael Schiavo, identifying him as having certain duties. The duties come across as expected or normative behaviors given the context and its moral order. In this exchange the Schindlers do not attempt to diminish Michael's rights, legal or otherwise, rather they point out the commitments that he had made previously and ask that he uphold these. The Schindlers are clearly aware that Schiavo holds the legal position under Florida law which granted him, as Terri's husband, sole guardianship and power of attorney of Terri's personal well-being and private affairs. In appealing to Schiavo's conscience to "do the right thing" the Schindlers are also acknowledging their own vulnerability in the situation (in that they do not hold any legal position with regard to Terri) and that Michael has the ability, and thus the duty to remedy this situation:

Long before and during the malpractice trial, you made a number of commitments to Mary and myself. One of your commitments was that award money was to be used to enhance Terri's medical and neurological care.

You also committed that the award proceeds would be used to provide a home for Terri so that Mary and I could live with her, and as her parents, we could provide the love and care that she deserves on a long term basis.

Since the trial and the ensuing award, you have chosen to ignore your commitments and have totally removed Terri from our lives. You have not communicated to us anything concerning her medical nor neurological status. ...

Regardless of your rationale, we believe you have a moral responsibility to include us in determining Terri's welfare. Lest you forget, we did raise her for 21 years, and also, from the time of Terri's seizure up to when you chose to alienate us, Mary was continually at you side, caring for you and Terri.

Indeed, Robert Schindler posits a supererogatory right to be involved in Terri's care and decision-making around the expenditure of proceeds from the malpractice case.

He states the nature of Michael's dutiful response quite directly as a "moral responsibility" in the last statement above. In this text, we also see the emerging narrative of the "embattled other" as the Schindlers find themselves facing the seemingly insurmountable situation as legally powerless actants. Not only did Schiavo refuse to communicate any medical information regarding Terri, but he had instructed all medical staff that they were to communicate with no one but him.

Later in the same letter, the Schindlers request that Michael consider "giving Terri back":

On a long term basis, we would like you to consider giving Terri back to us, so we can give her the love and care she deserves. Logically and realistically you still have a life ahead of you.

Give this some thought. Are you ready to dedicate the rest of your life to Terri? We are! Let us know your feelings (Schindler, 1993).

Here we see the Schindlers offer an alternate position for Michael; one suggesting that he might adopt an alternative storyline. Here the speech acts both suggest (albeit subtly) that he is not providing the love and care that Terri deserves and that he should not be expected to because he still has "a life ahead of him." Specifically they legitimize his right to walk away from the entire situation. The narrative implicitly offered is that of the "young and innocent afflicted with an unwarranted burden." Ultimately, Schiavo does not take up this storyline.

Schiavo's legal rights to make decisions for Terri are not, however without complication. Terri did not execute either a set of advance directives or a living will that would have served to secure a course of action of her own choosing. Lacking Terri's direct articulation of her desires should she be incapacitated, Michael's decisions were especially open to contestation. The Schindler's make three attempts over the course of some ten years to remove Michael as guardian.

Because the parties are no longer speaking to each other, observing the formation of the actant's identities in autobiographical talk is central to the analysis. Further because the texts are themselves the acts of legal opponents, an awareness of the distinction "between statements which are part of an autobiography, that is, which describe a life event from the point of view of the actor, and statements which are themselves life events" must be kept in mind (Harré & van Langenhove, 1999, p. 62).

Acts of Positioning Through Character Ascription and Identity Formation Through Colonization

Transcripts from 2001 interviews with both Schiavo and the Schindlers reveal the depth of the adversarial stances each has assumed. Michael Schiavo had petitioned the courts in May of 1998 for a discontinuation of Terri's life support.

Per Florida law, a vegetative state is considered a terminal illness and a guardian can petition for action to cease life support in the absence of written advanced directives. Because Terri did not have an advanced directive, a Guardian Ad Litem (GAL) was assigned to the case to represent her. In this instance the GAL recommends against the petition due to the potential conflict of interest regarding disposition of residual funds in Terri's trust. In fact, there was approximately $700,000 remaining in Terri's trust to which Michael would become heir. The GAL also notes that Michael had begun a serious relationship with a woman which may have affected his ability to serve in the best interest of Terri (Pearse, 1998). Still, in February of 2000, after multiple hearings Judge Greer orders the removal of Terri's feeding tube.

On the other side, the Schindlers had petitioned the court multiple times to remove Michael as Terri's guardian, to no avail. It was the contention of the Schindlers that Michael had been negligent in his care for Terri and that "his behavior was disruptive to Terri's treatment and condition." After Judge Greer's decision, the Schindlers submitted a motion based on new testimony and new evidence which aimed to reflect adversely on Michael's role as guardian. Though the specifics of the new testimony (presented during the year 2000) are not available for this study, a recent report of Terri's GAL suggests:

"It related to [Michael's] personal romantic life, the fact that he had relationships with other women, that he had allegedly failed to provide appropriate care and treatment for Theresa, that he was wasting the assets within the guardianship account, and that he was no longer competent to represent Theresa's best interests." (Wolfson, 2003, p. 16)

It is important to note that throughout these proceedings and for some time into the future, the Schindlers acknowledge their belief, in agreement with the clinical diagnosis, that Terri is in a chronic vegetative state.

Transcripts were obtained from the CNN show "Burden of Proof" which hosted Bob Schindler on May 3, 2001 and Michael Schiavo on May 7, 2001. These interviews were conducted days after Terri's feedings were terminated and then restarted when the Schindler's filed a civil action resulting in a temporary injunction. In these interviews the ascription of character is the dominant method for positioning the other side. In positioning themselves, each actant simultaneously uses inferred positioning (the result of the negative character of the other) and autobiographical narrative as a means of establishing identity and position. Further, each of the parties seeks to colonize Terri as an (historical) actant/extension of themselves, pulling her in to their project by claiming a special knowledge of her wishes via the special relationship they have with her.

Throughout the interview with Robert Schindler (interviewed together with his son Bobby, and lawyer Joseph Magri) there are assertions of the character of Michael Schiavo and statements of his mal-intent toward Terri. In the later interview, Schiavo similarly positions Schindler. Examples of the speech acts used to assign character are shown below:

Actant	Characteristic named or implied	Speech act employed
Schindler positioning of Schiavo	Careless guardian	"We have had people who deal with brain injury to see Terri… in their opinion Terri could be rehabilitated to improve to a better level than where she is now. … Unfortunately, we did not have the funds at that time, dependent upon the receipt of the malpractice trial money… when that came in; the money was not used for Terri's rehabilitation…"
	Disingenuous	During the malpractice trial… He "cried in front of the jury… told the jury that he was going to nursing school so that he could care of his wife for the rest of her life… now he wants to let her die."
	Opportunist	When asked why he would do this, being a young man Michael said, 'My wedding vows mean a lot to me.' … The first we heard of Terri's desire to die in these circumstances… was after the money came in."
Schiavo positioning Schindler	Selfish	"Schindlers testified that if anything became of Terri, that they would actually remove her arms and legs just to keep her alive… They would not carry out her wishes."
	Money-hungry	Michael, when asked why he is at odds with Terri's parents over such an important decision, "I believe that Mr. Schindler is very angry that he did not receive any money from the malpractice case. … I believe they are money-hungry, yes."
	In denial	"I think that they're seeing only what they want to see…. I mean, CAT scans don't lie." (Speaking of Schindler's claim that Terri responds to her mother.)

FIGURE 8.2. Examples of mutual character assignments made by Michael Schaivo and the Schindlers.
(Source: CNN Transcripts. Schindler, May 3, 2001; Schiavo, May 7, 2001.)

Both Schiavo and the Schindlers vehemently maintain that they are the ones that know Terri and what she would want. Schindler suggests that Michael is lying about what Terri has expressed regarding her wishes in such a circumstance as "That would be totally out of character for Terri to make comments like that… We don't think she ever made that kind of comment." Michael Schiavo states "It's Terri's wishes that she did not want to be like this." This assertion of knowledge as to Terri's wishes shows up quite readily in the storyline each party engages—that of "dutiful protector of the voiceless victim"—though with dramatically divergent courses of action proposed. Each party seeks to forward the storyline/project through speech acts which express their identity. Besides statements in which actants index and locate themselves in space and time, van Langenhove and Harré (1999) describe the various ways that actants explain their personal behavior:

There seem to be at least three distinct ways of explaining personal behavior: by referring to one's powers and one's rights to exercise them, by referring to one's biography (what one did, saw, etc. and what happened to one) and by referring to personal experiences that one has had as legitimating certain claims, for example 'expertise' (p. 24).

With Terri being central to the action but unable to participate directly in the conversation, she in effect falls within the psychological boundaries of both Schiavo's and Schindler's identity; what Benson (2003) calls the "psychological boundary of extension":

Psychological boundaries of extension are tied up with acts of possessing or of owning. They include what belongs to me (things, people, ideas, skills, rights, reputation, privileges and so on that I control and can call "my own"). They also encompass the ways in which I belong to others (forms of solidarity, group identity, obligation, and so forth that have claims on me.) (In Harré and Moghaddam, eds., p. 63).

In this way, Terri's rights are taken up by and directly linked to the constructed identities of those who see themselves as rightly "possessing" her. The relationship captures the past when Terri was able to communicate, but is also an evolving relationship. It is the very right to position Terri that is being contested. Further, the personhood of Terri is being contested vis-à-vis the identities of the opponent actants. In a way, the story is at once all about Terri and not about her at all.

As the rift deepens and the discourse comes in to the public, the world of meanings is more permeable to outside forces, which mold, shape and even form them through rhetorical redescription of the actions.

As the identities of the actants become more tightly constructed through the repeated, performative acts of autobiographical talk occurring in the public sphere (as opposed to discourse between the parties) it is entirely possible that the identity becomes less dynamic and more scripted—as if a set movement pattern of a chess piece—the script runs off of positions already established. In this view the action is not occurring in the battle between the Schindlers and Schiavo but rather in the nature of the uptake by external parties. In this context we see the evolution and formation of new moral commitments by the parties who are possibly being instrumentalized (with Terri, by extension) and colonized to forward other projects. As more actors enter the story, it is possible that at some point the Schindler's and Schiavo no longer have the option to renegotiate, as the momentum within the storyline is such that it can no longer be changed.

The Battle Over the Language—Discourse As Rhetorical Re-description

In the final strip, we pick up the story some three years down the road. In fact, the positioning of the parties by each other has not changed much, though there is notably more venom in the characterizations offered publicly. For example,

Schiavo suggests that the Schindlers are "courting the right wing activists" and that his life has been threatened. Schindler alternately claims that Schiavo is determined to have Terri "starved to death" and is denying her religious liberty as a practicing Catholic. The effects of outside actants on the narrative can be clearly seen via the changes in speech acts employed. A battle for the language is emerging.

To set the current legal context appropriately, one would need to know that by late 2003, the Schindlers are seeking to introduce new evidence to support their current belief that Terri is not in a chronic vegetative state but rather, in a minimally conscious state. The Schindlers gather several minutes of video footage of Terri, and release it to the media. Trusting that a lay public will interpret her movements, sounds and affect as they do, the Schindlers, through these video clips, give Terri *herself* an opportunity to reconstitute her personhood. It is an act done in hopes that Terri might gain a role as central actor in this drama. Where Schiavo insists that Terri is nothing more than a conglomeration of bodily functions and that she, being a "private person", would be mortified to know that a video of her "in this condition" was being shown, the Schindlers use the same video to demonstrate that Terri is responsive, interactive and "you know, cognizant... She's a person."

The video clips, taken as a set of performative acts opens the possibility for Terri to be interpreted directly, in a way previously unavailable. While it is clear that Terri is incredibly limited in her function, the meaning ascribed to the movements and behaviors we see, naturally fall to what is familiar. Specifically, wakefulness is most often (and correctly) experienced as synonymous with consciousness. That Terri might be wakeful and not be experiencing consciousness is difficult for most of the public to understand. Similarly, Terri's eye movements, vocalizations and limb movements are seen to be volitional and directly responsive to external stimuli. The perlocutionary effect of the video was remarkable, including its review by Senator Bill Frist, M.D., who later referenced it during his plea on the floor of the Senate for a federal-level intervention in Terri's case.

Another example of the varying speech acts used to contest the storyline is the use of the phrase "artificial life support" versus the alternative "assisted nutrition and hydration." This distinction becomes important when considering withdrawal of feeding. The terms are made more complicated by the fact that Florida law places the "vegetative state" in the category of terminal illness which is interesting when one considers that Terri, having lived in her condition for the last 15 years is clearly not in an active dying process (any more than any living person is in an active dying process—life is terminal, after all!) There are many people living with dysfunctions in swallowing who require alternate routes for fluids and food. In these cases, such assistance is not considered to be artificial life support but rather a functional support. Just one year earlier (March 2004) the Pope had clarified church doctrine to include assisted nutrition and hydration to persons in vegetative states as "natural, ordinary and proportional care" and as such, "morally obligatory." Further, the Pope contests the idea that to cease feeding is to allow a natural dying process to occur when he calls such an act "euthanasia by omission."

A related contention in the decision to withdraw feeding is the idea of the right to life versus issues of valuation based on presumed quality of life. The disability rights community, who took up the Schiavo case, is adamant that images of what constitutes a high quality of life must necessarily change as survival rates from catastrophic injuries continue to rise. Further, this group poses the challenge to an able-bodied public to see not the *disabled* person but the *person* who happens to have a disability.

Still, in the case of Terri Schiavo, her seemingly consistent clinical demonstration of non-reproducible responses along with her imaging studies would suggest that in fact, Terri has no awareness of her surroundings and is unable to communicate or interact in any meaningful way. The issue becomes the philosophical one of what constitutes personhood which centers on the dispute regarding the boundaries of the person. Is the person a body or is the person a consciousness? If the person is defined by consciousness than is the body without consciousness morally protected? Of related consequence is the idea of intrinsic worth; that is, is worth *intrinsic* to the person or is it *attributed* to the person. It is for this conversation that the anti-abortion activists took up the Terri Schiavo issue.

From Michael Schiavo's point of view, he was fighting for justice for Terri in the form of her privacy and her right to make the decision as a retrospective actant to end her life. In this way, Michael and many others see that Terri's *right* is that of dignity, and the fight is centered on the privacy one has in making decisions relative to maintaining dignity, in whatever way and by whatever means one sees fit. Unfortunately, in the absence of a written advance directives and in the case where family members contest a hierarchy of supposed intrinsic rights, right to life versus right to privacy, there is no where to turn except the courts. When the parties become emotionally entrenched in their narrative as the "embattled virtue" their duty to defend the vulnerable, as in the case of Terri Schiavo, can take years to reach conclusion. As noted earlier, the parties in this dispute saw two distinct readings of the same situation and were pursuing

Actant	Michael Schiavo Narrative	Schindler's Narrative
Seeker	Terri	Terri
Object Sought	Right to privacy/dignity	Right to life
Sender	Liberty/Justice	God/creator
Receiver	Terri/related others	Terri/related others
Helper	Michael/husband	Schindlers/parents
Opponent	Schindlers/parents	Michael/husband

FIGURE 8.3. Schiavo and the Schindlers represented according to Greimas' (1987) basic narratological scheme.

projects of dramatically different outcomes. Application of Greimas' (1987) basic narratological scheme to the dispute further demonstrates the strong parallels (Figure 8.3).

Conclusion

This is a very complex story. Positioning analysis allows us to make our way from the initial tragic events that destroyed Terri Schiavo, the person, to the final act when the body that had been Terri Schiavo was allowed to die.

The analysis shows a changing pattern of interweaving positionings and re-positionings as rights and duties of care for the body envelope that had formerly sustained the person were called in question. In the background we see a shifting pattern of personal attributions from the Schindler's to Michael Schiavo and reciprocally.

Without detailed material it is not possible to say anything worthwhile about motivations, in the sense of the kind of self-justifying discourse in which people engage when their actions are called in question. However, the amount of money made available by court action for the care of Terri Schiavo body as a former person appears and reappears in the background and is to some extent instrumental in the changing character attributions between the contending parties.

Also in the background is a deep philosophical question concerning the concept of a person. The 'body on the bed' once was material support of a person, Terri Schiavo. From the moment the accident destroyed essential parts of her brain this body was at best a former person. The Schindler family began to insist more and more vociferously that not only was it a former person but also the material location of a possible person, a revivified Terri Schiavo. The least said about the opportunistic intervention of politicians the better, though there is a positioning theory story to be told there as well.

Psychologically we are presented with the details of a public cognitive process involving several people and the medical and legal professionals who get called into the issue. Only with the help of a positioning analysis is it possible to follow closely the unfolding of the psychological substance of the affair, with its final denouement in the removal of the feeding tube.

References

Benson, C. (2003). The unthinkable boundaries of self. In R. Harré & F. Moghaddam (Eds.), *The self and others: Positioning individuals and groups in personal, political and cultural contexts* (pp. 61–84). Westport, CT: Praeger.

Greimas, AJ. (1987). *On meaning: Selected writings in semiotic theory*. Translation by Paul J. Perron and Frank H. Collins. London, UK: Pinter.

Harré, R., & van Langenhove, L. (1999). Reflexive positioning: Autobiography. In R. Harré and L. van Langenhove (Eds.), *Positioning theory: Moral contexts of intentional action* (pp. 61–73). Oxford, UK: Blackwell.

Pearse, RL. (1998). Report of Guardian Ad Litem. http://www6.miami.edu/ethics/schiavo/pdf_files/122998_Schiavo_Richard_Pearse_GAL_report.pdf. Accessed July 17, 2007.

Schindler, 1993. Personal communication to Michael Schiavo. Available at http://journals.aol.com/shjusticeforall/SavingTerriSchiavo/entries/2004/11/29/letter-to-michael-from-bob-and-mary-schindler/844. Accessed July 16, 2007.

Transcript, Michael Schiavo, CNN Burden of Proof, May 7, 2007, by Greta van Susteren. Available at http://transcripts.cnn.com/TRANSCRIPTS/0105/07/bp.00.html. Accessed July 17, 2007.

Transcript, Robert and Mary Schindler, CNN Burden of Proof, May 3, 2001, by Roger Cossack. Available at http://edition.cnn.com/TRANSCRIPTS/0105/03/bp.00.html. Accessed, July 17, 2007.

van Langenhove, L., & Harré, R. (1999). Introducing positioning theory. In R. Harré and L. van Langenhove (Eds.), *Positioning theory: Moral contexts of intentional action* (pp. 14–31). Oxford, UK: Blackwell.

Wolfson, J. (2003). *A report to Governor Jeb Bush in the matter of Theresa Marie Schiavo.* http://www6.miami.edu/ethics/schiavo/pdf_files/wolfson's_report.pdf. Accessed July 17, 2007.

Part 3
Intergroup Positioning

9
How Disadvantaged Groups Members Position Themselves: When They Might Appear to Work Against an Improvement in Status for Their Own Group

DONALD M. TAYLOR, JULIE CAOUETTE, ESTHER USBORNE AND MICHAEL KING

There is no more theoretically vibrant, and socially relevant, topic in modern social psychology than the study of intergroup relations. Until the early 1970s intergroup relations was an understudied, relatively neglected topic (see Taylor & Moghaddam, 1994). The only bright spot was the seminal research of Sherif (1966) which spawned realistic conflict theory, an influential theory, but one that is dominated by a focus on relations between groups of relatively equal power and status. Social identity theory (Tajfel & Turner, 1979, 1986 Tajfel), launched in the seventies, had a dual impact. First, it raised the profile of the psychology of intergroup relations as a topic, and second it shifted attention away from the study of equal status groups to relations between groups of unequal, often dramatically unequal, status. Such a refocus paralleled the real-world shift in attention from the cold war stand-off between two relatively equally powerful nations, to the world-wide uprising of cultural minority groups, including the more recent public concern with terrorism.

Scholars who address the social psychology of intergroup relations involving groups of unequal status share a theoretical assumption that serves as their springboard for new insights. The assumption, which lies at the heart of social identity theory for example, is that disadvantaged group members are motivated to improve the status of their group. Conversely, advantaged group members strive to protect their group's elevated status. When the status of a disadvantaged group improves, there are considerable material and psychological benefits for every disadvantaged group member. Tangibly, there may be increased opportunity for economic improvement, and psychologically, every member inherits the social currency associated with membership in a higher status group, which

149

in turn can be internalized as an important and positive component of their identity. Conversely, advantaged group members protect their status because of the economic and psychological benefits that accompany an elevated status.

These are the fundamental assumptions that guide current research and theorizing in the field of intergroup relations. Questions range from the role of prejudice, stereotyping and system justification in legitimizing the status of advantaged groups, to the conditions that give rise to disadvantaged group members taking individual or collective action designed to improve their status. We might conclude, then, that in terms of real-world intergroup relations, members of advantaged groups are motivated to guard their advantages while disadvantaged groups are motivated to improve the status of their group.

In this chapter, we focus on the motives of disadvantaged group members. Positioning theory, with its emphasis on social constructivism, and the fluidity with which an interaction can involve shifting motivations and redefined meanings, represents an interesting theoretical perspective on social interaction that challenges the fundamental assumptions of intergroup relations. Positioning theory stimulates scholars to reconsider why disadvantaged group members may not give the appearance of working to elevate the status of their group. It may also explain why disadvantaged groups might want to exaggerate their disadvantage. Through addressing these very different positionings by disadvantaged group members, we offer some insight into how the very societal structures that are designed to reduce intergroup conflict by fostering greater equality among groups may inadvertently be maintaining the unjust inequality they are professing to redress. An appreciation of the positioning complexities associated with intergroup relations may well point to new strategies for the resolution of intergroup conflicts.

In the present chapter, we focus our attention on a number of pivotal and frequently occurring positions that are taken by members of a disadvantaged group. Rather than describe all the various positions that disadvantaged group members might take, we focus on a number of important positions that might offer insights into understanding and resolving intergroup conflict. Our selective analysis is designed to provide the reader with a more in depth and focused analysis of some crucial, counter-intuitive intergroup positions. As well, our analysis is designed to be generalizeable to a wide variety of intergroup contexts, but we will use as examples those groups with whom we have had research and applied experience: Aboriginal peoples, visible minorities and women. We begin with a review of the positionings that are implied in current theory and research on the social psychology of intergroup relations. We then explore a series of positionings that, on the surface, might appear to be counter productive from the point of view of the motivations that are presumed to guide the behavior of members of society's more disadvantaged groups. Our focus on positioning theory will hopefully illuminate how even apparently counterproductive positions are designed to improve conditions for their group. Understanding these different positions may well offer insights into strategies for reducing intergroup conflict.

Assumed and Alternate Positioning of Disadvantaged Group Members

In the social psychology literature, the classic intergroup situation is one where the disadvantaged group's position arises from systemic discrimination at the hands of the advantaged group. Current theories of intergroup relations share the same framework concerning the motives of both the advantaged and disadvantaged group members. First, it is assumed that members of the advantaged group are motivated to "maintain their collective privilege" (Wright, 1997, p. 1277). The second, and complementary, assumption is that disadvantaged group members are motivated to improve their status by challenging the established hierarchy (Stephan & Stephan, 1996; Taylor & Moghaddam, 1994). Theoretically, then, the same basic motivation, the maximization of group status, is assumed to apply to members of all groups independent of their status.

Perhaps the most influential theory in the social psychology of intergroup relations is social identity theory (Tajfel & Turner, 1979, 1986), and the theoretical extensions it spawned including self-categorization theory (Turner, Hogg, Oakes, Reicher, & Wetherell, 1987). Social identity theory is a prime example of a theory whose roots are founded on the premise that group members are motivated to attain a positive and distinctive social identity. Its core premise is that members of low status groups are motivated to improve their status, and that high status group members seek to maintain their relative advantage.

Social identity theory, and its assumed positions, can be understood as resulting from two psychological processes. First, there is the natural, universal, human tendency to categorize and stereotype people. Empirical research addressing this tendency reveals that people position themselves and members of their group as sharing more positive characteristics than members of an outgroup (Stephan & Stephan, 1996; Taylor & Moghaddam, 1994). A second process that is central to social identity theory involves the universal motivation people have to secure for themselves a positive identity.

To understand the role of this process at a group level, one must recognize the important interplay between one's personal and collective identities. Collective identity is derived from group membership and plays an important role for a person's overall identity. Thus, for example, the status of a group will have an impact on a group member's self-esteem (Tajfel & Turner, 1979, 1986). With personal and collective identities interlinked, members of a group are presumed to share the motive of seeking (or maintaining) a positive social identity, which, in turn, supplies its group members with self-esteem. From these psychological processes, the assumption is that relations between groups can be understood as arising from a positioning whereby group members strive to maximize their status.

Alternate Positions of Disadvantaged Group Members

Social identity theory has provided invaluable contributions to the understanding of the dynamics of intergroup relations. Often, however, group members do not adopt their assumed position. That is, they do not appear motivated to raise the status of their group, and this poses a challenge for social identity theory.

From a positioning perspective, the puzzle is to understand why members of a disadvantaged group would appear to have no desire to improve their own status, or the status of their group. The counterintuitive element here is not only their seemingly passive acceptance of their disadvantaged position, but also their active support of the existing intergroup structure that reinforces and perpetuates their own disadvantage. It is as if these people have internalized and legitimized their "disadvantaged" position.

This position is exemplified by the classic study of Clark and Clark (1947), which showed that young Black children preferred White dolls over Black dolls. Subsequently, this form of negative self-stereotyping and outgroup preference has been observed among a variety of other disadvantaged minority groups in New-Zealand (Vaughan, 1978), South-Africa (Dawes & Finchilescu, 2002), and with selected Jewish populations (Sarnoff, 1951).

Not only has this counterintuitive positioning been observed in real-world contexts, but it has also been generated in the laboratory. In a series of experiments, Johnson, Schaller, and Mullen (2000) presented participants with a negative stereotype of a fabricated minority group. Through clever manipulation, participants were made aware of their own membership in this minority group, either before or after being exposed to the negative stereotype. Results showed that revealing participants' membership in the minority group before being exposed to the negative stereotype of the group prevented the development of a negative stereotype for one's own group. In contrast, participants maintained their bias against the minority group if they learned about their own membership in the minority group after the negative stereotype had been established. In this latter condition, minority group members did not appear motivated to even dispute, let alone improve, their group's status. An explanation is needed for this counterintuitive position.

New Positions, New Theories

It makes intuitive sense that disadvantaged groups strive to improve their condition. Yet, clearly, some groups do not. The recognition that leading intergroup theories inadequately account for this particular position has led to the development of a new theory focusing on the legitimacy of the status quo: system justification theory (Jost & Banaji, 1994; see also Jost, Burgess, & Mosso, 2001).

Social identity theory focuses on two psychological dimensions of the self: the personal and the group. System justification theory builds on this by considering a third dimension which is focused on the overarching social order (Jost & Banaji,

1994: see also Jost et al., 2001). Accordingly, people not only want to hold positive views about themselves, individually and as group members, but they also want to hold favorable impressions about the overarching social order. That is, people are motivated to justify the system. Justifying the social order might not seem very surprising from the perspective of advantaged group members; after all, they are benefiting from the status quo. However, there is considerable empirical support for the proposition that members of lower-status groups are also motivated to justify the very system which maintains group differences to their disadvantage (Jost & Banaji, 1994; Jost & Burgess, 2000; Jost & Major, 2001). Thus, it would seem that people are sometimes motivated to maintain a positive image of a system at the expense of self-esteem or collective-esteem, a psychological process akin to reducing cognitive dissonance (Jost, Pelham, Sheldon, & Ni Sullivan, 2003).

Since its inception, research has generated considerable support for system justification theory (Jost, Banaji, & Nosek, 2004). The theory has therefore been instrumental in interpreting why disadvantaged group members position themselves as supporting the status-quo, and do not appear motivated to improve their status. Thus, system justification theory has provided us with an alternative position, different from the position of disadvantaged group members that is assumed by most traditional theories of intergroup relations.

Need for a "Fluid" Theory

Social identity theory and system justification theory are two very influential theories designed to account for intergroup relations with an emphasis on groups of unequal status. When viewed from a positioning theory perspective, they each build their theoretical propositions from very different universal motivations. Social identity theory assumes that group members position themselves so as to maximize the status of their group. The motivation of disadvantaged group members from a systems justification perspective is to function within a predictable environment. This necessitates members of disadvantaged groups supporting the very social structure that defines their disadvantage.

Although system justification theory might fill a void left by social identity theory, this very strength might also be considered system justification's shortcoming: all it does is account for a new position. Although useful, it seems unreasonable to generate a new intergroup theory for every new group position that is recognized. As different positions are researched, it is apparent that intergroup relations is in need of a more integrated perspective accounting for the more traditional positions we have reviewed here, newly accounted positions, and beyond this, the conditions associated with systematic shifts among positions. Analyzing intergroup relations through the lens of positioning theory allows us to explore some of these new and shifting positions, and to appreciate the conditions that might exacerbate intergroup conflict, as members of a group shift from a system justification motivated position to one of social identity. In terms of addressing the implications for intergroup conflict, the issue to be resolved is when might members of a disadvantaged group shift from a position of system support to a position of challenging the system with a view to raising the status of their group.

In the following section, we will explore additional positions that appear on the surface to be counter-intuitive. We begin with a focus on positions that are motivated by the genuine desire of group members to improve their status.

Disadvantaged Groups and the Positioning Paradox

As traditional theories of intergroup relations suggest, disadvantaged group members are often truly motivated to improve their status. Given that an increase in group status is thought to lead to increased opportunity, increased collective self-esteem and thus increased psychological well-being, a group's default position would be to emphasize the strengths of their group in order to achieve recognition and status. However, when striving for higher status, disadvantaged group members may actually find that emphasizing their group's state of disadvantage is an effective position to obtain the most for their group, and themselves by extension. Thus, an interesting paradox arises: in order to maximize group advantage, group members may feel compelled to focus on the group's state of disadvantage.

The Positioning Paradox

When considering relations between advantaged and disadvantaged groups, modern Western society relies on an equity-based ideology. Equity in an intergroup relations context is based on a ratio of inputs to outcomes. That is, the ratio of a group's societal inputs to their received benefits should be equal to that of any other group. Thus, for example, it is inequitable for a group to receive less than another simply based on some ascribed characteristic, such as race or gender, which is unrelated to merit. Having recognized such inequities, advantaged group members in Western societies have implemented programs designed to foster equity. These include applying formal affirmative action programs to existing organizations and special grants and programs for particular disadvantaged groups in areas such as education, business and political representation. It is thought that given the appropriate resources and opportunities, members of disadvantaged groups will be in a position to increase their status. The implicit assumption is that these resource allocations will reduce the intergroup disparity, eventually leading to a society where there is genuine equality of opportunity.

Because of this focus on equity, eligibility for attention and resources from the advantaged group is based on a genuine need and obvious disadvantage. If we take into account the existence of sustained attention and resources, in order for a group to benefit from programs designed to reduce inequity, the group needs to project a public image of being disadvantaged. Indeed, gaining sufficient status might automatically make them ineligible for mainstream support. Consequently, members of both disadvantaged and advantaged groups may find themselves in a difficult position. Disadvantaged group members want to raise their group's status, yet actually accomplishing this goal indicates to the mainstream public that they no longer require resources or assistance from the advantaged group. Conversely, advantaged group members who wish to help a disadvantaged group can no longer justify their aid if the group appears to have gained sufficient status.

As a result of this paradox, the disadvantaged group and its individual members end up having to constantly shift their position, depending upon the context. These contexts may require positions that range from lauding the achievements of their group to describing their group as in a profound state of disadvantage. Thus, ironically, disadvantaged group members need to strike a balance between a genuine desire to improve their group's status, on the one hand, yet emphasizing the group's disadvantaged status, on the other.

In this instance it becomes clear that the same disadvantaged group member can position him/herself and his/her group in very different ways, all designed to promote the group's status. In our research and our more applied role in Aboriginal communities, we have encountered this positioning paradox frequently. First Nations, Inuit, and more recently Métis groups in Canada receive resources from the federal government with the hope on both sides that these resources will result in eventual equality for the advantaged and disadvantaged groups involved. It is easy to imagine how a member of an Aboriginal community involved in the promotion of his/her group's status would position him/herself in different ways depending on the context. When engaged in an interaction with other ingroup members, this individual might adopt the expected, default position and emphasize the group's strengths, why it deserves an increase in status, and what it has been able to accomplish thus far, in order to encourage a continued striving by group members for upward mobility. However, when engaged in negotiations with advantaged group members, the same individual might emphasize his/her group's position of disadvantage, the group's weaknesses, and the many obstacles it must overcome to attain equity with the advantaged group. Of course, this latter position is designed to emphasize that any support and resources that they are receiving are not only justified, but must continue. Whether it is conscious or not, disadvantaged group members know that in order to maintain the gains that come from being disadvantaged, they must at times emphasize that disadvantage.

Thus, the disadvantaged group does not have a rigidly defined position in society, and is not always engaged in promoting the group. On the contrary, members of the disadvantaged group, although motivated to increase their group's status, find that they sometimes must adjust their positioning so as to be more disadvantaged.

Support for the idea that group members can take on a variety of different positionings in an intergroup context is indirectly corroborated by research on collective social comparison. Taylor, Moghaddam, and Bellrose (1989) proposed that a group uses different targets of intergroup social comparison depending on their specific motivation. Here, social comparisons can be interpreted as a strategy for positioning one's group in a number of different ways. Firstly, if one's goal is to emphasize the strengths and achievements of one's group, then strategically it would be important to choose as a comparison group one that is worse off. Using such a downward social comparison strategy, group members position themselves as competent and able in order to justify to themselves and others why an increase in status is deserved. However, if the group's goal is to appeal to the advantaged group for equity in the form of additional resources, their target of comparison will undoubtedly be a group that is much better off. In doing so, they position themselves in a state of disadvantage, in order to legitimize appeals for more resources.

Finally, if the group's goal is to gain information about the group for genuine assessment purposes, social comparison is used to obtain accurate information in order to determine precisely where the group stands. Here, we see another possible position emerge. Rather than positioning themselves in a state of relative advantage or a state of relative disadvantage, group members can position themselves as genuine information seekers, wanting only to evaluate their true status. Depending on the goal of the interaction, members of a group can strategically influence how their group is perceived by others and even how group members perceive their own group.

Disadvantage as an Important Personal Resource

The continuous positioning and repositioning of a group's status can also be motivated by the simple fact that membership in a disadvantaged group can sometimes be used by group members as an important personal resource. Although still striving to increase the status of their group, the possession of characteristics associated with the group's disadvantaged status can often be a very valuable commodity.

Raising the status of a disadvantaged group often involves an empowerment process whereby a variety of new, group-specific, organizations are created and programs instituted. These may involve the creation of cultural centers, heritage language revival programs, or organizations designed to represent the group in terms of public policy. For example, there are a wide variety of such groups designed to empower the interests of visible minority groups, Aboriginal groups and women.

From a positioning perspective, disadvantaged group members who possess the prototypic group attributes (e.g. language and culture) are especially motivated to voice their group's disadvantaged status when negotiating with advantaged group representatives of the established order. The risk is that intergroup conflict might inadvertently be exacerbated if such a positioning is successful in prolonging affirmative action programs to the point that they provoke a backlash from members of the advantaged group.

Because of these affirmative action programs designed to foster equality, and a societal emphasis on the merits of disadvantaged group members, an individual from a disadvantaged group may find that they have an array of cultural and linguistic skills that are prototypical of, and symbolize, the characteristics that are a source of pride for the group. Members of a disadvantaged group who have these characteristics are positioned so as to attain a number of material and psychological benefits. For example, disadvantaged group members may have access to employment, resources, and even a sense of pride, at least partially because of their cultural knowledge. In fact, the cultural and experiential skills possessed by a disadvantaged group member may be highly valued because they personify the identity that defines the group. However, if the group's status were to appear sufficiently improved, and if the group's cultural uniqueness were to gain genuine respect, then a special celebration of the skills of the disadvantaged group might no longer be justified. An individual's cultural membership and the special skills they have developed in the context of their group may no longer have the same value.

An example of this phenomenon comes from affirmative action policies that recognize disadvantaged group members with particular skills. The skills of these group members are especially valued, and the group members receive employment and resources in the name of promoting equality for the disadvantaged group. Specifically, an Aboriginal person who excels at his or her traditional activities such as hunting or sewing, heritage language or at a traditional form of art may gain respect and material benefit because of these particular skills. In this case, an individual has been able to use their cultural membership and their culture specific skills as a form of currency in order to be successful. Their skills are meaningful and important in part because of the disadvantaged status of their group. However, if their group gains status, these culture-specific skills will no longer merit such celebration and will no longer have such critical value.

Membership in a group with a disadvantaged status can, therefore, be used as a material resource; however, it may also be possible for one's membership in a disadvantaged group to be an important psychological resource. Although traditional theories of intergroup relations would suggest that membership in a disadvantaged group has only negative psychological consequences for the individual, this may not always be the case. Indeed, social psychological research has shown that individual disadvantaged group members, including visible minorities, women, homosexuals, and the disabled do not in fact report pervasively low self-esteem (Crocker & Major, 1989). The recent societal emphasis on the celebration and encouragement of disadvantaged group members by the mainstream society may allow disadvantaged group members to take pride in their disadvantaged cultural identity. Because being a member of a disadvantaged group is a significant contributor to their identity, positioning oneself in a state of advantage may actually subtract from their cultural identity.

Again, the disadvantaged group member does not have a rigid role to play, but instead may need to project a number of different positions. Because of potential material and psychological gains that come from being a disadvantaged group member, it may at times be in their best interest to position themselves in a state of disadvantage. However, this paradoxical positioning can have implications for true equality.

Consequences of the Positioning Paradox

The structures in Western society that are socially constructed in order to foster equity are based on the assumption that disadvantaged groups will continuously, and actively, strive for higher status. However, after an analysis of the various positionings that a disadvantaged group and its members might take, it becomes evident that this underlying assumption may be misleading.

In many cases, both advantaged and disadvantaged groups have the goal of achieving equality. Members of disadvantaged groups work towards well-deserved and rightfully obtained material and psychological gains, and some advantaged group members may attempt to facilitate their progress. However, in order to continue to achieve at least short-term gains, we suggest that disadvantaged group members may, at times, have to position themselves in a continued state of deprivation, thus perpetuating their disadvantaged status. Admittedly, we cannot speak for the desires or actions of all members of every group, and we will elaborate on the positions of subgroups within disadvantaged groups in the following section. However, we suggest that at times positioning a group as disadvantaged may be appealing, as an improvement in the group's status may undermine the credibility of their disadvantage, devalue their particular skills, and make concessions from the advantaged group no longer justifiable. It may be the case that both disadvantaged and advantaged group members unwittingly maintain the inequality that they hoped to eliminate.

Our analysis thus far illustrates how the continuous positioning and repositioning of a groups' status may hold short-term advantages. However, in the current system, the end result may be the maintenance of inequality. Positioning one's group as disadvantaged, although immediately beneficial, may result in a long-term perpetuation of this disadvantage. Thus, the political structures in place for promoting equality need to be re-examined with the fluidity of positioning theory in mind. Positions in an intergroup context are actively negotiated and achieved, rather than ascribed and passively received (Tan & Moghaddam, 1999). A system designed to foster equity must recognize that disadvantaged and advantaged groups do not occupy rigidly defined roles in society; rather, their positions are in a constant state of flux. Depending on the intricacies of each interaction in which group members find themselves, and the specific goals of these interactions, a group's position will need to be slightly, and indeed under certain circumstances dramatically, altered. Fostering equality will undoubtedly have to involve the recognition of such flexibility in intergroup relations, and will depend upon an analysis of the various positions a group can take.

One concrete illustration of the need for fluidity in terms of positioning is the destructive cycle of disadvantaged group members needing to position themselves as disadvantaged beyond credibility. We have noted that disadvantaged group members are motivated to position themselves as disadvantaged when lobbying the advantaged group for a more equitable distribution of resources. If by adopting such a position genuine progress towards equity is made, disadvantaged group members may feel they are no longer needed. Their natural survival instinct will motivate them to continue positioning their group as disadvantaged in order to justify their mission, and in many cases their job, as an advocate for intergroup equality. What is needed is a structural mechanism such that when, in the course of lobbying the advantaged group for intergroup equity, genuine progress is made, new positionings are made available to disadvantaged group members. For example, a new positioning might involve members of advantaged and disadvantaged group members joining forces to educate other minority groups about how to best access societal resources.

The Positioning of "Elite" Disadvantaged Subgroups

In social psychological theory and research, with few exceptions (e.g. Five-Stage Model, Taylor & McKirnan, 1984), there is a tendency to assume that groups are homogeneous. We began our analysis by exploring the assumption that disadvantaged group members all have the same underlying motivation: to increase their group's status. Clearly, this may not always be the case, and further insights into the positioning of disadvantaged group members can be gained by considering the subgroups within a disadvantaged group. In this section, we will explore positionings that arise because not all disadvantaged group members are in fact identical, nor do they have identical motivations. Specifically, we will explore the positioning of what we will label the "elite" disadvantaged group members. We define elite disadvantaged group members as those group members who enjoy a relatively high status within their own disadvantaged group, because of their larger share of political, economic and social resources. These elite individuals can be considered as an advantaged subgroup encompassed within a societally disadvantaged group.

The Importance of Exploring the Specific Positioning of Subgroups Members: The Elite Disadvantaged Group Members

In researching discrimination and inequality, social psychologists have tended to focus on the average socio-economic differences between advantaged groups and disadvantaged groups. The distribution of socio-economic resources may overlap between groups (e.g. we may find highly successful African Americans, and very poor European Americans), but the crucial element to determine social inequality is the average difference between the groups. In other words, it is not because Oprah Winfrey, Colin Powell or Condoleezza Rice have made it to the top that systemic discrimination against African Americans, or women for that matter, has been eradicated.

This is an obvious point but one that is too often neglected. It is all too compelling to believe that the existence of highly successful individuals who belong to a disadvantaged group is tangible evidence that discrimination is no longer an obstacle for historically disadvantaged group individuals. For example, Kluegel and Smith (1986) have shown that most people only need to perceive that there are some opportunities for advancement in society for people to believe that others achieve the socioeconomic success or failure they "rightly" deserve. This basic perception can lead many people to believe that individual ability and hard work (i.e. meritocracy) can actually create opportunities and make up for any systemic barriers that might be faced. In order to challenge this common myth, much social psychological research has focused on exposing the continuing psychological effects of being disadvantaged. The result is that far less attention has been directed at the experience of those disadvantaged group members who are more successful. A notable exception would be the seminal research on "stereotype threat" that shows how even high achieving disadvantaged group members are prone to suffer from societal stereotypes (Steele, 1997).

Without undermining the recognition of continuing social inequality and group discrimination, the field of social psychology is now at a point where further investigation into the unique experiences of elite disadvantaged group members is warranted. Before exploring this new perspective of the positioning of elite disadvantaged subgroup members, it is necessary to review the history of research on subgrouping in the context of intergroup relations.

The Social Psychology of Subgroup Relations

It is difficult to find a coherent and integrated field of research related to subgrouping in social psychology, although the study of majority-minority influence does focus on minority subgroups (e.g. Martin & Hewstone, 2003). This is surprising because many social psychologists appear to be in the business of subgrouping: how many times do we encounter statistical analyses where participants are categorized into low and high group identifiers, effectively creating two subgroups, in order to explore the effect of differential group identi- fication? Although there is no clearly established field of subgroup dynamics, the relationship between a group and its subgroups does surface indirectly in different areas of social psychology. For example, the classic notion of superordinate goals involves the joining together of two groups to form a single, superor- dinate group with a shared goal. More recently, this theme has emerged in the development and testing of different theoretical models aimed at improving inter-group relations (e.g. the Common Ingroup Identity Model: Gaertner & Dovidio, 2000; Gaertner, Dovidio, Anastasio, Bachman, & Rust, 1993; the Mutual Inter-group Differentiation Model: Hewstone, 1996; Hewstone & Brown, 1986; for a comparison see Hornsey & Hogg, 2000). These models usually focus on a mainstream majority group and different ethnic minority groups, and conflict is reduced by creating superordinate group identification. Although most would recognize the benefits of emphasizing a common identity, the debate surrounds the question of whether social cohesion and harmony is most likely to be attained by encouraging the development of a shared identity. The problem is that a shared identity neglects subgroup identities which may be psychologically defining for individual subgroup members (see also Crisp, Stone, & Hall, 2006; Dovidio, Gaertner, & Validzic, 1998; Gonzalez & Brown, 2003; Hornsey & Hogg, 2000; Hornsey, van Leeuwen, & van Santen, 2003; Huo, Molina, Sawahata, & Deang, 2005).

Within this research framework, entire advantaged and disadvantaged groups are the subgroups that define society. But clearly, the "subgroups" of men and women or African American and European American are not themselves homogenous entities. In the present context, our focus is not subgroups within society, but rather subgroups within a disadvantaged group. More precisely, we will focus on the positionings that emerge when a subgroup of disadvan-taged individuals may have conflicting interests with other members of their own group, often because of their relative socio-economic advantage. Clearly, to attain intergroup harmony between diverse gender and ethnic groups, we need to explore the different individual and collective interests within these so-called "subgroups". Attention must be paid to the more neglected and subtle positionings within these major ethnic and gender groups.

While different levels of grouping and subgrouping are important to address, we focus here on elite subgroups within a disadvantaged group. The positioning issue for this influential group is whether they will position themselves as promoters of all members of their disadvantaged group, or whether they will position themselves so as to maintain their elite status and relative advantage compared to other members of their own disadvantaged group. We will examine closely one specific example of an elite disadvantaged subgroup, because there exists a rich accumulation of research: women who are successful in male-dominated careers. It will become clear that they often position themselves differently from other members of their own gender group, because of their acquired elite status.

Successful Women in Male-Dominated Careers

Women are underrepresented in high-status male-dominated careers, and one main cause for this exclusion is assumed to be systemic gender discrimination. Non-intuitively, some research has shown that at times it is women, and not men, who are more biased against other women (Cowan, Neighbors, DeLaMoreaux, & Behnke, 1998; Mathison, 1986). Furthermore, recent research has revealed that women may suffer even more when they are being discriminated against by other women. These women suffer more because it is difficult for them to believe that they are being a victim of discrimination when it is coming from a member of their own group (see Baron, Burgess, & Kao, 1991; Barreto & Ellemers, 2005; Ellemers, 2001; Schmitt, Ellemers, & Branscombe, 2003).

Research, inspired by this phenomenon, labeled the queen bee syndrome (Staines, Tavris, & Jayaratne, 1974), reveals how women who have been individually successful in male-dominated domains (an elite subgroup of women) position themselves differently from "regular" women. Accordingly, they often behave contrary to the interests of women as a group (e.g. Cooper, 1997; Ellemers, van den Heuvel, de Gilder, Maass, & Bonvini, 2004). Specifically, Ellemers and her colleagues studied the issue of why women were underrepresented among university faculty (a male-dominated environment). They were able to show that objectively there were no gender differences in the level of work commitment in their samples of male and female doctoral students. Yet, they found that female faculty members, but not male faculty members, tended to perceive female doctoral students as less committed to a scientific career than their male colleagues. Ellemers and her colleagues argue that, to make a successful career in a male-dominated environment, these female faculty members had to set themselves apart from their gender group: in fact, results showed that female faculty members adopted a masculine self-stereotype that emphasized how they are non-prototypical members women as a group. In other words, the position adopted by these women resembled the positionings men would usually adopt. Ellemers and her colleagues argue that a key explanation for this "queen bee" phenomenon resides in social identity theory. According to this theory, the individual upward mobility of female faculty is exemplified by these women's efforts to distance themselves from their group stereotype. This distancing leads female faculty members not only to perceive themselves as non-prototypical women, but may also elicit stereotypical views of other women. In more general terms, this means that in order to be successful, a disadvantaged group member needs to adopt a series of positionings that are more aligned with the advantaged group interests, and less with the overall interests of their own disadvantaged group. In our specific example, it means successful female faculty endorsing stereotypic views of other women, a positioning that would most commonly be upheld by male colleagues.

Ellemers et al. (2004) evoked social identity theory (Tajfel & Turner, 1979, 1986) to help explain the diverging motivations that subgroup members might have which translated into very different positions. Social identity theory describes how disadvantaged group members can increase their status either by individually gaining access to a more advantaged group, or by taking collective action to increase the status of their entire group. The Five-Stage Model of intergroup relations (Taylor & McKirnan, 1984) is more specific in outlining precisely how selected disadvantaged group members (elite subgroup) first attempt to pass into an advantaged group, and if successful they conform to the norms of the advantaged group. This is exemplified by women faculty members in the study of Ellemers and her colleagues. But the Five-Stage Model also argues that those individuals who are not successful in their attempt to individually move up into the advantaged group will return to their original disadvantaged group and will be motivated to instigate collective action designed to increase the status of their group as a whole. Tougas, Brown, Beaton & St-Pierre (1999) found that when women's attempts at upward individual mobility were unsuccessful, they were motivated, on behalf of their female colleagues, to support affirmative action in their workplace.

In sum, it seems that individuals' own experience in gaining higher status determines the way they view other group members and thus the way they position themselves (see Fajak & Haslam, 1998). If they gain higher status through upward individual social mobility, they position themselves by dissociating from their original disadvantaged group, and are unlikely to help their former group. But if attempts at individual mobility by a disadvantaged group member are unsuccessful, and they conclude that they are only able to gain higher status through collective means, then it seems that they are more likely to help their group by maintaining positionings consistent with their own group's interests. Direct empirical support for this claim comes from a series of experiments on tokenism (Wright & Taylor, 1998, 1999; Wright, Taylor, & Moghaddam, 1990). In these experiments, disadvantaged group members who were successful in gaining membership in the advantaged group effectively turned their back on their fellow disadvantaged group members. This positioning even arose when it was clear that the majority of disadvantaged group members were victims of blatant discrimination.

Different Subgroups, Different Interests? Group Interests versus Self Interests

We have now recognized two positions that can be taken by elite disadvantaged subgroups. The first position is personified by elite disadvantaged group members who, by conforming to the values and norms of an advantaged group, are able to individually attain a higher status. Researchers have argued that such individuals often oppose systematic social change (i.e. collective change that would most likely help the disadvantaged group as a whole), because they obviously did well within this unequal group hierarchy and are motivated to maintain it the way it is (see Gibson & Cordova, 1999). Just like advantaged group members, they are motivated to maintain the existing intergroup hierarchy from which they have clearly benefited. Like advantaged group members, they also maintain negative stereotypes about the disadvantaged group. But interestingly, they also seem to show an "in-subgroup" bias. To return to the Ellemers et al. (2004) example, while female faculty members negatively evaluate female doctoral students, they also evaluate other female faculty members more positively than male faculty members, effectively showing an in-subgroup bias (Brown & Smith, 1989; see also Cooper, 1997; Vonk & Olde-Monnikhof, 1998). It is clear that this elite subgroup has its own individual interests at heart, or at best the interests of its own limited subgroup, but definitely not the collective interests of the disadvantaged group at large. This is clearly reflected in the very different positionings they adopt.

The second position is one that is taken by those elite disadvantaged group members who faced systemic barriers that prevented them from successfully gaining membership into the advantaged group. As a result, they became "consciousness raisers" and they now advocate collective action on the part of their disadvantaged group in order to improve the interests of their group as a whole (cf. Tougas, Brown, Beaton, & St-Pierre, 1999). To illustrate, we can think of women who work for feminist movements, or other organizations whose goal is to promote social equality for women. Surprisingly, research suggests that such elite leaders can sometimes become alienated from the very disadvantaged group members they are attempting to help (Hornsey et al., 2003). For example, it is likely that by becoming leaders of women's movements, the power that accompanies their lofty position somewhat thwarts their genuine concerns for the common interests of women. To attain their goal of equality for all women, they may have to adopt a positioning that allows them to reach compromises with the advantaged group. These positions may be perceived as inadequate both by more "extremist" female activists, on the one hand, and by other "softer" activists, on the other. One interesting possibility, raised by Hornsey and colleagues would suggest that the leaders of women's movements come to believe that they are the only ones who know what is best for women at large. They further come to believe that they are the only ones making the efforts and sacrifices that are needed to meet the needs of all women. This may even lead them to believe that other women are just "dragging them down". They position themselves, therefore, as knowing what is "truly" best for the group. Accordingly, they can become frustrated and resentful that other women don't seem to share exactly their position regarding the plight of women, either because they don't share an interest in the cause or because their views on the cause and their plans of action are different. Counter intuitively, then, their best efforts to improve the status of their disadvantaged group backfire. In fact, research has shown that leaders who feel this resentment resort to decategorization, whereby these elite disadvantaged group members retreat to their individual identity so as to obtain more individual and immediate rewards and benefits for their actions (see Hornsey et al.). In other words, they choose to focus their positioning at the individual level, rather than the level of the group.

Conclusions

In this chapter, we have explored the motives of disadvantaged group members from a positioning perspective. It became clear from the outset that the explicit, and at times implicit, assumption of most theories of intergroup relations is limited. It is not the case that all disadvantaged group members are always motivated to improve the status of their group, and position themselves accordingly. Our motivational exploration led to the recognition of other positionings that range from benign acceptance of the status quo to actively reinforcing the disadvantages that so handicap groups who are victims of systemic discrimination. System justification theory pointed to a different positioning whereby members of a disadvantaged group come to support the social system that governs their own disadvantage. A positioning perspective led us to a further analysis of the different social contexts that confront members of disadvantaged groups. What emerged was a clear understanding of the positioning paradox that arises. When negotiating with the advantaged group, disadvantaged group members need to position themselves so as to emphasize their group's disadvantaged state. However, in the context of a meeting with other disadvantaged group members, a position of group progress and achievement needs to be taken. Finally, through an examination of the motives associated with elite members of the disadvantaged group, a variety of positions emerged. These ranged from highlighting group disadvantage or progress, to abandoning the disadvantaged group, to abandoning all forms of group positioning in favor of a purely individualistic position. Clearly, positioning theory allows for a potentially useful deconstruction of the motives associated with membership in a disadvantaged group.

Positioning theory also points to as yet underappreciated possibilities in terms of reconciling intergroup conflict. Once the goal of greater equity for a disadvantaged group has been realized, a number of disadvantaged group members, and indeed advantaged group members, will have lost their mission. People are, of course, reluctant to work towards their own redundancy. However, if emphasis was placed on changing positions not personnel, threats that retard the resolution of intergroup conflict might be avoided.

References

Baron, R. S., Burgess, M. L., & Kao, C. F. (1991). Detecting and labeling prejudice: Do female perpetrators go undetected? *Personality and Social Psychology Bulletin, 17,* 115–123.

Barreto, M., & Ellemers, N. (2005). The perils of political correctness: Men's and women's response to old-fashioned and modern sexist views. *Social Psychology Quarterly, 68,* 75–88.

Brown, R., & Smith, A. (1989). Perceptions of and by minority groups: The case of women in academia. *European Journal of Social Psychology, 19,* 61–75.

Clark, K. B., & Clark, M. P. (1947). Racial identification and preference in negro children. In T. M. Newcomb & E. L. Hartley (Eds.), *Readings in social psychology.* New York, NY: Holt.

Cooper, V. W. (1997). Homophily or the queen bee syndrome: Female evaluation of female leadership. *Small Group Research, 28,* 483–499.

Cowan, G., Neighbors, C., DeLaMoreaux, J., & Behnke, C. (1998). Women's hostility toward women. *Psychology of Women Quaterly, 22,* 267–284.

Crisp, R. J., Stone, C. H., & Hall, N. R. (2006). Recategorization and subgroup identification: Predicting and preventing threats from common ingroup. *Personality and Social Psychology Bulletin, 32,* 230–243.

Crocker, J., & Major, B. (1989). Social stigma and self-esteem: The self-protective properties of stigma. *Psychological Review, 96,* 608–630.

Dawes, A., & Finchilescu, G. (2002). What's changed? The racial orientations of South African adolescents during rapid political change. *Childhood, 9,* 147–165.

Dovidio, J. F., Gaertner, S. L., & Validzic, A. (1998). Intergroup bias: Status, differentiation and common ingroup identity. *Journal of Personality and Social Psychology, 75,* 109–120.

Ellemers, N. (2001). Individual upward mobility and the perceived legitimacy of intergroup relations. In J. T. Jost & B. Major (Eds.), *The psychology of legitimacy.* Cambridge: Cambridge University Press.

Ellemers, N., van den Heuvel, H., de Gilder, D., Maass, A., & Bonvini, A. (2004). The under representation of women in science: Differential commitment or the queen bee syndrome? *British Journal of Social Psychology, 43,* 315–338.

Fajak, A., & Haslam, S. A. (1998). Gender solidarity in hierarchical organizations. *British Journal of Social Psychology, 37,* 73–94.

Gaertner, S. L., & Dovidio, J. F. (2000). *Reducing intergroup bias: The common ingroup identity model.* Philadelphia: The Psychology Press/Taylor & Francis.

Gaertner, S. L., Dovidio, J. F., Anastasio, P. A., Bachman, B. A., & Rust, M. C. (1993). The common ingroup identity model: Recategorization and the reduction of intergroup bias. In W. Stroebe & M. Hewstone (Eds.), *European review of social psychology* (Vol. 2, pp. 247–278). Chichester: Wiley.

Gibson, D. E., & Cordova, D. I. (1999). Women's and men's roles models: The importance of exemplars. In A. J. Murress, F. J. Crosby, & R. J. Ely (Eds.), *Mentoring dilemmas* (pp. 121–142). Mahwah, Erlbaum.

Gonzalez, R., & Brown, R. (2003). Generalization of positive attitude as a function of subgroup and superordinate group identifications in intergroup contact. *European Journal of Social Psychology, 33,* 195–214.

Hewstone, M. (1996). Contact and categorization: Social psychological interventions to change intergroup relations. In C. N. Macrae, C. Stangor, & M. Hewstone (Eds.), Stereotypes and stereotyping (pp. 323–368). London: Guilford.

Hewstone, M., & Brown, R. (1986). Contact is not enough: An intergroup perspective. In M. Hewstone & R. Brown (Eds.), *Contact and conflict in intergroup encounters* (pp. 1–44). Oxford, UK: Blackwell.

Hornsey, M. J., & Hogg, M. A. (2000). Subgroup relations: A comparison of mutual intergroup differentiation models of prejudice reduction. *Personality and Social Psychology Bulletin, 26,* 242–256.

Hornsey, M. J., van Leeuwen, E., & van Santen, W. (2003). Dragging down and Dragging up: Relative group status affects responses to common fate. *Group Dynamics: Theory, Research, and Practice, 7,* 275–288.

Huo, Y. J., Molina, L. E., Sawahata, R., & Deang, J. M. (2005). Leadership and the management of conflicts in diverse groups: Why acknowledging versus neglecting subgroup identity matters. *European Journal of Social Psychology, 35,* 237–254.

Johnson, C., Schaller, M., & Mullen, B. (2000). Social categorization and stereotyping: 'You mean i'm one of "them"?' *British Journal of Social Psychology, 39,* 1–25.

Jost, J. T., & Banaji, M. R. (1994). The role of stereotyping in system-justification and the production of false consciousness. *British Journal of Social Psychology, 33,* 1–27.

Jost, J. T., Banaji, M. R., & Nosek, B. A. (2004). A decade of system justification theory: Accumulated evidence of conscious and unconscious bolstering of the status quo. *Political Psychology, 25,* 881–919.

Jost, J. T., & Burgess, D. (2000). Attitudinal ambivalence and the conflict between group and system justification motives in low status groups. *Personality and Social Psychology Bulletin, 26,* 293–305.

Jost, J. T., Burgess, D., & Mosso, C. O. (2001). Conflicts of legitimation among self, group, and system: The integrative potential of system justification theory. In J. T. Jost & B. Major (Eds.), *The psychology of legitimacy: Emerging perspectives on ideology, justice, and intergroup relations* (pp. 363–388). Cambridge, United Kingdom: Cambridge University Press.

Jost, J. T., & Major, B. (2001). *The psychology of legitimacy: Emerging perspectives on ideology, justice, and intergroup relations.* New York, NY: Cambridge University Press.

Jost, J. T., Pelham, B. W., Sheldon, O., & Ni Sullivan, B. (2003). Social inequality and the reduction of ideological dissonance on behalf of the system: Evidence of enhanced system justification among the disadvantaged. *European Journal of Social Psychology, 33,* 13–36.

Kluegel, J. R., & Smith, E. R. (1986). *Beliefs about inequality: Americans' views of what is and what ought to be.* New York, NY: Aldine de Gruyter.

Martin, R., & Hewstone, M. (2003). Social-influence processes of control and change: Conformity, obedience to authority, and innovation. In M. A. Hogg & J. Cooper (Eds.), *The sage handbook of social psychology* (pp. 347–366). London: Sage.

Mathison, D. L. (1986). Sex differences in the perception of assertiveness among female managers. *Journal of Social Psychology, 126,* 599–606.

Moghaddam, F. M. (1999). Reflexive positioning: culture and private discourse. In R. Harré & L. Van Langenhove (Eds.), *Positioning theory: Moral contexts of intentional actions* (pp. 74–86). Boston: Blackwell.

Sarnoff, I. (1951). Identification with the aggressor: Some personality correlates of anti-Semitism among Jews. *Journal of Personality, 20,* 199–218.

Schmitt, M. T., Ellemers, N., & Branscombe, N. (2003). Perceiving and responding to gender discrimination at work. In S. A. Haslam, D. Van Knippenber, M. J. Platow, & N. Ellemers (Eds.), *Social identity at work: Developing theory of organizational practice* (pp. 277–292). Philadelphia: Psychology Press.

Sherif, M. (1966). *Group conflict and cooperation: Their social psychology.* London: Routledge & Kegan Paul.

Staines, G., Tavris, C., & Jayaratne, T. E. (1974). The queen bee syndrome. *Psychology Today, 7,* 55–60.

Steele, C. M. (1997). A threat in the air: How stereotypes shape the intellectual identities and performance of women and African-Americans. *American Psychologist, 52,* 613–629.

Stephan, W. G., & Stephan, C. W. (1996). *Intergroup relations.* Boulder, CO: Westview Press.

Tajfel, H., & Turner, J. C. (1979). An integrative theory of intergroup conflict. In W. G. Austin & S. Worchel (Eds.), *The social psychology of intergroup relations* (pp. 33–47). Monterey, CA: Brooks/Cole.

Tajfel, H., & Turner, J. C. (1986). The social identity theory of intergroup behavior. In S. Worchel & W. G. Austin (Eds.), *Psychology of intergroup relations.* Chicago: Nelson-Hall.

Tan, S. L., & Moghaddam, F. M. (1999). Positioning in intergroup relations. In R. Harré & L. Van Langenhove (Eds.), *Positioning theory: Moral contexts of intentional actions* (pp. 178–194). Boston: Blackwell.

Taylor, D. M., & McKirnan, D. J. (1984). A five-stage model of intergroup relations. *British Journal of Social Psychology, 23*, 291–300.

Taylor, D. M., & Moghaddam, F. M. (1994). *Theories of intergroup relations: International social psychological perspectives.* Westport, CT: Praeger.

Taylor, D. M., Moghaddam, F. M., & Bellrose, J. (1989). Social comparison in an intergroup context. *Journal of Social Psychology, 129*, 499–515.

Tougas, F., Brown, R., Beaton, A. M., & St-Pierre, L. (1999). Neosexism among women: The role of personally experienced social mobility. *Personality and Social Psychology Bulletin, 25*, 1487–1497.

Turner, J. C., Hogg, M. A., Oakes, P. J., Reicher, S. D., & Wetherell, M. S. (1987). *Rediscovering the social group: A self-categorization theory.* Oxford: Blackwell.

Vaughan, G. M. (1978). Social change and intergroup preferences in New Zealand. *European Journal of Social Psychology, 8*, 297–314.

Vonk, R., & Olde-Monnikhof, M. (1998). Gender subgroups: Intergroup bias within the sexes. *European Journal of Social Psychology, 28*, 37–47.

Wright, S. C. (1997). Ambiguity, social influence, and collective action: Generating collective protest in response to tokenism. *Journal of personality and social psychology, 23*, 1277–1290.

Wright, S. C., & Taylor, D. M. (1998). Responding to tokenism: Individual action in the face of collective injustice. *European Journal of Social Psychology, 28*, 647–667.

Wright, S. C., & Taylor, D. M. (1999). Success under tokenism: Co-option of the newcomer and the prevention of collective protest. *British Journal of Social Psychology, 38*, 369–396.

Wright, S. C., Taylor, D. M., & Moghaddam, F. M. (1990). Responding to membership in a disadvantaged group: From acceptance to collective protest. *Journal of Personality and Social Psychology, 58*, 994–1003.

10
Wheels Within Wheels, or Triangles Within Triangles: Time and Context in Positioning Theory

Tom Bartlett

Introduction

As a discourse analyst, my humble dream is twofold: firstly, to understand language as action, to comprehend exactly what it is people are doing with and through language as they speak; and secondly, to interconnect all levels of discourse, from the rapid dynamics of real-time conversation to the slow rumblings of dominant discourses, the set texts of society. In this paper I will attempt to show how Positioning Theory can combine with discourse analysis towards these ends and how the combination can be applied to conflict analysis and resolution.

We can set out from the notion that discourse is fundamentally action as from an early age we seek empathy, a sense of worth and belonging amongst those with whom we have constant contact, chiefly through our shared discourse patterns. Through discourse we learn to behave according to the norms and practices accepted within our social milieu, in particular by those we love and respect. We learn not only to recognise the various discourse patterns around us and the rights and obligations they entail for different speakers, but also how to use these same discourse patterns ourselves according to the context, how to realise our behaviour through the appropriate language. These recognition and realisation rules (Bernstein 2000:16–18) are internalised and remain the basis of our behaviour, our means of social positioning through discourse. Positioning theory therefore helps us to understand and analyse language as action as it consistently relates individual acts of speaking to the taking up of social positions within context. This often entails drawing on ready-to-hand and familiar narratives that we recognise will achieve a certain effect in a certain setting. As Edwards and Potter (1992) point out, this means that we will not necessarily behave consistently across contexts, as how we react and how we respond are determined by the conjunction of contextual features. In essence, a speaker is not free to take up any position they wish with regard to the evolving storyline; rather, each speaker can only adopt those positions to which they are entitled through their symbolic capital (Bourdieu, 1991) as recognised by those present according to the subject matter and the setting. Moreover, this positioning will only be successful if the speaker is able to realise their social status through the appropriate linguistic means. To put it simply, speakers must use a style of language that makes clear their social standing and this standing must carry currency with the audience in context, as must the various acts they perform. This brings in deeply-rooted structural constraints that are not apparent in the basic positioning triangle and we can thus overlay the basic positioning triangle with these structural constraints to produce a "positioning star of David" (see Figure 10.1)

The relevance of this model will become apparent in the textual analyses that follow as I illustrate how Sam, a Guyanese indigenous leader talking to a conference of environmental scientists, and Gordon, a certificated biologist in a chinwag with me, use very different linguistic means to realise similar positionings as a function of their vastly different symbolic capitals in context. Conversely, we will also see how an attempted positioning by a powerful speaker was misinterpreted as a result of conflicting perceptions of the structural context, and hence the speaker's positioning, by her audience.

Turning to the different levels of discourse, I often get the feeling that analysts treat casual conversation, political speeches and ideological texts as though the role of language and the linking between language and society was different in each case. Some go as far as to make a distinction between the capital-D ideological Discourses that imbue society and small-d everyday discourse as talk. In response to this, I hope to show how Positioning Theory can be used to analyse all levels of discourse, highlighting the fact that the different levels employ the same basic mechanisms and vary only in the timescales over which they operate: in terms of the enduring social positions constructed and contested, the scope of the storyline invoked, and the scale and speed of each individual discourse act. Moreover, small-time discourse is spoken and interpreted in the shadow of the larger ideological Discourses which are, in turn, composed over time out of everyday discourse, with each short-term positioning triangle feeding into

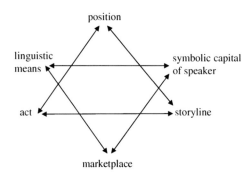

FIGURE 10.1. Structural constraints on positioning.

the longer term storyline (compare this with Rothbart and Bartlett's axiological model, this volume). Bearing in mind that each act of positioning occurs in a unique context, we have to conclude that positioning over different timescales implies differences of contextual constraints and affordances, and things become complex and messy when we consider that social actors may be operating over different timescales, and hence operating according to the strictures of different positioning triangles, simultaneously. This may lead to behaviour that is to say the least paradoxical and often contradictory when viewed through the lens of a single timescale. For example, we will see in one of the analyses that follow how Walter, a community leader, renounces control over a short-term situation as a means to strengthening his leadership within the wider cultural context.

In the remainder of the paper I will use positioning theory, as outlined here, to analyse various communicative events within crosscultural development discourse between the Makushi Amerindian population of Guyana, the national Government (GOG) and International Organisations (Bartlett 2001; 2003; 2004; 2005; 2006). In particular I consider the consequences of one small act that appears to have different meanings for different participants as a result of relatively bound sociostructural positionings maintained by higher level discourses that provide the macro and meso contexts for this micro act, so highlighting the necessary interplay between analyses of different levels of action. The focal event of the paper takes place in a meeting of the North Rupununi District Development Board (NRDDB), a community-based development organisation set up against a backdrop of the ambiguous relationship between the Amerindian populations on the savannahs and the highly-centralised power structures of Guyana (see Bartlett, 2003). More recently, social scientists from the Iwokrama International Programme for Rainforest Conservation and Development (Iwokrama) have been involved in a more participatory approach to development issues which saw the sustainability of the forest resources and the social sustainability of the local communities as inextricably linked. The following analyses bring out some of the tensions within this three-way interaction and the complex positioning responses of the various actors and my aim is to suggest that, in terms of conflict analysis and resolution, analysing actions from multiple perspectives, and hence complexifying the picture rather than idealising and reifying it, will lead to a better understanding of the context and an ability to act appropriately within it. There is a range of analytical tools to be deployed in describing and interpreting discursive acts and no one of these methods, nor even their combination, can provide a complete and coherent description and understanding of the complexities of contextualised social action. There is no silver-bullet solution to neatly categorised conflicts; rather, through multiple perspectives we can develop a feel for the game, a *sens pratique* (Bourdieu, 1990), that informs our involvement according to different timescales and the contextual variables involved: the symbolic capital at play in the social marketplace and the means of realising this capital effectively.

The Amerindian Act and the NRDDB Constitution

In the Amerindian Act of 1976, the Government of Guyana sets out in legal terms the framework for centralised control over Amerindian affairs and the scope of Amerindian self-determination within the larger state – in other words, it positions both sets of players and the relationship between them in terms of mutual rights and obligations. However, as suggested by the recursivity of the positioning triangle, the construction of this position is a reaction to an assumed contextual storyline, the interpretation of which becomes, in turn, an element of the evolving storyline. As well as constructing a framework for the legal interaction between the two groups, therefore, the Act also construes a particular version of Guyanese sociocultural reality which, as is the nature of such texts, lies somewhere between a reified past and an idealised future (see Bartlett, 2005 for fuller analyses of these texts). In comparison to real-time, dynamic activities, the Amerindian Act is a monolith, an extremely deliberative yet unresponsive statement of hypothetical intent, a yardstick against which real-time action can be measured. We can consider such formulaic statements of group purpose as ideological ideology: calculated representations of the mythical unity underlying a coherent and cohesive social order (roughly Foucault's conception of ideologies), stated in the essentialist and politically motivated language of the manifesto (ideology in the more common, negative sense of partisan politics). While such deliberative and publicly displayed texts are by nature largely static, acting as a background to more rapid, lower-level actions, they are also in and of themselves moves within a slow but ongoing dialogue of ideology and counter-ideology. The 2001 Constitution of the NRDDB will be analysed as just such an ideological response to the Amerindian Act; and it is the interplay of the two, the tension between them rather than the sum of their parts, that provides the contextual backdrop without which lower-level discourse/action cannot be fully understood.

Given the nature of the Amerindian Act and NRDDB Constitution as relatively undynamic statements realised "out of time" as the ideological background to real-time activity, we can analyse them as single acts, using quantitative linguistic methods to sketch a bare-bones model of the set of relations constructed and construed within each text, identifying and quantifying key grammatical roles ascribed to different participants in terms of the level and type of social agency they entail. The roles I focus on (after Halliday, 1994) are Actor, Patient,

TABLE 10.1. Relating participant roles to a typology of empowerment.

Initiator	Actor	Beneficiary	Comparable power relationship
	GOG/NGO	Amerindians	paternalism
Amerindians	GOG/NGO		advocacy
GOG/NGO	Amerindians		cooptation
Amerindians	Amerindians		transformation

Beneficiary and my own concept of Initiator. The conjunction of the different grammatical roles within a single process, the parts the different groups are assigned in the action, can be labelled in terms of more abstract relations between dominant and dominated group, as in Table 10.1 (Bartlett, 2005 after Cameron et al. 1992):

According to this schema, when outside agents act unbidden on behalf of a dominated group, there is a relationship of paternalism; where the dominated group initiates an action but the dominant group carries it out, we have advocacy; where the dominant group initiates an action but the dominated group carries it out, we have cooptation; and only where the dominated group both decides upon and carries out its own actions do we have a relationship of transformation. A quantitative comparison of grammatical agency as ascribed to the two groups within the Amerindian Act and the NRDDB Constitution reveals the pattern in Table 10.2, below.

As this table reveals, the rights and obligations that GOG constructs for itself are overwhelmingly protectionist: either directly paternalist, in providing for the Amerindians' needs (as GOG perceives them), or indirectly, in setting out their agenda for them. In contrast, the NRDDB Constitution constructs a relationship between the local population and the state that is overwhelmingly transformative, with advocacy by more powerful groups a necessary adjunct but paternalism and cooptation virtually invisible. Turning briefly to the relations between the two groups as construed through the Act's recalibration of an ongoing storyline, the first thing to note is that, by its very title, "The Amerindian Act of Guyana" defines the six distinct ethnicities it covers in essentially racial terms, undifferentiated amongst themselves yet inherently distinct from the rest of the population. And while several further sections construe the Amerindians as racially pure, these are tempered by implicit construals of corruptibility and the need for Government protection. For example, Paragraph 40f gives the Minister the right to make regulations "prohibiting any rites and customs which, in the opinion of the Minister, are injurious to the welfare of Amerindians". And in providing specific laws prohibiting the sale of alcohol to Amerindians (Paragraph 37), regulating the employment of Amerindians specifically as labourers (Part VII), and dealing with any non-Amerindian who "entices away or cohabits with the wife of any Amerindian" (Paragraph 41), there is further construal of the Amerindian population as debauched, sexually

TABLE 10.2. Power relations between GOG and Amerindians as constructed in the 2001 NRDDB Constitution.

	Amerindian act	NRDDB Constitution
Paternalism	30 (41.1%)	1 (3.7%)
Advocacy	1 (1.4%)	7 (25.9%)
Cooptation	39 (53.4%)	2 (7.4%)
Transformation	3 (4.1%)	17 (63%)
Total	73 (100%)	27 (100%)

Positions:

Amerindian rights to a level of autonomy;

Nation states right to constrain this;

GOGs obligation/right as protector.

Acts:	Storyline:
Amerindian Act as	Amerindian as precolonial soul and postcolonial
post-colonial manifesto.	yardstick; corrupted version of racial purity.

POSITIONING TRIANGLE 10.1. The Amerindian Act and post-colonialism.

fickle and incapable of non-manual work. In contrast, the NRDDB Constitution states that the Board's role within community development is to "facilitate and encourage...development initiatives", "to ensure that such initiatives provide benefits for and serve the interests of its constituent communities" and to "monitor the effects of the Iwokrama Programme and all other regional, national and international programmes" (emphasis in original). To summarise, the NRDDB Constitution can be said to promote the conditions for community-based development within the North Rupununi, contributing its part within a modern and diverse Guyanese entity – a position of cultural nationalism (May 2001:78), whereby minority groups focus on the moral regeneration of the community while developing their culture through processes of hybridisation, assimilation and accommodation. In contrast, the Amerindian Act construes the indigenous groups within Guyana as racially and geographically distinct from the mainstream, symbols of Guyana's precolonial past yet the passive recipients of government care and protection – a position of post-colonialism. The positions within the two documents are represented in Positioning Triangles 10.1 and 10.2.

Positions:

Amerindian rights to autonomy;

Amerindian obligations towards nation state.

Acts:	Storyline:
NRDDB Constitution as	Amerindian as developing traditions
cultural nationalist manifesto.	to meet social, political and scientific
	ends.

POSITIONING TRIANGLE 10.2. The NRDDB Constitution and cultural nationalism.

It is the tension between these two idealist positions that forms the backdrop for lower-level discourses, not only between the NRDDB and GOG, but also between the NRDDB and other any other NGOs, such as Iwokrama, whose participation, approved and monitored by GOG, cannot but become embedded within the complex storyline which these documents both reflect and rewrite.

Iwokrama and Makushi Narratives

The following texts represent a move away from the relatively explicit ideological ideology of the Amerindian Act and the NRDDB Constitution towards what I have elsewhere called implicit ideology (Bartlett, 2004, 2006), but would now prefer to call narrative ideology: the relatively coherent worldview of speakers as construed, sometimes unwittingly, through stretches of discourse. Text 1, below, comes from an interview I carried out with Gordon, senior research scientist at Iwokrama, and Text 2 provides extracts from a speech by Sam, a leader of the NRDDB, to the Iwokrama-sponsored Conference on Critical Issues in the Conservation and Sustainable and Equitable Use of Wildlife in the Guiana Shield.

Text 1. Gordon (Iwokrama Offices 24/4/01):

This is one of the (problems) about what's going on with Iwokrama the other day, you were there, at the meeting, when you know Uncle Henry saying "Oh, Iwokrama's so advanced, they've got so much more information about what's going on in Iwokrama forest," and I'm sitting there like I'm not, "Excuse me, but they don't know jack shit about the Iwokrama forest, in fact you know more about the forest than they do, but you also know much more about the North Rupununi, and in fact we've assimilated a lot of this information already. And we can write it down anytime, but, you know, you've got maps, you've got different things, you know where all the stuff is, you know everything [...] I mean you've got people coming in and doing surveys of parrots and macaws using methods that are unintelligible, cannot be, well, from the scientific perspective they're in fact useless, they're all gobbledygook [...] So where does this number come from? You might as well have pulled it out of your arse. However, nobody's going to ask that, because this is sci:entist did it. The authority is there because the Government here agrees with the scientists, because they know science is good. Now, if Uncle Henry comes along and says "Excuse me, but I think that you should harvest twenty-five birds a year" and doesn't want to explain exactly why they think that, or if they did try and explain it, it would completely out of the books, it would be relevant to this thing, but it wouldn't be accepted. And that's what's wrong. Because the twenty-five's probably much better than the middle of the – the effective number that's extracted from this thing with a model and a piece of shit here and a piece of crap there, 'cause that's all irrelevant.

This text can be analysed at three distinct levels which, as emphasised above, must be carefully distinguished and initially kept apart, to be brought together after individual analyses to provide a richer picture of discourse action in this context. Firstly, I will look at this text in terms of the narrative it relates and try

TABLE 10.3. Thread of Gordon's narrative on knowledge and power from Text 1 lines 1–10.

Actor	Process	Complement
Iwokrama	know	jack-shit about the Iwokrama forest
you (Uncle Henry/		
Makushi)	know	more (than Iwokrama) about the forest
	know	more about the North Rupununi
	have assimilated	a lot of information
we (Iwokrama)	can write	information
you (Makushi)	know	(information)
	have	maps and different things
	know	where all the stuff is, everything
people (scientists)	do surveys	
(imported) methods	are	unintelligible, useless, gobbledygook

to outline the positioning triangle that is being narrated within it. It is extremely important to remember that the storyline, positions and acts that Gordon narrates are quite distinct from the storyline that he is acting within and the position that he is enacting in real time through the act of telling his narrative. That will be my third layer of analysis; in between I shall outline a few of the tensions between Gordon's narrative and the ideological ideology of Iwokrama as embedded within the wider ideologies at play in the Guyanese and development contexts.

Probably the easiest place to begin analysing narratives is with the characters, events and relations within them, the storyline. Following Martin (1992), this involves finding various ideational threads within a text, following their development, and interrelating them. For example, in Gordon's interview we could say that the main narrative thread is the history of knowledge relations between the Makushi population, outside scientists and GOG, as shown in Table 10.3, a schematic representation of the first 10 lines of Text 1.

Pulling the various threads together, Gordon's narrated storyline has the overall theme that there is a history of imported knowledge being accepted by GOG despite its lack of accuracy and validation and despite the existence of superior knowledge within the communities. The history of relations between the Makushi, GOG and outside "experts" has, further, led to the Makushi's acceptance of this state of affairs and the downgrading of their own knowledge. This has come about because of the imbalance of rights and obligations (as narrated by Gordon), of each party's position with respect to knowledge and power, the gist of which is captured in the following extract:

However, nobody's going to ask that, because this is sci:entist did it. The authority is there because the Government (here) agrees with the scientists, because they know science is good. Now, if Uncle Fred comes along and says "Excuse me, but I think that you should harvest twenty-five birds a year," and doesn't want to explain exactly why they think that, or if they did try and explain it, it would completely (out of) the books, it would be relevant to this thing, but it wouldn't be accepted.

Implicit in Gordon's narrative is the idea that the existing problematic state of affairs can only be remedied by a realignment of these rights and obligations in favour of Makushi knowledge. In these terms, Gordon's interview is in fact a double narrative, a tale of positions as they currently exist and as they could and should be, and bridging the two states of affairs is the narrated (or at least implicit) act that will remedy matters: the recognition and acceptance of traditional ecological knowledge (TEK) by modern scientists and GOG. The positions within Gordon's narrative are roughly as in Positioning Triangle 10.3, below.

This is not to impute either accuracy or intention to Gordon, we are simply working within his narrative world; only once this analysis is complete can we move to consider the role of the narrative as an act at a higher level, asking why he (re)produced this narrative in this form at this time. However, it is not always clear in narratives such as these whether the speaker is referring to things as they perceive them to be (as part of the narrative) or stating how they should be (an act in itself at a higher level), and so we see how different levels of action are overlapping rather than discrete.

From the point of view of ideological ideology, we can contrast Gordon's narrative with the Amerindian Act, on one hand, and Iwokrama's agenda as it is dispersed over various sites on the other. This reveals several tensions across and between levels. For instance, Gordon's full-frontal real-time assault contrasts with both the negativity of the Amerindian Act and the more restrained approach of official Iwokrama literature and the frequent suggestion in official statements that Iwokrama, like GOG, maintains ultimate control, as in their Community Outreach Programme:

Iwokrama will continue to facilitate workshops on wildlife in the North Rupununi as requested by the NRDDB once the workshop subjects are considered to be consistent with the mission of Iwokrama
NRDDB and Iwokrama 1999:30

Positions:

GOG's right to choose knowledge source;

Historic/mythical power of imported knowledge;

GOGs obligation to choose an accurate and sustainable

method; Local community's right to own knowledge

system (TEK).

Acts:	**Storyline:**
GOG should switch to superior TEK;	Superior TEK; History of imposition
Makushi should recognise worth of	of imported knowledge; community
their own knowledge.	downgrading of own knowledge.

POSITIONING TRIANGLE 10.3. TEK. vs imported knowledge as narrated by Gordon.

Similarly, when I asked about Iwokrama's consultative processes, one local leader responded: "Well, they are working on that, I can see they are working hard towards it, but still like I said, I still think Iwokrama is somehow like trying to bend people towards their agenda." Gordon's narrative could thus be interpreted as protesting too much, overstating the importance of community knowledge as part of a higher level conflict with the dominant scientific and political discourses. Gordon's narrative act can thus be seen as embedded within the wider ideological issues, and could be represented as in Positioning Triangle 10.4, below.

And what is the storyline within which this narrative is performed as an act in its own right? This is the history of Gordon's and my relationship and the place of this interview in my fieldwork. The most striking features in this respect is the narrative's sense of almost exaggerated informality. While the narrative storyline of the failings of "expert scientists" and GOG is damning enough, the presentation of these ideas through language that is at once non-technical and extremely heightened in evaluative terms creates a sense of almost slapstick incompetence: scientists are not just poorly informed and mistaken in their research, they "don't know jack shit" and so produce "gobbledygook" which they "may as well have pulled out of (their) arse". This tone is intensified through present tense verbs and reported speech, making the narrative more immediate, more anecdotal, as with "and I'm sitting there like I'm not, 'Excuse me, but they don't know jack shit about Iwokrama'...". Swearing and irony almost swamp the narrative: as well as "jackshit" we have "bloody", "arse", "shit" and "crap" in this short extract alone, while irony is most obvious in the lengthened vowel of "this sci:ientist did it", and runs on into "the Government here agrees with the scientists, because they know science is good." This discursive style is adopted as a response to our relationship and the informal context of our discussion: we were both critics of an overtly "scientific" approach to the Iwokrama forest and

Positions:

Rights of Iwokrama as certified scientists;

Rights of community as specialists in TEK (within Iwokrama

parameters); Obligation of Iwokrama as arbiter between TEK and

GOG ideology.

Acts:	**Storyline:**
Undermine imported knowledge;	Excessively paternalistic attitude of
Overpromote TEK.	GOG; GOG/scientific disdain for
	TEK.

POSITIONING TRIANGLE 10.4. Gordon's interview as an embedded act at the ideological level.

the authoritarianism of GOG and both keen to be seen as accepted by the local community. We were also researchers and wanted our work to be taken seriously. Against this storyline Gordon's narrative serves to set us up (at least for the moment) as near equals, in terms of both status and knowledge (in this area) and so able to converse in a ribald manner, breaking down the potential barriers arising from Gordon's high position in Iwokrama compared with my status as research student and his vastly superior knowledge of both the science involved and the Guyanese context in general. Within this general relationship, we are further positioned as being painfully aware of the idiocies of some scientists and GOG attitudes, so aware that these can be taken for granted and presented simply through irony. These positions then serve to set Gordon up as, on one hand, a "good guy", knowledgeable yet down to earth, but also as a critic of GOG policy towards science, a right he has achieved, in my eyes at least, as audience, through both his knowledge as a certificated scientist and his acquaintance with the local communities on both a social and scientific level. Of importance here is how Gordon sets about creating this position through a constant downplaying of all that represents the very formal science in which he is certificated – a luxury he is afforded by that very certification. This is a luxury not open to Sam who, as we shall see below, is not averse to irony and informality but is at pains to create for himself a position of authority through speech acts that emphasise his knowledge and sobriety. Gordon's positioning at this level can thus be captured in Positioning Triangle 10.5.

Showing many similarities with Gordon's text in terms of theme, the following extracts from a presentation made to the Guiana Shield Conference by Sam, then Chairman of the NRDDB, show important contrasts at different levels. These are a result of the very different contexts within which the texts were produced and the social relations they contained. Whereas Gordon was a certificated scientist in an important position able to downplay his rights and knowledge, Sam is an uncertificated community elder speaking in front of professional

Positions:

Gordon as down to earth critic of "science";

Tom as sparring partner.

Acts:	Storyline:
Informal and mocking	Gordon's close relations to community;
style of interview.	and cynicism towards "science"; Tom's
	critical research agenda.

POSITIONING TRIANGLE 10.5. Gordon's interview as an interpersonal act of real-time discourse.

scientists working on sustainable development throughout the region, as well as representatives from various Amerindian groups in Guyana.

Text 2. Sam (Guiana Shield Conference 4–8/12/00):

Within communities there is much knowledge and many skills that can be applied to effectively manage natural resources. This knowledge can be the basis for developing future sustainable businesses based on natural resources. Some resources such as wildlife or ecotourism, that is like vines for handicrafts, honey, cashew, peanuts, dried fruits and others to be developed immediately. Other resources could be developed through partnership with NGOs and government agencies that help gather information needed to develop sustainable businesses. In this context it is important not to reinvent the wheel, but to learn from experiences of others […] Sometimes we wonder why Guyana as a whole country have not like clicked on that opportunity […] and we still are so economically stagnated […]The major strength of the communities lies in our knowledge of the area that we live in. We feel strongly that this knowledge is equal to scientific knowledge and should be recognised as extremely important […] And this brings to mind an example of what took place in Iwokrama, and what the satellite was showing in the images in the Iwokrama area is that a certain area had no sort of erm…greenheart, it showed like scrubby forest and so on. Our boys who work with Iwokrama was able to prove the satellite wrong, because when they went there, there were the biggest set, or the largest sizes of greenheart in the same area the satellite was telling you something else. So there is where the balance of knowledge came in […] It is our hope that NGOs such as Iwokrama, UNDP, CIDA, etc, etc, would be able to work directly with us in programmes that allow us and the NGOs to learn by doing rather than separating the theory from practice.

Within Sam's narrative we hear a similar tale to that told by Gordon with regard to the history of intellectual relations between the local communities and mainstream science. Though the subject matter is approached rather differently, we are still given the picture of the Guyanese government and certificated scientists failing to recognise TEK despite its superiority in certain areas. In Sam's narrative this is set against a backdrop of economic stagnation and the need for the two groups to collaborate to lift the country out of this situation. In terms of (projected) rights and obligations, this emphasis on building on existing community traditions and expertise represents both community choice and community action, with outside agencies merely "information gathering", providing "assistance" and "facilitating". The positioning within Sam's narrative is, then, something like Positioning Triangle 10.6.

This is very close to the position of the NRDDB Constitution in setting out a model of development within which traditional methods are modernised through contact with outside science yet remain grounded in the community and traditional knowledge (without "reinventing the wheel", in other words). At the level of ideological ideology, then, we can see how Sam's talk is embedded within the political as a reaction to the ideology of the Amerindian Act and also a contribution to the ongoing debate within the certificated scientific community regarding the relationship between TEK and imported science. Positioning Triangle 10.7, representing Sam's contribution within the context of

Positions:

Makushi knowledge of area (TEK); Imported knowledge

of marketing and western science; Limitations of western science;

Makushi right to recognition of and reward for TEK; Makushi

right to assistance; Makushi obligation to share TEK.

Acts:	**Storyline:**
GOG to take TEK seriously;	Guyana as economically stagnant despite resources;
Makushi/GOG/science partnership	Need for development; respect for TEK on one side,
of expertises; Praxis.	secrecy on the other; Successes of TEK over/in
	collaboration with imported science.

POSITIONING TRIANGLE 10.6. The narrative ideology of Sam's presentation.

ideological ideology, reaffirms some of the key themes in Gordon's interview, but with important differences.

Sam's narrative resembles Gordon's as an attempt to challenge the hegemony of imported scientific knowledge and authority, with both speakers relating first-hand examples of the failings of imported knowledge; however, he draws upon very different linguistic means to enact his discourse as face-to-face practice. While Gordon was able to paint his picture through overt mockery of the self-importance of mainstream science, a strategy made possible by his own position within that field and by the informal nature of his interview with me, Sam's position as an uncertificated speaker at a scientific conference prompts him to make his point subtly and with respect, through parables and anecdotes emphasising the complementarities between the two knowledge systems. This difference in attitude is also reflected in the language Sam uses, which is towards the technical end of the scale with phrases such as "sustainable business", "venture out into new products" and "economically stagnated", while the overall tone is markedly more formal than Gordon's: there are no swear words and few emphatic or exaggerated terms, but rather a sobriety that resonates with

Positions:

Rights of Iwokrama as certified scientists;

Rights of community as specialists in TEK;

Obligations of each to the other as collaborators.

Acts:	**Storyline:**
Point out limitations of imported knowledge;	Excessively paternalistic attitude of
Promote TEK.	scientific community.

POSITIONING TRIANGLE 10.7. Sam's interview as an embedded act at the ideological level.

Positions:

Sam as sober and knowledgeable;

Sam's right to contribute to conference;

Community elders as worthy collaborators.

Acts:	**Storyline:**
Account of complementarities of	Hegemony of imported science;
TEK and imported science;	Recontextualisation of TEK;
Contrast of current and desired states;	Conference as ongoing debate;
Call for authorities to share rewards of	Novelty of contribution to scientific
certificated knowledge;	conference from community
Call for communities to share benefits of TEK.	representatives.

POSITIONING TRIANGLE 10.8. Sam's presentation as an interpersonal act of real-time discourse.

the presentation of the subject matter and the semi-technical language. Tailoring his discourse to suit his audience, Sam comes across as a worthy collaborator who, as a respected member of the local communities, can also contribute to the joint effort of sustainable development by exhorting the communities to action, specifically through the sharing of their knowledge. Positioning Triangle 10.8 represents Sam's presentation as a real-time discourse act.

Texts 1 and 2 have shown that the positioning triangle within and upon which a speaker operates is constrained by both relatively stable sociocultural constructs such as race and education and contextual factors such as setting and audience. In the following example, examining discourse primarily at the microlevel of practical ideology, or real-time interaction, we see how these external factors can effect interpersonal positioning to such an extent that certain positions are not open to some speakers and efforts to position themselves in these ways can lead to serious misunderstanding.

Practical Ideology in Iwokrama-NRDDB Interaction

Text 3 comes from a workshop on resource management systems facilitated by Iwokrama at the request of the NRDDB. The purpose of the workshop was to relinquish some of Iwokrama's control over the development process and to promote local knowledge and management systems. In this section I want to focus on how long-term ideological debates over issues such as autonomy, paternalism and development, as illustrated in the previous analyses, are internalised within real-time discourse as tensions between narrative storylines and struggles over speakers' rights and obligations. In the extract we will look at, Walter, a community elder, is to take over the role of workshop leader/facilitator from the Iwokrama representatives. This is an important process given the storyline of outside domination that characterises such an exercise, from missionaries to governments and from teachers to development organisations. The importance of the event as an exercise in empowering the community is not lost on Walter, who talks of "identifying what we could do right away...what we can...what we are capable of doing...by ourself" and states that "Sara is not going to do it for us anymore...we've got to do it for ourselves." And for their part, Iwokrama have been making great strides in promoting an egalitarian discourse. Yet the following analysis suggests that the relatively permanent positions of the different protagonists within the wider sociopolitical structure are extremely durable and will resist negotiation and recalibration at the level of real-time micropositioning. Specifically, in the following text we apparently see how historical sociocultural and ethnic structures affect the interpretation of real-time acts so as to waylay the course of the workshop as a real-time event, with Walter's short-term positioning changing from control over the proceedings, in a role akin to chair, to the seemingly less prestigious role of contributing from the floor. Showing the complexities of triangles within triangles, however, this change can be analysed as a move in the maintenance of his position within a longer storyline. The first extract sees Walter in control of proceedings (for a fuller presentation and analysis see Bartlett, 2003):

W: It would be much easier if we have this, the well down there with a nice reservoir at that point. You have the pipes going all around and so forth. ((muttering)) (6s)

N: If you get this, the fish would take advantage of the situation and break free. And it would meet...what would be the expectations of government, which is to bring what more water we can into close reach of, within close proximity of members of the community. (11s)

W: Rainwater fresh at the home, is that what we saying? [...] Remember we talk about this here, right? Yesterday, the tank and the pipes going down and then getting taps going into every house; probably we get showers and flush toilets and so forth. Right? (14s)

The extract finishes with a long silence, a minor problem that becomes unintentionally and unpredictable exacerbated when Sara makes the following seemingly innocuous enquiry, following up on Walter telling her in private before the workshop that he was not feeling 100 per cent:

S: Walter, you managing okay? (18s) It's extra [...] Okay, we can do the first one in a minute, and then you can see that...

N: The thing with Guywa is Guywa adjust the whole situation, you know? (48s) ((muttering))

S: A'right...What is it?..No, Vanessa, you're not off the hook. Come back. (9s)

W: We're talking about the current fix..well..there

N: This thing got more detail now there than then.

> S: Do you want to come closer together and just sit among yourselves and do your own writing? In that small group rather than using this classroom style? (5s) Walter? You're not feeling so good, huh? CAN SOMEBODY...? Do you, do you want to sit and rest and have somebody else to do this?
>
> W: D'you want something?
>
> N: That'll do nicely.
>
> W: You want to say something?(7s)
>
> S: All right, if everybody sit together, Walter's not feeling so well. If we sit together maybe it would make it easier. Rather than standing up in front of everybody.

In this section Sara expresses overt concern for Walter and attempts to rearrange the format and setting to make life easier for him. However, although this intervention is framed in terms of Walter's plight, he has neither overtly expressed his ill ease at this point nor suggested a change in format; and Sara's use of "all right" sounds suspiciously like someone retaking control of a process that has gone a little awry. This rather high-handed though understandable behaviour effects the remainder of the sessions as Walter gradually reverts to a position of contributing from the floor, ceding the lead role to Sara, as illustrated in the following extract:

> S: Because drinking water is such a straightforward thing, these two collapse into one basically. I mean 'cause it's not like you're talking about logging or cutting down trees to do agriculture, right? So 1 and 2 would...
>
> N: Less time taken to.. for your water.
>
> S: Yeah. 1 and 2. Less time taken to acquire (our) water. So, less labour, right? (14s)
>
> S: Mm-hmm. Anything else? (6s)
>
> W: Encourage agr..kitchen gardens.
>
> S: Encourage agriculture, right? (20s) Anything else?
>
> W: Is it okay that hoping they erm..a flush toilet system?

It is very clear here (and even more so in the full transcript) that Sara has been repositioned as in control of the workshop, unconsciously on her part and abetted by the tacit repositioning of the Makushi elders. She reintroduces the activity in hand, encourages participation from the floor and suggests ways of saving time by condensing tasks, while Walter's "Is it okay...?" demonstrates how far he has formally ceded control. So, while this section works successfully in terms of facilitator-floor interaction, this success is achieved at a cost, as it is clearly now Sara that is back in control. In fact, Walter explained to me later in conversation that he had been aware that Sara was taking over but that he was caught between facilitating and contributing from the floor and, feeling that the non-traditional format did not allow him to combine these roles, he was not too unhappy at Sara resuming the facilitator role. But what caused this change in control over and

Positions:

Walter's rights as facilitator ;

Sara's obligations as co-worker.

Acts:	**Storyline:**
Question how Walter is feeling	Collaborative and egalitarian to
to show concern.	discourse relations between
	Iwokrama and NRDDB.

POSITIONING TRIANGLE 10.9. Sara's intended real-time positioning?

contribution to the workshop? It seems to me that the whole process stemmed from a misunderstanding of Sara's act in the second extract and so also the positioning it instantiated and storyline it evoked. From Sara's point of view her act was nothing more than as set out in Positioning Triangle 10.9.

From Walter's point of view, however, and possibly that of the majority of the participants, Sara's act seemed to be the outcome of very different positioning, as in Positioning Triangle 10.10. This triangle represent not the local perception of events, but a possible local perception of Sara's perception of events and therefore how they interpret her motives and how they respond to this.

This alternative understanding is, in part, caused by the long-term social structures, both in Guyana and the development paradigm in general, in which the discourse is embedded. The same role relations that allow Gordon to joke and mock because of his certificated authority, while Sam has to play it straight and formal, in this instance severely constrain the meaning potential open to Sara and lead to misunderstanding when these constraints are pushed. And once the initial misunderstanding occurs (and goes unnoticed) older traditions than Iwokrama's egalitarianism take over the proceedings. In response, Walter falls back on a role with which he feels more comfortable: being a prominent contributor from the floor. This is a role akin to that of elders within the more open discourse systems of the local Makushi population, held after sports and church and with a far less

Positions:

Sara/Iwokrama as leaders; Walter as trainee;

Iwokrama's right to lead the process;

Community obligation to listen.

Acts:	**Storyline:**
Sara retakes control over the proceedings by	Iwokrama expert scientists teaching
questioning Walter's ability and speaking for him.	new knowledge to Amerindians.

POSITIONING TRIANGLE 10.10. Local interpretation of Sara's intended real-time positioning?

clearly demarcated boundary between floor and chair. Viewed in these terms, Walter's move to the floor is not so much a volte face, contradiction or "retreat" from his earlier overt position of showing the capabilities of the local community within the imported discourse paradigm as it is a recourse to an alternative medium through which he can instantiate his community-based knowledge and authority, a retrenchment that allows him to guide the proceedings as best he can given the unintentional – though seemingly unavoidable – realignment of positions.

Discussion: Discourse, Positioning Theory and Conflict Analysis

The above discussion and analyses relate to conflict analysis and resolution with regard to analysis and intervention. In terms of analysis, what I have hoped to demonstrated through the variety of methods used to look at texts produced in different circumstances and their functions at different levels of action, is that there is no single correct analytical method and that there is no neat characterisation of interrelations between the NRDDB, GOG and Iwokrama. Each of the analyses brings out particular facets of these relationships, facets which may well be complex in themselves and become far more complex when considered together. While this does not allow us to draw a coherent picture, it does allow us a way into the big picture, an understanding of the general drift of events, often through analysis of the minutest details as the protagonists write straight in crooked lines. Instead of a neat synopsis of relations between these participants, then, we approach something closer to a vague understanding of what is going on, a "feel for the game" in Bourdieu's (1990) terms, a combination of heuristics and hermeneutics, an appreciation of the different storylines the different protagonists adhere to, and why, and the different narratives they latch onto and develop at different levels of action within such perceived contexts. In terms of intervention, providing alternative discourses within a conflict situation is not just a matter of providing new storylines, as the telling of these stories must be carried out in the appropriate narrative style by those with the appropriate symbolic capital to sway their audience in the particular context (see Rothbart and Bartlett this volume). Timescales are also important, and short-term goals must be considered within the context of longer-term strategies and positions. This approach would favour a topology of discursive activity, where different fora provide different marketplaces that allow for a variety of positions and narratives over and across levels of action.

As those opposed to analysing intention keep reminding us, we can never enter the minds of our subjects; but we do have the tools to outline the different positions they construe and construct through their discourse and to relate these to the different means at their disposal as a function of the sociocultural structures in which they operate. This, however, raises the question of the researcher's position as an outsider looking into an alien culture, the meanings and functions of which are refracted in new ways when viewed from within the researcher's own cultural storylines. But this is really the same point: there is no one correct, full or even best interpretation of events, each understanding serves its own purpose in context, as part of a storyline that engenders specific roles and contextualises further action. This does not mean that anything goes, and researchers have a duty to consider the repercussions of their own distinctive positioning and to discuss their understandings with the local community – bearing in mind, however, that the community members' own understandings are also situated, and that their responses to researchers' understandings are also discourses, further motivated positionings intertwined at many levels with the other discourses from the casual conversations to ideological documents that make up the sociohistorical context in which we all act. At best we learn to avoid reification and idealisation, developing an understanding of the complexities of social positioning while understanding that we can never see the whole picture, though we might begin to feel it and to act strategically and, over time, intuitively within it.

References

Bartlett, T. (2001). Use the road: The appropriacy of appropriation. *Language and Intercultural Communication, 1*(1), 21–39.

Bartlett, T. (2003). *The transgressions of wise men: Structure, tension and agency in intercultural development discourse.* University of Edinburgh: Unpublished Ph.D. Thesis.

Bartlett, T. (2004). Genres of the third space: The communities strike back. *Language and Intercultural Communication, 4*(3), 134–158.

Bartlett, T. (2005). Amerindian development in Guyana: Legal documents as background to discourse practice. *Discourse and Society, 16*(3), 341–364.

Bartlett, T. (2006). Linguistics and Positioning Theory within Conflict Analysis and Resolution: Work in Progress. *Social Justice: Anthropology, Human Rights and Peace, 6(1):* 113–133.

Bernstein, B. (2000). *Pedagogy, symbolic control and identity: Theory, research, critique.* Lanham, Boulder, New York and Oxford: Rowman and Littlefield.

Bourdieu, P. (1990). *The logic of practice.* Cambridge: Polity Press.

Bourdieu, P. (1991). *Language and symbolic power.* Cambridge: Polity Press.

Cameron, Deborah, Elizabeth Frazer, Penelope Harvey, M.B.H. Rampton & Kay Richardson. (1992). Introduction to *Researching Language: Issues of Power and Method.* London: Routledge.

Edwards, D. & J. Potter. (1992). *Discursive Psychology.* London: Sage.

Resolution: Work in Progress. *Social Justice: Anthropology, Human Rights and Peace, 6(1):* 113–133.

Halliday, M. A. K. (1994 2nd Edition). *An introduction to functional grammar.* London: Arnold.

Martin, J. R. (1992). *English text: System and structure.* Philadelphia and Amsterdam: John Benjamins.

May, S. (2001). *Language and minority rights.* Harlow: Longman.

NRDDB & Iwokrama. (1999). *Community-Based Wildlife Management in the North Rupununi.* Annai and Georgetown: NRDDB and Iwokrama.

11
Positioning and Military Leadership

ROBERT SCHMIDLE

Positioning theory is important as a source of categories for interpreting complex human activities. Since there is no more complex human activity than the command and control of military activities in war, we will examine the positioning of those in command of combat operations. The operations examined are set in Russia in 1812 and in Arabia in 1916. They are separated not only in time but also in character; one is a compressed series of direct attacks to confront and destroy an enemy, while the other is a prolonged series of indirect thrusts and parries to avoid confrontation in order to defeat an enemy. The value of positioning theory is based on developing a more nuanced understanding of the differentiated viewpoints of the participants in these events or more accurately, episodes. This understanding gives us more than a simple context for analysis of a particular episode; it provides a context in which a clearer view of emergent behavior in both the enemy and ourselves becomes evident across numerous episodes. Since these two operations are dissimilar not only in the style of execution but also in the style of leadership, they provide insight into the range of episode that we can interpret using positioning theory.

This project is not about how to solve the practical problems of the control of military operations, but rather it seeks to present a way to think about the conduct exhibited by the actors in episodes of the command of military forces. We begin with a brief overview of Positioning Theory.

Positioning Theory

Positioning Theory has been described as: "The study of local moral orders as ever shifting patterns of mutual and contestable rights and obligations of speaking and acting" (Harré & van Langenhove, 1999, p.1). More specifically, a position is defined as a

complex cluster of generic personal attributes...which impinges on the possibilities of interpersonal, intergroup and even intrapersonal action through some assignment of such rights, duties and obligations to an individual as are sustained by the cluster. (ibid., p.1)

In other words, my "position" is based on a relation to others in a particular situation in which I am assigned certain rights and duties, or have certain rights and duties conferred because of my position in an organization, or my personal character, history, and so on. That position is more accurately defined in a systemic sense, one that could be conferred by a formal organization chart, but one that is also relational in the sense of the actual influence that is exerted through discursive relations within and without the established lines of authority in an organization. Formal position assignments are often a poor guide to actual positions of the actors.

This notion of relation is central to understanding Positioning Theory. For example, a baseball player who can only hit a fly ball 300 feet would not be considered (or "positioned") as very competitive in the Major Leagues as his rights and duties as a player would be circumscribed. That same player's ability to hit a ball that distance, could, however, position him as the star of a local neighborhood team, with all the rights and duties that go with being considered a star player. So in order to understand Positioning Theory, we need to appreciate that: (1) prior assessments of personal skill, character and so on may be involved in positioning (2) there is a relative aspect to the positioning of the participants in relation to the other actors, the context, and the job at hand. Positions should therefore be understood as " ephemeral, disputable, and changeable" (Moghaddam, Hanley, & Harré, 2003, p. 11). All the participants additionally, and importantly, do not necessarily have a mutually shared understanding of those positions. Positioning Theory's relativistic nature is something that is displayed through the analysis of communicative discourse. As such Positioning Theory can be considered to be part of the confederation of ideas in Social Constructionism.

In order to understand the application of positioning theory we need to focus first on the concept of social constructionism. The importance of this concept to our study is that it "stresses that social phenomena are to be considered to be generated in and through conversation and conversation-like activities" (Harré & van Langenhove, 1999, p. 3). This notion is in line with a guiding precept of this project; that the social reality that we "experience" is not innately given or perceived, but is co-created or co-developed by the contributors to the discourse (or conversation). Understanding this we are led to conclude that the cognitive processes that influence the decisions we ultimately make are a product of a communicative discourse. Positioning Theory is a way of examining this discourse with regard to the various levels and types of positioning that the participants, intentionally or otherwise engage in. This assessment of social phenomena generated through conversation (discourse) also leads to an appreciation of the relative nature of the creation of such phenomena. That creation occurs not in a private soliloquy with oneself but in the interaction with others in a public context. That public interaction is through our use of language, or put another way " the intentional use of symbolic systems by human beings..." (Harré & van Langenhove, 1999, p. 3).

Central to my argument, therefore, is the postulation that the communicative discourse itself (as a symbolic system), does not represent some other cognitive process that is occurring or has occurred, but that the discourse itself is the cognitive process that we seek in order to better understand the events that took place. We evaluate military operations because they are the crucible in which human discourse is abruptly compressed and elongated, frequently causing misunderstandings that ultimately have lethal consequences. The participants in these events understand them in the context of episodes in which they occur. An episode comprises a series of events brought about by human action that have some unifying structure (Harré & van Langenhove, 1999). An example of an episode is the baseball game I referred to earlier. In this context, not only do the players create the game they are playing, through the continued deployment of rules, but also the rules themselves, as normative constraints, inform the behavior of the players in the episode of the baseball game.

The concept of an episode provides a vehicle that we can use to understand how the participants position themselves in a given situation. For instance, when a player is "at bat", we can select that as an episode. Positioning phase 1 involves taking up the allowable roles in the game. It has its own rules and customs that the participants (pitcher, catcher, and batter) are aware of as they position themselves within that episode. The catcher may choose to position himself as the quiet extension of the pitcher, or he may position himself as the aggressive, vocal instigator of the sequence, either way he does this inside the commonly understood (at least among the participants) episode of being "at bat." Positioning phase 2 involves the assignment in taking up the rights and duties, which define the property of the actions that make up the episode. The concept of episodes is important for this study because it provide a context for evaluating the intentional actions that occur as part of an event or sequence of events, including the unifying focus of the event.

Positioning Theory is the place from which we begin to examine the discursive process of creating and managing social reality (Harré & van Langenhove, 1999). That social reality is composed of many episodes, within those episodes the context for the actions that form that social reality, are both created and lived. Although Positioning Theory is not considered a general theory, it's application and usefulness as a heuristic tool is an underlying theme of this essay. It is the essential tool for studying the ephemeral micro-moral orders, which shape the fine grain of life.

Positioning Triangle

Within the construct of an episode there is an active and evolving relationship between the positions taken by the participants, the unfolding of the ongoing story-line, and the social force (or meaning) of the actions being taken. The "Positioning Triangle" portrays this triad of relations (Harré & van Langenhove, 1999).

Position 1 (Position 2,3...)

Social Force 1 (Social Force 2,3,,,)   Story-line 1 (Storyline 2, 3,...)

FIGURE 11.1. Positioning Triangle (Harré & van Langenhove, 1999).

The important thing about this triad of relations is that they are mutually influencing. For example, the positioning of a contributor to the discourse will have an effect on the social force (or illocutionary act, that is, what is meant in saying something) of an action, which in turn will be influenced by (as it too will influence) the evolving story-line of a particular episode (Austin, 1975, p.122). There is, however, not one position or one story-line or one illocutionary act, but numerous ones occurring simultaneously as well as sequentially at different levels in the creation and management of a fragment of social reality. There is, however, no assurance that all the participants in a given episode are dealing with the same understanding of the relative position or weight of influence of each of the legs of the triad (Harré & van Langenhove, 1999). In fact, it is more likely that they are not.

The Positioning Triangle also gives us a concept with which to gain insight into the potential changes that might occur if one of the vertices of the triad were altered. As we will see in our case studies, altering a vertex of the triangle and / or the relationship of the vertices will have consequences that appear both unpredictable and unintended. Positioning theory, understood in our context, will help anticipate what some of those consequences might be since it enables us to see the interconnectedness of an intentional act through the evaluation of positioning of the participants and the relevant story-line that make up the Positioning Triangle.

In this essay we use Positioning Theory to examine two case studies of military campaigns, Napoleon in Russia and T.E. Lawrence in Arabia. To begin, we will explore the decisions and actions of senior leaders of military organi-zations engaged in military operations. First we have the chance to evaluate the affect that their decisions had on the activities or episodes at the tactical levels of war where those decisions are executed. Second, we determine the extent to which those decisions were intended to influence other senior decisions makers more so than they were intended to influence the actual conduct of operations. Third, we examine the extent to which positioning of the partic-ipants, intentional or otherwise, contributed to the decisions that were made and the subsequent effect of those decisions on the actual operations on the ground. It is the interconnectedness of these episodes of communication between military commanders that is the focus of these case studies. We begin with Napoleon.

The Battle of Borodino

In Sept 1812 Napoleon Bonaparte fought a costly battle near the town of Borodino, which is approximately 60 miles west of Moscow. While the battle was ultimately a tactical stalemate, it represented a strategic event of immense importance. In the following examination we hope to better understand what influenced Napoleon's behavior and decisions in that episode of combat.

Positioning theory, as discussed previously, is: " based on the thesis that the type of participation that is open to any given member of the social group involved in the ongoing story-line that is unfolding in some episode is limited by a loosely defined set of rights, duties, and obligations" (Moghaddam, Hanley, Harre, p.10). Situational awareness, or the extent of understanding of a social reality, is the condition through which a position composed of those rights, duties, and obligations is occupied. That position, in this case study, defines the type of participation that Napoleon and each of his marshals is recognized as capable of manifesting.

Situational awareness, that is being aware of all possible information, or at least what is mutually understood by the participants to be relevant information about the activities at hand, allows a given contributor to position himself as "superior" to the others. That situational awareness will also give him greater influence over the ongoing story-line. His superior position also contributes to increased credibility and force in his illocutionary speech acts—those that portray meaning in what is said.

Purpose of Discourse

It is the episodes of discourse between Napoleon and his commanders that interests us. Specifically, we are interested in the relations, both discursive and directive, that Napoleon had with his lieutenants – Marshal's Ney, Davout, and Murat – leading up to, and during the battle of Borodino. I will attempt to show how positioning theory can help us better understand what is at work in these relationships.

It is my contention, with regard to the directive orders issued by Napoleon that most of them were issued to maintain his position as the one in charge, but were not believed, even by Napoleon, to be carried out completely, if at all. The implication of this line of thought is that when leaders are in a discourse with other leaders, whether they are in a senior to junior relationship or in one of more or less equality with contemporaries, that the positioning in that discourse focuses at times completely, on the maintenance of the discourse. For example, Napoleon will always be positioned, as superior to his marshals, whereas the marshals—Ney, Murat and Davout are, positioned as contemporaries who are relatively equal in the ongoing dialog about the battle. The maintenance of the discourse begins with the initial positioning of the participants, however, as the discourse continues the positions of the marshals and Napoleon change. It is my contention that one of the factors that determine their relative positioning in that discourse is the mutually attributed level of situational awareness. For example, if one of the marshals sends a report from the line of battle, the assumption is that his report and his recommendations are credible since he is in the best position to have the greatest awareness of the ongoing battle. More so surely than Napoleon, who at Borodino is away from the fighting and not even following events on the battlefield that closely, certainly not as closely as was his custom.

Suppose, however, that we look at that discourse as an attempt by the contributors to create and manage a micro world in which their positioning, and their story-line and their illocutionary acts are all designed to continue the existence of that micro world. If that were the case we might see only a coincident relationship between decisions by leaders at the most senior levels and execution of operations on the ground.

Levels and Networks of War

For the purpose of this essay we consider two different levels of war, the strategic and the tactical. The strategic is composed of senior political and military decision makers; in the case of the Emperor Napoleon there was only one decision maker since he was both the political and military leader of France. The other level is the tactical level; this level is composed of the soldier and his immediate leaders—those who are actually engaged in the fighting. Today we talk about a third level of war that has gained acceptance as part of the language of warfare. It is the operational level of war, that is the level at which commanders are concerned with translating strategic intent from policy makers (generally civilians) into tactical actions executable by military commanders. In Napoleon's case this was not an issue because he was acting as both the civilian head of government and the military field commander.

Although there is a connection between the different levels of warfare, it can easily be misunderstood because of an incomplete understanding of the multiple networks that make up the greater reality we know as "experience". In an effort to clarify, let us consider just two possible networks, a strategic network and a tactical network. It is my contention that decisions made in one network, at one level, will not necessarily affect the other in a direct, linear manner. While these two networks will obviously influence each other, the notion that they directly affect each other is problematic. For instance, a strategic decision, such as Napoleon's decision to invade Russia, while it does have an influence on tactical actions such as a cavalry charge at Borodino, does so only in the sense that one is being done in the context of the other.

There is a relation between these networks, but it is more normative than causal. If we consider the previous example where we looked at strategic and tactical actions, we see that tactical decisions by leaders positioned in strategic networks are in many cases, irrelevant to the long-term outcome of a given situation. For example, when Napoleon is positioned as the Emperor, he is acting in a strategic network, therefore his decisions and orders at the tactical level, given in that strategic context, are likely to be irrelevant to actions on the ground. This may explain Napoleon's frequent issuance of orders at Borodino that were adrift without a story-line, and therefore without context to make them "real." The relevancy that those decisions had was that they ultimately affected normative behavior, and not because they had a direct, casual affect on concurrent behavior. In this case the relative positioning of the contributors (to the respective networks in which they are operating), which is mutually established and maintained, was the normative structure in which communications between them existed. That position, in turn, determined the influence of the contributors (leaders) actions or decisions and its direction—up the chain of command to superiors, down the chain of command to subordinates, or across the chain of command to contemporaries. In other words, the positioning of tactical leaders in tactical networks is the normative or rule based structure that determines the kind and credibility of the communication they will have with members of the strategic networks.

Setting the Stage

As we examine Napoleon's campaign in Russia and specifically the battle of Borodino it is important that we recognize a fundamental distinction. That distinction is between the question of a "position" from the standpoint of the rights and duties to act, etc., and the question of the psychological and epistemic conditions supporting or justifying a "position." We shall be concerned with both in this study and will explore two separate story-lines. First, that " I" (Napoleon) am the Emperor of France and as such have the right to absolute command, second, that " I" (Napoleon) am a soldier engaged in the command of armed forces in a battle and have the duty to manage events in order to win that battle.

The Battle

At the time that he began the Russian campaign in 1812, Napoleon was arguably at the apogee of his power and influence; however his "position" was in question from the beginning.

It was utter folly to launch such a massive campaign
in a vast region where is was well known that food, supplies,
and fodder would be at a minimum, and roads of any
sort few and far between... Consequently,
few corps commanders could adhere to Bonaparte's orders,
which, moreover, sometimes went astray or at best were
delayed by the vast distances and the general confusion.
(Schom, 1998, p.599)

Napoleon can be seen here, early on in the Russian campaign, being positioned by his commanders as someone who is out of touch with the goings on at the execution level of the campaign. This positioning would continue throughout the planning and conduct of the battle of Borodino. It is interesting to note that already, in the beginning of the campaign, the illocutionary force of his messages had changed—his subordinates no longer saw them as "orders."

Situational Awareness: The Initial Positioning Act

When Napoleon met with his marshals on September 6, 1812, the day before the battle, there appeared to be two potential courses of action or plans for the attack. One plan was suggested by Marshal Davout who argued that: " he could strongly hit the exposed Russian left flank, swing around and envelop it, thus turning the Russian line" (Schom, 1998, p.610). Davout also pointed out that: " the mighty Russian guns were dug in and aimed facing the west, not the south or southeast" (ibid., p.610) implying that as he attacked from the southern flank the guns would be unable to fire on his troops without being repositioned.

Napoleon was keenly aware of Davout's ability and although he praised him in some quarters, he was always careful not to give him too much credit in public. He was clearly jealous of Davout's growing and well-deserved reputation (Schom, 1998, p.728). So when Davout offered his proposed course of action, he was positioned in the eyes of Napoleon and the other marshals, as having the right to propose courses of action because he was seen as a competent and credible tactician. The discourse of this council of war on Sept 6th however, evolved so that it eventually consisted of Napoleon issuing orders with the aim of confirming his position as the Emperor without much regard for the execution of events on the battlefield, i.e. his speech acts changed their illocutionary force. Why else would he chose a course of action—frontal assault against a heavily defended redoubt, although less risky intellectually, i.e. in terms of what was required of him and his leadership ability execute, that was clearly going to result in larger numbers of casualties. Napoleon's unimaginative tactics indicated his unwavering adherence to his defining operational framework of war—"being stronger at a given place." (Nicolson, 1985 p.75) What he lacked in this case was the situational awareness to see that the "given place" was not the heavily defended center of the Russian lines, but the exposed Southern flank.

Among the other marshals, Ney also offered an opposing voice to Napoleon's plan. Marshal Ney's reputation was that of a headstrong infantry commander who would, after the Russian campaign, be referred to as the "bravest of the brave." He had credibility as a tactician and his bravery was legend, but he was seen by Napoleon as " brave and nothing more...good at leading 10,000 men into battle, but other than that...a real blockhead" (*Napoleon Bonaparte*, p.739) The psychological attribute "blockhead" gave Ney's judgments little credence and led to a "position," but was not itself the position. Because of Ney's lack of credibility in the eyes of Napoleon, he had not much right to offer opinions, since little credence was placed in his opinion, although in this case the Emperor should have heeded his council.

The other marshal involved in this discourse is Murat. His relationship with Napoleon was one of tension and enmity. Napoleon thought him too independent and not servile enough, except when in the emperor's presence (De Caulaincourt, p.40). According to Caulaincourt, the Duke of Vicenza—whose memoirs of his experiences with Napoleon on the Russian campaign afford a unique view of Napoleon and his staff—Murat routinely offered opposing views to Napoleon. Speaking of Murat, Caulaincourt said: " He even ventured to make some remarks to this effect to the Emperor (about the large numbers of horses that had died or were so weak to be of little use to the cavalry, and how this would put the entire enterprise at risk in the weeks and months ahead) but his majesty did not care for reflections that ran counter to his projects and lent a deaf ear" (De Caulaincourt, p.63). In other words, unless the views were supportive, Napoleon positioned that person as having no right to venture an opinion, i.e., that person lost their "footing" in the discourse. According to Davies and Harré (1999, p.44), " we gain or lose our footing in conversations, social groups and so on, much as we gain or lose it on a muddy slope." Caulaincourt then observed that when Murat sensed Napoleon's disinterest " he changed the subject...by doing so kept to himself the wise reflections which he had voiced to us alone. He soon forgot them entirely" (De Caulaincourt, p.63).

So during the initial act of positioning while having the right to an opinion since they were credited with situational awareness, Davout and Ney openly questioned Napoleon about his choice of tactics. They positioned themselves as having both the right and the duty to intervene since each believed himself to know best what the situation was on the battlefield; Davout with his knowledge of the exposed Russian flank and the direction that the Russians guns are pointed, and Ney with his awareness of the effect that the thick forest would have on the cohesion of the attacking divisions. Murat remains silent however; content to position himself as "all duty" that is as a loyal, and capable cavalry commander.

On the morning of 7 Sept 1812 at the opening of the battle, no sooner had the artillery barrage started than it had to be stopped in order to move the guns forward, closer to the front lines so that their cannon balls could be effective against the Russian troops. Napoleon himself, the expert artillery tactician, had placed the guns, above the objections of his subordinate commanders, in those exact locations prior to the battle. After this error was evident to all, others were positioning him in quite the opposite way, perhaps as no longer having the right to be obeyed.

The thing that is perhaps most telling with regard to the implications of the positioning act on the basis of situational awareness is when Napoleon speaks of the battlefield as if it were a chessboard. This analogy to the chessboard is an important part in the developing story-line of this battle.

The chessboard analogy is an important part of our story because it shows that Napoleon was expecting to "see" clearly the layout of his and the enemies forces on the battlefield, in other words, he expected that he would eventually have perfect situational awareness. That expectation of perfect situational awareness, in turn, became a requirement for his decisions, while at the same time becoming a condition, through which a position of authority was occupied, i.e., the right and through which the story-line was developed.

So throughout the morning of September 7, 1812 the emperor waited, and waited for the perfect understanding, which in turn would make the perfect decision both evident and possible. Instead, what happened was that Napoleon made decisions, or did not make decisions, in order to appear to be in control of a situation that was actually beyond his ability to influence in any direct way. He could only influence the situation at Borodino by operating in one network at a time. In other words, if he wanted to make tactical decisions he needed to physically and mentally locate himself in a manner that allowed him to build situational awareness about what was happening in those tactical networks. In fact, what occurred at Borodino was that he was intellectually operating in the strategic network while trying to influence events in the tactical network.

Marshal Ney realized this was occurring when, on being told what Napoleon said about wanting to see the chessboard more clearly, burst out: " What's the Emperor doing behind his army? He doesn't see any of our successes there— only our reverses. Since he isn't fighting the war himself any longer and isn't the general any more, but wants to play the Emperor everywhere, why doesn't he go back to the Tuileries and let us be generals for him?" (De Segur, 1958, p.73) The secondary story-line that the battle was a game of chess, complimented the fatal mismatch between the strategic and tactical levels of war. The strategic level of war, as discussed earlier, is the one in which leaders are concerned with matters of grand strategy, such as the decision to invade Russia or to form an alliance with the Prussians. The tactical level of war, on the other hand, is the one in which leaders are concerned with the elements of execution of the grand strategy, such as the decision about where to employ artillery or whether or not to attack the Russians at Borodino frontally or from a flank. It is critically important for a commander to be aware of the level of war, i.e. the network, in which he is operating, because each has its own unique attributes and the linkage between them is often not easily discernible.

I would suggest that what is happening here is that Napoleon has been confused by trying to understand and operate in both the strategic and tactical networks. His playing the role of both general and emperor exacerbated this confusion about thinking in one network while trying to execute in another.

Being the Emperor

Due to this confusion on Napoleon's part, which contributed to his lack of situational awareness, the only decision he made all day that had an effect on the battlefield was the one regarding the employment of the reserve forces, which in this case were the Imperial Guard. He held back the Guard, not committing them to the battle, for strategic not tactical reasons, even though he was ostensibly trying to win the tactical battle of Borodino that was part of his strategic war against Russia. This was because even though the Guard may well have achieved a tactical victory that day, he could ill afford to risk losing them if he was to maintain his position as the Emperor of France. Napoleon's position as the Emperor is what gave him the right and the duty to make strategic decisions, such as the one to invade Russia. In this instance he made a tactical decision, i.e. not to employ the Imperial Guard in order to maintain his position as Emperor in that strategic network. So the dialog that he had with his marshals and others in his war council was for the principle reason of perpetuating that micro-world. The story-line in that micro-world was one in which Napoleon Bonaparte was, and remained, the Emperor of France. Regardless of how well Napoleon played the role of Emperor, he could not simultaneously and adequately play the role of field general.

There is an interesting parallel here to Adolph Hitler's positioning during Operation Barbarossa, the German invasion of Russia in June 1941. There are obvious similarities – both he and Napoleon initiated campaigns into Russia, suffered through brutal winter conditions, grappled the "Bear" in titanic military struggles and were ultimately defeated. However, there is a subtler, but no less powerful connection between the two. In comparing the campaigns we see Napoleon positioning himself as the Emperor while trying to make decisions as if he were a field marshal. Hitler, on the other hand, positioned himself as a field marshal when arguably he should have positioned himself as the Fuhrer. In each case they confused the level or network of war in which they chose to operate with the level of war in which others positioned them. Napoleon is acting like an emperor when he is positioned to be a general; Hitler is acting like a general when he is positioned to be the Fuhrer.

The Arabian Campaign 1916

In this next section we examine a military operation very different from the classic set-piece battle of Borodino. We focus on the central figure of T.E. Lawrence, a British officer who was different in nearly every imaginable way from Napoleon. As in the examination of Napoleon and his Marshals, what interest us are the relations between Lawrence and the Arab chiefs. Those chiefs are the ones who are actually directing the fighting against the Turks on the Arabian Peninsula in 1917. In order to understand those relations we look at three primary issues. First, the effects of the decisions that were made on the conduct of operations, second, the extent to which the decisions were intended to influence other decision makers, and third, the extent to which positioning of the participants contributed to the perpetuation of the micro world create by the discourse among those players. We will attempt to understand the positions of the participants through the same prism we used in the first study, that is the construct of situational awareness, or the level of understanding of a mutually created and commonly accepted reality. Finally we will apply the same notion of the strategic and tactical levels of war to better understand the networks in which Lawrence is operating. Those networks extend to his relations with both the Arab chiefs whom he was advising and with his distant and mostly disengaged British superiors.

Setting the Stage

T. E. Lawrence was neither an emperor nor a field marshal; rather he was a young British subaltern (a reservist no less) with a degree from Oxford. His uncommon depth of knowledge about the Middle East was gained from participating in archeological digs in the region prior to the outbreak of the First World War. At the time of the Arab revolt against the Turks in 1916 he was posted to British headquarters in Cairo, Egypt. There, his knowledge of Arabic language and customs positioned him as having the right to offer opinions about the region, but because of his lack of proper military experience, not about military operations. To most of the British officers in those days the "proper" experience for a subaltern was on the Western front in France fighting from the trenches and offering periodic sacrifices by charging headlong across open ground swept by cannon and machine gun fire. Napoleon would have understood these tactics, since he employed them at Borodino a hundred years before. These tactics could be characterized as the direct approach, of being "stronger at a given place" (Nicolson, 1985, p.75) and were the accepted Western way of war; to suggest anything contrary was, at the time, considered blasphemous.

Lawrence, on the other hand, was making the case to those in and out of his headquarters that the situation in Arabia was different and called for a more indirect approach in both strategy and tactics. While there were some senior officers who thought his ideas about encouraging an Arab revolt worthy of consideration, most of his superiors positioned him characterologically as "...generally impudent, often rude," (Asprey, 1994, p.179) weakening his right to advise. Lawrence believed that a revolt by the Arabs (encouraged and abetted by the British), as opposed to direct military confrontation, was the best way for the British to defeat Germany's ally in the region—Turkey. The Arab revolt did occur (initially without British involvement) in October 1916 with the capture of Mecca from the Turks, in what today is Saudi Arabia. Consequently, Lawrence on his own and without official orders visited the Arab sheiks that started the revolt. That visit marked the beginning of the creation, and subsequent positioning of "Lawrence of Arabia."

There are two story-lines that interest us in this study. First, that "I" (Lawrence) am the sole British advisor to the most important Arab sheik, Emir Feisal and have the right to offer opinions and advice about military operations, second that

"I" (Lawrence) am a soldier in Feisal's band of irregulars and have the duty to lead them to victory over the Turks.

The Initial Positioning Act

The initial positioning act is one in which Lawrence establishes his credibility as an advisor to Feisal. He does this by showing genuine respect for the uniqueness of Arab culture, while at the same time not imposing on them a Western point of view, thereby positioning himself as both not British and not Arab.

> I was sent to these Arabs as a stranger, unable to think
> their thoughts or subscribe their beliefs...If I could not
> assume their character, I could at least conceal my own,
> and pass among them without evident friction, neither a
> discord nor a critic but an unnoticed influence.
> (Lawrence, 1991,p.30)

The way in which Lawrence went about being an "unnoticed influence" was not always subtle, but was nearly always effective. He began by formulating a new way of interpreting and understanding war, one at odds with the traditional Napoleonic notion of absolute war whose end state was the physical destruction of the enemy army in battle. This traditional theory of war would clearly not provide a useful model in this case since the Arabs did not possess the means to physically destroy the Turkish army. By developing this new way of understanding warfare he positioned himself as having greater situational awareness (of the true nature of the conflict in Arabia) than his fellow British officers or the Arabs chiefs that he was to advise.

A New Theory of War

Lawrence proposed to understand the strategic and tactical imperatives of warfare by thinking about the three elements of war: "the Algebraical element of things, a Biological element of lives, and the Psychological element of ideas" (Lawrence, 1991, p.192). The algebraical element was the science of calculation, whereby he determined the number of soldiers required to defend a certain area of land or the number of soldiers required to defeat another army in a set-piece battle, like the one at Borodino. His calculations in this regard confirmed for him two important things. First, that the small numbers of Arabs engaged in the revolt could not expect to defeat the Turks in a pitched battle, and second that the number of Turkish soldiers needed to defend the entire Arabian peninsula was well beyond the number that the Turks had available to employ. These two numerical facts provided the impetus for the subsequently development of his unique strategy.

The biological element or what Lawrence later calls the " biological factor in command" (Lawrence, 1991, p.193) concerns the transformation of the illogical into the logical in a way that enables one to feel a level of certainty about making decisions. In other words the biological element is that which is informed by knowledge of the culture of both the Arabs and the Turks to a degree that helps make logical sense of seemingly illogical patterns of behavior. In explaining this notion he acknowledged that the previous "philosophers of war" who tied this element to the "effusion of blood" (Lawrence, 1991, p.193) were right to highlight the pervasive dialectic of life and death that is the nature of warfare. This is obvious enough, but Lawrence goes a step further and applies this dialectic more widely. He does this by taking the metaphor beyond the merely corporeal and applies it to the relationship between certainty and uncertainty and the subsequent effect of tying that synthesis to the logical process of decision-making. In our previous examination of Napoleon's decisions at Borodino we saw that this same tension between certainty and uncertainty was what drove the Emperor's impulse for greater situational awareness. This impulse he hoped would enable him to "see the chessboard (the battlefield) more clearly."

Lawrence describes the elements that contribute to the transformation from uncertainty to certainty in the following way: "The components were sensitive and illogical, and generals guarded themselves by the device of a reserve, the significant medium of their art" (Lawrence, 1991, p.193). In other words the reserve is the hedge against what one does not know, it is the "irrational tenth…and in it lay the test of generals" (Lawrence, 1991, p. Ibid). It is in this "space" of the "irrational tenth" that the positioning of the commander is of greatest interest, because it is here that the commander not only has the right to make decisions but also has the duty to understand the imperative against being rational in making those decisions. Napoleon at Borodino may have seemed to be behaving irrationally, but he made his decision about committing the reserve (the Imperial Guard) in a very rational way. In fact, in this case the situation demanded an irrational decision, one based on an unquantifiable "feel" for the situation on the battlefield and something that Napoleon had demonstrated a genius for in previous battles.

In terms of the different approach to warfare that Lawrence was postulating, the unifying theme of these three elements was the importance of in-depth knowledge of the adversary, which is always the prerequisite to developing any effective strategy. For example, in the case of the Arab revolt, Lawrence rightly saw that the Turks greatest vulnerability was the materials they needed to fight. Alternately the Arab's greatest vulnerability was manpower because they were far fewer in number and much more loosely organized. As "irregular" forces the Arabs were accustomed to fighting in small tribal bands and their effectiveness, as soldiers, would decrease exponentially if they suffered even a few casualties. This was because of the relatively large effect of even those few casualties on a small group both in terms of relative numbers and cohesion of the unit. The Turks, on the other hand were organized into larger more structured formations that had a greater capacity to absorb casualties and still retain the capability to operate as a unit.

Lawrence, when employing his own warfare principles, and in developing his knowledge of the adversary, discovered that the Turks were completely dependent on a fragile logistics system to sustain their operations. Based on this knowledge, Lawrence, who had no authority to direct, but did have the right and the duty to advise, created an unorthodox strategy for defeating the Turks. He proposed to disrupt and destroy their means of support, and not their army. Thus he transformed his theory of the indirect approach into an actual operational plan. This strategy showed deep understanding of the strengths and weaknesses of both the Arabs and the Turks.

The third and final of Lawrence's elements of war, the psychological element was described as " ...our "propaganda"...It was the pathic, almost the ethical, in war. Some of it concerned the crowd...some of it concerned the individual" (Lawrence, 1991, p.195). Lawrence draws out an important notion in this section when he describes how he thought the Europeans' interest in the art of war was misplaced because they were more concerned with the weapons with which men fought. He on the other hand thought they should focus on understanding the beliefs with which men fought, since it was beliefs that motivated the behaviors of men. This element was, in his mind arguably the most important of the three and the hardest to categorize however undeniable it's central role in warfare. Taken together these three elements, the algebraical, the biological, and the psychological, created the foundations that supported his theory of the indirect approach. An approach that was like" a thing intangible, invulnerable, without front or back, drifting about like a gas?" (Lawrence, 1991, p.192).

Levels and Networks of War

In 1916 greatly outnumbered irregular Arab forces were fighting a war on the Arabian Peninsula against regular Turkish forces. Because of the dearth of fighters there was no advantage to the Arabs in engaging the Turks in the way Napoleon had engaged the Russians—by direct assault. Lawrence points out the contrast by observing: " Napoleon said it was rare to find generals willing to fight battles; but the curse of this war was that so few could do anything else" (Lawrence, 1991, p.196). As a result of his position as an advisor Lawrence had the right to put forth a strategy that privileged the metaphysical or more irrational indirect approach over the material or more rational direct approach. He also had the duty in his position as a soldier to carry out tactical actions necessary to insure the success of that strategy. Those tactical actions contrarily privileged the material over the metaphysical. Unlike Napoleon, he seems not to have confused the two.

The following passage indicates how Lawrence was able understand his position in both the strategic and tactical levels of war. Early in his service with the Emir Fiesal's band of Arabs, Lawrence was leading a small raiding party on a long march over a period of weeks. In the course of this march there was increasing tension between men of the different tribes that made up his party. On one particular occasion, it reached a breaking point, which Lawrence later described: "My followers had been quarreling all day; and while I was lying near the rocks a shot was fired...one of the men was lying stone dead with a bullet through his temples" (Lawrence, 1991, p.181). He quickly determined that the killer was a man named Hamed. Since the killing stemmed from an ongoing feud between two tribes in his group, Lawrence, as the leader of the group and not belonging to either tribe was positioned as the one whose duty it was to execute the murderer. Lawrence recalled the incident in the following passage

> It must be a formal execution, and at last, desperately
> I told Hamed that he must die for punishment and laid
> the burden of his killing on myself. Perhaps they would
> count me not qualified for feud...for I was a stranger
> and kinless.
>
> (Lawrence, 1991, p.181).

Positioned as the leader of the group by Fiesal he was also additionally positioned by the men in the group as being a "stranger and kinless" and therefore as having both the right and the duty to pass judgment and administer the punishment. This episode of a tactical action, is certainly in stark contrast to the indirect approach he championed as the necessary strategy to defeat the Turks. It also suggests that Lawrence, far better than Napoleon, understood the dichotomous relationship between the strategic and tactical levels of war and his rights and duties in each. This understanding also enabled Lawrence to have much greater situational awareness in carrying out the ongoing day-to-day operations that ultimately lead to the success of his strategy.

Finally, we explore the difference in the behavior of the two men through the lens of positioning theory and gain insight into their understanding of the implications of positioning. First we turn to Napoleon and observe him the night before the battle of Borodino. Napoleon had doubts in the hours before the battle that his orders were being obeyed but he did nothing to try to change his position from being the Emperor to being the field general (De Segur, 1958, p.63). If he were to change his position he would have injected himself into the tactical network where orders are executed in order to insure that they were being obeyed. He clearly seems not to have understood the relation between the networks of war. Lawrence however did understand that if he was to have influence as an advisor and as a strategist he must be positioned as one who is obeyed.

The distinction between the two becomes even more evident when we look at positioning and the right to be obeyed in these episodes. Napoleon during the evening before the battle did nothing more than simply ask one of his guards what orders he had received. He consequently made no attempt to insure that his (Napoleon's) orders were being carried out. Lawrence on the other hand reacted quite differently when faced with a situation that similarly demanded obedience.

He did far more than simply inquire of his men what they thought they had been ordered to do; he shot and killed one of them to insure the obedience of the rest.

Conclusion

The application of positioning theory to military leadership offers a conceptual framework in which to examine leaders in varied situations to better understand positioning in local moral orders. We have seen that positioning can be intentional or unintentional, occurring at different levels and created through discursive practices. In the case studies we also examined the relationship between positioning in strategic (metaphysical) and tactical (material) networks. This relationship is most evident when we come to understand that while there is positioning at one level to insure the continuation of the metaphysical micro world of the participants, there is also positioning at another level that reflects the material world of the participants. The positioning at the material level has the objective of ensuring that the actions necessary to achieve the tactical victory that is the duty of generals are occurring so that the strategic victory that is duty of statesmen (and emperors) is accomplished.

Napoleon's failure to prevail at the battle of Borodino was due to privileging of his position in the metaphysical realm at the expense of his position in the material realm. It is of course in the material realm where actions relevant to the conduct of battle occur. He tried unsuccessfully to operate in both realms without understanding the relationship between the positions he occupied in each. Lawrence's success on the other hand came about because he understood the overriding importance of his position in the material realm and privileged it accordingly above the metaphysical. The lesson for contemporary civilian and military decision makers is that their positioning at the strategic level of warfare is quickly irrelevant to empirical events "on the ground" without a deep and concomitant understanding of the relationship between the two. That understanding clearly reveals the necessity of having a credible position at the tactical (execution) level of war if they are to accomplish the duty conferred by their position.

References

Asprey, R. B. (1994). *War in the shadows: The guerilla in history*. New York, NY: William Morrow and Company, Inc.

Austin, J. L., *How To Do Things With Words*, Harvard University Press, Cambridge, 1975.

Caulaincourt, Armand, *With Napolean In Russia*, William Morrow and Company, New York, 1935.

Davies, B., & Harré, R. (1999). Positioning and personhood. In R. Harré & L. van Langenhove (Eds.) (1999), *Positioning theory: Moral contexts of intentional action* (pp. 32–52). Oxford, UK: Blackwell Publishers. [Original version published 1990, Journal for the Theory of Social Behavior, *20*, 43–63].

De Segur, P. P. (1958). *Napoleon's Russian campaign*. Cambridge, UK: The Riverside Press.

Harré, R., & Van Langenhove, L. (1999a). The Dynamics of Social Episodes. In R. Harré & L. Van Langenhove (Eds.), *Positioning theory* (pp. 1 – 13). Oxford: Blackwell.

Harré, R., & van Langenhove, L. (1999b). *Positioning theory: Moral contexts of intentional action*. Oxford, UK: Blackwell.

Harré, R., & van Langenhove, L. (1999c). Epilogue: Further Opportunities, In R. Harré & L. van Langenhove (Ed.), *Positioning Theory*. Oxford, UK: Blackwell Publishers.

Lawrence, T. E. (1991). *Seven pillars of wisdom*. New York, NY: Random House, Inc.

Moghaddam, F. M., Hanley, E., & Harré, R. (2003). Sustaining intergroup harmony: An analysis of the Kissinger papers through positioning theory. In R. Harré & F. M. Moghaddam (Eds.), *The self and others: Positioning individuals and groups in personal, political, and cultural contexts* (pp. 137–155). Westport, CT: Praeger.

Nicolson, N. (1985). *Napoleon 1812*. New York, NY: Harper & Row.

Schom, Alan, *Napolean Bonaparte*, Harper Perennial, New York, 1998.

12
Discursive Production of Conflict in Rwanda

NIKKI R. SLOCUM-BRADLEY

Introduction: Identity, Norms and Legitimization in Conflict

An estimated 800,000 Rwandan Tutsis and moderate Hutus were killed in 100 days in 1994. Rwandan media were accused of inciting the hatred and giving directives to kill that led to what has been described as 'the fastest and most comprehensive genocide known to mankind' (Kimani, 2000). A state of 'war' had been declared in Rwanda when the alleged offensive broadcasts and publications took place. The Rwandan Patriotic Force (RPF), comprised mainly of the children of Tutsis who had fled previous massacres in Rwanda, had invaded the country, purportedly in an attempt to gain the return of thousands of Tutsi refugees like themselves. What was – and what should be - the role of the media in the Rwandan and other 'wars' around the world? How should the rights of the press be weighed against a universal duty to protect human rights, when these rights and duties may be contradictory? The freedom of expression and the freedom of the press are constitutional rights in many countries, and in the United States even so-called 'hate media' proponents legally can and do publish their views (Kimani, 2000). However, if such material can make a decisive impact on people's decisions to commit crimes, what is the responsibility of the publisher, writer or broadcaster?

The International Criminal Tribunal for Rwanda (ICTR) convicted three persons in what was collectively referred to as the 'Media Case', which focused on these individuals' responsibility for the genocide on the basis of their control of a radio channel and a newspaper in Rwanda (Della Morte, 2005). However, the fundamental questions underlying the case remain open and hotly debated. The present chapter examines these questions in greater detail and attempts to illuminate the relationships between media discourse, (ethnic) identities, and conflict.

Identity and Conflict

Various theories attempt to explain the role of identities in conflict between individuals and groups. One of the most influential theories in psychology is Social Identity Theory (Abrams & Hogg, 1990; Hogg and Abrams, 1999), which proposes that people strive to achieve a positive social identity and, if they feel it is inadequate, they will take steps to remedy it (Moghaddam, 1998: 485). Accordingly, a person's social identity is defined as 'that part of a person's self-concept which is derived from membership in social groups' (Moghaddam, 1998: 486). Given an 'inadequate' social identity, meaning one that is not sufficiently 'positive' and/or 'distinct', people will draw upon various strategies to change the situation (for a concise summary of strategies and the conditions under which they are employed, see Moghaddam, 1998: 485-488). One strategy is to directly challenge the out-group, in order to improve the relative status and power of one's in-group. Thus, an explanation of ethnic conflict in accordance with social identity theory presumes that people 'identify' with their 'ethnic group' (in-group) and that they compare themselves with other ethnic groups (out-groups), which they are prepared to denigrate in order to augment their own group's relative power and status, and thereby boost their social identity.

Another explanation is provided by rational choice theory, which is based upon the assumptions that people have fixed, ordered 'interests' (generally as pre-defined by the researcher), and their behavior maximizes the fulfillment of these interests, under the presumed condition of competition for scarce resources. In this view, ethnic groups are seen as instrumental coalitions formed in an attempt to compete and achieve one's interests.[1] One of many issues left unaddressed by both rational choice and social identity theories is the conditions under which people will define their 'identity' in terms of, or form a coalition based upon the category of, their 'ethnicity'.

Alternatively, socio-biologists (see Wilson, 1975; Van den Berghe, 1987) argue that ethnicity is a direct cause of conflict. According to this perspective, a person's ethnicity (phenotype) reflects his or her genotype, such that those who share a common ethnicity also have more genes in common than those of a different ethnic heritage. Individuals will act aggressively towards those who are more dissimilar, because this strategy is more likely to ensure that their own genetic material is passed on. In contrast, in discussing the role of ethnicity in conflict, Van Hoywehgen and Vlassenroot (2000) argue that ethnicity cannot be the cause of a conflict, but that 'ethnic identity narratives justify behaviour' (p. 112) and are usually employed by elites in order to gain political or economic benefits. In this view, the value of 'ethnic' solidarity is constructed as an 'interest' (to use the terminology of rational choice theorists) in narratives, in order to achieve other ends. Kaufman (2001) also examines the key role of narratives, which he refers to as 'ethnic myth-symbol complexes', in forming 'ethnic hatreds', which he claims can lead to ethnic violence under opportune conditions. The importance of examining narrative in order to understand the roots of conflict is pinpointed in the conclusion of Van Hoywehgen and Vlassenroot's (2000) research:

While the motives of a rebel movement or militia may be easily traced, it is often less obvious why people at the grassroots level can be mobilized and called to respond to the appeals of entrepreneurs. Therefore not only the general logic of the conflict has to be identified, but also that of 'local micro-politics'. Only then will we get a real grip on the logics of ethnicity and violence in contemporary Africa (p. 114).

In order to understand how ordinary people are recruited to commit mass murder, and thus learn to prevent this, it is necessary to understand how the media inspires hatred and incited killings and other 'crimes of humanity'. This is done by creating a certain social reality, in which it becomes not only acceptable, but even one's duty to undertake the actions in question. In other words, through discourse, a social reality is constructed that entail norms that are conducive of the actions perpetrated.

Similarly, Fujii (2002) argues that, by skillfully exploiting the resources of the past and the opportunities of the present, the génocidaires were able to construct a world where genocidal thinking was the norm, and to make that world the only consequential reality for victim and killer alike (pp. 2–3). The author draws upon Katzenstein's (1996) definition of a norm as 'the standard of appropriate behavior for actors with a given identity (p. 5)', which highlights the link between an actor's identity constructs and corresponding norms for action, rather than utility-motivated behavior. Such an approach is also endorsed by Florini (1996), who argues, 'Norms are obeyed not because they are enforced, but because they are seen as legitimate (p. 365)'.

Legitimacy and Identity

Like 'identity', 'legitimacy' is often treated as something that people, institutions, organizations or regimes 'have' or do not 'have'. Scholars have even distinguished between different types of 'legitimacy' (see Scharpf, 1999). However, like 'identity', 'legitimacy' is a concept that is used by people to achieve social tasks. In fact, the concept is often used to legitimise or de-legitimise! Processes of legitimisation and de-legitimisation can be accomplished in several ways. First, actions are legitimised by attributing actors with the right or duty to act in such a way. A (potential) victim of an attack has the right to defend herself. Thus, insofar as her action - for example, striking the attacker with a baseball bat - is defined as an act of 'self defence', then her actions have been legitimized. The example highlights the importance of meaning construction in the processes of legitimisation and de-legitimisation by demonstrating the logic inherent in metaphors, as issue to which we will return later.

The legitimisation of actors can occur through the attribution of rights and duties to an actor in a specific context. In contrast, de-legitimization occurs when a specific set of rights and duties is withheld from an actor, or when these are rescinded. Actors also can be legitimised when positioned as having properly fulfilled the duties attributed to them. In the same vein, actors are de-legitimised when positioned as having failed to fulfil duties attributed to them. For example, when a radio journalist says that Hutus who flee are cowards and they rather should stay on their land and defend their country, he attributes Hutus the duty to stay on their land and fight. He accuses those who flee of not fulfilling their duty. The journalist thus de-legitimizes both the action of fleeing as well as the actors who have fled.

Narrative Analysis in Conflict Studies

Given the importance of these processes of (de-)legitimization, as well as the use of narrative in generating norms for action, an analytical framework for understanding the role of 'identities' in conflict should ideally capture both of these elements. While Kaufman (2001) analyzes the narratives surrounding three cases of ethnic conflict, his narrative analysis lacks a systematic framework. Other studies (see Des Forges, 1999; Fujii, 2002; Gulseth, 2004) have examined the role of the media in the Rwandan genocide from theoretical approaches popular in communications studies, such as the Jowett and O'Donnell (1999) 'ten-step plan', which Gulseth (2004) characterizes as the 'dominant paradigm of American communication research'. This plan and similar approaches identify various steps and categories of 'propaganda'. In studies that apply these approaches, various texts are defined as 'propaganda' and thus analyzed within an analytical framework specifically for analyzing propaganda. For example, Gulseth (2004) draws upon Jowett and O'Donnell's definition of propaganda as, 'a deliberate and systematic attempt to shape perceptions, manipulate cognitions, and direct behavior to achieve a response that furthers the desired intent of the propagandist' (Jowett and O'Donnell, 1999:6, in Gulseth, 2004, p. 27). There are two main problems with this theoretical approach.

First, the identification of a particular text as 'propaganda' and the decision to analyze the text with the method for analysis of 'propaganda' become circular: either the text is pre-defined as 'propaganda' and thus the method is applied; or the method (for analyzing propaganda) is applied and the analyst concludes that the text is indeed 'propaganda'. The second problem is the analyst's ability to apply and verify the criteria given in Jowett and O'Donnell's definition of 'propaganda'. It is impossible to verify intentions or motivations, because these are constructs. As the textual analysis below will reveal, any statement can be made about a person's or group's 'intentions', 'desires', 'wants' or 'goals', but none can be verified.[2] Hence, explanations that (merely) claim to reveal purported 'motives' fail to illuminate the mechanisms of meaning construction and thus provide no scientific value.

Positioning Theory as an Analytical Framework

Positioning Theory (Harré & Van Langenhove, 1999) is a useful tool for a systematic analysis of narrative or discourse, the mechanism of meaning-creation, which also highlights the attribution of rights and duties to actors. It accomplishes this by illuminating the mutually influential relationship of 'positions' attributed to actors, storylines, and the 'social force' of utterances and acts. Here, the 'social force' is what is accomplished socially through an utterance or act, such as blaming, encouraging, thanking, complimenting, accusing, and so forth. Positioning Theory is thus an ideal tool to illuminate both the processes of norm construction and legitimization.

A Positioning Theory approach to studying discourse of the Rwandan genocide entails the application of an analytical framework, the Positioning Triad, which has proven useful in revealing how social reality is generated in general. That is, the method is not specific to a particular kind of discourse, so the discourse need not be pre-categorized, as 'propaganda' or otherwise. In accordance with this approach, all discourse contributes to the construction of social reality (and thus 'frames', 'shapes' or 'manipulates' it). However, no claims need to be made about an actor's 'intentions' in so doing. To the contrary, regardless of an actor's intentions, his or her interlocutor co-determines the 'social force' of an utterance or act. Accordingly, George may 'intend' to 'incite' anger through the illocution of an insult (social force) aimed at Hillary, but he will not succeed if Hillary laughs in reply. A retrospective 'objective' description of the exchange will consequently not portray it as, 'Hillary was insulted by George', but rather as 'Hillary laughed at George'. This illustration of the co-construction of social reality also demonstrates the nature of the relationship between an illocution and its social force.

In accordance with these insights, the present paper treats statements of intentions, motivations, or goals as 'storylines', one element of the Positioning Triad. These storylines, like others, have a social force and position actors. While the social force and positionings can be verified, one cannot verify what a person's 'real intention' is. When an author takes a stance on the 'intentions' of a person or group, which has often been done in studies on the Rwandan genocide, (s)he is merely creating a storyline of his or her own. The author's storyline is no more valid than those of texts (s)he is analyzing.

While an illocution may 'incite' or 'encourage' (social force) a particular action, it can never 'cause' it. The analytical distinction defines causation as a determinate relationship (under certain conditions) between two events. In accordance with Positioning Theory, the relationship between two social forces is not causal but normative. One social force may make another appropriate. For example, if George compliments Hillary on her choice of clothing, it may be appropriate for her to reply with an expression of gratitude. However, one social force does not 'cause' another: Hillary can choose to slap George instead. Someone 'encouraged' to kill another person can refuse. Thus, an understanding of the normative context generated should be taken neither as a stamp of approval, nor as a suggestion that other options were not available to actors. One option is to counter the meaning-system proposed – that is, the positionings and the resulting normative framework – with an alternative meaning system that provides alternatives for action.

Inherent to meanings systems is an intrinsic 'logic', according to which certain actions are appropriate and others not. Such meaning systems can be captured in simple metaphors, such as the 'self defense' example given above or the phrase, 'ethnic cleansing'. The term 'ethnic cleansing' implies that the target to be 'cleansed' is 'dirty' or 'impure'. What does one logically do to impurities? One eradicates them. The simple logic hidden within the metaphor suggests (normatively) appropriate action. Thus, RTLM radio journalists refer to Tutsis as 'cockroaches' and propose that they should be 'exterminated'. This logic will be highlighted in the analysis below.

The characterization of the discourse in RTLM's radio broadcasts as 'hate speech' by the ICTR and various scholars (Gulseth, 2004; ICTR, 2003; Schabas, 2000) warrants a brief discussion of the role of emotion in the discursive production of conflict. Within the current approach, emotions are but one of many psychological phenomena produced in discourse, the production of which 'depends upon the skill of the actors, their relative moral standing in the community and the storylines that unfold' (Harré & Gillet, 1994: 27; Harré & Van Langenhove, 1999: 4). Accordingly, discourse does not cause emotions, or other mental phenomena, like attitudes. Rather, emotions are 'immanent in the relevant discursive activities themselves' (Van Langenhove & Harré, 1999: 16).

Scholars have long debated over the nature of racial and ethnic differentiations. In arguing that the 'ethnicization' of the terms 'Hutu' and 'Tutsi' is politically constructed, not primordially vested, Fujii (2001) depicts the status of the terms 'Hutu' and 'Tutsi' before they became 'ethnic' labels and follows the process of reinterpretation to understand 'how these terms came to represent 'ethnic' rather than 'social' identities' (p. 2). The author Des Forges (1999) provides various interpretations of the history of Hutu and Tutsi relations (see also Fujii, 2002). Within the approach presently advocated, such histories can all be treated as different storylines that position the actors (including Tutsi and Hutu) in different ways. While these may provide useful background information, the concern of the present paper is to illustrate the meanings given to 'Tutsi' and 'Hutu' in the discourse of RTLM broadcasts.

Positioning Analyses

In order to illuminate the process of meaning construction during the 1994 Rwandan genocide, the present study uses the Positioning Triad as a framework to analyze the discourse of RTLM radio broadcasts. While the present study uses radio transcripts due to their power, influence and availability, in the present approach, media is not to be treated as qualitatively different from any other discourse. The transcripts, translated from Kinyarwandan into English and French, were obtained from the ICTR. Important to note is that the analysis is intended to be illustrative, not exhaustive or 'representative' of all discourse that constituted the conflict. The following positioning analyses also

TABLE 12.1. Legitimization and Consequences in Meanings Systems Generated Through RTLM Discourse.

Storyline	Positions	Social force	Legitimization and consequences
Tutsis want power & will take everything from Hutus.	Tutsi: Abusers, thieves Hutu: Victims	Warning, accusation	Hutus have right to defend themselves. →SL: Hutus are defending their country.
Tutsis kill 'Rwandans' indiscriminately & cruelly.	Tutsi: foreigners, wicked savages, barbaric, criminal, animals Hutu: Rwandan, innocent	Warning, accusation	Hutu have right to purge Tutsi from Rwanda.
We (RTLM) tell the truth; the other (Tutsi mélange) is lying.	Tutsi: liars Hutu: honest	Warning, accusation	Hutus have the right to be trusted; Tutsis should be mistrusted.
Hutus are fighting for democracy.	Tutsi: minority, uncompromising, suicidal Hutu: majority, just	Claim of injustice	Hutu majority has right to maintain power. Tutsis have no right to power. →SL: Tutsi effort is suicide.
Tutsis have attacked Rwandan sovereignty – & want to destroy the country.	Tutsi: war machine, terrorists, nihilists, foreigners Hutu: victims, Rwandan	Claim of injustice	Rwandans (Hutus) have right to purge Tutsis from country to defend their national sovereignty.
Hutus want peace, but Tutsis want war.	Tutsi: greedy, hawkish Hutu: reasonable, dovish	Accusation, Claim of injustice	Tutsi are violating duty to support peace; Hutus are fulfilling this duty.
God is on the Hutu's side & wants Tutsi to perish. Good vs. evil.	Tutsi: evilHutu: good	Affirmation	Tutsi are sinning; Hutu are righteous.
Whites abandoned the Hutu & seek to destroy Rwanda.	Whites: attackers, selfish Hutu: victims	Accusation, Warning	Rwandans (Hutu) have right to defend themselves & shouldn't rely on 'Whites'.
Tutsi abuse children.	Tutsi: cruel	Accusation	Tutsis violate duty to respect human rights.
Tutsi teach children to hate Hutu.	Tutsi: security threat Hutu: victims	Warning	Tutsis violate duty to support peace.
Tutsi oppress Hutu.	Tutsi: oppressors Hutu: victims	Accusation, Warning	Tutsi violate Hutus' rights; Hutus should fight for their rights.

highlight the processes of legitimization and logics inherent to the meanings systems generated. The results are summarized in Table 12.1: Legitimization and Consequences in Meanings Systems Generated Through RTLM Discourse. The analysis presented below begins with an illustration of how various groups and individuals are amalgamated into one group, which is positioned in various ways, including as 'the enemy'. The rest of the analysis is organized by storylines.

Positionings of Tutsi/ Inkotanyi/ Inyenzi/ Rwandan Patriotic Front (RPF)

The terms 'Tutsi', 'Inkotanyi' 'Inyenzi' and 'Rwandan Patriotic Front' (RPF), although sometimes distinguished, more often than not were used inter-changeably in RTLM broadcasts. In other words, the Tutsi were positioned as Inkotanyi and Inyenzi and were equated with the RPF. 'Inkotanyi' – in most contexts – is the word used for the group against which the Rwandan Armed Forces (FAR)[3] was fighting. In one radio text, it is defined as follows: 'The people against whom we are fighting are of three types. Their common name is "the Inkotanyi"' (Author's translation from French; RTLM 21/05/1994; ICTR 99-52-7, p103/10C, K0143653). The term 'Inyenzi' literally means 'cockroaches' in the Kinyarwanda language. Kimani (2000) elaborates upon the development of the term's use:

In the years preceding the 1994 genocide, Tutsis in Rwanda were often called by the slang epithet 'Inyenzi', which means 'cockroaches.' Tutsis who fled Rwanda during the pogroms that followed the revolution of 1959, in which a Tutsi monarchy was overthrown, had originally used the term themselves. These exiles tried to come back into Rwanda in 1960's using force. They allegedly used the term Inyenzi to imply that, like the tenacious household pest, they would invade secretly at night. However, when the term was revived in the 1990's to refer to RPF, a new army of invading Tutsis, Inyenzi developed a separate and sinister meaning. According to Human Rights Watch researcher Alison Des Forges, it came to imply vermin to be exterminated and removed from the Rwandan household.

It is with the assertion, 'There is no difference between the RPF and the Inyenzi' that the RTLM journalist, Gaspard Gahigi, introduced a radio interview of the historian, Ferdinand Nahimana. He followed this with the query, 'Perhaps as a historian you could explain the relationship between the RPF and the Inyenzi to our listeners?' The historian confirms the journalist's initial assertion and elaborates upon it (International Monitor Institute, 2003).

The equation of Tutsis with this mélange is evident in the following passage, in which the radio journalist, Kantano, tells a story about a member of Interahamwe[4] taking a bribe from a half-Tutsi man in exchange for his life, and he warns (social force) against so doing:

Another man called Aloys, Interahamwe of Cyahafi, went to the market disguised in military uniform and a gun and arrested a young man called Yirirwahandi Eustache in the market, a merchant who has been selling things at the market for 18 years. In his Identity Card it is written that he is a Hutu through he acknowledges that his mother is a Tutsi. ...This man Aloys and other Interahamwe of Cyahafi took Eustache aside and made him sign a paper of 150000 Frw. ... If you are a cockroach you must be killed, you cannot change anything; if you are Inkotanyi you cannot change anything. No one can say that he has captured a cockroach and the latter gave him money, as a price for his life; this cannot be accepted. If someone has a false identity card, if he is Inkotanyi, a known accomplice of RPF, don't accept anything in exchange; he must be killed (RTLM transcripts K0143676).

Tutsis were thus positioned, without distinction, as members of the military group, RPF, as 'cockroaches', and as 'inkotanyi', the enemy of the Rwandan government military, the FAR. This mélange, as positioned by the radio journalists, will henceforth be referred to as the 'Tutsi mélange'.

In addition to the confounding of the above groups into one common 'enemy', the Tutsi-mélange was also positioned in various other de-humanizing, criminalizing ways. These include being positioned as arrogant, contemptuous and crazy:

'The contempt, the arrogance, the feeling of being unsurpassable have always been the hallmark of the Tutsis. They have always considered themselves more intelligent and sharper compared to the Hutus. It's this arrogance and contempt which have caused so much suffering to the Inyenzi-Inkotanyi and their fellow Tutsis, who have been decimated. And now the Inyenzi-Inkotanyi are also being decimated, so much so that it's difficult to understand how those crazy people reason...' (Kantano Habimana, RTLM, 31, May 1994; ICTR 99-52-T, p. 103/17D).

The following anecdote uses analogy to position the Tutsi-mélange as liars:

'...When you say to a girl of easy virtue, "Miss, you are licentious", she denies it. That is not serious. But when she gets pregnant, she can no longer refute the fact. The Inkotanyi have reached that point. They are like a young girl pregnant with an illegitimate child, thus providing irrefutable proof to those who were accusing her of lustful behavior. All this would have been more tolerable if the Inkotanyi were only not guilty of licentiousness. When you tell them: "You, Inkotanyi, you kill people, you kill people atrociously, you indulge in torture", they resort to flattery with their smooth tongue, pride, arrogance' (Kantano, RTLM, Audio-Tape No. 0009, K0169266).

The RTLM journalists positioned them as nihilists who want to destroy everything:

Unfortunately the Inyenzi-Inkotanyi do not want life to continue, they want everything in this country to come to a standstill, schools, health centers, hospitals, everything (Kantano Habimana, RTLM 02/07/1994; K7 20 Tape no. 0215, KT00-0936).

The Tutsi-mélange was also positioned as a group of terrorist evil-doers with suicidal tendencies:

'The Good Lord is really just, these evil doers, these terrorists, these people with suicidal tendencies will end up being exterminated' (Kantano Habimana, RTLM, 2 July 1994; ICTR 99-52-T, p 103/40D).

Furthermore, they were positioned as 'wicked savages', a 'barbaric war machine', and cannibals:

...What is even more distressing is that ... I have already told you this, we have often said so ... the methods of execution used by the Inyenzi-Inkotanyi ...they kill in a cruel manner ...they mutilate the body ... and remove certain organs such as the heart, the liver and the stomach. This is what I was telling you yesterday, that the Inyenzi-Inkotanyi could be eating human flesh ... no, there is no doubt about that anyway, since ...what do they do with all the organs they remove from the bodies? They do eat human flesh ...the Inyenzi-Inkotanyi eat human beings... so much so that we have little hope of finding any remains... (Valérie Bemeriki, RTLM, 14 June 1994; ICTR 99-52-T, p 99F).

Building upon these de-humanizing positionings, they were, in various ways, more directly positioned as animals. In addition to the 'cockroach' positioning, the Tutsi mélange is referred to as a 'species', 'dogs' and 'weevils':

'Be advised that a weevil has crept into your midst.' (Gahigi Gaspard, RTLM, 14 March 1994; ICTR 99-52-T, p 36/54B)

To position people as animals is to de-legitimize them, since animals are generally not accorded the same rights as human are. As discussed above, the logic intrinsic to the metaphor that Tutsis are pests is that these 'cockroaches' should be 'exterminated'. This conclusion was repeated frequently by RTLM radio journalists, as exemplified in the following passage:

...They are hard to please, they are wicked... It is obvious that they were created to gulp our Rwandan blood and to kill. It is in their nature. It is thus a waste of time to continue pleading with them... Let them take up guns, we will do the same. Let the Inyenzi's fate be sealed, as is already the case. Storming around, running all over the hills, saying that they have captured here and there, killing the population that is running away from them, that does not make any sense. Actually, when the time for elections comes, it is not those banana-trees, frogs, Muhazi's fish or the corpses they have thrown in Muhazi which will go to the polls. No. It will be our people who are surely on our side and whom we should help regain possession of their property. So, we have no other choice but to fight the Inyenzi-Inkotanyi and to exterminate them (Valérie Bemeriki, RTLM Tape no. 0035 (KT00-0876), 20/06/1994).

Another radio journalist draws the same conclusion and explicitly justifies his reasoning with a claim that the group is of a single ethnicity:

One hundred thousand young men must be recruited rapidly. They should all stand up so that we kill the Inkotanyi and exterminate them. ... The reason we will exterminate them is that they belong to one ethnic group. Look at the person's height and his physical appearance. Just look at his small nose and then break it (Kantano Habimana, RTLM Tape No. 0134 (KT00-0490), 04-05/06/1994).

Thus, the conclusion to kill thousands of innocent individuals was facilitated by the internal logic of the meaning system promulgated in the radio broadcastings and by the amalgamation of various groups and individuals into a large, diffuse and pervasive 'enemy'. While the rest of the analysis is organized into storylines, this amalgamated positioning, here referred to as the Tutsi-mélange, should be kept in mind.

Storyline: Tutsis Seek Power and Property

Through the employment of various storylines, the Tutsi-mélange was accused (social force) of having various dubious motivations. For example, the positioning of the Tutsi-mélange as 'barbaric' and 'savage' was also used to question their 'real' motivations for fighting, which the RPF had claimed was to achieve a power-sharing government and right of return for Rwandan Tutsi refugees. The following excerpts reveal a motivation storyline that the Tutsi are only interested in gaining power and property, a repeated theme in the broadcasts:

[The Inkotanyi] hide behind an old woman so if someone shoots them, the bullet will hit the old woman and the Rwandan Armed Forces dare not do that. These people hide inside houses, like real bandits, and will rather die without food. Anyway, they are bandits. So they stay with their hostages, some of whom dies. I heard about one Thaddée, I still hear about…other persons whom they found inside the houses… the occupant was a Hutu, he would be cut into pieces with a machete or burnt alive. Whoever was an Interahamwe or a member of the CDR, who is not a member if PL LANDO, PSD, MDR RUKOKOMA or PSD/NZAMURAMBAHO, has his fate sealed. There are currently some unfortunate people in Remera who have not been able to escape the killers. They were savagely killed…. These desperate Inkotanyi found some people in their houses and preferred to lock them up and leave them to die of hunger. That clearly shows that the Inkotanyi love property and power and not the people (Kantano Habimana, RTLM K0163176, 12/04/1994).

Here, use of the metaphor 'bandits' captures the notion that the Tutsi-mélange wants to steal what is not rightfully theirs, be it power or property. Tutsi-mélange wants to steal what is not rightfully theirs, be it power or property. In the same vein, and given the importance of agriculture to the livelihood of the people, the journalists frequently make the explicit accusation and warning (social forces) that the Tutsis intend to steal the Hutus' crops:

The cockroaches are running there in our cassava plantation, where they are digging out bananas, eat [sic] and make beer from bananas they didn't plant… (Kantano Habimana, RTLM 28/05/1994; ICTR 99-52-T, p 103/11B, K0143679).

Thus through the accusation that they trespass upon the rights of others, the Tutsi are de-legitimized. The logical conclusion is that the Hutu have the right to defend what is rightfully theirs.

Storyline: The Tutsis Lie While the Hutus Tell the Truth

Further undermining the legitimacy of the Tutsi-mélange and their claims is a storyline that, while the Hutu are telling the truth, the Tutsi are lying. The Hutu are thus positioned as having integrity and being trustworthy, while the Tutsi are devious and to be mistrusted. This de-legitimizes the Tutsi for not fulfilling their duty to be honest while legitimizing the Hutu for fulfilling the same duty. In the following passage, the accusation (social force) that the Tutsi-mélange tells lies is used to cast doubt upon their purported motivations. The radio journalist's answer is the storyline that their 'real' motivation is to acquire power:

The main common point between that war of UNAR's members and this Inkotanyi war is the telling of lies to the population. To lie that you control the town while you do not. To lie that you control the country while you do not. To lie that the armed forces should join you. … What we inherited from Parmehutu is the integrity, the truth, and those were the reasons for which the Revolution took place. The rejection of inequality, of the lie, of pretending to be superior or (inaudible), while the residents want the truth. It is the same thing now except that when the war broke out, most of us thought that it was in connection with the problem of the repatriation of refugees. Is it still the same situation? At the beginning of the war, the Inkotanyi said that they wanted Habyarimana. Now that they have killed him, what are they fighting for? They are fighting for the power they used to have before 1959 and which they think they can re-conquer. The situation is getting more and more clear [sic]. What is clear now is that this war revealed their true objective (Karamira Froduald, RTLM 17/05/1994, ICTR File 0008, K0143606).

The same storyline is also used to de-legitimize RTLM's rival radio station, radio Muhabura, and its claims:

I salute the journalists of radio Muhabura (which belongs to the Inkotanyi), adversary radio of great importance that affronts RTLM via the sound waves. Dear journalists, we are listening attentively to the ridiculous rumors you are spreading. We must refute them at all cost. You have said this morning that I declared that persons who are fleeing must be seized and killed. You lie, you clumsily capture information like someone who actually lives in the bush (Author's translation from French) (Habimana Kantano, RTLM 29/05/1994; ICTR 99-52-T, p 103/15C, K0143708).

Storyline: Tutsi Attack on Rwandan National Sovereignty

By positioning the members of the Tutsi force as foreigners from Burundi, the RTLM radio journalists generate a storyline that the Tutsi-mélange is attacking Rwanda's national sovereignty. The actions of the force are de-legitimized, because as alleged foreigners they fail to uphold their duty to respect the 'sovereignty' of another nation. The implicit logic is that the Hutus have the right to purge them from Rwanda:

The day we will attack them and chase them away from Bujumbura, they should only have themselves to blame because they will have provoked us. In any case, Rwanda has the right of pursuing them. If you are attacked from outside your country, you have the right to pursue the attackers into their country of origin. So, if we use our right of pursuit and chase Burundian Tutsis from power in Bujumbura they should not blame us because they will have provoked us (Kantano Habimana, RTLM Tape No. 0134 (KT00-0490), 04-05/06/1994).

This meaning construction concomitantly legitimizes the use of violence on the part of the Hutus in order to 'defend their right to sovereignty'. As reflected in the positioning of the Tutsi-mélange as nihilists, exemplified above, the journalists further warn (social force) that, in its 'attack on Rwanda', the Tutsi-mélange wants to destroy the country, which can be seen as an elaboration of this storyline.

Storyline: The Hutu Majority is Fighting for Democracy

In positioning the Hutu as the 'majority', RTLM journalists position them with the right to govern, in accordance with the rules of a democracy. In contrast, the Tutsi-mélange is positioned as the (numerical) 'minority', and thus with the duty to respect the rights of the majority. The storyline invoked is that the Hutus, positioned as the majority group, are fighting for democracy:

If Hutus unite and understand that Tutsis should abandon their thirst for power forever, then clearly, no foreigner will rule Rwanda. We are the ones who should rule, in full democracy. It is therefore clear that if one ethnic group in the country takes an uncompromising stand while it constitutes the minority, the majority cannot roam around asking for help saying that the minority ethnic group has attacked them. This would be utter foolishness. This is disgraceful in the eyes of the international community, which says that if an ethnic group rises against us, we should fight back and subjugate it, and if we lose, we should allow it to govern. It is then impossible for the Tutsi minority, which is 8%, to defeat the Hutus and to rule the country just because it is backed by Museveni (Kantano Habimana, RTLM Tape No. 0134 (KT00-0490), 04-05/06/1994).

This storyline legitimizes the Hutu and their actions, because they are portrayed as fighting for the rights due them by virtue of the rules of democracy: the majority rules. It simultaneously de-legitimizes the Tutsi with the accusation (social force) that they are trespassing upon the rights of the majority (and hence fail to uphold their duty).

Storyline: Tutsi Oppressed Hutu and Will Do So Again

Further questioning the motivations of the Tutsi-mélange, the journalists frequently evoked the storyline that the Hutu had previously been oppressed by the ruling Tutsi (minority) elite. In one broadcast, a radio journalist recounts the following narrative:

Let me take my own example, for I was born a Hutu; my father is a Hutu, my grandfather is a Hutu, my great grandfather is a Hutu and all my mother's parents are Hutus. I can go up the genealogy of my family back to about the ninth generation. They are Hutus. They brought me up as a Hutu, I grew up in Hutu culture. I was born before the 1959 revolution; my father did forced labour, as Charles said. My mother used to weed in the fields of the Tutsis who were in power. My grandfather paid tribute-money. I saw all those things, and when I asked them why they go to cultivate for other people, weed for other people when our gardens were not well maintained, they would tell me: 'that is how things are: we must work for the Tutsis' (Jean-Bosco Brayagwiza, RTLM, 12 December 1993; ICTR 99-52-T, p 103/101B, 0101e).

This storyline is projected into the future with the accusation and warning (social forces) that the Tutsi's intention is to re-take power and again oppress the Hutu (majority):

It is not only today that the PRF's Inyenzi Batutsis want to take and monopolize power in order to oppress the Hutus and cast democracy out of the window, the Batutsi's superiority complex has been around for a very long time. Thus, they established schools like the famous Astrida Secondary School in Butare and the Ishuri ry'Indatwa, the elite Nyanza School in Nyabisindu, opened in 1907. The schools were not for everybody, much less for the Hutus, who had been enslaved for centuries and had no access to these schools. According to the feudal colonial legend, the schools were meant for only those born to govern, in other words, Tutsi children considered as the most intelligent. It is this superiority complex which set the Tutsis apart because, even today, many of them are still convinced of their intellectual superiority to the rest of the Rwandans (Georges Ruggiu, RTLM 12/04/1994; ICTR 99-52-T, p 103/4B, 0004, K0163183).

The projection of the intention to 'oppress' again de-legitimizes the Tutsi's actions, since inherent to 'oppression' is a lack of respect for the rights of the oppressed. Concurrently, Inherent to being the 'oppressed' is having the right to fight for one's rights.

Storyline: The Tutsi Effort is Suicide

Given their positioned status as a small minority, as well as the purported strength of the FAR, the journalists conclude that the efforts of the Tutsi-mélange can be equated with a suicide mission:

Tomorrow the delegates of the FAR will engage with the Inyenzi-Inkotanyi. I recommend them to smoke cannabis to effectively brave these thugs who have invaded our fields to steal our crops. They will gain no political benefits from the war. They will never win elections. It is in their interest to stop the combats because they continue to commit suicide (Authors translation from French) (Habimana Kantano, RTLM 29/05/1994, ICTR 99-52-T, p 103/15C, K0143711).

The terms 'suicidal' and 'crazy' are repeatedly used to le-legitimize the actions of the Tutsi-mélange by suggesting they go against the 'common sense' - that is, the logic inherent to the meaning systems propagated by the RTLM journalists.

Storyline: Hutu Want Peace, But the Tutsi Want War

In RTLM broadcastings, the Tutsi-mélange is positioned as greedy – as wanting more that is rightfully theirs. The conclusion drawn is that, despite the Hutu's desire for peace, the Tutsi initiated and prolong the state of war, due to their unreasonable demands:

It is not for the Rwandans to impede the peace of Rwanda. But as it appears, the RPF's attitude is making things difficult for us. ...As for the party MDR, we wish peace for all the Rwandans. We wish the war would end. Such has always been our wish. However, the one that does not want to put an end to it and that is what the UNAR did, is losing. He is losing property and people. Because when you look at those [Arusha] agreements, they gave to the RFP more than what it would have got from elections. For the sake of people's peace. And now, it wants even more than what it had been given when we consider how the war was launched and how it is conducted. We hope that they will understand and display common sense and protect their relatives and ensure peace in Rwanda (Froduald Karamira, RTLM 17/05/94, ICTR 99-52-T, p103/8B, K0143609).

Herewith, the onus for the suffering of the people under wartime conditions is attributed to the Tutsi, and they are positioned as not upholding their duty to support efforts for peace. Hutus, in contrast, are legitimized as fulfilling this same duty.

Storyline: God is on the Hutus' Side

RTLM journalists evoke the storyline that God is on the Hutu's side:

The Good Lord is really just, these evil doers, these terrorists, these people with suicidal tendencies will end up being exterminated (Kantano Habimana, RTLM, 2 July 1994; ICTR 99-52-T, p. 103/40D).
The Rwandan God is on our side, he is not far away and I believe he will continue to help us in our misfortune, our serious misfortune which has no parallel in the world. How can a minority, a small group of people assemble bandits to chase the authorities elected by the majority of the population out of power? That has never happened anywhere and I hope such will never happen to the Rwandans. The God of the Rwandans will save us from this (Kantano Habimana, RTLM 12/04/1994; ICTR 99-52-T, K0163180).

Inherent in this storyline is the positioning of the Hutu as good and the Tutsi as bad/evil, as is made explicit in the following broadcast excerpt:

Continue with vigor; we cannot accept that the bad triumph over the good. Continue in solidarity and pray that God will answer our prayers (Author's translation from French) (François Nsengiyunva, RTLM 17/04/1994, ICTR 99-52-T, 2432bis).

This is perhaps the ultimate legitimization technique, in the eyes of some, since the will of God is not to be questioned - enough said!

Storyline: Whites Abandoned Hutu and (Also) Seek to Destroy Rwanda

In contrast to God, who is purportedly on the Hutu's side, the journalists must explain the international community's intervention on behalf of the Tutsi. To give meaning to this development, they evoke the storyline that 'Whites' – and Belgians in particular – have (again) abandoned the 'Rwandans' (e.g. Hutu).

The whites have just abandoned us and that is no surprise! What relationship is there anyway between us and them? If you depend so much on them, you will eat trash. You should not rely on their assistance or their lies because they are always after their own interest (Kantano Habimana, RTLM 12/04/1994; ICTR 99-52-T, K0163180).

In the radio broadcasting the accusation (social force) is made that Belgians, like the Tutsi-mélange want to destroy Rwanda:

It is a pity that the Belgians seek to destroy Rwanda by beginning with the main entrance [the airport]! ... The Rwandan government should be ready to request that the Rwandan ambassador to the UN file a complaint against Belgium because it has attacked Rwanda (Author's translation from French) (Nsengiyunva François, RTLM 17/04/1994, ICTR 99-52-T, 2428-9 bis).

Especially given Rwanda's past under Belgian colonial rule, this storyline undermines the legitimacy of the 'Whites' and their actions. Intrinsic to the metaphor 'abandonment' is the accusation (social force) that the abandoner has failed to uphold his duty to provide solidarity.

Storyline: Tutsi Abuse Children

Another storyline evoked is that the Tutsi-mélange abuses children. This storyline de-legitimises the Tutsi through the accusation (social force) that they do not fulfill their duty to protect and respect the rights of children.

It is sad to hear that the cockroaches (RPF) take 12 year children, young children, to the battlefield and give them difficult tasks because there are children, still ignorant, and not yet intelligent enough. The child may think that he can pass through the shootings or fly. They make him pass in fire and when they shoot, they tell him that nothing bad can happen to him (Kantano, RTLM 16-17/05/1994; ICTR 99-52-T, p103/2B, K0143489).

Since children are portrayed, and generally seen, as innocent and helpless, the accusation positions Tutsi as particularly savage.

Storyline: Tutsi Teach Children to Hate Hutu

In addition to abusing children, in the following excerpt from an RTLM programme, a journalist generates the storyline that Tutsi are teaching children to hate Hutu:

Jeanne is a sixth-form teacher at Mamba, Mamba in Muyaga commune. Jeanne is not doing good things in this school. Indeed, it has been noted that she's the cause of the bad atmosphere in the the classes she teaches. She had a husband named Gaston, a Tutsi, who took refuge in Burundi. He left, but when he reached the other side, he started to plot against the Hutus of his commune; he arranged their murder through this woman, his wife, Jeanne. He is doing everything possible to launch attacks in Muyaga commune, through this woman named Jeanne, who is a teacher at Mamba, in Muyaga commune. She did not stop at that, she teaches that to her students; she urges them to hate the Hutus. These children spend the entire day at that, and it corrupts their minds. We hereby warn this woman named Jeanne, and, indeed, the people of Muyaga, who are well know for their courage, should warn her. You therefore realize that she is a security threat for the commune (Valerie Bemeriki, RTLM, 2 June 1994; ICTR 99-52-T, p 103/20B, 0020e).

This storyline is closely related to the one that Tutsi want war, as it also positions the Tutsi-mélange as failing to uphold the duty to support peace.

Storyline: Tutsi Hate the Hutu

The duty to support peace is also violated by the Tutsi according to this storyline, in which not only are the Tutsi teaching children to hate Hutu, but in general Tutsi hate Hutu. This storyline was invoked by playing a song entitled 'I Hate the Hutus', as well as through alleged interviews.

We have just been listening to a song called 'Nanga abahutu' (I hate the Hutus). We shall now listen to a journalist named Rwatubogo, François Rwatubogo, of the newspaper La Medaille Nyiramaciviri, who also says: "I hate the Hutus. I too hate the Hutus, who are wicked, wicked due selfishness, poverty, jealousy and ignorance [sic]. A selfish Hutu can forget his kin, those belonging to the same ethnic group as he does. He can conspire against his country to fill his belly, and that is why the Tutsis say, 'The Hutu consults his soothsayer about what to eat rather than what will kill him' (Kantano, RTLM 17-18/05/1994; ICTR 99-52-T, p103/9D, K0169274).

The song referred to, written and sung by Simon Bikindi at the height of the war, includes the following lyrics:

I hate those Hutus, those de-Hutuized Hutus, who have given up their identity, dear comrades. I hate those Hutus, those Hutus who walk blindly. Fools, naive Hutus committed in a war of which they do not know the cause. I hate those Hutus who can be brought to kill and who, I swear, kill Hutus, dear comrades. And if I hate them, it's all for the better (Hirondelle News Agency, 2006).

The storyline serves to create a belief that Tutsi hate Hutu, which at the time was likely to have the perlocutionary force of inciting anger in Hutu so that they would 'retaliate' against the Tutsi (Hirondelle News Agency, 2006).

Conclusion

In summary, the analysis reveals how, through various acts of positioning, duties and rights were attributed to actors in a way that served to de-legitimize the Tutsis (including everyone identified as falling within the framework of the Tutsi-mélange), and other actors allegedly on their side, and to legitimize Hutus and their actions. Tutsis (and their allies) were de-legitimized through invoked storylines and positions, in which they were accused (social force) of trespassing upon the rights of others or otherwise failing to fulfill their duties. In being positioned as the 'minority', rights were withheld from them. In contrast, Hutus were attributed rights, and thus legitimized, by being positioned as the 'majority'. Their actions, in particular the use of violence, were legitimized through storylines that interpreted these actions as 'self defense'.

The inherent logic common to the meanings generated by the RTLM journalists is that the Tutsi-mélange should be 'exterminated' or 'kicked out', as illustrated by Ruggiu's conclusion in the following excerpt:

...This is... the time when the Rwandan people become more and more conscious that the RPF is no more than a barbaric machine, a war machine and that increasingly [people] in Gitarama, Butare, here in Kigali and yesterday, people of Byumba, they too, have begun to organize themselves. The population is determined to fight the Inyenzi-Inkotanyi and kick them out of the country (Georges Ruggiu, RTLM Tape No. 0134 (KT00-0490), 04-5/06/1994).

To reinforce this conclusion, the journalists engaged in a great deal of cheer-leading (social force) in which they encouraged Hutus to hunt out and eliminate Tutsis:

...You inhabitants of Kimisaga, start looking for them within the APACE premises in Kabusunzu. You people of Nykabanda, be vigilant, search the footpaths thoroughly and see if there are any Inkotanyi there. Go after them and ferret them out. Those of you at the roadblocks should go on checking particulars so as to avoid any surprises. Take heart, continue checking because anyone fighting the Inkotanyi should remain vigilant and should not slumber or even drink water since they always lie in wait for the slightest breach to sneak in (Habimana, RTLM 12/04/1994, ICTR 99-52-T, p 103/4B, K0163175).

Thus, to eradicate the Tutsis, according to the meaning system constructed by the RTLM journalists, was not only legitimate but the 'logical' thing to do.

How can the logic inherent to a particular meaning system be countered? One can propose an alternative metaphor: Instead of 'impurities', a minority can be an 'enrichment' to society. Because an enrichment is something to be treasured and nurtured, the logic of the metaphor suggests a fundamentally different alternative for (normatively) appropriate action. While a meaning system cannot be evaluated for its truth-value (e.g. there is no 'real' storyline), it can be evaluated according to the possibilities for action that it makes viable.

Returning to the question posed at the beginning of this chapter regarding the rights and responsibilities of media, this insight suggests certain duties for not only journalists and other media voices, but for all meaning-makers: It is every person's duty to examine the kind of reality engendered through their meaning constructions. It is the actual and potential consequences of this reality - the actions it facilitates - against which the rights to freedom of speech and freedom of press are to be weighed. Furthermore, when confronted with a violence-promoting meaning system, it is the duty of every individual to counter this with a meaning system that promotes tolerance and non-violent alternatives for action. A first step toward this skill is the ability to illuminate what is accomplished socially through discourse. This chapter has illustrated the utility of the Positioning Triad as a tool for systematic analysis of social realities – those lived and those dreamt of.

Abbreviations

ICTR - International Criminal Tribunal on Rwanda
RTLM - Radio Télévision Libre des Milles Collines
RPF - Rwandan Patriotic Front
FAR - Rwandan Armed Forces (The acronym is based upon the French translation.)

Notes

1. Kaufman (2001) provides a critique of various strands of rational choice theorists' explanations of ethnic war.
2. One can, however, say something about the 'correctness' of an interpretation according to a given cultural system.
3. At the time of the 1994 genocide, the FAR was the government-backed military
4. *Interahamwe* is a Hutu paramilitary organization that was backed by the Hutu government during, and heading up to, the genocide.

References

Abrams, D., & Hogg, M. A. (1990) (Eds.) (1990). *Social identity theory: Constructive and critical advances*. London: Harvester Wheatsheaf.
Della Morte, G. (2005) De-Mediatizing the Media Case. *Journal of International Criminal Justice*, 3(4), 1019-1033. Oxford: Oxford University Press. URL: http://jicj.oxfordjournals.org/cgi/content/abstract/3/4/1019.
Des Forges, A. (1999). *Leave none to tell the story: Genocide in Rwanda*. New York: Human Rights Watch. URL: http://www.hrw.org/reports/1999/rwanda/index.htm#TopOfPage.
Florini, A. (1996). The evolution of international norms. *International Studies Quarterly*, 40, 363-89.
Fujii, L. A. (2001). *Origins of power and identity in Rwanda*. Paper prepared for the annual conference of the International Studies Association, 20–24 February 2001, Chicago, IL, USA. URL: http://www.isanet.org/archive/fujii.html.

Fujii, L. A. (2002). *The diffusion of a genocidal norm in Rwanda.* Paper prepared for the annual conference of the International Studies Association, 24–26 March 2002, New Orleans, LA, U.S.A. URL: http://www.isanet.org/noarchive/rwanda.html.

Gulseth, H. L. (2004). The Use of Propaganda in the Rwandan Genocide: A Study of Radio-Télévision Libre des Mille Collines (RTLM). Thesis for the Cand. Polit. Degree at the Department of Political Science, University of Oslo.

Harré, R., & Gillet, G. (1994). *The discursive mind.* Thousand Oaks: Sage.

Harré, R., & van Langenhove, L. (eds.) (1999). *Positioning theory: Moral contexts of intentional action.* Oxford, UK: Blackwell.

Hirondelle News Agency (2006). Rwanda: Trial of Rwandan Singer Bikindi Opening Next Week At the ICTR. AllAfrica.com. 11 September 2006. URL: http://allafrica.com/stories/200609141118.html.

Hogg, M. A., & Abrams, D. (Eds.). (1999). *Social identity and social cognition.* Oxford: Blackwell.

International Criminal Tribunal for Rwanda (2003). The Prosecutor v. Jean-Bosco Barayagwiza, Hassan Ngeze and Ferdinand Nahimana, Case no ICTR-99-52-T. URL: http://69.94.11.53/ENGLISH/cases/Barayagwiza/CaseProfile/Cp281103.htm

International Monitor Institute (2003) Kantano Habimana and Humor as a Weapon. URL: www.imisite.org/rwanda.php.

Jowett, G. S., & O'Donnell, V. (1999). *Propaganda and persuasion.* London: Sage.

Katzenstein, P. J. (ed.). (1996). *The culture of national security.* New York: Columbia University Press.

Kaufman, S. J. (2001). *Modern hatreds: The symbolic politics of ethnic war.* Ithica and London: Cornell University Press.

Kimani, M. (2000). The Media Trial Accounting For the Rwandan Genocide - Impressions of the 'Media Trial'. ICTR Reports, December 5, 2000. Internews.

Moghaddam, F. (1998) *Social Psychology: Exploring Universals Across Cultures.* New York: W. H. Freeman and Company.

Schabas, E. A. (2000). Hate Speech in Rwanda: The Road to Genocide. *McGill Law Journal*, *46*(141), 142–171.

Scharpf, F. (1999). *Governing in Europe: Effective and democratic?* Oxford: Oxford University Press.

Van den Berghe, P. (1987). *The ethnic phenomenon.* New York: Praeger.

Van Hoywehgen, S., & Vlassenroot, K. (2000). Ethnic ideology and conflict in Sub-Saharan Africa: The culture clash revisited. In R. Doom & J. Gorus (Eds.), *Politics of identity and economics of conflict in the great lakes region* (pp. 93–118). Brussels: VUB Press.

Van Langenhove, L., & Harrè, R. (1999). Introducing Positioning Theory. In R. Harré & L. Van Langenhove (Eds.), *Positioning theory* (pp. 14–31). Oxford: Blackwell.

Wilson, E. O. (1975). *Sociobiology: The new synthesis.* Cambridge, MA: Belknap Press.

13
Rwandan Radio Broadcasts and Hutu/Tutsi Positioning

Daniel Rothbart and Tom Bartlett

In the field of international relations, threats are typically characterized as realpolitik tactics, deployed as instruments of power by nation-states. In reality, any threat is a form of coercion, control, power, manipulation, or possibly terror. This is particularly true of large-scale conflicts that persist for generations. In such cases threats can have a destructive effect on the ways protagonist groups define their identities and their essential differences. Over time, threats can shape, and reshape, a sense of group identities. Thus implicated in identity formation, threats can quickly escalate to function as a major source of violence.

In this chapter we examine how the Rwandan genocide of 1994 was fuelled by a qualitative shift in the anti-Tutsi ideology of Hutu extremists, and how this ideology heightened threat narratives in Hutu-Tutsi identities. The ideology of racial hatred in Rwanda has its historical roots in colonial rule. When the Belgians took control of Rwanda in 1916, they instituted policies that distorted racial divisions between Tutsis and Hutus. Tutsis were presumed to have "nobler," more "naturally" aristocratic dimensions than the "coarse" Hutus. Belgians placed Hutus in forced labor camps, road construction, and forestry crews and by the 1930s Tusti leaders enjoyed a complete and unprecedented monopoly of "traditional leadership positions" in Rwanda (Article 19:10). This situation was reversed, however, after a Hutu uprising in 1959, which left the majority of Tutsi chiefs dead or in exile and ushered in the "Social Revolution" of 1959. In the legislative elections of September 1961 there was widespread political violence against the Tutsi and Hutu parties won 83% of votes nationwide, a figure corresponding to the percentage of Hutu in the general population (Article 19:10–11). Full independence came on July 1, 1962 and in the legislative elections of 1965 only the Hutu-based MDR-Parmehutu party of President Grégoire Kayibanda fielded candidates.

Thus racial hatreds persisted even after Rwanda acquired full independence (Gourevitch, 1998, Chapter 4). Reversing the extreme pro-Tutsi ideology of Belgian rule, by the late 1980s and early 1990s Hutu extremists were portraying Tutsi as essentially degenerate and demonic and after the October 1990 invasion of the Uganda-based Rwanda Patriotic Army (RPA), a group of mainly Tutsi exiles (Article 19:13), some Hutu extremists were claiming that Hutu survival demanded the elimination of the Tutsi from Rwanda.

In this inquiry into the propagation of Hutu/Tutsi difference we employ the concepts and themes of positioning theory (Harré & Moghaddam (Eds.), 2003b; Harré & van Langenhove (Eds.), 1999b). A position is a set of right and obligations that are kept alive through storytelling practices and realised through speech and other acts. In the case of Rwanda, storytelling occurred through newspaper articles and radio broadcasts by anti-Tutsi ideologues in the years preceding the 1994 genocide. This anti-Tutsi media captivated some sections of the Hutu population's attentions with increasingly elaborate character assassinations of individual Tutsis, stories of past atrocities, and narratives of Tutsi plans for conquest. Positioning theory explains how Tutsi identity, already suspect to sections of the Hutu community was objectified as degenerate, criminal, and vicious through the storytelling power of those articles and broadcasts. Indeed, these media offered a sense of empowerment that comes from righteous hatred of an enemy and fomented violence among oppressed Hutus as the demonization campaign by anti-Tutsi propagandists further fabricated identity differences through the categories of virtues and vices.

A transforming moment in the radicalisation of Hutu opinion was the assassination of President of Rwanda, Juvenal Habyarimana in a plane crash near Kigali's airport on April 6, 1994. The country erupted into an orgy of violence and the systematic campaign of extermination by the interahamwe (Hutus death squads) resulted in approximately 800,000 murders and more than two million displaced from their homes. However, in this chapter we hope to show how the political propaganda that precipitated the 1994 genocide was not a new phenomenon but a shift in the anti-Tutsi ideology of the 1950s (above) which claimed that Tutsis had always dominated Hutus, exploiting a caste system of institutionalized injustice and brutality against them. Such an ideology perpetuated myths of the Tutsi as "power-hungry" and "terrible warriors," an "intelligent," "tricky," "double-dealing," and "dishonest" people whose presence in Rwanda served as a direct threat to the Hutus as genuine Rwandans.

More ancient distinctions were also mythologized and propaganda-centered notions of Tutsi-Hamite and Hutu-Bantus "races" flourished, deepening divisions. The myth of the "feudal" Tutsi seen as a "race of arrogant lords" was solidified. Many scholars attribute this myth to the work of a former seminarian, Gregoire Kayibanda (Semujanga, 2003, p. 172). He developed a racist ideology without race—in actuality, Hutus and Tutsis cannot legitimately be separated by race. Whatever physical distinction could be observed in past centuries had been obliterated through generations of intermarriage. The belief in a separate ethnic identity is at best highly suspect. According to the Genocide Convention of the ICTR Statute, an ethnic group is "a group whose members share a common language or culture." But Tutsis and Hutus share the same religion, language, and culture.[1]

In the 1990s racial hatreds were aggravated through various state-sponsored media. The periodical Kangura was particularly inflammatory. Distributed free of charge by state facilities, Kangura enjoyed wide popularity. It quickly became an outlet for anti-Tutsi propaganda, such as the racist document "The Ten Commandments." Although originally intended to unite the Hutus behind President Habyarimana and his party, the Hutu extremists used the Commandments to fuel Hutus' hysteria, to legitimize a strategy of extermination. Some of the commandments revealed "knowledge" of the Tutsi defects (Semujanga, 2003. pp. 196–7). For example, Commandment #1 reads:

Every Muhutu (Hutu) must know that Umututsikazi, wherever she is, works for her Tutsi ethnic group. Therefore, any Muhutu who weds a Mututsikazi, who makes of a Mututsikazi his concubine, who makes of a Mututsikazi his secretary or his Protégé is a traitor.

These commandants appeal to Hutus to understand Tutsi character, evident in "every Muhutu must know...." The other commandments include references to Tutsi as power-hungry, wicked, and deceitful. Hutu propaganda stated that as part of the Tutsi campaign of conquest, Tutsi women would try to seduce Hutu men to create hybrid descendants. The impact of such discourse can be interpreted in terms of an axiology of difference, and in this space we illustrate the dynamic nature of such an axiology using Positioning Theory and the tools of discourse analysis, as outlined below.

An Axiology of Difference

The naïve assumption that group identity exists independently of a set of beliefs, shared history, myths, symbols, and rituals must be abandoned. Group differences typically require a shared repository of beliefs about how the world is organized, and is typically viewed in terms of normative dualities, such as safe/dangerous, home/foreign, sacred/profane, and evil/virtuous, among others. The notion of realpolitik is itself a utopian idealization which attempts to separate political power from agents' value-commitments.

According to Erving Goffman's celebrated study, stigmatization is a process of creating differences that lead to social separation, moral denigration, and criminal culpability of various forms (Goffman, 1963). The process of stigmatizing individuals takes on special significance in the public media. When disseminated through radio, television, print media, and internet, threat narratives take on the aura of legitimate "news" and foster a sense of global, fixed, essential, and eternal differences. These stories explain the malicious deeds of the threatening Other, not by the fleeting circumstances of the social setting, but rather by their uncontrollably malicious, degenerate, or demonic behavior. They are portrayed as vicious, wicked, immoral, criminal, uncivilized, reprehensible, blameworthy, scurrilous, felonious, nefarious, infamous, villainous, heinous, atrocious, accursed, satanic, diabolic, hellish, infernal, fiendish, demonic, and depraved. As the threat narratives denigrate the Other, they reinforce the moral superiority of the ingroup. Exploits of those attempting to thwart advances of the invaders are glorified as pure, noble, angelic, saintly, or occasionally even godlike.

The question "Who are they [as a collectivity]?" calls for an understanding of the character, commitments, and plans of the Other. Such a manipulated understanding shapes and solidifies beliefs about group differences. That is, group positioning associated with threat narratives establishes an axiology of ingroup virtues and outgroup vices, and this axiology acquires a cognitive power for conflict protagonists. Storytellers organize the salient events of the past according to the categories of group virtues and vices. The collective axiology is used to "educate" the faithful to the "true" sources of hostilities, guide them in taking the right course of action, and prepare them for the struggle ahead.

An axiology of difference was thus created in Rwanda through a nexus of three kinds of constructions: icons, myths, and normative order (IMN). Such a nexus establishes moral imperatives, requiring of its followers vigilance against the threatening Other. In the case of anti-Tutsi ideology, such a nexus imposes a pre-formed logic of threat and survival, a logic that links "knowledge" of the threatening Other with an injunction for action. The "reality" of axiological difference is linked to the normative imperative for right and wrong in the face of the Tutsi threat. The cognitive force of this logic can be overpowering, fostering in some cases blind obedience and a suppression of individuality. The IMN nexus and resultant constructions are a formal cause of protracted conflict (Rothbart & Korostelina, 2006).[2] The threatening Other is characterized as eternally untrustworthy, committed to destruction, and capable of conquest. A pre-formed logic for action is solidified, as it fosters a sense of inevitable conflict. The narrative of inevitability follows from demands for vigilance, obedience, strength, and sacrifice (Frohardt & Temin, 2003). In some cases, the story of impending strategic incursion and conquest by the Other establishes the rationale for pre-emptive attacks against the "invaders" as a measure of "self-defense."

Normative Order

A normative order is framed through axiological categories of virtue and vice, right and wrong, and good and bad. Such an order provides a kind of global orientation, enabling an individual to locate him/herself in relation to others living in a dangerous world. Consider as examples the adherents of a fundamentalist religion, professional soldiers committed to national security, and militant members of national group. On such identity-grounds, the faithful are separated from "impure" Others through narratives of violence circulated throughout the group that establish and enshrine dualistic categories (virtues/vices, right/wrong, good/bad), and in so doing, provide coherence to the struggle of "us versus them" (cf. Moghaddam, 2006 on the topic of terrorist mentalities). In some cases, the threatened group acquires feelings of purity in their mission, and absolution of their past criminal acts. Threat narratives reassure the faithful of their own moral standing, or even of their moral supremacy, in a world populated by evildoers. Their positions are secured, their mission is sanctified, and their sacrifices are glorified.

A normative order has a temporal dimension. Protagonists of conflict live simultaneously in the past, future, and present. They continuously engage patterns and repertoires from the past, project hypothetical pathways forward in time, and adjust their actions to the exigencies of emerging situations (Emirbayer & Mische 1998, 1012). In some cases of identity-based conflict, all actions of the ingroup cohere with an idealized vision of "the good," a vision often projected backwards and forwards in time simultaneously. An act deemed heroic, for example, exhibits certain virtues that link past deeds to aspirations for a better world, inspiring later generations to continue along the same "righteous" path. The notion of the right course of action is inseparable from a vision of betterment, of promoting good and preventing bad. And such a vision is tied to the mythic narratives of the past.

Mythic Stories

Protagonists of conflict often recount the suffering of ingroup members in order to confirm that threats from the Other are "real." A history of malice enables the propagandists to develop and promote a pattern of the Other's degenerate character. Inflammatory accusations can be formed readily by fabrications of their criminal behavior. The scale and scope of the past injustices can be easily exaggerated, although at times grounded on real acts of oppression. The frequency of inflammatory reports, and the repetition of negative images of the Other exert a controlling force over the collective psyche.

Over the course of intergenerational storytelling about evil deeds, particular episodes become venerated, almost sanctified. These mythically reinforced events are lifted above the tide of history, and come to dominate the landscape of the ingroup's sacred past. Within the ingroup's collective imagination certain traumatic encounters with the Other occur in mythic time, outside of chronological history. Sacred events overshadow and supersede the mundane experiences of daily life. Certain places, times, and episodes are revered and relived, acquiring an explanatory power, offering insight into life's tragedies, sufferings, and pain.

This relation between the mythic past and axiological differences is depicted in the following Figure 13.1:

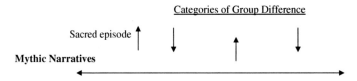

FIGURE 13.1. Mythic time.

This figure represents the interdependency of mythic narratives and notions of group difference in axiological terms. This axiology of difference constitutes a teliomorphic model of the social world, that is, a second-order idealization of first-order narratives.[3] This model is not static. It continually changes from the infusion of new, potentially sacred, episodes. In turn, the application of the teliomorphic model to new circumstances rests on the process of narrative exemplification of mythic episodes through their retelling in new events. In this figure the symbol "↑" represents a sacred episode that is recounted through generations of storytelling. The process of applying the model to a subsequent episode is represented as ↓, which depicts the transition from second-level teliomorphic model to first-level determinations of right and wrong, good and bad. The application of an axiology of difference to present or future scenarios thus confers a sense of stability to ingroup identity, and consistency (even fairness) in the implementation of norms. The virtues of justice demand uniform application of the axiological order, establishing a moral requirement for consistency, that is, always doing the right thing under similar conditions. Below we will exemplify the dynamics of this model using Positioning Theory, in which actions, including discourse, are seen as realising socio-psychological positions which are taken up in response to a storyline, with these actions feeding back into the evolving storyline.

Iconic Forms

Axiological differences are often fleshed out in riveting forms by employing icons of vice. The images of evil deeds are quickly converted to the icons of collective vice. Such icons transcend the locality of their empirical origins, and function as a graphic template for recognizing the enemy's character. In protracted conflict, where the group differences are given an aura of eternal truth, the icons of vice become prototypes of the essentially unjust, immoral, uncivilized, or possibly inhuman character of the Other.

Animal images are often used by racists as a means for demonizing the Other, for establishing the essential criminality, malicious nature, or degenerate character of the outgroup. Associating the Other with various animal images over a prolonged period can bring these iconic forms into common consciousness and so present the in-group with a default framework for interpreting the actions of the Other, which interpretations go on to strengthen the iconic representation of the Other as ruthless killers. In Rwanda for example the images disseminated by Hutu propagandists of the Tutsis as "filthy vermin," "snakes" and "cockroaches" transferred the eternal, biological associations of such creatures' malicious character onto the Hutu people. Again, the media provided a suitable instrument for solidifying this essential polity between the Hutus and Tutsis.

Using Discourse Analysis on Narratives of Sacred Events in Mythic Time

This section of our chapter develops the work of Rothbart and Korostelina as outlined above and uses discourse analytical methods to exemplify the processes captured in schematic form in their teliomorphic model (above). In particular, we focus here on accounts of real-time events, the relationship of these to narratives of sacred events set in mythic time, and their gradual assimilation into these mythic narratives. Such recontextualisation is a linguistic operation; however, the linguistic means for achieving this transformation are neither straightforward nor common property. Firstly, at the linguistic level they involve not only the renarrating of historical events within a mythical framework of time and space, but also the legitimation of this retelling through the interpersonal and rhetorical resources of language. Secondly, such linguistic legitimation is effective only for those with the appropriate symbolic capital (Bourdieu, 1991), the sociocultural prestige that lends to certain speakers an aura of authority in particular fields of discourse and before the relevant audience. Discourse, in these terms, is the mediational means through which speakers are able to realise their embodied symbolic capital as power in action within a specific "linguistic marketplace" (Bourdieu, 1991).

The linguistic analyses that follow therefore focus on textual devices for representing and evaluating reality, for situating events in time and space within a particular rhetorical or generic form as a socialising strategy, and for operationalizing the external symbolic capital of the speaker. Following the theory of Systemic Functional Linguistics (Halliday & Hasan, 1985), we can label these three parameters field (the representational), mode (the generic/textual) and tenor (the interpersonal). For events and situations (field) to be accommodated within a mythic and sacred storyline, they must be recontextualised in an appropriate form (mode) by legitimate speakers (tenor). For example, mythic language realises capital as power within groups for whom myth is a socialisation convention, provided the speaker is recognised as a "legitimate mythologiser" and the audience (and other elements of the marketplace) are appropriate. Once legitimated, such discourse becomes an "interpretative repertoire" for future events within that discourse community (Potter & Wetherell, 1987:172). These repertoires provide easily accessible narratives that speakers use to rationalise, justify or condemn their actions and those of others to a particular audience at a particular time, the community proxy for individual cognition, at times replacing individuality with blind obedience to the norm.

The following analyses, chronologically ordered to suggest the dynamics of media representations that precipitated the genocide, attempt to show the evolution of such interpretative repertoires within the framework of an axiology of difference based on sacred myths and events. They suggest a drift in discourse style along two parameters. There is a movement from a narrative style primarily concerned with recounting current events and recent history, using ethnic generalisation and essentialism as support, to a style that chiefly promulgates such stereotypes in the form of caricature and myth. This shift occurs in parallel with a movement from a textual authority derived from history, science and the law to a call for widespread grassroots vigilantism based on the authority of calls to tribal and family loyalty and the "common knowledge" of eye-witness testimony. However, the chapter does not claim to provide a complete picture of media discourse in the build-up to the Rwandan genocide and its role in that tragedy; it is intended to illustrate how a fuller discourse analysis might offer a rigorous and nuanced understanding of how a shift in perceived identity differences acted as a prelude to the genocide. Here we focus on what we see as the key linguistic aspects of the axiology of difference: the discursive construal of "mythic time" and "sacred events" and the evolution of these through the accommodation and assimilation of real-time events and circumstances through the dynamics of narrative exemplification. From this perspective the storyline, positioning and evoked acts of Hutu extremists evolved from the long-term situation sketched in Figure 13.2 to the far more radical position of Figure 13.3 in the period immediately prior to the genocide. Employing the analytical framework of positioning theory (Harré & Moghaddam, 2003, Chapter 1), the three points of the triangle represent the following: the storyline of past and current events that is maintained and developed in the minds of protagonist groups and which provides the interpretative repertoire against which future events will be evaluated and the rights and duties of the protagonists determined; the position of the protagonists in terms of their rights and duties and those of out-groups as determined by the evolving storyline; the actions that protagonists carry out or are supposed to carry out in light of the evolving storyline and the interpretation of their rights and duties within it. Importantly, the storyline can be reconstrued by those with the appropriate symbolic capital (Bourdieu, 1991) and couched in culturally powerful rhetorical styles so as to skew the interpretative repertoires of a group. If this occurs, the roles protagonists take up will follow almost as given and the

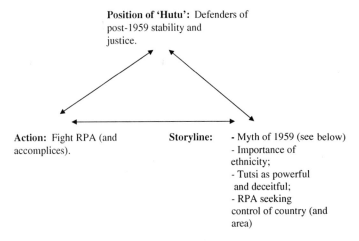

FIGURE 13.2. Post 1959 anti-Tutsi ideology.

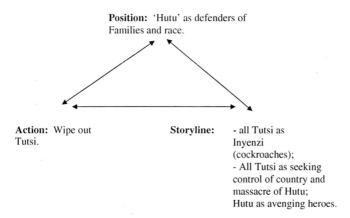

Position: 'Hutu' as defenders of Families and race.

Action: Wipe out Tutsi.

Storyline:
- all Tutsi as Inyenzi (cockroaches);
- All Tutsi as seeking control of country and massacre of Hutu; Hutu as avenging heroes.

FIGURE 13.3. Anti-Tutsi ideology in the immediate pre-Genocide period.

actions they carry out will not only appear justified but the only honourable path. Thus, a small shift in storyline as the source of a group's interpretative repertoire can lead to a significant reinterpretation of their roles and so onto an escalation of violence as the acts appropriate to these rights and duties are recalibrated. The purpose of the discourse analysis offered here is to track how these shifts occurred and to suggest a strategy for developing counter-discourses.

Returning to the Rothbart/Korostelina teliomorphic model, these two figures aim to capture in broad terms different stages of development in the mythic history of the Hutu extremists, storylines that are structured around axiological differences and which inform the positions taken up and used to justify extreme acts. We can use this model to trace the dynamics of change as a process of interaction between the mythic bases of belief/identity and situated narratives as the means of accommodation and assimilation between current events and the evolving myth. Figures 13.2 and 13.3, however, are not meant to represent an initial and a final state, but rather a direction. There is never a point where one storyline exists in isolation; nor is there a chain of storylines/triangles leading from one position to the next: at any time positioning is occurring at many different levels in relation to various goals and timescales. In other words, positions are not discrete and drifts are not steady and unidirectional; all we can say is that these are general tendencies and that the dynamic nature of positioning as well as the complexities of life in real time preclude analyses that are too neat. The following analyses, then, are intended to show how detailed consideration of linguistic features might be used to strengthen or challenge more global analyses. These analyses are focused around: (i) two discourse representations of the evolving axiological myth, from December 1990 and March 1993, a few months before the genocide; and (ii) media reports of the Government massacre of Bagogwe Tutsi in January 1991 as an illustration of narrative exemplification. These are followed by analyses of broadcasts from

Radio-Télévision Mille Collines (RTLM) during the genocide itself and the relationship of these to the evolving myth is discussed.

Some important caveats apply:

1. The texts used have already been chosen by previous authors to illustrate their conclusions;
2. They are not full or exhaustive;
3. They have been translated from Kinyarwanda to French to English.
4. The texts are sometimes excerpts that have been cut from longer texts and so lose some of their continuity.

The first texts come from the newspaper Kangura. Kangura was a familiar voice in creating and reaffirming myths of ethnic divisions in Rwanda, calling on Hutu to protect their rights against the Tutsi who, they repeatedly proclaim, were intent on taking over the country and disrupting the "natural balance" that had existed since the revolution of 1959. As Foreign Minister Casimir Bizimungu says on Radio Rwanda on 8th October 1990 (Article 19:25):

This terrorist organisation [Rwandan Patriotic Army] has as its only aim the establishment of a minority regime embodying feudalism with a modern outlook. The Rwandan people will not agree to reverse history, leading the nation's dynamic forces back to feudal drudgery and enslavement.

As this and the following passages suggest, pre-1959 Rwanda and ancient history often intermingled to create a single image of Tutsi rule as disorderly, barbaric and threatening to Hutus. This myth draws strongly on the idea that the Tutsi are not truly a Rwandan race, that they are at worst invaders and at best outsiders who have infiltrated Rwanda and who continue to dissimilate in order to receive more of their quota of jobs as scientifically assigned within the existing Hutu order. In Texts 1 and 2 we see how this myth is developed through historical narratives with an air of scientific authority and neutrality.

Text 1. Kangura 4. November 1990:21 (Chrétien et al.:109):
In the history of Rwanda the first arrivals are the Twa (Pygmies) who dedicated themselves to hunting and gathering; then the Hutu (Bantus) arrived who cleared the forest in order to farm there and who established a social organisation; finally the Tutsi came (nilotic, Ethiopides) who devoted themselves to cattle-breeding. Why does one want to change our history?
Who would have the right to change the history of the country?

Text 2, from a month later, repeats the ploy of using quasi-scientific language to mask racist discourse but this time uses this neutral language as a springboard into a more explicitly evaluative stance:

Text 2. Kangura 5. December 1990:7–8. (Chrétien et al.: 110):
1 The first inhabitants of Rwanda were the Twa, followed by the Hutu (7th century).

2 A long time after, the Tutsi infiltrated and quickly took power by a system of vassalage based on

3 the cow. Power was monarchical and feudal, and the other ethnic groups were reduced to

4 servitude: abused at will and exploited without mercy. The regime was oppressing and bloody.

5 For example, the queen mother Kanjogera, in order to rise from her seat,

6 would lean on two swords planted in the shoulders of two Hutu children...

7 The hypocrisy and the spirit of domination of the Tutsi extremists seem to be limitless

8 when those who have remained in the country are characterized by falsifying their identity

9 so as to occupy, beyond the positions already granted to them according to regional and ethnic

10 balance, a share of the positions that belonged to Hutus.

11 The Rwandan refugees never felt ashamed to keep on lying knowingly

12 that the Tutsi ethnic group was discriminated against.

13 They are, however, well represented in all sectors...

As stated above, we can analyse the development of this text along the three parameters of field, roughly the subject matter, including attributions of agency; tenor, focusing on the forms of authority that underlie the discourse and on evaluative language; and mode, the rhetorical styling of the discourse, labelled

TABLE 13.1. Phasal analysis of Text 2.

Lines	Phase	Field	Tenor	Mode
1–6	1	Early history of Rwanda and arrival of different ethnic groups. Control by Tutsi.	Straightforward, authenticity based on formal knowledge. Restrained, pseudo-factual negative evaluation.	Recount of historic events.
5–6	1.1	Mythological trope of savagery as exemplum of Tutsi control.	No evaluative language per se.	Recount of mythical events.
7–13	2	Untrustworthiness and dissimilation of modern Tutsi in claiming powerful positions not due to them; rationality of post-1959 system of allocation.	Authority of discourse based on personal opinion and purported visible evidence. Language more explicitly negative in evaluation.	Present Generalisation - extremist Tutsi treated as an abstract class.
11–12	2.1	Characterising Tutsi discrimination under Hutu as myth. Tutsi as liars.	Strongly evaluative language.	Past Generalisation/ Recount or recent past.
13	2.2	Reaffirmation of post-1959 justice.	Return to factual style. Authority of the system.	Generalisation/ Commentary on present state of affairs.

according to Cloran's (2000:175) schema.[4] The force of these variables in practice is a function of the symbolic capital of the speakers and the cultural significance of the rhetorical style in the specific linguistic marketplace. A change in any one of these three variables leads to a new phase (Gregory, 1988) of the discourse. Table 13.1 shows the different phases of Text 13.2 and their progression. The numbering of the phases (e.g. 1, 1.1, 2...) reflects the idea that one phase can be embedded in another as a subcomponent, an excursion rather than a change of course.

In the first paragraph we see what looks like a historical account of the origins of the Tutsi in Rwanda in which the depiction of Tutsi power as feudal and monarchical reads as authoritative, using an academic style to talk of historical groups and events. However, this neutral style is used to frame a more powerful mythical representation with the introduction of the Queen Mother Kanjogera, a powerful icon in representations of the RPA as wanting to return the country to pre-1959 backwardness (where the barbarism of mythical history and the perceived disorder of the 20th century social system are not clearly distinguished). The text thus moves from the historical concepts of vassalage and servitude to the more emotive oppressive and bloody onto the individualised icon of the evil Queen Mother with her swords stuck in the backs of innocent Hutu. Myth is thus embedded in pseudo-scientific reporting and borrows some of the credibility that style establishes.

The second paragraph can now complete the move by equating the icon of the Queen Mother and her ruthless domination to the Tutsi extremists of today (though, importantly, the qualification of extremists is still present). The personal opinion of "seem"[5] is soon hidden by the narrative example of Tutsi duplicity and the evocation of those who cheat the quotas afforded them by the post-1959 order and so subvert the system, seen as a model of modernity and justice when juxtaposed with the vassalage and bloodthirstiness of Tutsi rule. The language here is explicitly pejorative, until the return to the more neutral "fact-based" style of line 19. This phase of the text illustrates how objective facts can be accommodated to stereotypes: not only are the statistics showing the underrepresentation of Tutsi in powerful positions false, it is claimed, but the reason they are false is that the Tutsi cheat. This presumably reveals Tutsi deception, here only in terms of gaining employment, but is later developed to devastating effect to suggest that all Tutsi are accomplices and hence potential RPA soldiers.

In short, this brief passage shows the mixing of pseudo-factual language, myth and moral condemnation, as well as the identification of characters and events from history with narratives from the present. It also demonstrates the force of stereotype in overcoming more objective accounts of the status quo. It fits in with the first positioning triangle (Figure 13.2 above) by positioning the Hutu/government as defending the gains of 1959 against the backwardness of Tutsi extremism, while setting the ground for the move to the more radical second positioning (Figure 13.3). One of the principal ways this second positioning gains prominence is through extension of the already powerful duplicity myth to denigrate the entire Tutsi population – not just the extremists of the above text. The following issue of Kangura demonstrates this:

Text 3. Kangura 6. Dec 1990:10–11 (Chrétien et al.:290–291).
In truth, no one is unaware that we have been attacked by enemies of Rwanda who are called inkotanyi.[6] These enemies of the country prepared themselves a long time ago, since they were pushed back at the time of the first attacks, they didn't stop there, they went to prepare a war which will not leave anybody alive (simusiga). In preparing that war, they have constituted a network of accomplices among business people, among the military and the civilians, among the Rwandan journalists and foreigners.

At roughly the same time as texts such as the above are developing the myth of Tutsi duplicity, universal collusion with rebel forces and predictions of massacres, the parallel idea is developed that the Tutsi do not truly represent Rwanda, either historically as Nilotic interlopers, or in the present day, as they readily renounce their identity, are accomplices of "enemies of the country", and are even plotting to colonise the entire region of Central Africa and enslave the Hutu (Article 19:67). This combination of narrative moves is brought into prominence after the RPA capture Ruhengeri for a day in late January 1991, liberating prisoners there (Article 19:29). The following texts demonstrate how this event is narrated to reinforce and develop the sacred myths outlined above. The first is a Radio France International report (24/1/91) from newly appointed director of the state information department ORINFOR, Ferdinand Nahimana, under whom "the radio [Radio Rwanda] broadcasts tended to become more virulent and distorted" (Article 19:29):

...these attackers included a number of Libyan commandos...the proof comes from the information we received precisely from those who fled Ruhengeri prison, who say the Arabs had freed them.

This report might well be for international consumption, but it also contributes to the myth of Tutsi as less Rwandan than the Hutu. While for this myth the idea of accomplices refers to outside agents, it is later also used to refer to insiders as notions of agency are muddied and a general notion of uncertainty and fear is promulgated. Kangura 9, from January 1991 (Chrétien et al.: 291–292), narrates the events as follows:

The accomplices of Ruhengeri have taught us a lesson, we should understand that if we persevere in being unconcerned we will be exterminated by the accomplices of the inkotanyi...
... Before I arrived at [the] center of Ruhengeri town city, I met with the warrant officer Sukiranya who runs the prison of Ruhengeri. He told me how we first have been attacked by well placed accomplices who always knew how to hide among the others. He assured me that the weapons used by the inkotanyi had been in Ruhengeri for a long time...

This text explicitly claims that the agents behind this act were not merely the RPA but their political and civilian accomplices who for some time had been storing weapons, intended for Hutu extermination. Thus the author simultane-ously accommodates the event to the myths of Tutsi dissimilation and duplicity and their plans for regional domination while portraying the war as one of all Tutsi against all Hutu. This last point is brought home in all its ferocity in the following statement from a leaflet issued in response to Ruhengeri by the Minister of Interior and the Préfet of Ruhengeri (Article 19:34):

Go do a special umuganda [communal work]. Destroy all the bushes and all the Inkotanyi who are hiding there. And don't forget that those who are destroying weeds must also get rid of the roots.

In January 1991, shortly after this leaflet was issued, the government carried out a massacre of Bagogwe Tutsi. The pro-government narrative of this massacre shows the power of axiological stereotyping in assimilating events into mythical storylines. In September 1991, one month after news of the massacres reached the public, the pro-government paper La Médaille Nyiramacibiri "denied that any Tutsi had been killed but instead claimed that the Bagogwe were responsible for widespread violence in north-west Rwanda" (Article 19:69–70):

They are the ones who have sparked the violence in Mutura region by provoking the population, beating and killing a soldier just as the inyenzi had stepped up their attacks …the fury of the Bagogwe is stronger than that of lions…Why do certain Tutsi like blood?

While the above texts demonstrate a movement towards eye-witness testimony as a powerful source of interpersonal authority and grassroots justice as an appropriate arena of action, both of which seem to be critical to the genocide, the growing segregation of Rwandan society along ethnic lines continues to be rationalized along pseudoscientific lines. To demonstrate how the movement in discourse in the period leading up to the genocide represents a shift in the dominant myths in Rwanda society and the alternative authorities that underpin them, a more detailed analysis follows of a text which appeared in Kangura in March 1993, not long before the genocide. This text demonstrates the same conflation of historic myth and present-day fact as Text 2. But, whereas in the earlier text myth is used to illustrate opinions presented as history, here myth and icon are given preference over pseudo-science, while casting blame on Tutsis in general as a race, inherently deceitful and bloodthirsty, and calling for Hutu vigilance. These are the dominant discourses of RTLM during the genocide, as will be illustrated below. Text 4 takes the term inyenzi, cockroaches, as applied to the Tutsi, and develops it to the full:

Text 4. Kangura, March 1993:17–18:
 1 We began by saying that a cockroach cannot give birth to a butterfly. It is true. A cockroach
 2 gives birth to another cockroach…
 3 The history of Rwanda shows us clearly that a Tutsi stays always exactly the same, that he has
 4 never changed. The malice, the evil are just as we knew them in the history of our country.

 5 We are not mistaken in saying that a cockroach gives birth to another cockroach. Who can make

 6 the distinction between the inyenzi (cockroaches) who attacked in October 1990 and those in the

 7 years of 1960? They all are linked, some are the grandchildren of the others. Their wickedness

 8 is the same. All these attacks have as their objective to restore the monarchy and feudalism. The

 9 unimaginable crimes that the inyenzi of today commit against the citizens remind one of those

10 made by their ancestors: killing, plundering, raping girls and women, etc.

11 If in our language someone calls something a snake that by itself is enough. That means many

12 things. A Tutsi is somebody who seduces by his word but whose wickedness is incommensurable.

13 A Tutsi is somebody for whom the desire of revenge never dies out, somebody whom you can

14 never know what they think, who laughs when he suffers atrociously. In our language, a Tutsi is

15 called a cockroach because it takes the advantage of the night, who makes use of concealment to

16 achieve his goals. The word inyenzi also points out the frightening snake whose venom is

17 extremely powerful. The fact that the Tutsi chose these names is very significant for those who

18 want to understand…

19 The first Republic knew to defend itself thanks to Gregoire Kayibanda, who knew very well the

20 misdeeds of the Tutsi. The second Republic has been falling since its birth into the trap of

21 Inyenzi-ntutsi. The Tutsi closed the eyes of the Hutu, especially those who played a key role in

22 the government, they distracted them in "peace" and the "unity" of which they themselves do not

23 believe. They gave them their women bizungerezi who plunged them into a kind of definitive

24 drunkenness. While the Hutu were busy with Community work, while they were dancing,

25 the Tutsi were preparing the attack which will bring them back to power. When the Hutu were

26 brutally awoken, Rwigema and his friends had crossed the Katigumba border. That's what the

27 Hutu called a surprise attack.

28 But for the courage of a few men the Inyenzi would have taken over the country.

29 While the bizungerezi were lulling the important Hutu of this country, the children of the Tutsi

30 studied to university level, it's amongst them one finds today doctors, teachers, lawyers, church

31 leaders…

32 I'm not speaking of business, these are those who control the economy of the country.
33 During this time, the Hutu split up among the Bakuga, the Banyanduga, Interahamwe, Inkuba,
34 CDR orbakombozi. The Tutsi is calm.
35 If the Hutu don't pay attention, the Tutsi will dare to steal from them the Revolution which they
36 achieved in 1959.

The phasal analysis of this text is given in Table 13.2. This text contrasts with Texts 1 and 2 in that historical narrative plays a secondary role to the

TABLE 13.2. Phasal analysis of Text 4.

Line nos.	Phase	Field	Tenor	Mode
1–17	1	Mythic history of Rwanda based on metaphor of cockroach.	Common sense, with Kangura itself and previous discourse as authority.	Generalisations of evil Tutsi character.
1–2	1.1	Introduction.	Own commentary and past texts as basis of authority.	Commentary on own discourse.
3–4	1.2	Tutsi characteristics through history.	Uncited pseudo-history as authority, strongly pejorative language.	Generalisations on Tutsi character.
5–10	1.3	Conflation of present, pre-1959 and ancient history. Legendary crimes of Tutsi in power.	Common knowledge and popular history as authoritative; highly evaluative language.	Commentary on common sense projecting a Recount of recent history.
11–18	1.4	Evil traits of Tutsi justifying use of term *inyenzi*, cockroach.	Authority of common sense as embedded in popular myth and language.	Commentary on folk wisdom projecting Generalisation on Tutsi character.
19–36	2	Comparison of vigilance of First Republic with the carelessness of the Second Republic leading to covert Tutsi domination.	Authority of writer *per se*? History? General knowledge and observation?	Recount of recent history projecting Commentary on present 'crisis'.
28	2.1	Prediction of what might have been.	…	Conjecture.
29–34	2.2	Comparison of Hutu divided amongst selves while Tutsi work and infiltrate.	Observation as authority.	Recount of recent history and Commentary on present 'crisis.'
35–36	2.3	Prediction of Tutsi domination as a result of present carelessness.	Call to order based on observation of present and immanent threat of Tutsi.	Prediction of return to Tutsi domination.

mythology and icons within which it is framed–the established metaphor of the Tutsi as cockroaches. This metaphor simultaneously denigrates the Tutsi while conflating the population in general with the RPA through its play on inyenzi (cockroaches) and inkotanyi (RPA fighters, Tutsi militia in the past), a generalizing strategy repeated through the bracketing together of the monarchy, the battles of 1960 and the present struggle. In terms of the axiological model, above, in Texts 1 and 2 myths are used to provide an interpretative framework for current events and recent history while in Text 4, above, the myth is the given with narrated events playing an illustrative and hence supportive role. Moreover, here the word of the speaker, the evidence of the readers' eyes own and common sense are the only authority behind the argument, as opposed to the pseudo-science of the earlier text. Iconography and myth take precedence over historical narratives and rhetorical questions replace the need for proof (Who can make the distinction...?).

In this context, the government of Kayibanda (ll.41ff) is as much mythical as historical and provides the metaphor of the forefathers whose examples are to be followed in preference to the leaders of today, lulled by the deceptiveness of the Tutsi, now an established fact, into a kind of "definitive drunkenness." The deceptions included the notions of peace and unity, notions that the Tutsi exploited (as demonstrated above) and so lack legitimacy. The storyline within the second positioning triangle (Figure 13.3) is by this stage well in place: a narrative constructing the Tutsi in general, prompted by their inherent blood-thirstiness, as seeking domination over the Hutu population in general.

This narrative may not represent a huge shift from the earlier, long-standing account, with most of the mythology and iconography predating the genocide by many years. However, the constant reiteration and refinement of these narrative shifts creates a new interpretative repertoire within which the Hutu population in general, or at least those who joined the militias, have their position, as a set of rights and obligations, recalibrated away from supporting the government's fight to preserve the gains of 1959 against the RPA rebels towards a more radical positioning in which they see themselves as defenders of the Hutu race and their own families against the Tutsi population as a whole. Such an urgent narrative does not rely on the authority of history or science, but reacts to the repeated calls of those close to the ground and implies a moral authority derived from military heroism and community solidarity. It is in this role as "the drumbeat behind the violence" (Article 19:116) that Radio-Télévision Mille Collines (RTLM), set up on 8th July 1993, comes into its own and completes the movement from the authority of (pseudo-) science and the battle against the RPA and "accomplices" to a discourse of Hutu versus Tutsi, grassroots justice and peer pressure underwritten by notions of loyalty to everyday heroes. In the case of RTLM, the storyline and interpretative repertoire fomented by the repeated maligning of the Tutsi, no matter how incredible, underpinned the extreme Hutu positioning traced above and the horrendous acts this inspired. This notion is captured in the following statement, made after the conflict by a self-confessed Interahamwe militiaman (Article 19:5):

I did not believe that the Tutsi were coming to kill us…but when the government radio continued to broadcast that they were coming to take our land, were coming to kill the Hutu – when this was broadcast over and over – I began to feel some kind of fear.

RTLM manufactured a relevant style by setting itself up as representing the grassroots, creating a forum for public venting, and thus inspiring their loyalty. According to the French historian Gérard Prunier (interviewed by Article 19:86–87):

RTLM was geared to people on street corners – if it was beamed to peasants, it was for the young ones. Their parents would have disapproved. It was for 20-year-olds and under. RTLM's target was gangs, young thugs…

The older message was "we need to set things right after they went wrong under the feudal monarchy". The younger generation did not care about this. It meant nothing to them…you have to get the support of the people not yet born in the revolution of 1959…The ideas [for ethnic hatred against] Tutsi had been around for years. RTLM presented them in a form more palatable for the younger generation.

RTLM used street language.

In terms of assimilating individual events into the mythic storyline, the RTLM response to the assassination of Hutu President Ndadaye of Burundi on 21st October 1993 draws on all the axiological themes we have seen so far, as it calls on the Hutu population in general to respond to the Burundi situation, for which agency is extended from the RPA, as part of the regional master plan mentioned above, to be seen as a threat from Tutsi in general. RTLM (October 1993) quotes from an article from the pro-government newspaper Ijambo (Article 19:88–89):

The fact that the Rwandan army has not yet launched an attack on Burundi is a sad thing. They should go and destroy the quarters of the Inkotanyi in Burundi, if they agree that the Hutu also have the right to live in Rwanda and Burundi…

All Rwandan Hutu are asked to contribute. Those who can use a gun, let them cross the border, those who cannot, let them learn, those who cannot yet, let them contribute money to buy guns and bullets.

The call for grassroots action with its authority derived from eyewitness accounts, group solidarity and the heroism of peers is brought to the fore in RTLM's April/May 1994 interview with Marie-Claire Kayirange, who became a roadblocker after being holed up for 3 days (Article 19:117–119):

God willing…I managed to get out and left. But I told myself that I would continue to fight…I was fighting without a gun, I did not even know how to use it, I used traditional weapons. So you see, everybody is fighting. Women cannot rest. The advice I give others is that they get military training and have the courage to fight the enemy.

Conclusion: Towards a Counter Discourse

This analysis of anti-Tutsi ideology reveals the effects of a racial law of Rwandan history. According to this law, a Hutu's life is touched by the lives of ancestors, descendents, contemporaries, tracing a path from the past to the future that "demonstrates" essential Hutu/Tutsi differences. Again, the differences are axiological, as revealed through the IMN nexus depicted above. From such a law, Hutu extremists sought compliance from their followers to eliminate the Tutsi threat. As the genocide progressed, RTLM descended further into a role of intelligence centre for the extremists, revealing the identity and whereabouts of "accomplices" as they sought to escape. Calls were made for the international community to jam its broadcasts. Article 19, the anti-censorship group, endorses this idea in this extreme case, but goes on to suggest that it would have been better to provide alternative discourses before the genocide, broadcasting in Kinyarwanda from outside the Rwandan border (Article 19:161ff). This is an important point, and where discourse analysis, as sketched out in this chapter, might usefully combine with the model of an axiology of difference in developing the idea that providing alternative storylines is not enough; for these to be taken up by the community as a whole they must draw on (and counterbalance) prevailing myths and narratives and be underwritten by appropriate forms of authority.

Acknowledgement

Special thanks go to the editors of this volume for their invitation to contribute to important work. We would like to acknowledge our colleagues at our home institutions for their insight on topics central to this chapter. We are particular grateful to Krista Rigalo and Fidele Lumeya for their excellent translation of transcripts of Hutu radio broadcasts that served as the primary text of our analysis.

Notes

1. The International Criminal Tribunal of Rwanda addressed the problems of Tutsi racial identity. After dismissing various attempts to objectify the differences between Hutus and Tutsi through ethnic, national, and racial indicators, the Court ruled that the categories of protected peoples are not subject to "objective" (etic) definitions of an ethnic group. The court relied instead on "subjective" (emic) indicators established by the Rwandan people themselves. (P. J. Magnarella 2002, p. 318).
2. For Aristotle, the formal cause is sometimes understood as the "definition," i.e. what it is to be a thing of a certain kind. The formal cause of ethnic-based conflict centers on an axiology of virtues and vices that establish borders and orders of protagonist groups (Rothbart & Cherubin 2008).
3. This notion of teliomorphic model used in this context represents a liberal extension of Rom Harré's notion, that is a model that seeks to improve upon the subject matter being modelled. See his seminal work on the centrality of modelling in the sciences, *Principles of Scientific Thinking* (1970, Chapter 2).
4. This is a modified version of Cloran's highly structured methodology that would not be appropriate for translated texts.
5. With the caveat mentioned that this is a translation from a translation.
6. This was originally the name of a 19th Century formation of Tutsi fighters. The term *inyenzi*, cockroach, which is to become a powerful metaphor, is based on this term.

References

Bourdieu, P. (1991). *Language and symbolic power.* Cambridge: Polity Press.

Cloran, Carmel. 2000, Socio-semantic varation: Different wordings, different meanings. In Unsworth, Len (Ed.). *Researching Language in Schools and Communities: Functional Linguistic Perspectives.* London and Washington: Cassel.

Emirbayer, M., & Mische, A. (1998). What is Agency? *American Journal of Sociology, 103*(4), 962–1023.

Frohardt, M., & Temin, J. (2003). Use and Abuse of Media in Vulnerable Societies, USIP, Special Report No. 110, October 2003.

Goffman, E. (1963). *Stigma.* Englewood Cliffs, NJ: Prentice-Hall.

Gourevitch, P. (1998). We wish to inform you that tomorrow we will be killed with our families. New York: Picador.

Gregory, M. (1988). Generic situation and register: A functional view of communication. In J. D. Benson, M. Cummings, & W. Greaves (Eds.), *Linguistics in a systemic perspective.* Amsterdam: John Benjamins.

Halliday, M. A. K., & Hasan, R. (1985). *Language, context and text: Language in a social-semiotic perspective.* Victoria: Deakin University Press.

Harré, R. (1970). *Principles of scientific thinking.* Chicago: University of Chicago Press.

Harré, R., & Moghaddam, F. (Eds.). (2003b). *The Self and Others: Positioning individuals and groups in personal, political and cultural contexts.* Westport, CT and London: Praeger.

Harré, R., & Moghaddam, F. (2003a). Introduction: The self and others in traditional psychology and in positioning theory. In R. Harré & F. Moghaddam (Eds.), *The self and others* (pp. 1–11). Westport, CT: Praeger.

Harré, R., & van Langenhove, L. (1999a). The Dynamics of Social Episodes. In R. Harré & L. van Langenhove (Eds.), *Positioning theory* (pp. 1 – 13). Oxford: Blackwell.

Harré, R., & van Langenhove, L. (1999b). *Positioning theory: Moral contexts of intentional action.* Oxford, UK: Blackwell.

Harré, R., & van Langenhove, L. (1999c). Epilogue: Further Opportunities, In R. Harré & L. van Langenhove (Ed.), *Positioning Theory.* Oxford, UK: Blackwell Publishers.

Magnarella, P. J. (2002). Recent Developments in the International Law of Genocide: An Anthropological Perspective on the International Criminal Tribunal for Rwanda. In A. L. Hinton (Ed.), *Annihilating Difference: The Anthropology of Genocide.* Berkeley: University of California Press, Chapter 12.

Moghaddam, F. M. (2006). Interobjectivity: The collective roots of individual consciousness and social identity. In T. Postmes & J. Jetten (Eds.), *Individuality and the group: Advances in social identity* (pp.155–174). London, UK: Sage.

Potter, J., & Wetherell, M. (1987). *Discourse and social psychology: Beyond attitudes and behaviour.* London: Sage.

Rothbart, D., & Cherubin, R. (2008). Causation as a Core Concept in Conflict Theory. In S. Byrne, D. Sandole, J. Senehi, & Ingrid Staroste-Sandole (Eds.), *Conflict analysis and resolution as multi discipline: Integration and synergy across disciplines.* London, UK: Routledge Press.

Rothbart, D., & Korostelina, K. (2006). Moral denigration of the other. In *Identity, Morality, and Threat: Studies of Violent Conflict.* Lexington Books, Rowman and Littlefield Publishers, Inc.

Semujanga, J. (2003). *Origins of Rwandan genocide.* Amherst, NY: Humanity Books.

14
Nuclear Positioning and Supererogatory Duties: The Illustrative Case of Positioning by Iran, the United States, and the European Union

FATHALI M. MOGHADDAM AND KATHRYN A. KAVULICH

Although positioning theory has for the most part been applied to inter-personal relations, there has also been some attention to reflexive or intra-personal positioning (e.g., Tan & Moghaddam, 1995) as well as to inter-group positioning (e.g., Tan & Moghaddam, 1999a). The dynamic nature of positioning theory makes it particularly applicable to long-term inter-group relations that involve groups maneuvering for advantage in changing social, political, and economic circumstances. This is in contrast to the mainstream inter-group theories that have been adapted for testing almost exclusively through laboratory experiments lasting one hour or so (for a broader discussion, see Moghaddam, Hanley, & Harré, 2003).

In an earlier study (Moghaddam & Kavulich, 2007), we applied positioning theory to explore the dynamics of changing relationships between the Islamic Republic of Iran (IRI), the European Union (EU) and the United States (US), with a focus on Iran's nuclear program from September 1, 2004 through November, 29, 2004 (the date of the adoption of Resolution 291104 by the International Atomic Energy Agency, IAEA, Board of Governors, which marked a temporary decline in tensions between the main parties). The period of the present study is January 1, 2006 to May 9, 2006, the end date marked by the release of a letter from the new Iranian President, Mr. Mahmoud Ahmadinejad, to the U.S. President, Mr. George W. Bush. A number of important changes took place in the time period between the two studies reflecting the dynamic, fluid nature of inter-group relations in real world contexts.

One set of changes involve the internal dynamics of Iran. Mr. Ahmadinejad became the new president of Iran in June 2006, and immediately embarked on a policy that is closer to the radical line of the Khomeini era of the 1980s than to the outwardly moderate line associated with the former president, Mr. Mohammad Khatami in the 1990s. In February 2006 Iran drastically reduced access by IAEA officials to Iran's nuclear facilities and personnel. Mr. Ahmadinejad referred to the Holocaust as a 'myth', declared that Israel will be 'wiped off the map', demanded that Israel give up its nuclear weapons, and affirmed the right of Iran to conduct nuclear research despite strong US opposition.

This radicalization of Iranian policies coincided with a higher profile for Islamic radicalism around the world. For example, there were mass protests and attacks against Western interests in many Islamic communities around the world in early 2006, in reaction to the publications of 'blasphemous' cartoons of the Prophet Mohammad in a Danish newspaper. There was also a rise in anti-Americanism among Muslim communities. For example, between 2000 and 2006, the percentage of Muslims holding a favorable opinion of the United States declined from 75 to 30 in Indonesia, 52 to 12 in Turkey, 46 to 62 in Nigeria, and 25 (2002 percentage) to 15 in Jordan (Pew Research Center, 2006).

A second set of changes involve the dynamics of the situation in the West and internationally. On the one hand, radicalization of Muslims in Western Europe, symbolized by weeks of riots involving Muslim youth in France, led France and Germany to move closer to the 'hard line' positions of the United States and the United Kingdom. Thus, Iran now faced a more united front of Western powers, as well as threats that the United States might use ariel bombardment to attack Iran's nuclear research centers. On the other hand, President Bush and Prime Minister Blair had lost the support of the majority of their own populations (in the U.S.A and the U.K., respectively) and were much weaker domestically, whereas the sharply increased price of oil and the tacit support of Russia and China now made Iran far stronger internationally. Also, Mr. Ahmadinejad won popularity among nationalists at home for (supposedly) standing up for Iran's 'national interests'.

It is in the context of these complex socio-political changes that we embarked on a second phase of our study of positioning involving Iran, the USA, the EU, and other agents. Iran's nuclear program actually has its origins in the pre-revolution era, during the reign of the Pahlavi dynasty (1926–1978). Despite being seen as enjoying full American support, the last Pahlavi king, Mohammad Reza Shah (ruled 1941–1978), failed to win American support for launching a nuclear program in Iran and had to do so relying on German technology in the 1970s (for a more in-depth discussion of the background to Iran's nuclear program, see Moghaddam & Kavulich, 2007). The 1978–79 revolution brought to power Ayotollah Khomeini (1900–1989) and his followers, who adopted strongly anti-American rhetoric. Mr. Ahmadinejad has explicitly revived the earlier, revolutionary rhetoric, particularly as it pertains to rights, what is demanded of others, and duties, what is owed to others.

A series of events intensified the struggle between the governments of the Islamic Republic of Iran and the United States, joined later by the UK, France and Germany, in the period 2003–2006. After reports that Iran was operating a covert nuclear weapons program, IAEA inspectors examined nuclear facilities in Iran and in June 2003 the IAEA chief Mohammad ElBaradei reported that Iran had failed to report certain (apparently covert) nuclear activities and materials.

Iran was suspected of hiding a program to produce weapons-grade uranium. Under pressure from the United States and other countries, in December 2003 Iran attempted to ease tensions by signing the Additional Protocol to the Nuclear Nonproliferation Treaty, which allowed more intrusive inspections of its nuclear facilities. Inspections gained a new urgency by early 2004, because of reports that Iran had received atomic weapons know-how and technology from Pakistani nuclear scientist Abdul Qadeer Khan, the 'father' of the Pakistani nuclear bomb. Under mounting pressure from the United States and the European Union, in November 2004 Iran announced the voluntary and temporary suspension of uranium enrichment.

Between the start of the voluntary suspension of uranium enrichment and the resumption of uranium enrichment by Iran in January 2006, negotiators from the UK, France and Germany made a number of offers to Iran, to accept economic incentives to stop uranium enrichment. Russia also made an offer to enrich uranium for Iran in Russia. These offers served as the 'carrot'. The threat of US led sanctions, and possible military attacks on Iran by the US or Israel, served as the 'stick'. Iran rejected the 'carrot', and on February 4, 2006, the IAEA board voted to report Iran to the United Nations Security Council.

Positioning Using Rights and Duties

In the present study we explore the positioning that takes place involving Iran, the USA, the EU, and other major actors. Our particular focus is on rights and duties, which are involved in all positioning acts. In some cases the parties involved accept each others understanding of what are the respective rights and duties of each party, but often there are negotiations, disputes, and continuing re-formulations. In the case of Iran and nuclear technology, the disputes are serious, and the threat of large scale hostilities loom in the background. Clearly Iran has less power and is the minority group relative to the USA, the sole superpower and the majority group in this context.

We argue that the dispute between Iran, the USA and the EU over nuclear power hinges particularly on supererogatory duties, duties that individuals and groups are not obligated to carry out, but receive credit for if and when they do carry them out. For example, nations are not (yet) obligated to convert their public transportation systems from using fossil fuels to renewable energies, thus this is not an agreed upon formal duty. However, those nations that do make serious efforts to make this conversion are lauded, because their actions are interpreted as fulfilling supererogatory duties.

However, like all duties, supererogatory duties are negotiable. In this case, on the one hand Iran attempts to present its 'voluntary suspension' of uranium enrichment as the fulfilment of a supererogatory duty, and therefore laudable. On the other hand, the United States and (to a lesser extent) the EU attempt to position Iran as having lost the trust of the 'family of nations' and not eligible for having its actions interpreted as fulfilling supererogatory duties. The implication is that only those who meet certain moral standards can be eligible to position themselves as fulfilling supererogatory duties. This two stage processes, first, claims about moral character and, second, positioning acts, is highlighted by the illustrative that is the focus on this chapter.

Predicting Scripts

In the battle to win support for their particular interpretations of supererogatory duties, what script will parties to the dispute follow? Are there any predictions we can make on the basis of positioning by minority and majority groups in other contexts? On the one hand, one can emphasize the context dependent nature of positioning, as well as the endless variations that scripts could follow. From this perspective, each case of minority-majority relations and the positionings involved will be different. From an alternative perspective, however, minority-majority relations have certain characteristics in common, and there will be commonalities in positioning processes involving groups with lesser and greater power. The common characteristic of relatively less and greater power could lead to certain universals in support for rights and duties.

The United Nations Universal Declaration of Human Rights is one of many documents that asserts there to be universal rights (Alverado, 1999). Of course, what is present on paper does not necessarily reflect the actual state of affairs in everyday life. First, declarations of human rights written on paper are often violated, both by Western and non-Western countries, including the United States. Many sources testify to this, an example being annual Amnesty International reports. If declarations of human rights represent a theoretical ideal that exists at least on paper, can we identify any universals with respect to rights in actual behavior? This question has both theoretical and applied importance and has now received some research attention (see papers in Finkel & Moghaddam, 2004). A second, related point is that declarations in general have focused on rights rather than duties: are there universal aspects to duties?

One line of argument (for example, see Louis & Taylor, 2004) is that rights and duties reflect group norms, which can and often do vary across groups, as indicated by cross-cultural and anthropological research. Further, group norms can be shaped by those who enjoy the greatest power in society. Thus, rights and duties are constructions, shaped by those in power to reflect their own interests. This relativist viewpoint casts serious doubt on the idea of universals in rights and duties, since the implication is that as power shifts, group norms shift, with resultant changes in rights and duties over time and across groups.

However, an alternative argument is that although there exist major differences in rights and duties over time and across groups, there are also a small but important number of universals. One such universal is that during times of instability and potential change, priority is given by minority groups to rights and by majority group to duties (Moghaddam, 2004). In short, the expectation is that Iran, in addition to interpreting its 'voluntary suspension' of uranium enrichment as a fulfilment of supererogatory duties, will highlight its 'right to nuclear power', while the USA and its allies will highlight the 'more urgent' duties of Iran to abide by its 'international obligations', and by doing so help maintain the status quo in power relations.

An important question arises at this point: who is to judge the correctness of the claims made by Iran, the USA, the EU and other parties? Perhaps the most important judge is the so-called 'international community', and each of the parties attempts to position themselves as allied with the international community.

Positioning Using 'The International Community' As Higher Authority

The post 9/11 era is associated with a new competition to win 'hearts and minds' around the world, involving persuasion of the masses in Western and non-Western societies. At the same time, there is greater emphasis on the so-called 'international community', consisting of all nations that belong to the United Nations 'family'. Being part of a family implies conformity to family norms and obedience to authority figures.

But a common characteristic of family life is also rebellion against authority figures. The international community is in some ways on paper a 'family or a partnership of equals, but like most such relationships some members are 'more equal then others'. The five permanent members of the United Nations Security Council (The United States, Russia, China, the United Kingdom, and France) are certainly 'more equal than others', and the United States has the greatest influence.

This arrangement was put into place after the Second World War, but a great deal has changed since then. For example, India is now a rapidly expanding industrial power of over a billion people, and Germany has been re-united and is the largest economy in the European Union. India and Germany are among a number of countries pushing for changes in power relations in the 'international community'. Besides, the Non-Aligned Movement is no longer pre-occupied with positioning in a Cold War context and, instead, is attempting to act as an organization representing poorer countries battling 'exploitation' by richer countries, symbolized by the United States.

Thus, the positioning undertaken by Iran is better understood in the context of international relationships very broadly. By positioning itself as allied with others in the Non-Aligned Movement, not only the likes of 'revolutionary' Venezuela but also 'moderate' India, Iran is attempting to present itself as part of an international movement to bring about change in power relations and to challenge the 'authority figures' in the family of nations. Of course, the main priority of this Non-Aligned international movement is to protect and enhance the rights of the poorer nations. In the next section we examine how representatives of Iran, the United States and other entities attempt to achieve advantageous positions by reference to the international community.

In the following section, because of space limitations only one example is given of each type of statement made to achieve a particular positioning strategy.

Positioning on the Issue of the Assumed 'Wishes of the International Community'

Iran

There are three strategies that we want to highlight in particular with respect to how Iran positions itself using the international community. First, Iran presents itself as a 'good family member' that meets all the rules and regulations of the international community. Thus, Deputy Foreign Minister Mehdi Mostafavi stated that:

"Iran's nuclear research is based on rules and regulations of international organizations (such as) the International Atomic Energy Agency (IAEA) and the Non-Proliferation Treaty (NPT) which gave the country the inalienable right"[1]

This brief statement achieves three goals: Iran is positioned as a 'good family member'; second, it is the family that gave Iran its rights; third, these rights are 'inalienable', and so by implication they cannot be taken away by others.

A second positioning strategy in this context is the attempt to portray Iran's opponents as not being good family members and, indeed, not accepting the rules of the family. For example, Vice President for legal and parliamentary affairs Ahmad Moussavi stated that,

"The countries possessing nuclear warheads, which themselves have not signed the International Atomic Energy Agency (IAEA) nuclear Non-Proliferation Treaty (NPT) and are not committed to international laws, intend to deprive Iran of access to nuclear energy for peaceful purposes"[2]

Iran's opponents are positioned as 'outside the family', as not being 'committed' to the rules of the family, and of trying to deprive Iran of rights given to it by the family. Besides, Iran is only trying to abide by the family rules and conduct projects 'for peaceful purposes'.

A third strategy we highlight refers to what is perhaps a more sensitive and subtle issue: enjoying the confidence of the family. Iranian officials have leveled the charge that, given the situation in post-war Iraq (a topic we return to later in this discussion), the United States is no longer a trusted member of the family. For example,

"It has become obvious that in dealing with our nuclear programme, the United States has lost the confidence of the international community."[3]

Interestingly, the issue of 'confidence' and 'trust' is central to the positioning attempted by other countries, particularly the United States.

US and Allies

Representatives from the United States have attempted to portray Iran as untrustworthy. For example, Secretary of State Condoleezza Rice said that...:

"This is not a question of Iran's right to civil nuclear power. This is a question that the world doesn't believe Iran should have the capability and technology that could lead to a nuclear weapon"[4]

The attempt here is to counter Iran's repeated claims that it has the right to develop nuclear power for peaceful purposes, a right given by the international community. First, the claim is made that the dispute is not at all about this right 'to civil nuclear power'; this is implied to be a 'red herring'. Rather, this is about, first, 'the world', the family of nations, not trusting Iran. In particularly, this untrustworthy 'family outcast' should not have access to a dangerous weapon. Iran is being positioned as a 'black sheep' who will harm others if he manages to get hold of a weapon. This 'threat is repeated in numerous ways by various officials, for example

"That's a threat, a serious threat. It's a threat to world peace."[5]

Moreover, the United States is presented as concerned with the health of the family and being forced to take,

"Strong steps to make certain that we maintain the credibility of the international community"[6]

The implication is that if the family does not discipline Iran, the 'black sheep', then the family will not have credible authority and will suffer. A similar use is made of the international community by British officials, who use the threat of action by the Security Council as additional pressure on 'the black sheep' of the family. For example,

"But Iran should also be under no doubt that if it continues to defy the wishes of the international community, that the Security Council will respond"[7]

In this example, the 'wishes of the international community' are placed as being above the wishes of individual members, and the Security Council is the authority figure in the family who will put rebels back in line. This theme is continued in the next statement from the same British official, Foreign Secretary Jack Straw.

"We will now be asking the Security Council to increase the pressure on Iran so that the international community can be assured that its nuclear programme is not a threat to peace and security"[8]

Britain is being positioned here as just another member of the international community, asking the 'authority figure' of the Security Council to protect peace and security for 'the family'. Iran is positioned again and again as the rebellious family member, as the one who is threatening the lives of all of the family. Europe is presented as part of a united family, collaborating to keep the 'rebel' member, Iran, under control.

"It has significant support in the European Parliament since we are more and more aware that Iran poses a threat – not only to the Iranian people but to global peace, democracy, and stability."[9]

Thus, the 'psychological-moral' characteristics of the pseudo-person, Iran, are the grounds on which the right to have a nuclear program is disputed.

Positioning and 'Supererogatory Duties'

The above analysis allows us to return to a subtle but important point about supererogatory duties and the position(s) that enable a party to have fulfilled them. The act of making a claim about having fulfilled a supererogatory duty itself depends on a position with associated rights (and duties). Others can dispute one's position as having the right to claim having fulfilled a supererogatory duty; for example, if the act that seems to fulfill the duty is obviously self-serving.

Consider, for example, the case of the Smiths, a wealthy family who decide to donate a large sum of money for a university research project. In making the announcement at a press conference, the family position themselves as having fulfilled a supererogatory duty. They were not obligated to make the donation, and they went 'beyond the call of duty' to do so. However, it is their money and they have a right to choose how they use it. They could build another villa in the south of France, or buy a home in Iffley Village, but instead they have donated money for university research, and this is laudatory.

Imagine now if it is discovered that the wealth of the Smiths is derived from the drug trade. This information can lead people to re-label actions taken by the Smiths. Critics would content that actions taken by the Smiths do not constitute the fulfilment of supererogatory duties, because the Smiths do not meet the moral requirements to position themselves as fulfilling such duties; they have forfeited their right to such a claim. The same action (donating money for university research) is now interpreted in a different manner.

Similarly, in the case of Iran, the U.S.A and its allies are claiming that Iran does not have the right to claim it has fulfilled a supererogatory duty (the voluntary suspension of uranium enrichment). On the contrary, critics contend that, as the 'black sheep' of the family of nations, all such claims by Iran should be dismissed, and Iran should be placed under strict control until it has earned the trust of the 'family of nations'.

A 'Calming Voice of Moderation'

In the face of dramatic announcements by representatives of the United States and the EU, Russia and China, two other 'authority figures' in the 'family of nations', have attempted to position themselves as moderate, reasonable voices. On the one hand, they have thrown cold water on the hot passions and (purportedly) 'extreme' claims of the United States and its supporters. For example, a Russian representative commented:

"I want to calm the international public – Iran has no intercontinental ballistic missiles."[10]

By referring to 'intercontinental ballistic missiles', the Russian representative is introducing a mocking tone and criticizing exaggerated claims about an 'Iran threat'.

Similarly, a Chinese representative has reassured that,

"There's still room for resolving the Iran nuclear issue through diplomatic negotiation and the International Community should not abandon these efforts."[11]

The appeal here is still to the international community as authority figure in the family, but an authority figure that should keep on the track of negotiations rather than serve as a threat.

Rights, Duties, Iran and The International Community

Positioning with reference to the international community becomes more complex when rights and duties are incorporated. We discuss this issue first in the case of positioning by Iran, and then positioning by the United States and its allies.

Iran

Iranian representatives give priority to rights, but go beyond this by claiming that they have a duty to uphold these rights,

"We are not permitted to ignore our rights and to retreat in confrontation with the illogical pressure of the West ..."[12] (Prime Minister Mahmoud Ahmadinejad)

The claim that 'we are not permitted' raises the question, by whom? Who gives the permission? The answer is the Iranian nation, the masses. This becomes clear in the following statement, IRNA Jan 24, 2006

"The hegomonic powers tend to deprive Iran even of its right to study and research, despite the fact that the nation stood against arrogance 27 years ago by launching the Islamic revolution and gave thousands of martyrs to avoid being subject to ruthless decisions"[13] (Iran's Ambassador to Tajikistan Nasser Sarmad-Parsa)

In this case, the 'threat' is described as being from 'hegomonic powers' rather than the 'Security Council', and the target of this threat is the Iranian nation, which has given 'thousands of martyrs'.

The 'hegomonic powers' are further challenged by the Iranian Prime Minister rejecting their 'natural' right to question Iran's intentions.

"President Ahmadinejad is asking, 'why only you [Western powers] should send inspectors for human rights or nuclear issues to Iran – we want to inspect you and report on your activities"[14] (Ayatollah Ahmad Jannati, secretary of the Guardian Council of the Constitution)

This appeal is to those in the 'family of nations' who do not enjoy power in the present system, and who are more likely to be the 'targets' of control than those who control.

The United States and Its Allies

While Iranian representatives focused on rights and argued that the international community and international law gives Iran the right to develop nuclear power for peaceful purposes, the United States and its allies focus on duties, and particularly the duty of Iran to demonstrate the peaceful nature of its nuclear program. Consider, for example, this statement from Jack Straw, the British Foreign Secretary:

"The onus is on Iran to act to give the international community confidence that its nuclear program has exclusive peaceful purposes, confidence, I'm afraid, that has been sorely undermined by its history of concealment and deception"[15]

Mr. Straw is positioning Iran as obligated to show that its nuclear program is exclusively peaceful in purpose, but also arguing that Iran is unable to carry out this responsibility because its 'history of concealment and deception' means it is not to be trusted. Here, again, moral character is cited in support of a positioning act.

The same focus on duties is reflected in statements by United States representatives. For example, referring to the IAEA vote to report Iran to the UN body, and the demands entailed in the vote (including that Iran suspend enrichment activities and grant inspectors access to Iranian nuclear facilities), US undersecretary of state R. Nicholas Burns said,

"Iran is going to have to meet these conditions and show it has taken a fundamentally different course"[16]

In this case, Iran is positioned as obligated to take a 'fundamentally different course' in order to meet the demands of the 'family of nations'. Thus, the 'black sheep' of the family is being told to 'mend its ways', and an example is presented as to the model to follow:

"Libya is an important model as nations around the world press for changes in behavior by Iranian and North Korean regimes"[17] Secretary of State Condoleezza Rice, following the news that the US will restore diplomatic links with the Libyan regime headed by Col. Muammar el-Qaddafi. Secretary Rice positions Iran and North Korea, two 'rebellious' family members, as going against the wishes of 'nations around the world'. Lybia, a country that recently abandoned its nuclear program, is positioned as a former 'black sheep', one that has mended its ways and now sets an example for other rebellious family members.

It is interesting to note that the Iranian opposition groups have also given priority to Iran's duties. The following is an illustrative example of this point:

"Ardeshir Zahedi, who signed the Non-proliferation Treaty on behalf of Iran, believes that making use of peaceful nuclear energy is a natural and absolute right of Iran. However, this is on the condition that nuclear technology is at the disposal of a regime that honors and abides by its international obligations"[18]

Zahedi presents rights as being conditional on meeting duties, with the implication that the Iranian 'regime' has lost the right of 'making...nuclear energy' because it has not met its obligations.

These positioning strategies by the different parties are made more complicated by a new development: the tragic events in post-war Iraq and its consequences for the influence and prestige of the United States, and the ability of the United States to effectively position itself and others.

Concluding Comment: The Iraq Factor and Conflict Resolution

The United States and its allies have attempted to position Iran as a 'black sheep' of the family of nations, as a family member that has tried to deceive in the past and is not to be trusted with technology that could be used to make dangerous weapons. The duty of Iran, it is argued, is to satisfy the family of nations that it has changed its ways. Until Iran meets its obligations, the rest of the family will not allow Iran to enjoy the right to develop nuclear technology. But the war in Iraq and enormous mis-management in post-war Iraq have made it far more difficult to successfully complete this positioning strategy.

Prior and during the 2003 invasion of Iraq, the United States claimed that it had solid proof that the Iraqi regime was developing and stockpiling weapons of mass destruction. This proved to be a false claim. Since the invasion, images of Abu Ghraib Prison and the mistreatment of Iraqi prisoners, as well as increasing violence that has cost over one hundred thousand Iraqi lives and thousands of American lives, has diminished American influence in the 'family of nations'. This has allowed critics to question the trustworthiness of American claims about Iran being a 'black sheep' of the 'family of nations'. In raising questions, critics have repeatedly cited the case of Iraq. This is how one analyst explained the situation:

"Those who want to give Iran the benefit of the doubt use the Iraq experience as a reason for doing so: the misuse of intelligence, the mistakes in the intelligence and the way the war has progressed"[19]

Mark Fitzgerald, a non-proliferation expert at the London-based Institute for Strategic Studies.

Moreover, the mismanagement of the war in Iraq and related blunders by the Bush administration have shifted perceptions among people in many parts of the world of what constitutes a 'danger to world peace'. While in the United States in 2006, 46% of the population saw Iran as the greatest danger to world peace and 31% saw the U.S. in Iraq as posing the greatest danger, in the U.K., France and Spain, people saw the U.S. in Iraq as a greater danger to world peace than that posed by Iran (Pew Research Center, 2006). The perception of the U.S. as a danger to world peace was even stronger in major Islamic countries. For example, the percentage of people who saw Iran as a danger to world peace in Indonesia, Egypt, Jordan, Turkey, and Pakistan was 7, 14, 19, 16, and 4; but in the same countries the percentage of people who saw the U.S. in Iraq as a danger to world peace was 31, 56, 58, 60, and 28 respectively.

The increase in anti-American sentiments, and the mismanagement of the situation in Iraq, has made it far more difficult for the United States to succeed in positioning Iran as the black sheep of the 'family of nations' and having forfeited the right to position itself as fulfilling supererogatory duties. Indeed, the United States has weakened the possibility that America will be seen as fulfilling a supererogatory duty – that of 'policing the world' and maintaining peace.

An implication of this analysis for conflict resolution is that the conflict management avenues available to a member of a majority group, even one as powerful as the United States, are to a large extend dependent on the rights and duties associated with its own generally accepted position. Because of the mismanagement of the situation in Iraq, the perceived mistreatment of Islamic prisoners by American guards, and so on, the United States is perceived to have lost certain rights – such as the right to act as 'the policeman of the world'. This has weakened the U.S. challenge to Iran's claim to have fulfilled a supererogatory duty.

Notes

1. 'Iran to Continue Nuclear Research: Official.' IRNA. Tehran, Iran. January 24, 2006.
2. 'VP: Iran Determined to Safeguard Its Nuclear Right.' IRNA. Tehran, Iran. January 24, 2006.
3. 'UN Security Council to Meet on Iran Nuclear Crisis.' Agence France Presse. France. May 3, 2006.
4. 'Iran Nuclear Move Draws UN Ire.' Financial Times. London, UK. April 13, 2006.
5. 'China, Russia United on Iran, UN Statement Elusive.' Reuters News. Beijing, China. March 21, 2006.
6. 'Iran Nuclear Move Draws UN Ire.' Financial Times. London, UK. April 13, 2006.
7. Woodcock, Andrew. 'Straw Urges New Efforts over Iran Nuclear Row.' Press Association Newsletter. March 13, 2006.
8. 'Officials Comment on Iran Nuclear Issue.' Reuters News. April 28, 2006.
9. Bryant, Lisa. 'Iranian Resistance Group Seen as Leverage in Nuclear Dispute.' Voice of America. USA. January 24, 2006.
10. 'Russia Tries to Defuse Iran Crisis; IAEA Inspectors Visit Enrichment Facility.' Daily Star. Beirut, Lebanon. April 8, 2006.

11.   Jize, Qin. 'Iran Issue: Still Room for Solution.' China Daily. Beijing, China. March 31, 2006.
12.   'West Treating Iran's Nuclear Dossier Politically.' IranMania News. London, UK. January, 26, 2006.
13.   'Khatami Defends Iran's Nuclear Plan.' Reuters. Kuala Lumpur, Malaysia. February 11, 2006.
14.   Engdahl, F. William. 'A High-Risk Game of Nuclear Chicken.' Asia Times Online. Kowloon, Hong Kong. January 30, 2006.
15.   Sciolino, Elaine and Cowell, Alan. 'Russia and China Demand Iran Freeze Nuclear Activity, but Reject Referral to U.N.' New York Times. New York, US. Jan 17, 2006.
16.   Anderson, John. 'Iran to Face Security Council.' The Washington Post. Washington, D.C., U.S. February 5, 2006.
17.   Brinkley, Joel; Wald, Matthew; and Weisman, Steven. 'U.S. to Restore Diplomatic Links with the Libyans.' New York Times, May 16, 2006.
18.   Kayhan Newspaper (London), 'It is Iran's certain right to have atomic energy for peaceful purposes' March 16, 2006. (Our translation)
19.   Moore, Molly. 'Permanent Members Russia, China Favor Less Formal Action on Atomic Program.' Washington Post. Washington, DC, U.S. January 22, 2006.

References

Alverado, R. (1999). *A common law: The law of nations and western civilization*. Aaltenm, The Netherlands: Pietas press.

Finkel, N., & Moghaddam, F. M. (Eds.). (2004). *The psychology of rights and duties: Empirical contributions and normative commentaries* (pp. 105–134). Washington, DC: American Psychological Association Press.

Louis, W. R., & Taylar, D. M. (2004). Rights and duties as group norms. In N. Finkel & F. M. Moghaddam (Eds.), *The psychology of rights and duties* (pp. 105–134). Washington, DC: American Psychological Association Press.

Moghaddam, F. M. (2004). The cycle of rights and duties in intergroup relations: Inter-objectivity and perceived justice re-assessed. *New Review of Social Psychology,* 3, 125–130.

Moghaddam, F. M., Hanley, E., & Harré, R. (2003). Sustaining intergroup harmony: An analysis of the Kissinger papers through positioning theory. In R. Harré & F. M. Moghaddam (Eds.), *The self and others: Positioning individuals and groups in personal, political, and cultural contexts* (pp. 137–155). Westport, CT: Praeger.

Moghaddam, F. M., & Kavulich, K. A. (2007). Nuclear positioning: The case of the Islamic Republic of Iran, the European Union, and the United States of America. In J. Valsiner & A. Rosa (Eds.), *The Cambridge handbook of socio-cultural psychology* (pp. 576–590). New York: Cambridge University Press.

Pew Research Center (2006). *Conflicting views in a divided world. How global publics view: Muslim-Western issues, U.R. role in the world, Asian rivalries*. Washington, DC: Author.

Tan, S., & Moghaddam, F. (1999a). Positioning in intergroup relations. In R. Harre & L. van Langenhove, *Positioning theory* (pp. 178–194). oxford, MA: Blackwell.

Tan, S. L., & Moghaddam, F. M. (1995). Reflexive positioning and culture. *Journal for the Theory of Social Behavior, 25,* 387–400.

Tan, S. L., & Moghaddam, F. M. (1999c). Positioning in intergroup relations. In R. Harré & L. Van Langenhove (Eds.), *Positioning theory: Moral contexts of international actions* (pp. 178–194). Boston: Blackwell.

Tan, S. L., & Moghaddam, F. M. (1999b). Reflexive positioning: culture and private discourse. In R. Harré & L. van Langenhove (Eds.), *Positioning theory* (pp. 74–86). Oxford, England: Blackwell.

15
Conceptual Frame for a Psychology of Nonviolent Democratic Transitions: Positioning Across Analytical Layers

CRISTINA JAYME MONTIEL AND DANIEL J. CHRISTIE

This paper presents a conceptual framework for a psychology of active nonviolent democratic transitions by integrating an ecological model (Bronfenbrenner & Morris, 1998) with positioning theory (Harré & Moghaddam, 2003a). Nonviolent democratic transitions refer to state-society transformations or turning points characterized by the destruction of an authoritarian political system and creation of an open political system by using peaceful means. Hence, our focus is on peace by peaceful means where the former peace refers to positive peace or movement toward socially just ends and the latter peace refers to negative peace or the absence of war through the nonviolent management of conflict (Galtung, 1969, 1996).

At the height of the Cold War, authoritarian regimes dominated civilian populations of the Majority World through the actual or threatened use of military force. In contrast, the last quarter of the 20th century witnessed a shift from authoritarian and militarized state political structures, to more open political systems. The phenomenon of nonviolent political transitions opened up democratic space in Eastern Europe, Southeast and East Asia, Latin America and South Africa. Figure 15.1 provides examples of nonviolent democratic transitions in a span of 20 years, from 1986–2006.

Major texts on nonviolence, including those by Gandhi (1957/1927), Sharp (1973), Pelton (1974), Holmes (1990), Kool and Keyes (1990), Sponsel and Gregor (1994), Ackerman and Kruegler (1994) and Ackerman and DuVall (2000), have approached the topic from a range of perspectives including anthropological, historical, political, sociological, strategic, as well as, pragmatic. Our analytical perspective is at the intersection of two theoretical frameworks: ecological theory (Bronfenbrenner & Morris, 1998), which nests nonviolent actions in larger social and political structures, and positioning theory (Harré & Moghaddam, 2003b), which analyzes the positions occupied by actors within social structures and the perceived rights and duties associated with those positions.

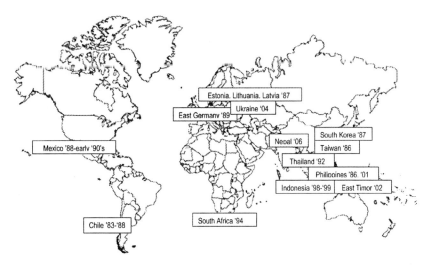

FIGURE 15.1. Map showing nonviolent transitions in the majority world from 1986 to 2006.[1]

We begin this chapter with an examination of the nature of nonviolent democratic transitions, as contrasted with violent transitions. Then, we demonstrate the descriptive value and explanatory power of an eco-positional analytical framework.

The Nature of Nonviolent Democratic Transitions

Nonviolent democratic transitions use peaceful means to destroy an authoritarian structure and create a more open political system. These power shifts involve a political strategy that utilizes peaceful and indigenous social power, rather than armed and foreign-based force. Force emanates from organizing and mobilizing large numbers of prodemocracy groups, in order to produce, not reduce, social conflict. Open social strain makes manifest social resistance that was previously latent or underground as mass movements challenge the status quo power arrangement of state authoritarianism. Like armed conflict, nonviolent action is mass-based, contentious, and coercive vis-à-vis the authoritarian state (Bond, Jenkins, Taylor, & Schock, 1997). Instead of relying on militarized methods to consolidate and expand political power, active nonviolence utilizes creative innovations to challenge the authoritarian state (Ackerman & Duvall, 2000; Bond et al., 1997; Zunes, Kurtz, & Asher, 1999). Because it is peaceful and mass-based, yet forcefully contentious and structurally framed, active nonviolent political transitions can challenge the violent approaches that characterize authoritarian systems, while offering a viable alternative to homegrown armed liberation struggles, and militarized foreign-backed power shifts.

The forceful removal of a dictator is necessary but not sufficient for democratization, especially if regime change leads to another domestic authoritarian system like a junta or a foreign occupation. In these instances, the authoritarian system remains intact, even if the palace occupants change. Further, reliance on homegrown armed liberation struggles or foreign-backed regime change can destroy the local social fabric, traumatize, and render dysfunctional large numbers of peoples who are needed to play constructive roles in developing civil society.

In contrast, democratic transitions typically engender several stages or turning points (Kuzio, 2001; Linz & Stepan, 1996). The first stage of transition, referred to as democratization, involves confronting an authoritarian regime, winning the contestation, and assuming state power. A combination of factors contributes to the downfall of authoritarian regimes: loss of its public legitimacy or support, fractiousness within the ruling elite especially the military, and foreign pressures (Przeworski, 1986).

After pro-democracy forces win state power, the next step in pursuing peace by peaceful means requires state-building or strengthening political and economic institutions crucial to the operation of a viable democratic state. Democratic transition also involves nation-building, especially in multiethnic states like Bosnia, Lebanon, and Iraq to mention a few. When nation building occurs, individuals within a society undergo a transformative identity process in which social identities become more inclusive and disparate groups come to share feelings of belongingness and a common sense of who they are, where they are from, and where they are going collectively. A nation is not necessarily equal to the people of a state (Linz & Stepan, 1996), especially in territories where state boundaries have been imposed by foreign powers without regard for the ethnic contours of the local population.

Properties of the Conceptual Frame

While the explanatory power of scientific psychology has relied on the reduction of behavior and cognition to neurophysiological activity, comparable efforts have not been made to link human agency to larger units of social organization. Our approach to a psychology of nonviolent democratic transition does so, borrowing generously from human development ideas that view behavior and cognition as time-sensitive (Elder, 1998) and embedded in larger units of social organization (Bronfenbrenner & Evans, 2000). We appreciate how developmental science offers a conceptual orientation that synthesizes research in formerly disparate human-inquiry disciplines, emphasizing continuous interactions across levels of analysis, time frames and contexts (Cairns, Elder, & Costelo, 1996). Our analytic frame also draws extensively from positioning theory (Harré & Moghaddam, 2003a), which emphasizes the collaborative construction of social reality by actors. These embedded collaborative processes contrast sharply with an approach that seeks to explain the behavior of individuals under static, well-controlled situations.

Three characteristics mark the conceptual frame for a psychology of nonviolent democratic transition: (a) varying layers of analytical units, (b) continuously interacting with each other, (c) across changes in time and power-situations. Figure 15.2 shows the eco-positional model with analytical units involved in nested and interactive relationships.

Varying Levels of Analysis

The model recognizes that the size of the analytical units varies from global systems to the individual activist. Four layers are specified. On the periphery are two macro layers consisting of global and state systemic conditions. A third analytical unit is at the meso or middle level which hosts the pro-democracy movement. This is a collection of different social movements that share the goal of toppling the authoritarian regime and building more open political space. Social movements are conglomerations of individuals who share collective goals (Klandermans, 1997) and a collective identity (Polletta & Jasper, 2001; Simon & Klandermans, 2001; Taylor, Bougie, & Caouette, 2003b), as they engage in collective action. Democratic transitions temporarily bring together protest movements of different ideological orientations, class and gender compositions, and inclinations toward political violence. The process of consolidating these social movements is called mesomobilization (Gerhards & Rucht, 1992). At the micro level we find individual activist-leaders. Further, a sub-outer layer of

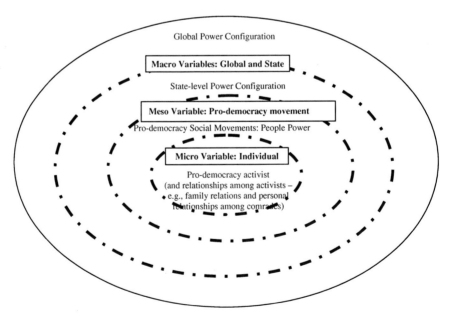

FIGURE 15.2. Analytical units in a nested and interactive model of a psychology of nonviolent transition.

the micro level hosts intimate relations, including family relations and personal relationships among comrades.

Each analytical unit corresponds to a social science discipline, with the macro units typically staked out by political science, meso levels by sociology-anthropology, and micro units by psychology. Compared to the disciplines of sociology and political science, psychology has had the weakest contributions to a multidisciplinary view of nonviolent democratic transition. However, both political scientist Migdal and colleagues (Migdal, Kohli, & Shue, 1994) and sociologist Giddens (1994) have proposed views that combine macro contextual conditions with rapidly-changing micro situations. They show how the transformation of political systems entails micro-level human dynamics that are not discernable with a molar analysis that takes place exclusively at the level of the state or social structure. Borrowing from Migdal, we view society as a unit embedded within a state. The state-society relation is bidirectional, though our analysis emphasizes the role of social organization at the societal level as a means of nonviolently challenging repressive political structures. Giddens (1994) likewise emphasizes societal considerations in viewing democracy. He defines four spheres of democracy, namely personal life, social movements and self-help groups, organizations, and the larger global order. Political change from authoritarianism to democracy thus takes place on all four levels of analysis.

Nested in macro political and social systems are human collectives and individuals who are engaged in pro-democracy action. During democratic transitions, individual acts are carried out by activist-leaders while collective acts are carried out by pro-democracy social movements.

We differentiate act from action, where the act connotes the social meaning of a behavior and action implies the personal meaning of such a behavior from the view of the individual/collective enactor (Harré & Moghaddam, 2003a). The private or personal meaning of a political behavior may or may not be congruent with the public or political meaning of the same behavior to others in the political environment. For example, during the Philippine People Power I in 1986, a number of military leaders viewed their protest action as a military-led coup against Marcos. On the other hand, civil society viewed the military's collective act as supportive of the civilian-led nonviolent revolution.

Along with Gandhi (1951) and Sharp (1973), we posit the importance of one's interior life and subjective disposition, as necessary ingredients for an individual's nonviolent action. We likewise recognize that psychological explanations of nonviolence are highly developed along this angle, because the very nature of psychology as a discipline focuses on individuals as the basic analytical unit (Kool & Keyes, 1990; Mayton, Diessner, & Granby, 1996). A larger, more inclusive, unit of analysis is comprised by collectively shared subjectivities and attendant nonviolent political power (Ackerman & DuVall, 2000; Gandhi, 1951; Sharp, 1973; Zunes et al., 1999). Consistent with the concept of collectivity, we note that nonviolence during democratic transitions is referred to as People's Power, not Person Power. At the meso and macro levels of analysis, however, psychology walks on relatively unfamiliar ground, because the discipline remains steeped in individualistic paradigms of human behavior.

Reciprocal Continuity Across Levels of Analysis

Human developmentalist Elder (1998) defines transition as any change in state. When marked by a significant change of direction, transitions are turning points as well. The concept of transition connects the smaller analytical layers of human agency (Bandura, 2001) with macro contextual conditions (Elder, 1998). Individuals bring to each transition their histories of human experiences and dispositions, select themselves into a transition process, and are influenced by the social change (Elder, 1998). In the same vein, we posit a parallel yet distinct phenomenon occurring at the collective level. Social movements bring to the democratic-transition experience their organizational histories and cultures, opt to participate in the destruction of an authoritarian system and creation of open political space, and are influenced by the process and outcome of such a major political transition.

A key concept of the model is reciprocal continuity, which implies that there is continuous bidirectional exchange between each analytical unit and its surrounding environment (Elder, 1998). All four analytical levels interact with each other in this bidirectional fashion, and the nearer the analytical unit, the more frequent the interaction. For example, activists regularly interact with social movements and vice-versa. Bronfenbrenner and Morris (1998) refer to enduring interaction in one's immediate environment as proximal processes. However, during a democratic transition period, interaction across analytical units can take place beyond the immediate proximal environment. In fact, to produce social strain, transitions may host nonconventional and disruptive interactions that do not follow traditional proximal processes. For example, an activist-leader can relate with the authoritarian state on a personal rather than collective basis; or a social movement can align with international solidarity networks without state sanction.

Psychological phenomena during political transitions likewise arise as interaction effects. The nature of interaction on this level is more complex, because it not only considers exchange across analytical layers, but also includes interaction between subjectively-intended action (Bandura, 2001) and political effects of a public act. We use positioning theory to explain complex psychological interactions during democratic transitions.

Positioning Theory

Understanding Psychological Situatedness During Democratic Transitions

Psychological states during democratic transitions are not only context-dependent, but also situation-specific. Context refers to the general and continuing multilayered interactions among the activist, pro-democracy movement, state, and global environment. On the other hand, "Situation is spatiotemporally specific. It is a particular concrete physical and social setting in which a person is embedded at any one point in time" (Ashmore, Deaux, & McLaughlin-Volpe, 2004, p. 103). Because democratic transitions host rapid changes across analytical layers, and because the goal of transition is to alter conventional (macro) state contexts, the model attends to both contextual and situational conditions.

The concept of positioning can be used to explain psychological conditions nested in dynamic political environments during nonviolent democratic transitions. Because of its conceptual flexibility, positioning theory can be useful in understanding rapidly changing social situations (Taylor et al., 2003b) across different analytical units (Tan & Moghaddam, 1999).

Like roles, positions engender a set of expectations in the form of rights and duties that constrain actions and cognitions. However, unlike role theory and its static conception of rights and duties, positioning theory captures the fluidity and temporal-spatial variability of positions. Moreover, roles exert long term influences on expectations while positions take a more fine-grain analysis of the situation-specific nature of action and cognitions (Harré & Slocum, 2003). An activist, for example, may play the role of a leader but as specific situations arise the leader may stake out a wide range of positions such as a confidant, strategist, organizer, and even follower.

In relation to democratic transitions, positioning theory illuminates that which is subjectively experienced by the individual activist, members of pro-democracy movements, and those who occupy the authoritarian state. We use conceptual tools identified by positioning theorists as useful in describing subjective phenomena – storylines, positions, and speech and other acts/actions (Harre & Moghaddam, 2003a; Harré & Slocum, 2003).

Storylines refer to subjective scripts located in the individual or collective minds of participants who are interacting with each other. Such storylines are embedded in the political cultures and subjective histories of the interacting participants. Histories include isolated individual/collective experiences, as well as historical interactions between and among the participants. The subjective narratives are fluid and change as the interaction unfolds.

Speech and other acts/actions refer to the smallest unit of interaction in our interactive model, as storylines unfurl and positions change. During political transitions, such acts/actions refer to politically significant behaviors that disrupt and dismantle the authoritarian regime or support and construct a new democracy. An action connotes subjective meaning in relation to the individual/collective actor who carries out the behavior, while an act is the meaning of the same behavior in relation to others in the actor's social context. Many of these acts/actions take the form of verbal or written utterances that carry social or illocutionary force. Table 15.1 lists examples of oral and written utterances during nonviolent democratic transitions.

In addition to these speech acts, other powerful expressions for political interaction are actions without talk (e.g., joining a candle-light procession),

TABLE 15.1. Examples of oral and written utterances during nonviolent democratic transitions.

Analytical unit	Examples of oral and written utterances
Individual level: Activists	Verbal utterances; personal email and cell phone text messages; secret notes smuggled from prison; underground meetings and debates
Collective level: Pro-democracy social movements	Leaflets and manifestos distributed during protest rallies; pastoral letters; underground radio and print media; email and cell phone text messages; final decision after meetings; streamers and placards; press releases
State level	Government pronouncements through radio, television, and newspaper media under state control; secret files and orders to state political and military machinery; transcripts of "debates" in state-controlled legislature, judiciary, and executive offices
Global level	Statements of foreign leaders and visiting state officials.

purposive inaction (e.g., boycotts; not moving away from the path of a tank), and purposive silence (e.g., not praising the dictator). Especially in asymmetric conflicts where enemies are Goliathic, other forms of non-utterance interactions arise with powerful forcefulness.

Positioning Crosses Analytical Levels

During democratic transitions, positions arise simultaneously and bidirectionally across various analytical layers. Imagine different types of points in space, with different units of analysis. The points are nested from micro to macro units. Each point takes on meaning in relation to itself, and also in relation to points in other analytical layers surrounding the embedded set of points. The power of positioning theory lies in its capacity to analyze simultaneously-occurring human phenomenon that interact with each other across analytical layers during democratic transitions. For example, the political action and act of one activist-leader – e.g., holding a placard at a protest rally – is defined in relation to the enactor (self-meaning), other comrades in the same social movement, other social movements under the umbrella of the pro-democracy movement, and in relation to the authoritarian state. On another level, collective political action and the act of one social movement like, say a manifesto condemning a foreign superpower's back-up of the local dictatorship, is defined in relation to the group as a whole (collective group-meaning), individual activists in the same group, other movements in the larger pro-democracy movement, and also in relation to the state and global powers. Finally, one state action, like massive arrests at a funeral of a grassroots mobilizer, acquires different meanings to an activist, one's comrades, different social movements in the united front, the state itself, and global powers. Because authoritarian systems have strong states, the state is a significant actor and meaning-interpreter in the positioning that goes on during nonviolent democratic transitions.

Table 15.2 shows how a single individual, collective, state or global act takes on at least six different positions and meanings in the democratic transition. Columns A to D are the analytical units that may carry out a political action, while Rows 1 to 6 are the levels that interpret acts A to D. A psychology of nonviolent democratic transition may attend to each cell in the matrix, and to the nature of multidirectional interactions across the six rows.

A research agenda on a psychology of nonviolent transition may focus on any cell in the matrix as a central dependent variable or independent variable. As in other embedded phenomena, "the multilevel nature of human development invites different points of entry ... (that) frequently link or cross levels.... Studies commonly employ different points of entry in the same research, though framed by the entry point of its central question" (Elder, 1998, p. 944). The analytical entry of a psychology of nonviolent democratic transition may be at any layer of the nested political system. However, outcomes of nonviolent democratic transitions are usually located at the juncture between pro-democracy movements and the state, as political groups contend with the state through a united front.

Storylines are Temporally Situated

The role of timing during transitions has been discussed in the context of human development. Elder (1998) points out that "Human lives are socially embedded in specific historical times and places that shape their content, pattern, and direction" (p. 969). Further, Elder proposes that "the temporal relation between lives and trajectories varies according to the timing of transitions" (p. 981). We borrow from Elder's ideas about the importance of temporality in embedded human systems undergoing transition. The nature of positions and storylines associated with political acts and actions depends on temporality. During nonviolent democratic transitions, time matters in at least three ways – (a) storylines within each analytical unit change across time, (b) subjective histories of reciprocal interactions accumulate through time, and (c) storylines are sequentially situated.

Storylines within each analytical unit change across time. Each analytical layer hosts storylines that unfold along a time coordinate. As time passes, storylines change on the global, state, social movement, and activist-leader levels. Because conditions vary across time points, contextual correlates of nonviolent democratic transition say, a decade ago, need to be tested again years later. For example, the Philippines' second People Power in 2001 operated under more democratic state conditions brought about by the success of People Power I in 1986. Before 1986, the Marcos Dictatorship controlled television stations; communications about protest actions were disseminated through pastoral letters of the Catholic Church read during Sunday mass homilies. However, the 2001 prodemocracy

TABLE 15.2. Positioning by the activist, social movement, state, and global unit of analysis during democratic transitions.

Analytical unit positioned in relation to political act (1 to 6)	Enactor of a political act (A to C)			
	Individual Activist: Act A: e.g., activist holding a placard at a protest rally	Social Movement: Act B: e.g., movement's manifesto condemning US back-up of local dictatorship	State: Act C: e.g., state forces' massive arrests at a political funeral	Global Forces: Act D: e.g., US President Carter declares, "Our commitment to human rights must be absolute" (Carter, 1977).
(1) Activist self	Position A1 – meaning of *action* to one's self	Position B1 – meaning of group act to activist	Position C1 – meaning of state act to activist	Position D1 – meaning of global act to act vist, e.g., political prisoners begin to enjoy more relatives' visiting rights
(2) Other comrades	Position A2 – meaning of activist's act to one's comrades	Position B2 – meaning of group act to one's comrades	Position C2 – meaning of state act to one's comrades	Position D2 – meaning of global act to one's comrades, e.g., motivated to struggle for democracy
(3) Social movement of activist	Position A3 – meaning of activist's act to one's social movement	Position B3 – collective meaning of group *action* to the social-movement enactor	Position C3 – collective meaning of state act to a specific social movement	Position D3 – collective meaning of global act to a specific social movement

(4) Other social movements in the pro-democracy untied front	Position A4 – meaning of activist's act to other social movements	Position B4 – collective meaning of group act to other movements in the united front	Position C4 – collective meaning of state act to other social movements in the united front	Position D4 –collective meaning of global act to other social movements in the united front
(5) State	Position A5 – meaning of activist's act to state forces (this may influence the state's counter-hit against a specific individual)	Position B5 – meaning of collective act to state forces (this may influence the state's counter-hit against a specific social movement)	Position C5 – meaning of state *action* to state	Position D5- meaning of global act to state
(6) Global (Superpowers, UN, international NGO's)	Position A6 – meaning of activist's act to pro and anti-state global forces (unless the individual is an international figure, there is little impact on this level)	Position B6 – meaning of social movement's act to pro and anti-state global forces (this may influence foreign funding decisions and consequently the logistical resource base of the social movement)	Position C6 – meaning of state's act to pro and anti-state global forces (this may influence foreign aid/funding decisions and consequently the logistical resource base of the state forces)	Position D6 – meaning of global act to pro- and anti global forces (this may influence US and other international political and financial support vis-à-vis the authoritarian state and/or prodemocracy forces)

movement against President Estrada made full use of sympathetic local television facilities to cover the Senate investigation of Estrada's plunder case. Note how state-level conditions allowed for different forms of political communication by prodemocracy movements during People Power I and II.

Because each analytical layer changes across time, explanatory scripts of nonviolent transitions must have a time referent, anchoring any given political moment not only to the different macro-micro analytical units, but also to the time-point that hosts the event. For example, in order to explain why Marcos helicoptered to Hawaii after four days of People Power, one would inquire about what was happening on the global, state, social-movement, and individual level during this political moment. A lens calibrated with time-referents would reveal temporal conditions like a (global) phone call from US President Ronald Reagan to Marcos, (state) defection of a key Air Force wing to the People Power camp, (social movement) millions of people on the streets blocking the Marcos tanks, and (individual-activist) a university law professor successfully persuading his military-general brother who was commanding the Marcos tanks not to turn the tanks on the People Power crowd.

Most political situations during democratic transitions change rapidly and can hardly be predicted. However, there are also some patterned changes-across-time associated with each analytical layer. We now point out a few changes in the global, state, social-movement, and activist-leader layers that occur regularly across time.

In recent years, global power configurations changed across three significant stages: the Cold War, the demise of the Cold War, and the post-September 11 "war on terrorism". At the state level, during transition, the state changes from an authoritarian to a more open political system. Further, the process of state democratization entails smaller steps such as destroying the authoritarian regime, state-building, and nation-building (Kuzio, 2001; Linz & Stepan, 1996). Pro-democracy movements also undergo changes as a collective. Klandermans (1997) identifies different types of movement cycles. Sequences that are most relevant to the temporality of pro-democracy movements are event-related and exhibit growth-decline cycles. A political/cultural event can be predicted to generate much dynamism among movements. Examples of such events in the context of the Philippines' People Power I were electoral exercises, anniversaries of anti-colonial victories, and visits of the pope. Growth-and-decline cycles refer to the life stages of a movement as it is born, grows stronger, then degenerates. Growth is marked by rapid recruitment, intense commitments, and successful mobilizations. Signs of organizational decline include high membership departures (Klandermans, 1997) or defections, internal fractiousness, and the drying up (or personal pocketing) of logistical resources especially from foreign sources. For the activist-leader, there is at the very least the developmental stage of the individual that identifies time-coordinates, as one grows from adolescence, to young adulthood, to full adulthood. For the activist, we posit developmental changes that occur over time and move the activist from a conventional form of reasoning about social injustices to a more principled position within the context of human rights (Crain, 2005; Kohlberg, 1984).

Figure 15.3 illustrates the temporality of context across different levels of analyses. In order to understand the nature of democratic transition, one would need to identify what changes across time arise not only within a single analytical layer, say the global arena, but also alongside and in-interaction-with other time-based changes on the other macro and micro levels of human phenomenon like the state, the social movement, and the activist-leader. For example, the 1986 People Power I occurred when the Global level was in the midst of a Cold War, the Philippine state was a dictatorship, prodemocracy movements grappled with strong underground liberation movements, and the average age of radical activists was approximately 30 years old. People Power II in 2001 took place when the Cold War had subsided, the Philippine state operated under a new democracy, armed ideological struggles had lost a large amount of their social power, and lead activists were already parents who not only joined the rallies but also brought along their teenage children to the protest actions.

Subjective histories of interactions accumulate through time. Positioning theorists have raised the importance of a person's or group's historical experience

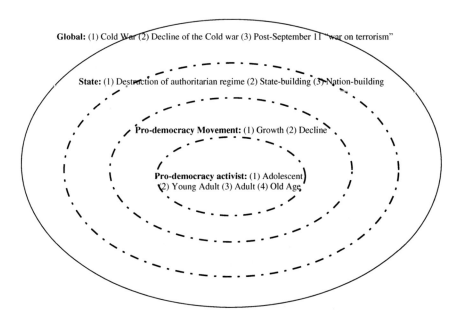

FIGURE 15.3. Positioning is time-contextualized: Examples of what's going on in the context of each analytical unit at the time of a political act in the pro-democracy movement.

in the production of storylines (Davies & Harré, 1990; Tan & Moghaddam, 1999). During nonviolent transitions, subjective histories shared by agents interacting in the political arena partly shape the meaning of their political actions and acts. More specifically, the meaning of personal/collective actions during democratic transition depends on the subjective interactive histories of Points 1 and 2 that are positioning in relation to each other. We describe history as subjective because we see it as a constructed reality on both the personal and social levels. History is likewise interactive because it emanates from a remembrance of past interactions between participants in the political process.

The centrality of memory in fueling conflicts has been well documented (Cairns & Roe, 2003). On the individual level, subjective history can be located in one's personal memory while on the social-movement level, we deal with politicized collective memories (Halbwachs, 1938; Liu & Hilton, 2005; Schuman & Rodgers, 2004). During transitions, state memories refer to the collective memories of officials who occupy state power. These constructions are selective, and contain politically-convenient episodes and persons (Jovic, 2004).

Storylines, like collective narratives, do not emerge from nowhere; as Salomon (2004) points out, the most important source of collective narratives is a group's history and the way in which a group construes its past. An event that occurred centuries ago, say during colonial times, can play into an ongoing storyline, if it is recalled in present time.

Collective memories are often suffused with emotions and aimed at delegitimizing opponents (Bar-Tal, 2003) while legitimizing, motivating, and idealizing the acts of proponents (Devine-Wright, 2003). These collective memories are located in political space and time and can serve as a catalyst of change and resistance to change. For example, during protest rallies, Philippine prodemocracy assemblies chanted inspirational political songs that reactivated memories of liberation struggles against the country's former colonial rulers Spain and the US. Collective singing about courageous people's struggles against past oppressions drenched the social movement with the emotional fervor needed to contend a militarized authoritarian state. At the political moment when song revived history, the accumulated past fused with the present and became a source of cultural inspiration in the current social combat.

Storylines are sequentially situated. Storylines are deeply embedded in smaller time-units surrounding the situation of a political act. An act/action is partly defined by what precedes it and what comes after it, in a reciprocally continuous manner. Timing likewise couches meanings related to opportunities and threats in the fluid political environment. For example, during martial law in the Philippines, the timing of political detainees' hunger strikes coincided with globally-publicized events such as papal visits, in order to maximize opportunities of international media coverage.

Time-proximity directly relates to the amount of impact on meaning and position. Political acts and actions immediately before and after a particular act/action strongly influence the position and meaning of the act/action. In order to understand the subjective meaning of a personal or collective act, one needs to consider the repertoire of acts and actions by all analytical layers, within smaller time-units, before and after the act that is being meaningful described.

Storylines and Positioning are Power-sensitive

The process of nonviolent democratic transitions involves social conflicts in the political arena. Contentiousness and power-competitions mark interactions among activists, within and between social movements, and between pro-democracy forces and the authoritarian state. Even within the state, there is fractiousness among hardliners and moderates. Storylines and positioning within these storylines unfold in the shadow of power. Hence, understandings of subjective meanings during transition cannot remain blind to the color of power. We cite three ways in which storylines and positions are power-sensitive. First, the power to position the other is unequally distributed across individuals in a group, and social-movements in a pro-democracy united front; second, subjective meanings of acts and actions are related to one's power position in the conflict; and third, major storylines during transition are about political power.

The power to position is unequally distributed in a group. Positioning theorists have raised the issue of power inequalities during social conflicts (Harré & Slocum, 2003; Tan & Moghaddam, 1999). In asymmetric conflicts, powerful social utterers take on more rights, duties and obligations to define positions in the unfolding storyline. The social contentions revolve around competing story-lines and positions claimed by different conflict participants on the individual and collective levels. During nonviolent democratic transitions, fluid power configu-rations host changing power-holders among activists, social movements, and the state.

Even within analytical units, power competition arises in order to assert proclaimed storylines and their corresponding embedded positions. Hence, one would note a variety of competing and contentious storylines, not only between the state and anti-state forces, but also among activists and among social movements in the same united front. For example, during the Marcos Dicta-torship, the Philippine social democratic movement suffered serious organiza-tional fissures caused by the internal debate about whether to take up arms or remain nonviolently opposed to the state. Organizational factions, leadership struggles, and everyday political intrigues defined themselves in relation to individual and collective positions taken along the two contending storylines about the mode of struggle.

Subjective meanings of acts/actions are related to one's power position in the conflict. One's storyline about the conflict is linked to one's power-location in an asymmetric relationship (topdog or underdog). As Bourdieu (1979/1984) succinctly states, "agents have points of view in this objective space which depend on their position within it" (p. 169). Evidence from the Mindanao war in the Philippines supports Bourdieu's claim. A study of Muslims' and Christians' understandings of the Mindanao conflict showed that only the marginalized Muslims saw themselves in a low-power position, while the dominant Christians did not see any intergroup inequality. Further, Muslims traced the causes of the war to unjust political structures, while Christians claimed that the Mindanao conflict arose from internal dispositions of the antagonistic groups. Hence, there were at least two social constructions of the causes of war – the story from above, and the narrative from below (Montiel & Macapagal, 2006).

Storylines during nonviolent democratic transition are about political power. During nonviolent transitions, different contending storylines arise about the production, distribution and utilization of political power. Storylines about power production are about methods of political confrontation, and narrate how to source power in order to change or maintain the authoritarian regime. Social movements and activists who support nonviolence use storylines about producing social power based on huge numbers of peaceful and organized people. Other participants on the political scene like the state and the armed liberation movements and activists carry storylines about producing power through militarized methods like the government's armed forces or underground guerilla tactics.

Storylines about power distribution describe political goals during the transition. In general, activists and pro-democracy movements carry storylines that promise a future where political power is shared with a broader mass of people. On the other hand, the state carries storylines about centralizing rather than distributing political power.

On the social-movement level, storylines are embedded in the group's collective action frame, or shared meanings and goals about political action (Klandermans, 1997). Collective action frames are formed in three ways, beginning with the social construction of shared meanings on the problematic situation, followed by a discourse on who is the enemy and finally, a push for collective action to bring about change (Benford & Snow, 2000). For example, prodemocracy united fronts evolve their collective action frame by first socially constructing shared meanings of political oppression, followed by a discourse blaming the authoritarian head of state as the people's Enemy, and then building up a nationwide call to remove the authoritarian leader and open up democratic space.

A third storyline emerges after the authoritarian regime falls, and more democratic political space opens up – storylines about the utilization of power. With pro-democracy activists occupying power positions in the newly democratized government, storylines arise about how to use state power in an appropriate way. Coming to the foreground at this stage of transition are narratives about government and social-movement corruption (i.e., the misuse of power) under the new government. Another storyline after the fall of the regime and during state-building has to do with staying out of the state, or joining the state. Competing social movements and activists hold different versions of this storyline, and intense intergroup conflicts among former pro-democracy allies spring from contradictory storylines about remaining outside the new state or utilizing power from within the state.

The Philippine experience with People's Power showed the power of story-lines during nonviolent democratic transition. The first People's Power in 1986 revolved around the distribution of political power, beyond the confines of the Marcos dictatorship. In 2001, People's Power II toppled President Estrada along the narrative of power utilization – positioning Estrada as a state leader who misused state power through massive corruption, and hence was undeserving of the rights, duties and obligations of the country's presidency.

Conclusion

Nonviolent democratic transitions involve the use of socially-contentious yet peaceful means to destroy authoritarian systems and produce more democratic space. Such political transitions demonstrate that large-scale intrastate conflicts can be resolved without massive killings. Other models of political transitions out of authoritarian regimes, like militarized foreign occupations in the name of democracy or armed liberation movements, also claim to resolve intrastate conflicts. However, militarized interventions merely change the palace occupants, fortify authoritarian systems, and traumatize civilian populations.

A psychology of peaceful power-shifts necessitates the recognition of rapidly-changing political meanings across interactive analytical layers, ranging from the global context, transitioning state, prodemocracy movements, and the activist leader. Because of its conceptual flexibility, positioning theory addresses these paradigmatic issues and illuminates the psychological study of democratic transitions.

The theory's propositions about changing storylines, positions and illocutionary forces can tackle not only different analytical layers of individual/collective human phenomena but also extremely fast rates of social psychological change during political transitions. Positioning theory likewise allows for the understanding of dynamic and temporary situational factors, in addition to relatively-stable contextual variables. In intrastate conflicts, individuals and collectives contend with each other intensely as conflict escalates, hence dynamic situation effects can be more crucial than static context effects.

Finally, positioning theory elucidates how meanings of political acts/actions during intrastate conflict resolution are couched in temporality and power-arrangements. During democratic transition, political subjectivities are tempo-rally embedded in three ways: (a) storylines within each analytical unit change across time; (b) subjective histories of interactions accumulate through time; and (c) storylines are sequentially situated. Further, political meanings are likewise power-sensitive in the following ways: (a) the power to position is unequally distributed in a group; (b) subjective meanings of acts/actions are related to one's power position in a conflict; and (c) storylines during nonviolent transition are about political power.

Acknowledgement

We gratefully acknowledge the support given to the first author by Ateneo de Manila University's 2005 Loyola Schools Scholarly Work Faculty Award.

Note

1. Background map, courtesy of www.worldatlas.com, used with permission.

References

Ackerman, P., & DuVall, J. (2000). *A force more powerful: A century of nonviolent conflict.* NY: Palgrave.

Ackerman, P., & Kruegler, C. (1994). *Strategic nonviolent conflict: The dynamics of people power in the twentieth century.* Westport, CT: Praeger Publishers.

Ashmore, R. D., Deaux, K., & McLaughlin-Volpe, T. (2004). An organizing framework for collective identity: Articulation and significance of multidimensionality. *Psychological Bulletin, 130,* 80–114.

Bandura, A. (2001). Social cognitive theory: An agentic perspective. *Annu. Rev. Psychol., 52,* 1–26.

Bar-Tal, D. (2003). Collective memory of physical violence: Its contribution to the culture of violence. In E. Cairns & M. D. Roe (Eds.), *The role of memory in ethnic conflict* (pp. 22–93), New York, NY: Palgrave.

Benford, R., & Snow, D. (2000). Framing processes and social movements: An overview and assessment. *Annual Review of Sociology, 26,* 611–639.

Bond, D., Jenkins, J. C., Taylor, C. L., & Schock, K. (1997). Mapping mass political conflict and civil society: Issues and prospects for the automated development of event data. *Journal of Conflict Resolution, 41,* 553–579.

Bourdieu, P. (1984). *Distinction. A social critique of the judgment of taste.* (R. Nice, Trans.). Cambridge, MA: Harvard University Press. (Original work published 1979).

Bronfenbrenner, U., & Evans, G. W. (2000). Developmental science in the 21st century: Emerging questions, theoretical models, research designs and empirical findings. *Social Development, 9,* 115–125.

Bronfenbrenner, U., & Morris, P. A. (1998). The ecology of developmental processes. In W. Damon (Series Ed.) & R. M. Lerner (Vol. Ed.), *Handbook of child psychology: Vol. 1. Theoretical models of human development* (5th Ed., pp. 993–1028). New York: Wiley.

Cairns, E., & Roe, M. D. (Eds.). (2003). *The role of memory in ethnic conflict.* New York, NY: Palgrave.

Cairns, R. B., Elder, G. H., & Costello, E. J. (1996). *Developmental science.* Cambridge: Cambridge University Press.

Carter, J. (1977). Inaugural Address of President Jimmy Carter. http://jimmycarterlibrary.org/documents/speeches/inaugadd.phtml

Crain, W. C. (2005). *Theories of development.* Upper-Saddle River, NJ: Prentice-Hall.

Davies, B., & Harré, R. (1990). Positioning: The discursive production of selves. *Journal for the Theory of Social Behavior, 20,* 43–63.

Devine-Wright, P. (2003). A theoretical overview of memory and conflict. In E. Cairns & M. D. Roe (Eds.), *The role of memory in ethnic conflict* (pp. 9–34). New York, NY: Palgrave.

Elder, Glen H. (1998). The life course and human development. In W. Damon (Series Ed.) & R. M. Lerner (Vol. Ed.), *Handbook of child psychology: Vol. 1. Theoretical models of human development* (5th ed., pp. 939–991). New York: Wiley.

Galtung, J. (1969). Violence, peace and peace research. *Journal of Peace Research, 6,* 167–191.

Galtung, J. (1996). *Peace by peaceful means.* London: Sage.

Gandhi, M. K. (1951). *Non-violent resistance.* New York: Schocken Books.

Gandhi, M. K. (1957/1927). *An autobiography: The story of my experiments with truth.* Boston: Beacon Press.

Gerhards, J., & Rucht, D. (1992). Mesomobilization: Organizing and framing in two protest campaigns in West Germany. *American Journal of Sociology, 98,* 555–596.

Giddens, A. (1994). *Beyond left and right: The future of radical politics.* Stanford: Stanford University Press.

Halbwachs, M. (1938). Individual psychology and collective psychology. *American Sociological Review, 3,* 615–623.

Harré, R., & Moghaddam, F. (Eds.). (2003b). *The self and others: Positioning individuals and groups in personal, political and cultural contexts.* Westport, CT Praeger.

Harré, R., & Moghaddam, F. (2003a). Introduction: The self and others in traditional psychology and in positioning theory. In R. Harré & F. Moghaddam (Eds.), *The self and others* (pp. 1–11). Westport, CT: Praeger.

Harré, R., & Slocum, N. (2003). Disputes as complex social events: On the uses of positioning theory. In R. Harré & F. Moghaddam (Eds.), *The self and others* (pp. 123–136). Westport, CT: Praeger.

Holmes, R. L. (Ed.). (1990). *Nonviolence in theory and practice.* Belmont, CA: Wadsworth Publishing Company.

Jovic, D. (2004). 'Official memories' in post-authoritarianism: An analytical framework. *Journal of Southern Europe and the Balkans, 6,* 97–108.

Klandermans, B. (1997). *The social psychology of protest.* Cambridge: Blackwell.

Kohlberg, L. (1984). *The psychology of moral development.* San Francisco: Harper & Row.

Kool, V. K., & Keyes, C. L. M. (1990). Explorations in the nonviolent personality. In V. K. Kool (Ed.), *Perspectives on nonviolence* (pp. 17–38). New York: Springer-Verlag.

Kuzio, T. (2001). Transition in post-communist states: Triple or quadruple? *Politics, 21,* 168–177.

Linz, J., & Stepan, A. (1996). *Problems of democratic transition and consolidation: Southern Europe, South America, and Post-Communist Europe.* Baltimore: The Johns Hopkins University Press.

Liu, J., & Hilton, D. (2005). How the past weighs on the present: Social representations of history and their role in identity politics. *British Journal of Social Psychology, 44,* 537–556.

Mayton, D. M., Diessner, R., & Granby, C. D. (1996). Nonviolence and values: Empirical support for theoretical relationships. *Peace and Conflict: Journal of Peace Psychology, 2,* 245–253.

Migdal, J., Kohli, A., Shue, V. (1994). *State power and social forces: Domination and transformation in the Third World.* New York: Cambridge University Press.

Montiel, C., & Macapagal, E. (2006). Effects of social position on societal attributions of an asymmetric conflict. *Journal of Peace Research, 43,* 219–227.

Pelton, L. H. (1974). *The psychology of nonviolence*. New York: Pergamon Press.

Polletta, F., & Jasper, J. M. (2001). Collective identity and social movements. *Annual Review of Sociology, 27*, 283–305.

Przeworski, A. (1986). Some problems in the study of the transition to democracy. In G. O'Donnell, P. C. Schmitter, & L. Whitehead (Eds.), *Transitions from authoritarian rule: Comparative perspectives* (pp. 47–63). Baltimore: The Johns Hopkins University Press.

Salomon, G. (2004). A narrative-based view of coexistence education. *Journal of Social Issues, 60*, 273–287.

Schuman, H., & Rodgers, W. L. (2004). Cohorts, chronology, and collective memories. *Public Opinion Quarterly, 68*, 217–254.

Sharp, G. (1973). *The politics of nonviolent action. Part two: The methods of nonviolent action*. Boston: Porter Sargent Publishers.

Simon, B., & Klandermans, B. (2001). Politicized collective identity. A social psychological analysis. *American Psychologist, 56*, 319–331.

Sponsel, L. E., & Gregor, T. (Eds.). (1994). *The anthropology of peace and nonviolence*. Boulder, CO: Lynne Rienner Publishers.

Tan, S. L., & Moghaddam, F. M. (1999). Positioning in intergroup relations. In R. Harré & L. Van Langenhove (Eds.), *Positioning theory: Moral contexts of international actions* (pp. 178–194). Malden, MA: Blackwell.

Taylor, D., Bougie, E., & Caouette, J. (2003a). Applying positioning principles to a theory of collective identity. In R. Harre & F. Moghaddam (Eds.), *The self and others: Positioning individuals and groups in personal, political, and cultural contexts* (pp. 197–215). Westport, CT: Praeger.

Zunes, S., Kurtz, L. R., & Asher, S. B. (1999). *Nonviolent social movements: A geographical perspective*. Malden, MA: Blackwell.

Part 4
Conclusion and Glossary

16
Afterword

FATHALI M. MOGHADDAM, ROM HARRÉ AND NAOMI LEE

Robert Kennedy, 'I would think that the war would never be won militarily. Where it's going to be won really is the political war...'

Lyndon Johnson, '...we get the Canadians to go in and tell Hanoi that our objectives are very limited. That we don't want to take'em over and we don't want to be the power in that part of the world, that all we want to do is get'em to leave these other folks alone and then they'll do better by then. And we're going to talk to Pearson (the Canadian Prime Minister) today in New York about getting the Canadians to go into Hanoi on that front. We're going to Khrushchev with suggestions as to what we think they ought to do and can do. We're going to London with our trying to open some new diplomatic routes...'

The publication of the Lyndon Johnson White House Tapes (Beschloss, 1997), from which the above discussion of 1964 is excerpted (pp.375–377), provides fascinating insights into various attempts to position the U.S. Government during the Vietnam War, using third parties, such as Canadians and the British. Over three decades later, a similar positioning effort is ongoing, this time involving the Bush Administration's policy in post-invasion Iraq and its attempts to persuade 'the enemy' (and the world) that '...we don't want to be the power in that part of the world, that all we want to do is get'em to leave these other folks alone and then they'll do better by then...'. The storyline in Iraq is eerily reminiscent of the Vietnam years, with the ghostly echo of Robert Kennedy saying '...the war would never be won militarily. Where it's going to be won really is the political war...'.

Since the U.S. led invasion of Iraq in 2003, we have repeatedly heard that the more important war is about 'winning hearts and minds'. Two interpretations of this rhetoric need to be noted. First, by referring to 'winning hearts and minds', speakers are signaling that at a strategic level their efforts are really not all about guns and bombs, that they have more than just a military goal. Second, speakers are positioning themselves not only as more sophisticated but also as morally superior to those who are simply concerned with military solutions. Furthermore, the very idea of 'winning hearts and minds' presumes that the emotions and opinions of the 'enemy' somehow inferior to those of the American way of life.

Such claims about 'winning hearts and minds' underline the fact that even in the heat of battle, with war raging in Vietnam in the 1960s and Iraq in the post 2003 era, for example, the parties in disputes continue to try to better position themselves to gain the moral high ground. Given the centrality of positioning processes before, during, and after conflicts, it is appropriate to ask: what is the role of positioning theory in resolving real-world conflicts such as the conflicts in Iraq, and Vietnam before that?

Our answer to this question is bold and provocative: what Robert Kennedy called 'the political war' and in more recent times has been more broadly referred to as the fight to 'win hearts and minds', in Iraq and elsewhere, is just another instance of positioning, and of highlighting the central role of positioning in both conflict escalation and resolution. Conflicts can become resolved when a third party succeeds in getting both contending groups to interpret the things said and the actions performed from the point of view of the positionings that underlie each. The conflict becomes a display of a local distribution of rights of the outside forces to define superior political and moral values and the duty of the recipients of their attentions to adopt them.

The studies reported in this book provide some indications of the role and power of positioning theory toward resolving conflicts. In this final discussion, we briefly highlight the conflict resolution role of positioning theory, pointing out certain limitations and potentialities.

The Positioning Theory Approach: From Mental States to Meaning-Making Practices

Psychological approaches to conflict typically treat actors' interests, attitudes, and personality characteristics as the drivers of conflicts. Positioning theory helps us see how such factors are supple constructs that actors fashion through communicative processes, as they make motivational attributions, produce character ascriptions, and place each other into storylines and positions that distribute rights and obligations unevenly. Typically treated as prime movers, potent psychological concepts are recognized by positioning theorists as defined in the course of conflict and producing social effects. Hence, positioning theory illuminates how meaning-making practices (e.g. the creation of actors' motives, interests, etc. through language) lie at the heart of conflict. For example, Slocum-Bradley (Chapter 12) demonstrates how an analysis of communicative practices and their social consequences has a rigor not obtainable in conventional, speculative analyses of actors' mental states.

This analytical shift, from mental states to communicative practice, suggests a move to interventions at the level of discursive practice. At this plane of activity, practitioners of conflict resolution can facilitate reshaping storylines to redefine the social meaning of actions and reconfigure arrays of rights and duties. But a preliminary step is to determine what needs to be done in a conflict situation: not all conflicts need to be resolved.

When Conflict Resolution Is Demanded, and When It Is Not

Many conflicts come about in situations when both parties have some claim to demand that their side holds a monopoly of the moral right. Sometimes a disinterested onlooker would agree. These are the kinds of conflicts that call for 'conflict resolution'. However there are other situations, also unfortunately more common than one would wish when there is a sharp imbalance between the moral position of one party vis á vis that of the other. In these cases far from conflict resolution being the proper aim, conflict amplification is morally demanded. For example, Moghaddam and Ginsburg (2003) discussed a case of bio-piracy involving the Ayahuasca plant, which is venerated throughout the Amazon region of South America. Despite the long history of this plant being used for medicinal and spiritual functions in South America, in 1986 a U.S. patent was awarded to an American company, giving the company exclusive rights to sell and develop new varieties of the plant. When indigenous South American tribes learned of this patent, they mobilized to fight for their rights.

What is the role of the outsider in such situations? Surely the morally correct course of action is to help the minority group, in this case indigenous South Americans, to mobilize and to fight for their rights. Rather than pacify the minority group(s), surely in such cases our moral obligation is to help mobilize them and help them to win the conflict (with the help of outsiders, the South American indigenous groups did mobilize and the U.S. patent for Ayahuasca was eventually revoked).

Sporting competitions are alternative versions of real life conflicts. However, neither side in a football match has moral right on its side. But only one side can win. In these cases we are quite happy to propose ways in which the coaches can amplify the conflict.

Positioning In Other Types of Conflict

In several of the studies reported in this volume the distinction between conflicts that are already ongoing and those that are potential or incipient can easily be seen. Redman's study illustrates this very clearly. The study of conflict management must deal with incipient as much as ongoing conflicts. How do we prevent a conflict escalating, defuse it so to say, when there is no imbalance of moral good to be struck? And how do we inflame a potential or incipient conflict when one side is, according to the generality of human beings, making the preliminary moves to engaging in immoral actions?

In this regard, the value of Positioning Theory emerges at two levels of reflection. For those who are concerned with understanding the roots of long standing conflicts, the ability to reach into the often unacknowledged background assumptions, beliefs and traditions is an essential tool. We believe that in many cases the apparent causus belli is superficial, hiding deeper divisions and antagonisms than the protagonists acknowledge. More often than not these turn on moral issues, such as the acceptable or equitable distribution of rights and duties among the contending parties. Sometimes the dispute turns on incompatible story-lines with which people make sense of local events. The myths and legends of a community, such as the important role that the 'martyrdom at Karbela' almost fourteen hundred years ago continues to play in the lives of Shi'a Muslims in contemporary Iraq and Iran (Moghaddam, 2006, pp. 52–56) are often roots of conflicts deeper than the way that people understand the issues of rights and duties that are the apparent source of dispute.

Another way this contrast between the superficial and the deep roots of conflict is evident in the Schiavo case (Chapter 8). Each party to the conflict formed a view of the character and motivations of the opponents in such a way that any discussion of the actual distribution of rights and duties with respect to the injured woman could never even be begun. Here we can see the powerfully destructive way that entrenched character attributions lead to the taking up and rejecting of positions that share the apparent discussion of rights and duties which actually conceals the underlying opinions that each party has formed of the other.

Yet again, it may be that an intuitive grasp of the centrality of positions in maintaining social order and also in undermining it can lead to very successful management of complex social relationships. In Chapter 11 on the way that Positioning Theory can illuminate the forms of military command, Napoleon's conflicted taking up of incompatible positions, as Emperor and as Field Commander was disastrous. He succeeded in transforming an incipient conflict into a real one. Lawrence's subtle management of positioning between himself and his Arab allies avoided positioning incompatibilities and contradictions. He succeeded in halting any slide from an incipient into a real conflict. This must surely account in no small measure for his success in the Turkish campaign, and Napoleon's failure in Russia.

The urge to understand may come from a disinterested scientific curiosity, such as might motivate a historian or sociologist interested in the origins and sustaining forces of a seemingly intractable and irresolvable conflict. Could such understanding have any role to play in the efforts that well meaning outsiders may be making to bring an existing conflict to an end in a way that will meet the needs and wishes of the contending parties? Of course, we know that there is a method of conflict resolution that usually succeeds, at least in the short run. That is the suppression by force of one or both of the parties to the dispute. The British Raj maintained inter-communal peace in the Indian subcontinent by force, or at least in later times by the threat of it. In some cases, such as the massacre of St Bartholomew's Day in France in 1572, a conflict can be resolved by the murder of enough of the members of one of the contending parties to ensure the exodus of the rest. Peace reigns, more or less in the graveyard. How much better in every way it would be if there were a method of research and a system of concepts by the application of which a 'bird's eye view' of conflict could be achieved!

Understanding and Resolving Conflicts

However, getting a good understanding of the roots of a conflict does not necessarily lead to its resolution. This brings us to the other level of reflection – the matters that antagonists might be brought to consider by bringing the insights of Positioning Theory to bear on their situation. One must bear in mind that what may seem to an outsider to be one situation may not be seen in that way by those in contention. Social constructionists have pointed out that the very same events, as seen from an outsider's point of view, may be seen as one thing by one party and as another by the other. This point is highlighted by the statement, 'One person's terrorist is another person's freedom fighter'. Who are the U.S. led forces fighting in Iraq? Terrorists or freedom fighters intent on liberating Iraq from foreign invaders? Was 9/11 a murderous terrorist attack or a daring commando raid (see Moghaddam, 2006, p.2)

It is hardly news that most conflicts are irresolvable and if they end it is because the impetus to keep the conflict going has disappeared. For example, studies of how terrorism ends show that often it is because of changes in economic conditions or other factors that alter the circumstances of the conflict, rather than because of the psychological characteristics of those in terrorist cells (Cronin, 2006). The research of Donal Carbaugh (1999) highlights a similar phenomenon: the ending of a conflict over the appropriate use of a hillside that simply faded away as people gradually drifted into a compromise between developers and conservationists.

Positioning Theory and 'Lay' Practitioners

Positioning Theory is sometimes put into practice by 'lay' practitioners in conflict situations, but those who resolve the conflict make no use of the explicit formulations of the theory. An example involves the longstanding conflict between Catholics and Protestants in Ireland has run on for at least four hundred years. It has been exacerbated by aggressive acts from both communities, not least the savagery of Oliver Cromwell's suppression of the uprising of 1649, with its iconic story of the massacre at Drogheda. The Protestants with their Orange Order still march to celebrate their victory at the Battle of the Boyne. The recent outburst of the 'troubles', over the last thirty years, has shifted its footing around one central positioning issue, the assumptions of overriding rights and duties by one of the contending parties and their denial to the other. Positioned thus the IRA repositioned itself as having the right to engage in an armed struggle. To many people's surprise and to great general satisfaction it looks now as if a final repositioning of the Catholic and Protestant communities has come about, each conceding rights and duties to the other to accomplish a common moral order. This shows up in the recent decision of the Sin Fein party to recognize the courts and the police force of the Province as legitimate for all citizens. The Prime Ministers of the UK and of Eire were deeply involved in the 'peace process'.

From the point of view of social psychology we can see each of them working within an informal version of Positioning Theory. Story-lines were revised, social meanings of words and actions reconsidered and the redistribution of rights and duties was undertaken. Each of these analytically distinct phases was intricately intermingled with the others throughout the chequered history of these negotiations. That these efforts met with a measure of success illustrates what is possible when a conflict is seen in Positioning Theory terms, even if the theory is never mentioned explicitly.

We have emphasized the ephemeral nature of positions. They differ from roles, and other long term determinations of rights and duties to act. Using Henricksen's (Chapter 3) useful notions of the crystallization and dissolving of positions one can capture the process by which positions become roles. When this shift has occurred the conflicts founded on position incompatibilities are even more intransigent. Roles become part of the cluster of attributes determining a person's sense of self. Reflecting along these lines leads to the question of whether conflicts can be 'nipped in the bud' when someone realizes that carrying on an interaction from a certain array of positions will slide from a dispute into a full blown conflict.

Conflict resolution ought to be as much about identifying and halting incipient conflicts as about the resolution of conflicts that are already underway. Redman's analysis (Chapter 6) illustrates this process very clearly. During the conversation concerning the setting up research opportunities there are several moments when positioning moves appear and incipient conflict becomes a possibility. However, as the conversation unfolds positions are abandoned before they have crystallized into something from which an easy return is impossible.

Throughout these studies there runs an important principle. Positioning is usually, overtly or tacitly, a two stage process. In the first stage at least some of the people engaged in an interaction are attributed certain traits of character, histories, intentions and so on. On the basis of these attributions rights and duties are distributed to those involved. In many cases no conflict emerges because everyone is satisfied both with the attributions and the consequent assignment of rights and duties. Not always so. Grattan's study (Chapter 8) of the unfolding of the Schiavo case shows how the motivations mutually attributed by the people engaged in the problem of what to do with Terri Schiavo, left unexamined and unresolved, led inexorably to a conflict so deeply embedded in contradictory positions that no resolution was possible, except as a fait accompli by the courts.

Position Theory, Leadership, and Dominant Narratives

Perhaps the most important long-term contribution of Positioning Theory to conflict resolution will be in changing the language that the lay public uses in discussing conflicts. Positioning Theory is intuitively appealing and its terminology is easily incorporated in everyday conversations. The spread of Positioning Theory ideas will make it possible for the lay public to better identify and react to factors that enhance conflict, such as the role of destructive leadership, leadership that gains influence through conflict and diminishes in influence during times of peace. Of course, in some contexts leaders help to continue dialogue and avoid conflict (for example, see the study on Henry Kissinger's negotiations with Chinese and Soviet leaders, Moghaddam, Hanley, & Harré, 2003). But leaders can also have a destructive role, through their power in shaping the narratives used in society to position both ingroup and outgroup(s).

The key to the Positioning Theory contribution to understanding destructive leadership is, first, the insight that the course of conflict escalation (and de-escalation) is in important ways influenced by narratives and, second, leaders can have tremendous influence on the narratives that become dominant in interpersonal and intergroup relationships. Consider, for example, the use President George W. Bush made of terms such as 'axis of evil', 'weapons of mass destruction', and 'war on terror', in preparing the political ground for the U.S. led invasion of Iraq in 2003.

The insight that narratives impact on the course of conflict escalation and de-escalation should be considered in the wider contact of the idea that narratives shape all psychological experiences. This is exemplified in the notion of false consciousness, which arises when a subordinate group understands the world in such a way that their own group interests are harmed, and indeed they fail to see themselves as a distinct and separate group with interests that are contradicted by the interests of the dominant group. False consciousness arises through the subordinate group adopting the dominant narrative that, for example, depicts society as meritocratic and open, and that justifies group-based inequalities.

The concept of false consciousness has been adopted to apply to the plight of minority groups broadly, rather than just to social classes. For example, feminist psychologists have adopted this concept to argue that the picture of the world offered by traditional psychology reflects male interests, and women act against their own group interests when they adopt traditional psychology (see Chapter 17 in Moghaddam, 2005). This is a rather ironic turn of events, because in classical Marxism all forms of intergroup conflict other than class conflict (including conflicts based on sex and ethnicity) are manifestations of false consciousness, that ultimately serve to perpetuate the class system.

Psychology has in important ways contributed to false consciousness. For example, from the beginnings of modern psychological research on intelligence, starting with the studies of Francis Galton, to contemporary studies, such as The Bell Curve (Hearnnstein & Murray, 1994), a consistent theme has been that intelligence is largely inherited, and that group based inequalities reflect group differences in intelligence. A recent twist in this line of argument has been that because more intelligent individuals rise to the top and then marry other more intelligent individuals, and because less intelligent individuals fall to the bottom of the status hierarchy and marry other less intelligent individuals, stratification is becoming more rigid. Paradoxically, so the argument goes, the openness of society is enhancing group based inequalities.

The rhetoric linking intelligence with status is reinforced by the entire higher education system. Despite well documented inequalities, resulting in children from economically advantaged families having huge advantages in competition for places in the most prestigious schools (Niemann, Y. F. & Maruyama, 2005), the dominant narrative in the education system is one of 'equality of opportunity' and 'open competition'. The clear message to the larger society is that the education system is meritocratic.

A subtle aspect of false consciousness is that it is not assumed to involve a conspiracy: the ruling class is not assumed to be conspiring to 'fool' the lower classes. Rather, the narratives legitimizing the social system are adopted by all classes. In this case, narratives of legitimacy justify group-based inequalities and prevent inter-group conflict. However, this conflict-avoidance process does not necessarily result in a morally justifiable peace.

Finally, A Note Regarding Future Research

The application of Positioning Theory to conflict resolution highlights the importance of both synchronic and diachronic axes of social episodes. We can examine single time points in conflict and map coherent triads of storyline-acts-positions. We can also look for meaning through the sequential ordering of positioning triangles, as Bartlett (Chapter 10), for instance, has done. Synchronic analyses give priority to the structure of the social episode, while diachronic analyses show how meanings unfold over time. The diachronic axis emphasized in many of the studies of this volume suggests promising ways of extending the positioning triangle through time.

The present volume was organized along the axis of scale of conflict, from intrapersonal to international. Future research might investigate how positioning theory can be applied to various stages of conflict, including reconciliation. A focus on reconciliation is particularly important because many of the major tragic conflicts around the world, including in the Near and Middle East, never arrive at a genuine reconciliation. Rather, violent conflict erupts, then dissipates as the sides lose energy and resources, only to erupt again some time later, when the sides regain energy and gather enough resources.

With respect to methodology, it is useful to keep in mind that Positioning Theory allows for a variety of different methods to the study of conflict. Certainly, the centrality of meaning-making practices in conflict does demand rigorous analysis of talk and text. However, although Positioning Theory provides a framework by which to analytically organize storylines, acts and positions, it does not restrict itself to understanding how sequences of talk and text are interpreted. The studies presented in this volume make use of a variety of well-established discourse analytic and other linguistic methods. Thus, future research could proceed along these and other methodological paths.

References

Beschloss, M. R. (Ed.) (1997). *Taking charge: The Johnson white house tapes*, 1963–1964. New York: Simon & Schuster.

Carbaugh, D. (1999). Positioning as display of cultural identity. In R. Harré & L. van Langenhove (Eds.), *Positioning theory* (pp. 160–177). Oxford: Blackwell.

Cronin, A. K. (2006). How Al-Qaida ends: The decline and demise of terrorist groups. *International Security, 31,* 7–48.

Hearnnstein, R. J., & Murray, C. (1994). *The bell curve: The reshaping of American life by difference in intelligence.* New York: Free Press.

Moghaddam, F. M. (2005). The staircase to terrorism: A psychological exploration. *American Psychologist, 60,* 161–169.

Moghaddam, F. M. (2006). *From the terrorists' point of view.* Westport, CT: Praeger Security International.

Moghaddam, F. M., & Ginsburg, S. (2003). Culture clash and patents: Positioning and intellectual property rights. In R. Harré & F. M. Moghaddam (Eds.), *The self and others: Positioning individuals and groups in personal, political, and cultural contexts* (pp. 235–249). Westport, CT: Greenwood.

Moghaddam, F. M., Hanley, E., & Harré, R. (2003). Sustaining intergroup harmony: An analysis of the Kissinger papers through positioning theory. In R. Harré & F. M. Moghaddam (Eds.), *The self and others: Positioning individuals and groups in personal, political, and cultural contexts* (pp. 137–155). Westport, CT: Praeger.

Niemann, Y. F., & Maruyama, G. (2005). Inequalities in higher education. *Journal of Social Issues, 61,* 407–426.

Glossary of Terms Integral to Positioning Theory

Accountive positioning explicitly accounting for prior positioning acts as itself a social act.

Acts the social meaning of actions.

Action any intentional activity.

Body positioning locating the body in social and physical context.

Duty a demand placed by others on the person who owes it.

Deliberate self-/other positioning Locating self or other in terms of agency, point of view, or biographical details as a move to gain advantage.

Explicit positioning to carry out a positioning act intentionally and overtly.

Forced positioning positioning someone in the eyes of others against the will of the person so positioned.

Gender positioning to carry out a positioning act such that gender differences are made salient.

Illocutionary force the act one commits through an utterance. [from J.L. Austin (1962). How to do things with words. Oxford, UK: Clarendon Press.]

Implicit positioning to carry out a positioning act in an unconscious manner.

Indirect positioning using mental, characterological, or moral traits to place a person or group into a position. Also referred to as Presumptive positioning.

Mutual positioning when what one person says simultaneously positions self and other or ingroup and outgroup.

Local moral order the dynamic, collaboratively negotiated cluster of rights and duties associated with particular positions embedded in a storyline.

Malignant or malevolent positioning when what is said about a person leads others to think about and treat that person in harmful ways.

Malignant social psychology positioning that compromises the personhood of an individual and can lead to negative reactions, such as hostility and learned helplessness.

Metapositioning to explicitly reposition. See also Accountive positioning and Explicit positioning.

Moral positioning positioning someone into a recognizable social role, e.g. mother, doctor.

Performative positioning challenging or revising previous positioning acts. See also second and third order positioning acts.

Perlocutionary force the social and other consequences that follow from a speech act (Austin, 1962).

Personal positioning positioning someone in terms of their individual attributes and particularities (e.g. forgetful, generous, witty), in contrast to positioning by reference to supposed collective attributes, such as class or ethnicity.

Position a cluster of rights and duties that limits the repertoire of possible social acts available to a person or person-like entity (such as a corporation) as so positioned.

Positioning acts (first, second, and third order) Relationally situating at least two people (self and other) into a local moral order according to some storyline. First order positioning is an initial act of positioning. Second order positioning involves questioning and negotiating a first order positioning act made within the same conversation. Third order positioning is an act of repositioning made in a new context from that in which first order positioning took place.

Positioning theory concerned with the social and psychological processes by which local moral orders are collaboratively constructed and collectively upheld, and with the way the actions of participants are constrained to flow in accordance with normative and moral systems.

Positioning triangle a metaphor for understanding the social significance of positioning acts, the three corners of which are positions, acts (such as speech acts), and storylines.

Presumptive positioning See Indirect positioning.

Reflexive positioning when a person positions herself or himself

Right a demand placed on others by a person who believes that these others have a reciprocal duty to satisfy it.

Self and other positioning positioning oneself as contrasted with being positioned by others, and with positioning others.

Social force See Act.

Story lines a loose cluster of narrative conventions according to which a social episode unfolds and positions arise.

Strategic positioning attributions of rights and duties that are to the advantage of the person who performs the positioning acts.

Subject positions the beliefs concerning possibilities of action, and such psychological accompaniments as feelings and so on of someone positioned in a certain way.

Name Index

Subject Index

Breinigsville, PA USA
15 June 2010
239893BV00003B/24/A